The Jew Accused

The Jew Accused

Three Anti-Semitic Affairs (Dreyfus, Beilis, Frank) 1894–1915

ALBERT S. LINDEMANN

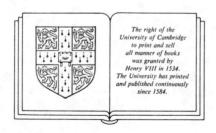

The right of the
University of Cambridge
to print and sell
all manner of books
was granted by
Henry VIII in 1534.
The University has printed
and published continuously
since 1584.

CAMBRIDGE UNIVERSITY PRESS

Cambridge

New York   Port Chester   Melbourne   Sydney

Published by the Press Syndicate of the University of Cambridge
The Pitt Building, Trumpington Street, Cambridge CB2 1RP
40 West 20th Street, New York, NY 10011, USA
10 Stamford Road, Oakleigh, Melbourne 3166, Australia

First published 1991

Printed in Canada

Library of Congress Cataloging-in-Publication Data
Lindemann, Albert S.
The Jew accused : three anti-Semitic affairs (Dreyfus, Beilis,
Frank), 1894–1915 / Albert S. Lindemann.
p.   cm.
Includes bibliographical references and index.
ISBN 0-521-40302-2
1. Antisemitism – History. 2. Blood accusation. 3. Dreyfus,
Alfred. 1859–1935 – Trials, litigation, etc. 4. Antisemitism –
France. 5. Beilis, Mendel, 1874–1934 – Trials, litigation, etc.
6. Antisemitism – Soviet Untion. 7. Frank, Leo, 1884–1915 – Trials,
litigation, etc. 8. Antisemitism – Georgia – Atlanta. I. Title.
DS145.L59   1991   91-27101
305.892'4044 – dc20   CIP

A catalog record of this book is available from the British Library.

ISBN 0-521-40302-2 hardback

Contents

Plates

Acknowledgments

This volume has benefited from a large number of careful and penetrating readings from colleagues, students, and friends. I would like to give special thanks to an old friend, Professor Peter Kenez, of the University of California, Santa Cruz, for an early reading that persuaded me to expand upon matters at first neglected and to rethink many positions. As in his readings of my previous books, he has helped in many ways that he would not suspect. Professor William Rosenberg, of the University of Michigan, Ann Arbor, another old friend who has given valuable readings to previous works of mine, gave a final reading of great sensitivity and penetration, persuading me to rethink a number of positions and rephrase crucial passages. Yet another valued friend, Professor Irwin Wall, of the University of California at Riverside, also read the manuscript in its final stages and saved me from many errors, blunders, and infelicities.

A number of my colleagues at the University of California at Santa Barbara have shown, time and again, that collegiality of scholars can be more than an empty phrase. I am deeply grateful to professors Morton Borden, Alexander Deconde, Harold Drake, Joshua Fogel, Otis Graham, Robert Kelley, Laura Kalman, Sears McGee, Joachim Remak, Jeffrey B. Russell, and Ken Mouré of the History Department for rigorous but unfailingly supportive readings.

Thanks of a different sort go to Professor Richard Hecht, of Religious Studies, who encouraged me, several years ago when we began to teach a course on anti-Semitism together, to try my hand at research and writing in this field of history. His many remarkably patient readings of this manuscript as it evolved, as well as his humor and good nature in our ongoing discussions of anti-Semitism and Jewish history, have been invaluable.

Warm thanks, also, to professors Geza Jeszenszsky and Tibor Frank, Fulbright Exchange scholars from Hungary, for their readings, and for help in understanding Hungarian history and translating Hungarian materials. Professor Frank suggested the present title, *The Jew Accused*. All of these scholars, representing a considerable range of expertise in European and American history, have made it possible for me to consider subjects that I might otherwise have believed beyond reach.

My editor at Cambridge University Press, Frank S. Smith, has shown an eagle eye for stylistic clutter, redundancy, and questionable tangents.

His advice on both style and content has been consistently excellent. The book is a little shorter and immeasurably better for his efforts. My copy editor, Alan Gold, discovered yet additional passages that could be made clearer, more consistent, and more polished; his diligence and high professional standards have had an influence on nearly every page. The anonymous outside reviewers for the press pointed out a number of flaws, both of fact and formulation. My sincere thanks to them.

My decision to ask for evaluations of the manuscript from those without Ph.D's in history has proven to be a most rewarding one. I could not imagine more perceptive, rigorous, and informed readings than those given me by Robert English, Milton Hammer, Morton Maizlish, and Michael Mallen. Among the many students of mine, both graduate and undergraduate, who have read drafts of the manuscript, I would like to single out Caron Cadle and Steven Korbin for their meticulous attention to both style and content. The others, scores of them over the past several years, are too numerous to list, but conversations with them, their remarks and various reactions, too, have had an important influence in the final product, particularly, I believe, in helping to make this volume accessible to a wide audience. My wife, Barbara, has, as always, been my first, last, most candid, and most perceptive critic, perhaps because she knows my inner thoughts – and failings – better than anyone else. Without her constant support and affectionate indulgence, this book would never have been completed.

These many readers have ably pointed out factual errors, alerted me to questionable passages, and challenged interpretive perspectives. When they disagreed with me, they usually persuaded me to change my mind – more often than it is comfortable for me to remember. They were sensitive to tones and nuances that at first escaped me but that are crucial in a work like this. For the factual errors that remain, for the inappropriate phrase or missed nuance, and, of course, for the interpretations, I remain solely responsible.

Santa Barbara

1

Introduction

I set out to write this book for a number of reasons, but primary among them was the growing fascination and plain excitement I felt as I became familiar with the extraordinary trials of three Jews, Alfred Dreyfus, Mendel Beilis, and Leo Frank. The sensational charges against these three men, the passions of their accusers and defenders, the hundreds of thousands of people swept up in the "affairs" that developed from the trials add up to an irresistible and an instructive story. It is one that far transcends the personal tragedies – however cruel and outrageous – of the three men and their families, and it is one that has never been told in a comparative perspective, as part of a larger whole in the generation before World War I.

There has recently been much discussion, and lamentation, concerning how the writing of history has been, in the words of one historian, "institutionalized."[1] It is a revival of an older and recurring discussion in the historical profession. Roughly translated, the charge is that the discipline of history has been taken over by overspecialized academic historians and in the process has become fragmented within itself and sadly remote from the concerns and consciousness of society at large, of ordinary educated readers. Critics charge that professional history is too often arcane, pedantic, and, alas, simply unreadable. Against such charges professional historians, when they pay any attention to the complaints, reply that history written by dilettantes suffers, with rare exceptions, from crippling defects: conceptual superficiality, factual unreliability, and an inclination to cheap sensationalism.

There is much more content and complexity to these debates than it is appropriate to explore here,[2] but it has long been my concern and hope, as a professional historian, to break out of the stereotypes they suggest, even while recognizing an element of truth in them. The story of the Three Affairs offers a marvelous opportunity to do so. Many educated readers will have heard something about the Dreyfus Affair (1898–1900);

---

[1] See, for example, Theodore S. Hamerow, "The Transformation of History into an Academic Discipline Has Diminished Its Role," *The Chronicle of Higher Education*, vol. 34, no. 43, A40. Also, Theodore S. Hamerow, *Reflections on History and Historians* (Madison, Wis., 1987).

[2] For a wide-ranging and provocative discussion of the matter, see Peter Novick, *That Noble Dream: The "Objectivity Question" and the American Historical Profession* (Cambridge, 1988).

few pages of modern history offer as much color and fascination. Revolving around the story of a Jewish officer in the French Army unjustly accused of espionage, it has the qualities of a mystery novel, one that Agatha Christie could not top. Indeed, many of the leading characters of the Affair are so unbelievable that few novelists would have the audacity to create them. The dizzying twists and turns of events, the plots and counterplots, the elaborate puzzles stagger the imagination – and, as anyone who has read an account of the Dreyfus Affair will no doubt add, sorely tax the memory. Many of the mysteries associated with the Affair remain unanswered to this day. A recent scholarly study of it remained on the best-seller list in France for several years.[3]

The less widely known Beilis (1911–13) and Frank (1913–15) affairs offer even more colorful – and lurid – reading. They involve, respectively, charges of ritual murder by Jews for Christian blood and charges of murder as a result of Jewish sexual perversity, the latter culminating in a lynch mob storming the walls of a state prison to hang the unfortunate Jew whose throat had already been cut several weeks before by a fellow prisoner. These affairs, too, riveted the attention of contemporaries and commanded front-page attention both inside and outside the countries involved. The Beilis and Frank affairs also offer us shockingly unexpected revelations, bizarre characters, and almost comically complex twists and turns. Indeed, in all of the affairs an initial and most demanding task, as I see it, is to offer an overview of their labyrinthine complexities. Still, I have not slighted the essential facts, for only through them can some sense of the exquisite ironies and subtleties of the cases be achieved.

What is most significant and, finally, most interesting about the affairs is not really the sensational details but larger issues. Among them are the nature and power of modern anti-Semitism, the sometimes tragic conflict between the freedom of the press and the protection of individual rights, the genesis of modern mass politics, the reaction of individuals to extreme situations, and the inevitable ambiguities of campaigns for truth and justice when political advantage is to be gained from them. I am most of all concerned to explore the elusive qualities of modern anti-Semitism and to suggest some revisions of both popular and scholarly beliefs about it.

In that latter regard, these pages try to show (1) how a comparative approach to the Three Affairs offers perspectives and insights that are hidden to those who have considered each affair individually, (2) how, even though these are appropriately termed "anti-Semitic affairs," the role of anti-Semitism in them was more ambiguous and less decisive than generally believed, and (3) how Jews, although unfairly accused and vic-

---

[3] Jean-Denis Bredin, *L'Affaire* (Paris, 1983); English translation, *The Affair: The Case of Alfred Dreyfus* (New York, 1986).

timized in these years, were by no means merely passive victims; they fought back against their tormentors and exercised power in ways that are little appreciated. A final concern that connects to each of the above is to examine the interplay of fantasy and reality in modern anti-Semitism: on the one hand, "fantastic" visions, deriving from inherited prejudice and religious imagery of Jewish power and malevolence; on the other, "real" conflict between Jews and non-Jews, related to ordinary competition (economic, social, political).

This effort at historical reinterpretation is less the result of a systematic reconsideration of the relevant primary documents of each case – that would have been a gigantic task – than of a study of the proliferating monographs, articles, and secondary works that touch upon the affairs and the background to them. I have, of course, reexamined many of the primary documents that were of central importance in these affairs, but what is most needed at present is to synthesize the insights of specialists in a range of fields and to make those insights available to a wider audience.

The Dreyfus Affair was *the* affair. It set the tone for the reaction of contemporaries to the Beilis and Frank affairs, and the treatment of the Dreyfus Affair by many historians has also much influenced how historians, far fewer in number, have interpreted the subsequent two affairs. But in the reactions of contemporaries and of historians to the two later affairs the powerful model of the Dreyfus Affair has involved some important problems, ones that will be more completely scrutinized in subsequent chapters but that may be usefully summarized at this point.

The Dreyfus Affair was seen by many contemporary believers in Dreyfus's innocence (the Dreyfusards, as they came to be known) as a titanic struggle between the forces of Justice and Injustice, between Truth and Mendacity, between Tolerance and Prejudice, between Progress and Reaction. The term *intellectual* in France dates from the time of the Affair. It was first used derisively against the Dreyfusards, but they then adopted it, proudly presenting themselves as the voice of reason and intellect over tribalistic instinct.

For many contemporaries the Affair took on the qualities of a medieval morality play, with Good and Evil arrayed starkly against one another, and so also has it been presented by many works of modern history.[4] However, the more one plunges into its mysteries and paradoxes, the more the issue of Good and Evil becomes confused. The morality play turns out to be subtler in its themes than is at first apparent. It emerges

---

[4] Probably the most widely read account of the Affair in English, Nicholas Halasz, *Captain Dreyfus, the Story of a Mass Hysteria* (New York, 1955) is the most striking in this regard; his account offers ample illustration of how an ostensibly factual account can introduce a large element of imaginative rearrangement, of how much history and imaginative fiction have in common. The work will be further discussed below.

as closer to a modern stage drama, full of ambiguities, uncertainties, and moral dilemmas. We find that the "heroes," even the best of them, are flawed by ignoble instincts and dubious motives. And the "villains" are in some very important cases redeemed by heroic or otherwise estimable traits. Even some of the worst of them were not quite the conniving fiends that a number of accounts would lead us to believe. Mostly we find human beings that are a perplexing mix of sometimes repellent and sometimes admirable qualities, drawn into a vortex of passionate ideological and national allegiances, personal ambitions, lamentable blunders, and plain honest mistakes. So it was, to varying degrees, in all three affairs.

A central theme of the Dreyfus Affair as it will be presented in these pages has little to do with the familiar verities of how good people must struggle against evil ones. It is, rather, that preconceived belief, ideological intoxication, can tragically cloud the mind, weaken the reason, and pervert the moral sense of good people as well as of evil ones. Even otherwise honest and decent people are prone to believe what they want to believe, what they somehow need to believe, and not what a dispassionate examination (however elusive a conception that is) of evidence indicates, above all if such an examination might lead to awkward conclusions.

Belief that is impelled or contorted by desire and psychological need is far more typical than belief that leads to awkward conclusions. It is that latter stance, of embracing the awkward truth no matter what the consequences, that must be considered heroic – and rare. If we are to find heroes, in the most rigorous sense of the word, we must look for those whose personal interests were actually damaged by coming to the rescue of Dreyfus (or Beilis or Frank), not those who perceived personal or political opportunity in taking up the cause of public martyrs. Such heroes are to be found in all the anti-Semitic affairs discussed in this volume but often in some unexpected quarters.

What is an anti-Semitic affair?

My use of the term *affair* in these pages may require some elucidation, even for those who are familiar with it in application to major political controversies. To borrow from the title of an excellent study of the Dreyfus Affair, it was "more than a trial"[5] – much more, as were the trials of Beilis and Frank. One may, of course, speak of the Dreyfus "case" or the Beilis "case," even of the "*cause célèbre*" that developed from each of them.

[5] Robert Louis Hoffmann, *More Than a Trial: The Struggle over Captain Dreyfus* (New York, 1980).

The thesaurus offers the following as synonyms for *affair*: *contention, struggle, rivalry, quarrel.* Each of those terms suggests important aspects of the affairs. "Affair," then, refers to exceptionally divisive matters, where opposing sides are driven by overpowering emotions. But more important, in an affair issues that transcend the trial itself come into play.

Obviously, a highly emotional response is natural in trials of Jews accused of ritual murder or espionage or murder in the pursuit of perverse sexual gratification, as were Beilis, Dreyfus, and Frank. Murder trials of almost any sort will engage emotions, but they do not usually evoke the kinds of involvement that the Beilis and Frank trials did. Espionage trials invariably provoke widespread, emotional interest, but they do not necessarily become affairs. Even ritual murder trials with Jews as defendants have not usually developed into affairs.

To become an affair, then, a trial must engage powerful and also conflicting emotions in large numbers of people over an extended period. It must attract important numbers of prominent individuals who are willing to devote their energies to winning "justice," a concept that has diametrically opposed meanings for the opposing sides, since each side sees itself as motivated by selfless, high ideals. An affair must mobilize large numbers of ordinary citizens to the extent that they are willing to sign petitions, attend rallies, or engage in action in the streets. They must passionately believe in the guilt or innocence of the accused and also be persuaded that justice is not being served.

Finally, and most important, for a trial to become an affair it must have ideological implications. It must, in other words, develop into something more than a strictly legal issue of innocence or guilt. Participants in an affair see themselves as selflessly involved in a larger struggle, one that meshes into their general political convictions, into their view of the world. Political parties and interest groups join the fray, as do newspapers and journals, artists and intellectuals, trade union leaders and business executives.

Thus, the trial of the confessed Jewish spy, Jonathan Pollard, who was sentenced to life imprisonment in March 1987 for having passed thousands of top-secret documents to Israeli agents for large sums of money and other perquisites provided by the Israeli government, did not provoke an affair inside the United States. True, many Israelis subsequently elevated him to the status of hero, and some American Jews tried to mobilize opinion against what they perceived as an overly harsh sentence. But his case did not engage a sufficiently large part of the population, pro and con, in the United States for it to be termed an affair as I am using the word.[6]

---

[6] Cf. William Bole, "The Pollard Affair: Did the Punishment Fit the Crime?" and Burton Levine, "Justice for the Pollards," *Present Tense*, vol. 16, no. 2, Jan.–Feb. 1989, 12–19;

The case of the "thrill" murderers, Loeb and Leopold, rich Jews whose guilt was also not in question, did not provoke an anti-Semitic affair. The repulsiveness of their crime, dubbed the "crime of the century" by contemporaries (1924), naturally attracted widespread attention and evoked some anti-Semitic grumblings but no fundamental split in opinion, no mobilized factions, no major ideological linkage, no significant assertion that this was a typically Jewish crime.

Even the trial of Julius and Ethel Rosenberg (1951), accused of passing atomic secrets to the Soviet Union, which did develop into a political affair, still did not become a distinctly *anti-Semitic* affair. To be sure, it was closer to one than the previous two examples, since in this case the Rosenbergs did not confess to being spies and, more important, many Americans believed that their trial was unfair and that their arrests were tinged with anti-Semitic motivations. That the judge and the chief witness for the prosecution, as well as the prosecuting and defense attorneys in the case, were themselves Jews, and that prominent and influential Jews like Roy Cohn worked with great tenacity to see them convicted and executed, helped to diminish that trial's potential as an anti-Semitic affair. Similarly, that Pollard was spying for a friendly rather than an enemy power helped to diminish the seriousness of his crime in the eyes of most Americans who followed the case. Had he turned the secrets over to Iran or Libya, even if the money paid him had been less than what the Israelis provided, American opinion would almost certainly have turned more strongly against him.

In short, the trials of Jewish criminals, spies, and murderers dot the pages of modern history without developing into anti-Semitic affairs. Often those trials were sensational, the crimes odious, but when the guilt of the defendants was widely recognized by Jew and non-Jew, right and left, when their activities were unable to awaken opposing factions and link to larger issues, no anti-Semitic affair could result.

Themes, interpretations, goals

A larger number of pages in this volume are devoted to the historical background to the Three Anti-Semitic Affairs than to the affairs themselves. I want to make as clear and explicit as possible why I have done so, and why I consider the historical background to be a key part of the contribution of this volume. The most important reason, and the one that is most difficult to put forth briefly, has to do with an issue already

Andy Goldberg, "The Proud Parents," *The Jerusalem Post, International Edition*, week ending Apr. 1, 1989, 6; Wolf Blitzer, *The Territory of Lies* (New York, 1989).

described as central: the elusive nature of modern anti-Semitism. In particular, how is one to explain outbursts of anti-Semitism in modern times? Are they fundamentally unpredictable and mysterious eruptions, or do they somehow fit into a comprehensible pattern of the past? Is it possible, at least retrospectively, to see anti-Semitic events building in the same way that we can see a revolution or a war building? Was the Dreyfus Affair a "surprise," something that somehow "leaped out" of history, or did it "make sense," given conditions in France in the 1890s?

These questions touch upon tangled controversies in the historical profession, especially among those who write Jewish history, ones that cannot be followed at length here. My position throughout this volume will be that we can understand anti-Semitism in the same way that we can understand other modern isms, and we can understand anti-Semitic events like the Dreyfus Affair, or, indeed, the Holocaust, just as we can understand World War I or the Russian Revolution. The Three Affairs can be set in a historical context that makes them, if not predictable, at least as comprehensible as other events in history. I do not accept that such analysis tends to justify anti-Semitism, as some have maintained, although I do think it often sheds a more textured light on individual anti-Semites, making them appear more a part of the human family, not stick-figures or bugbears. The idea of trying to shed that kind of light is also regarded with suspicion by many.[7] My belief is that a calm, balanced, and unflinching effort to understand anti-Semitism and anti-Semites is in the long run the best defense against the views they try to propagate. Shrinking from that effort, taking refuge in dogmatic moralizing, finally plays into the hands of anti-Semites, since many of them charge Jews with trying to prevent an honest and objective examination of anti-Semitism.

Yet what it means to "understand" in this regard is admittedly problematic. Many authors who present hatred of Jews as an ultimately mysterious eruption, an effect without understandable causes, are arguing something more plausible and sophisticated: that anti-Semitism itself is fundamentally irrational, a fantasy of twisted minds. Its deepest causes cannot be found in the activities of real Jews but only in baseless fantasies about them. Insofar as anti-Semitism is to be comprehended, it must be through an analysis of the Gentile mind, a dissection of the pathologies of western Christian thought that have over the ages powerfully condi-

---

[7] Robert J. Lifton reports that when he began his study of Nazi doctors, "some [made] . . . a compelling case for leaving the whole subject alone. Their argument was that Nazi evil should merely be recognized and isolated: rather than making it an object of study, one should simply condemn it. Psychological study in particular, it was feared, ran the risk of replacing condemnation with 'insights.' " Robert J. Lifton, *The Nazi Doctors: Medical Killing and the Psychology of Genocide* (New York, 1986), xi.

tioned non-Jews to hate Jews. "The Jewish Problem is really a Gentile Problem," as a familiar phrase has stated the issue – one-sidedly and simplistically, I believe. Hannah Arendt has called attention, in characteristically mordant tones, to the inclination of some Jewish observers to uphold "the perfect innocence of the [Jewish] victim, an innocence that insinuates not only that no evil was done [by Jews] but that nothing at all was done by them which might possibly have a connection with the issue at stake."[8]

A further refinement of the argument that hatred of Jews is irrational is to be found in some of the most penetrating analyses of modern anti-Semitism, a refinement that seeks to link the twisted minds of individual anti-Semites to what might be termed pathological tendencies in the economy, society, and state of late nineteenth-century Europe and America. These pathological tendencies have, it is argued, intricate connections with capitalist development, with the introduction of modern techniques of production, the overturning of older ways and habits. Europeans and Americans who were threatened by these transformations began to act "hysterically," in the process refashioning centuries-old religious fantasies about Jews into a more modern secular language.

This argument takes on a myriad of forms and degrees of sophistication, but it often comes down to the assertion that the grievances of the "losers" (small shopkeepers, for example) in modern economic development are irrational, in that they represent a past that was doomed by the march of history to disappear. Such tormented and deluded people were drawn to a simple but also false explanation, one derived from fantasy or inherited prejudice: The Jews were the cause of their misfortunes. Anti-Semitism is thus best understood as a spasm of a sick, moribund society, or a death-rattle of doomed classes. Again, although this is a more sophisticated argument, one that I accept to an important extent, I will express reservations about it, especially in its treatment of capitalist development as pathological and in its presentation of the "losers" as wholly irrational.

The background chapters for each of the affairs attempt to give appropriate attention to real historical forces as much as to the fantastic productions of anti-Semitic propagandists. More precisely, these chapters examine the intricate interplay of the two and the important differences in that interplay from country to country over time. As I see it, the most challenging job for the historian is to unravel fantasy and reality, to appreciate how they connect, to evaluate the relative importance of each in given, concrete situations and in historical evolution. I do not belittle the role of irrational hatred, but I will also explore the degree to which hostility to Jews was related to more mundane factors. These are factors

---

[8] Hannah Arendt, *The Origins of Totalitarianism* (New York, 1963), 5.

that led to tension and hostility among other groups in society, without their being qualified as irrational, fundamentally incomprehensible, or primarily the product of a powerful and autonomous ideology.

I do not argue, however, that hatred of Jews has been essentially the same as hatred among other groups in history. Anti-Semitic ideology derives from a set of images and myths that are central to the identity of the Judeo-Christian West, ones that have been constantly refashioned over the centuries. The anti-Jewish hatred that derives from them is at some level unique and may be said to have a life of its own, however elusive to define. Nevertheless, developments in the material world have a decisive impact on the ways those images and myths are refashioned and thus on the nature of anti-Semitism – and, perhaps most important, on its concrete implications, for example, in violence against Jews. We need to understand the myths and the way they are manipulated, their psychological appeal, but I find the evidence weak that they are essentially ahistorical, self-perpetuating, or primary movers in history. It is rather the experiences of real people in the real world that nourish them and give them life. On the other hand, those experiences not only nourish anti-Semitic visions but also counter them: When real Jews do not correspond to those visions, which is often the case, the visions are put into question. That, too, is a major theme of the relations of Jews and non-Jews in modern times.

A closely related justification for these substantial background chapters is much easier to provide. My concern is not only with anti-Semitic affairs but also with what they represented in a broader sense. The interplay of Jew and Gentile in modern Europe and America is a fascinating and many-sided story, one that reveals the nature of modern times in graphic and unaccustomed ways. I conceive of this as a work of comparative history, one that seeks to gain insights into the histories of given nations (French, Russian, and American primarily, but also Hungarian, German, and Austrian) in the light of contrasting national development. One particularly revealing way of looking at national development, I believe, is in terms of how nations respond to the presence of Jews within their borders and how Jews define themselves as citizens of those nations. This approach provides a special kind of window, revealing crucial differences that may not appear so sharply when one looks at a set of countries from other perspectives. However, not only differences emerge; similarities between countries so ostensibly dissimilar as the United States and Russia also become apparent. And it is these similarities, I believe, that have been overlooked or at times purposely obscured. In this, and in a number of other ways, I think the reader will easily perceive how this work deals with much more than the Three Affairs.

2

The historical setting in Europe and America

The rise of the Jews in the nineteenth century

Late nineteenth-century anti-Semitism, and the relationships of Jews and non-Jews more generally, cannot be understood without an appreciation of what will hereafter be referred to as the "rise of the Jews" in Europe and America. Anti-Semites, of course, perceived rising Jews as a kind of specter, and those perceptions had interesting parallels to the fears in other quarters of a rising working class or a rising Germany. Obviously, in the Jewish case it was a restricted and paradoxical rise, one that stood in marked contrast to the suddenly revealed vulnerability of Jews implicit in the title of this work, "The Jew Accused."

The rise was nonetheless real and historically significant. The material comfort and social success of Jews, the emergence of a numerous Jewish bourgeoisie in western Europe and the United States by the late nineteenth century, were part of a remarkable ascendance of the Jews since the late eighteenth century, when they began to achieve civil equality. Relevant statistics and other details of this rise will be provided in subsequent chapters, but it is clear that in the long history of the Jews, the rise of the Jews in the nineteenth century has few parallels in terms of the rapid transformation of the condition of Jews – in absolute and relative numbers, in wealth, in fame, in power, and in influence. Jewish ascendance in Hellenistic Alexandria or in Golden Age Spain obviously suggest themselves as comparable, but the modern rise was almost certainly more important. The extraordinary energy emanating from the Jewish people as a whole, and, more palpably, from countless prominent individuals of Jewish background, is one of the most important and often overlooked phenomena of modern times.

Some Gentiles welcomed this rise; some opposed it. Others, probably the majority, remained ambivalent if they noticed it, as many obviously did not. Whether they finally welcomed or opposed it depended very much on the specific shape it assumed in individual countries, as well as on the culture and traditions of those countries – and, indeed, on turns of events that must be termed historical accidents. But had this rise of the Jews not occurred, there would not have been modern anti-Semitism in the specific forms it assumed from country to country in the last decades of the nineteenth century, nor would there have been modern philo-Semitism, also much influenced by the rise of the Jews, by the sense that Jews were a force for good in the modern world.

The controversial issue of a "rising tide" of anti-Semitism in Europe and the United States, to be further explored in subsequent chapters, cannot ignore the "rising tide" of the Jews throughout the nineteenth century, and especially in the generation before 1914. It can, of course, be argued that since the days of Moses and Pharaoh, it has been, time after time, the perceived threat of "rising" Jews that has provoked hatred and violence against them. But the dimensions of the modern rise exceed those of the past.

Again, to make these observations is not to suggest that Jews, by "rising," are themselves to blame for modern anti-Semitism, although some ultraorthodox Jewish spokesmen have made that argument,[1] nor is it even to argue that Jews in some vaguer sense were the fundamental cause of it, as some Zionists have argued. Other ethnic groups, for example, the Irish in the United States, "rose" without evoking an ideology of hate that is really comparable to anti-Semitism in texture, intensity, or duration. The following chapters will be centrally concerned with examining the nexus of factors that spawned modern anti-Semitism and with criticizing simplistic accounts of it. Nevertheless, to point out that the rise of the Jews was an important prerequisite for modern anti-Semitism helps us to avoid another inadequate approach, alluded to in the Introduction, that is, to argue that modern anti-Semitism had little or even nothing to do with a Jewish reality, that it was based entirely on Gentile fantasy about Jews, on a wholly irrational and mysteriously self-perpetuating fear of them and what their rise implied for non-Jews.

Irrationality there certainly was, as there was a kind of self-perpetuating fantasy, but specifically modern anti-Semitism, as it first appeared in the late nineteenth century, is best conceptualized as a potent mixture of fantasy and reality, of crude caricatures of Jews constantly nourished by daily perceptions and often accurate portrayals of them. To be sure, the claims of modern anti-Semites, from the 1870s on, that they opposed Jews only for "real," racial reasons, and not on the basis of bigoted religious fantasies, were often transparently false. Similarly, their claims that anti-

---

[1] Cf. Allen Nadler, "Piety and Politics: The Case of the Satmar Rebbe," *Judaism*, vol. 31, 1982, 135–51. The Rebbe's judgment, based on traditional rabbinical texts, has to do with the oath that the Jews were supposed to have made to God to remain politically passive after the destruction of the Temple; the Gentile nations similarly agreed not to oppress Israel "too much" if that promise were not broken. The Holocaust was God's punishment of the Jews for breaking their promise, for becoming politically active. Cf. in addition, Amos Funkenstein, "Theological Interpretations of the Holocaust," in François Furet, ed., *Unanswered Questions: Nazi Germany and the Genocide of the Jews* (New York, 1989), 276–7.

Semitism was a scientific attitude based on the new science of race, one that revealed the malevolent inner essence of the "Semitic race," could not long stand scrutiny. But many Gentiles felt threatened by the rise of the Jews, and some had good reason to feel threatened, for Jews were in truth encroaching on arenas that had previously been exclusively Gentile, and Jews were helping to make life as those Gentiles had traditionally experienced it difficult or impossible.

Some non-Jews were able to react to the rise of the Jews as a real phenomenon, one that could be measured and evaluated as other real phenomena were. Other non-Jews were inclined to react to the rise of the Jews with a shriller tone and to exaggerate its dimensions, often grotesquely. For some such non-Jews, the Jewish Question became a consuming monomania. As one of them graphically expressed himself, Jews, who at the end of the eighteenth century had had such a debased status that they "paid the same tax as swine at village gates," were by the early twentieth century "the masters of Europe . . . they make and unmake governments, they have closed down Catholic churches, they have grabbed the country's entire wealth, the press, the professions, our children's education – they own everything."[2]

In short, and to pick up the terms set down in the Introduction, the rise of the Jews as a measurable, ordinary, and limited phenomenon nourished a fantasy, a specter, where Jews were perceived as taking over the world. Those who wished could easily tap an elaborate ideology of Jew-hatred, one that borrowed from both Christian myth and certain ideals of classical antiquity, both of which emphasized the destructiveness of Jews, their hatred for non-Jews, and their determination to dominate or enslave Gentiles. In its Christian form the emphasis was on "deicide," the charge that Jews had killed Christ and continued to hate Him and all He represented. In the form derived from classical antiquity, it was the charge of *misanthropeia*, a rejection of brotherhood with other peoples – ultimately related to the charge of deicide and the stubborn refusal of Jews to accept brotherhood in Christ.

But those who believed malevolent Jews were taking over the world were mostly on the fringes of society, isolated fanatics. For the most part the more influential Gentiles by the middle of the century were inclined to sympathy, however ambiguous, for newly emergent Jews, and they denounced anti-Semitism as bigotry unacceptable in a modern, civilized nation. Jews were granted civil equality and generally welcomed as modern citizens, increasingly recognized for their ample contributions to national strength and praised for their role in modern civilization. Such

[2] Quoted in Zeev Sternhell, "The Roots of Popular Anti-Semitism in the Third Republic," in Frances Malino and Bernard Wasserstein, eds., *The Jews in Modern France* (Hanover, N.H., and London, 1985), 128–9.

Gentiles were mostly, though not exclusively, men of the bourgeois-liberal left and center; they often saw Jews as useful allies in their own struggle to implement a liberal program.

A tiny minority of extremely wealthy Jews established close relations with the old ruling aristocracy – the connection of the Rothschilds with Metternich is perhaps the best-known example – but those ties did not mean that the conservatives and reactionaries of the old aristocracy supported the idea of civil equality for all Jews. Individual Jews also certainly had friendly relations with the common people, but, again, those relations did not translate into significant popular support for Jewish emancipation.

The linkage of Jewish emancipation with the program of the liberal middle class resulted in a problem for Jews, in that bourgeois-liberal Gentiles had enemies. People who were in one way or another threatened by the rise of the liberal left and the rise of the middle class were naturally inclined to anti-Semitism, to see the Jews, in short, as the friends or allies of their enemies. In a broader way, Jews, as newcomers and former outsiders, were seen as beneficiaries of all that was new and modern, of all that was undermining traditional habits or familiar things. And, again, although that perception lent itself to exaggeration, it was not pure fantasy by any means.

Opponents of liberalism, whether on the conservative right or on the socialist left, were not all hate-filled fanatics and were not all necessarily drawn into the intoxicating visions of Jews as deicides standing outside the rest of human society. Much of what they treasured in traditional life had humanistic and aesthetic substance. It is certainly justified to describe modern anti-Semitism as an ideology of narrow, cancerous resentment, of sometimes grotesque fantasy, and of appalling implications. But however uncomfortable it is to recognize it, not all of those whom historians have classified as anti-Semites were narrow bigots, irrational, or otherwise incapable of acts of altruism and moral courage. They represented a bewildering range of opinion and of personality types.[3] They have sometimes been dismissed by means of one-dimensional stereotypes, ironically much in the same way that they dismissed Jews.

The rise of the Jews developed in several stages, in general ways paralleling stages in modern history as a whole (for example, a "liberal" period distinguished by the growing eminence of the Jewish bourgeoisie was followed by a period that saw the rise of the Jewish masses in those areas where there were Jewish masses). It had many ambiguous or contradictory aspects, also in general ways paralleling trends in modern history. One such aspect was that while a significant minority of Jews became richer,

[3] Cf. Albert S. Lindemann, "Anti-Semitism: Banality or the Darker Side of Genius?" *Religion*, vol. 18, 1988, 183–95.

more educated, and more powerful, a significant minority became poorer, more vulnerable, and more desperate. To an important degree, the astonishing rate of Jewish population growth underlay both the rise of the Jews and their pauperization – and even the special extremes of richness and poverty, power and powerlessness. The existing structures of state and society in Europe, especially in eastern Europe, where the population increase was the most marked, were unable to absorb these new Jewish multitudes, their energies, hopes, and ambitions. But at the same time, this two-sided fortune was typical of the age, when populations almost everywhere began to mushroom. Non-Jews also experienced unprecedented wealth and disastrous pauperization. In their case, too, existing structures were simply overwhelmed. The new age posed unprecedented problems for almost all members of society.

To suggest that Jews were subject to impersonal forces that neither they nor any of their contemporaries understood touches on another area of considerable debate in the historiography of anti-Semitism: How much are Jews to be seen as passive objects, as opposed to active subjects, in history?[4] For the purposes of this study it is necessary to make clear that, however one cares to define Jewish power before the end of the nineteenth century, however much Jews themselves believed that since ancient times they had remained powerless outsiders in history, now great numbers of them began, by their own reckoning, by their own definitions of themselves, to enter the mainstream of history and to become active, often passionate participants in it. Gentile reaction to that dramatic entry was at times correspondingly passionate.

In attempting to understand modern anti-Semitism, we do best to speak of a complex, many-sided interplay of Jew and non-Jew, not of a passive Jewish "object" and an active non-Jewish "subject," not simply of suffering Jews and oppressive non-Jews, not even of Jewish martyrs (or heroes) and Gentile villains. Just as it was argued above that modern anti-Semitism was not only the product of Gentile fantasy but also of a definite reality (the rise of the Jews), so these rising Jews began to exercise power, even if that power was not nearly so extensive as anti-Semitic fantasy would have it.

The interplay of Jew and non-Jew in modern times entailed much more than mutual oppression, of negative and fanciful images of one another. There was much that was positive and hopeful about the relationship. Throughout modern times negative and positive images of Jews have competed with one another in the eyes of Gentile observers, as indeed negative and positive images of non-Jews have competed with one another within the Jewish world. To focus only on the negative, whether from

[4]Cf. David Biale, *Power and Powerlessness in Jewish History* (New York, 1986).

the Gentile or Jewish perspective, is both inadequate and distorting. And here we come to a central point: The Three Anti-Semitic Affairs were as much about Gentile–Jewish cooperation as they were about Jewish–Gentile conflict.

The transformation of the condition of the Jews had much to do with the growing admiration by Jews for their Gentile surroundings, an admiration that was facilitated by what might be termed an invitation by Gentiles to join them in a modern civilization that would put aside the hatreds of the past. Only rarely in their long history had Jews been so profoundly and yet subtly challenged in their basic identity and sense of worth as when they began to merge into Gentile society in the course of the nineteenth century. Widespread adoption of non-Jewish culture led to fundamental changes in Jewish religious practices, and, finally, to a widespread indifference to traditional religion among Jews, an indifference that paralleled but exceeded the move away from religion in the Gentile world.

In certain periods a significant minority of Jews, especially among the wealthier classes, intermarried with non-Jews and converted to Christianity. These transformations sometimes were associated with a kind of Jewish anti-Semitism, or what has been called self-hatred, a facile epithet applied to an often excruciatingly complex reality. In its milder forms this sentiment expressed itself as a shame or embarrassment about many aspects of Jewishness and a consuming concern for what Gentiles might think of Jews. Jews often went to great lengths to hide from non-Jews the aspects of Jewish life that had become embarrassing for them, a natural enough inclination, at any rate, when anti-Semites were exaggerating or seeking to exploit resentment about those aspects. But what is considered embarrassing is, of course, highly subjective; some Jews took pride in what others sought to disguise. Still, the feeling of many Jews, especially in western Europe, about their Jewish identity was epitomized by the much-quoted quip of the poet Heinrich Heine: "Those who would say that Judaism is a religion would say that being a hunchback is a religion." For him Judaism was not a religion but a "misfortune."

Modern anti-Semitism and modern mass politics

Hostility to Jews and Judaism has a long history in Europe and in the ancient world, but the beginnings of a specifically modern variety of Jew-hatred in both Europe and America may be situated in the last quarter of the nineteenth century. Those beginnings are linked to other characteristically modern phenomena, such as industrialism, populist nationalism, the decline of traditional religion, and the growth of modern cities.

Before this period, hatred of Jews was couched in terms of religious belief. Religious expressions of Jew-hatred persisted in the late nineteenth century, especially in the more traditional areas, but modern anti-Semites more typically rejected religious anti-Semitism and emphasized instead that Jews were a harmful race. Premodern religious antipathy, in other words, centered on Jews as religious dissidents – deicides, or "Christ killers." Modern anti-Semites claimed to hate Jews as a foreign, unassimilable, and destructive race rather than as members of a religious community that hates Christ and Christians.

Modern anti-Semites have typically claimed to resent or hate Jews for "real" reasons, for things that the Jewish race does in the economic and social spheres, for example, as distinguished from "unreal" reasons having to do with religious fantasy. Thus, modern anti-Semites charge Jews with exploiting and cheating non-Jews, taking their jobs from them, gaining control over the stock market, the press, and even the state itself, whereas premodern anti-Semites were concerned with religious and metaphysical matters, with the alleged demonic rituals of Jews, their outrageous beliefs, their guilt not only for having murdered Christ but for hating him and all Christians, for wanting to "kill" Christ and all he stood for, time and again.

The very word *anti-Semitism* was coined in the 1870s, when racial-nationalistic antipathy to Jews (the "Semitic" race) began to find a new political expression in Europe, when the dominant liberal and conservative parties of the previous decades were being challenged by parties that sought to attract the restive lower orders. At this time political parties were formed and political platforms worked out that attempted to rally masses of voters by means of anti-Semitic messages, holding Jews responsible for the ills of the time. The Dreyfus, Beilis, and Frank affairs, for all their differences, were very much part of modern politics and of the new kind of racial anti-Semitism, used for political and other purposes, that arose in the late 1870s and early 1880s.

The last two decades of the nineteenth century constituted a period when modern mass movements and politics began to make an appearance in Europe and the United States, with substantial and revealing differences from country to country. "Modern mass politics" refers to new, democratic-populist and socialist forms of expression, as distinguished from the more elitist, liberal, and individualist politics that prevailed in much of Europe and the United States during the 1850s, 1860s, and early 1870s. By the 1870s broad masses of the population began to assert themselves in new ways, slowly at first but with growing visibility by the turn of the century. They did not actually take over leadership positions in the nation-states of Europe or the United States, but they constituted a distinct new presence; they showed a new energy and confidence, and they appeared to many observers to be the voice of the future. Jewish masses, no less than non-Jewish, began to participate in these new political movements, although the term "Jewish masses" has little meaning except in regard to eastern and central Europe, since elsewhere Jews had by this time become mostly members of the comfortable middle class or bourgeoisie.

There were major differences from country to country in the development of mass politics. The United States was at the forefront, whereas in Russia political developments seemed in comparison retarded by a century. One important qualification must be registered to that generalization: The impressive Jewish mass movements that arose in the generation before World War I were largely indigenous to Russia or were Russian in inspiration, even when transplanted to the United States, where they thrived and took on new forms.

In the United States there was no particular "question" or problem in the way that the term was understood in Europe, since Jews were accepted as American citizens without debate, and their presence in the country, their rise in the course of the nineteenth century, provoked no notable outcry, no major anti-Semitic movements. (In the more rigorous sense of the term, having to do with the painful dilemmas that Jews experienced as they blended into U.S. society, there was, of course, a Jewish question in the United States as well.) In Russia, throughout the nineteenth century and the early twentieth, Jews were viewed by the authorities and by much of the rest of the population as a foreign, separate, exploitative, and distressingly prolific nation, thus necessarily subject to special legislation to keep them "under control." They never achieved civil equality under the tsars. In German-speaking central Europe, Jews gained citizenship, or civil equality, only incrementally in the course of the nineteenth century, each step accompanied by a searching, often divisive debate. It was there that one may speak most appropriately of a Jewish Question in the sense of a contentious matter debated at length by major thinkers. It was German thinkers, both Jewish and non-Jewish, who exercised the widest influence in this matter.

Modern mass political movements in Europe were characteristically antiliberal. That hostility to liberalism had many sources, but primary among them was the discredit of the free-market policies of the 1850s and 1860s because of the economic recession of the mid-1870s through the early 1890s. At the time, the recession was known in Europe as the Great Depression. It was sparked by a stock market collapse and bank failures in 1873, which were in turn linked to a number of financial scandals in which individual Jews played a visible, sometimes notorious role. The discredit of liberalism in the economic realm often provoked hostility to Jews because of the central role some of them played in the stock market and in other closely related aspects of midcentury economic innovations, such as railroad building.

Agriculture in these years was a particularly troubled area, in both Europe and America, although one of very great diversity and by no means universal distress. Since Jews often lived in what was widely perceived as exploitative relationships to poor peasants (for example, as grain or cattle merchants, middlemen, moneylenders, or as managers of tenant farms), rural resentments against them intensified in the late nineteenth and early twentieth centuries, especially since Jews were able to benefit from the play of market forces in many previously isolated rural areas. However, peasant anti-Semites were decidedly less important – less focused, less articulate, less ideological – than anti-Semites in urban areas, where modern industry and market forces more generally had a more notable impact.

Urban unemployment rose markedly in these years, and manual laborers in the cities and towns turned to left-wing, antiliberal parties of various sorts. The socialist parties in Europe, to a large extent Marxist or collectivist, were the first to arise and finally the most successful of these parties. However, resentments against Jews on the part of the urban working class, and on the part of the socialists that sought to organize workers, were relatively weak. Liberal and conservative politicians sometimes lumped the anti-Semitic parties together with the socialists; both were depicted as attacking the established order and liberal economic principles, the free market and private ownership of the means of production, and both were believed by liberals and conservatives to appeal to the lower orders on the basis of vulgar prejudice and base, material concerns. Yet there were major differences between the socialists, especially the Marxists, and the new anti-Semitic parties.

The anti-Marxist Christian social parties (also called Christian socialist but in fact substantially different from the socialists) were another branch of the new, antiliberal, mass parties, and they also sought to attract the support of the urban working class. Since the Christian social parties remained aligned with the Christian churches, both Catholic and Protestant, they were somewhat less threatening to respectable society, but they, too, were critical of the fruits of the free-market economy, and they often attacked the role of Jews in the economy. In fact, the distinction between anti-Semitic parties and the Christian social parties was often elusive, since in practice almost all Christian social parties attacked Jewish influence in modern life, usually lumping it together with more generally secular trends of the day. Nevertheless, anti-Semites who prided themselves on being modern typically sought to distance themselves from specifically religious hatred of Jews, to attack the Jewish race rather than the Jewish religion. But the distinctions in practice often did not hold up; there was much confusion of themes and theories among anti-Semites at the end of the nineteenth century. The so-called new right, or revolutionary right, to be further discussed below, recruited among anti-Semites and Christian socials, and attempted to introduce greater ideological coherence amid this confusion.

The new mass parties, whether socialist, Christian social, secular anti-Semitic, or new right, opposed liberal principles and practices in a number of other arenas, beyond economic policies. The Social Democratic Party in Germany, for example, organized itself into an impressive collectivist apparatus, actively supported by hundreds of thousands of dues-paying, card-carrying members. The German party was closely associated with the even larger German trade union movement. In both there was a pervasive sense that only through class solidarity, through close co-operation of thousands of workers, could their poverty and oppression be effectively combated.

The new mass parties were unquestionably inclined to appeal to emotion, to popular resentments over the injustices of the capitalist system. Marxist theory asserted that bourgeois society could finally be brought down only by violent action on the part of the organized working class; appeals to reason and to the common interests of the working and owning classes were dismissed as ineffectual and utopian. The anti-Semites had an easier answer to the social and economic problems of the day: Get rid of the Jews; strip them of their pervasive economic power and newly acquired civil equality; keep them in their place in those countries, like Russia, where they did not enjoy civil equality and were clamoring for it. Only then would the evils of bourgeois-capitalist society disappear, or fail to develop further, since those evils derived from the domination of Jews over that society.

Nineteenth-century liberals considered the masses, and thus the new mass parties, to pose a danger to liberty and the social order. A concern with protecting and expanding liberty had been characteristic of liberals earlier in the century, but the main enemy at that time had been the conservative ruling order, and at that time middle-class liberals had been willing to turn to the masses for support in a common struggle to destroy the old order. As the century progressed, and as much of the liberal program, particularly economic liberalization, was put into practice, liberals, both Jewish and non-Jewish, were ever more inclined to perceive a new, rising danger from below, especially from the industrial proletariat, rather than from above.

By the late nineteenth century liberals in many countries began to edge to the right, to establish alliances with the older ruling elites, a tendency that often entailed splits in the liberal camp into right and left wings. Such alliances were all the more easily accomplished since liberals had never wholly dislodged members of the older political elites from many positions of power, particularly at the national level, as distinguished from municipal or regional levels, and even more particularly in the ranks of the military and diplomatic corps.

In western and central Europe, in part because it had been the liberals who had sponsored civil equality for Jews, Jews became overwhelmingly liberal in political preferences. More to the point, liberalism was a natural enough tendency for Jews, since they had by this time become over- whelmingly middle class and associated with commercial and industrial enterprise. Jewish liberals did not differ markedly from Gentile liberals in most regards; they were also disturbed by the growing power and new militancy of the lower orders. Jews may have been even more suspicious than non-Jews of lower-class political organizations since the mob had been turned violently against them on countless occasions since the late Middle Ages. Similarly, Jews had throughout history depended upon the ruling elites, kings and nobles, to protect them. Many prominent Jewish financiers in the nineteenth century were closely allied with the old aristocracy or the monarchy.

Many prominent and highly visible socialists, such as Karl Marx and Ferdinand Lassalle, were also of Jewish origin. However, these, like the financial magnates, were exceptional individuals rather than men who were typical of the Jewish community in western and central Europe. Since Jews in western and much of central Europe had become members of the comfortable, property-owning bourgeoisie, Jewish liberals them- selves were at the forefront of those who attacked the socialists and other representatives of the emerging lower classes. With the rise of political anti-Semitism, Jews felt threatened not only as Jews but as property owners – in fact, almost certainly at first more as property owners than as Jews.

The relations of classes, races, and religious groups were substantially different in the United States, and, of course, the country had no aris- tocracy or monarchy. Nevertheless, the German-Jewish bourgeoisie there resembled western European Jews in its attachment to liberalism and its distaste for populist or socialist ideas – the latter of which came to America to a large degree with the massive Russian-Jewish immigration that began in the last two decades of the nineteenth century.

On a few occasions in Germany, so alarmed were Jewish liberals by the rapidly growing socialists that they were even willing to cooperate temporarily with anti-Semitic factions in order to defeat socialist candi- dates for political office. More commonly, Jewish liberals, especially in Austria-Hungary, opportunistically sought to discredit socialist critiques of capitalism as tinged with religious-racial bigotry, as inherently anti- Semitic. It was true that anti-Semitic motifs found their way into socialist rhetoric, especially during the early part of the century, in the assertion that "capitalism is Jewish." On the whole, however, Marxist socialism took a principled stand against anti-Semitism, contemptuously dismissing it as the "socialism of fools." Christian socialism, on the other hand, was more lastingly and unambiguously anti-Semitic.

The lower-middle class and anti-Semitic ideology – the 1880s

Those scholars who have studied anti-Semitism in the nineteenth and twentieth centuries are nearly unanimous in describing it as most characteristically an urban petty-bourgeois or lower-middle-class phenomenon, especially in western and central Europe. The major exception is in eastern Europe, where the middle classes were much less numerous, as also were cities and towns; there anti-Jewish resentment was found among those strata of the gentry that felt threatened in one way or another by the rise of the Jews. But in the rest of Europe Jews made an irresistible, almost inevitable target for anti-Semitic agitation among non-Jewish artisans, shopkeepers, and clerks who believed that their livelihood was being destroyed by Jews, that their country was being taken over by these alien upstarts. Members of the lower-middle classes who aspired to upward mobility into the professions often found that their children could not gain access to higher education because of the greatly disproportionate numbers of Jews there. Shopkeepers resented the "unfair" competition of Jewish-owned department stores.

Among those who arose to speak on behalf of the lower-middle class, to offer an ideological interpretation of its dilemma, and, finally, to organize a movement to fight on its behalf, was Wilhelm Marr (1819–1904). His writings have come, in most histories, to epitomize the new or modern racist anti-Semitism of the 1880s. He was the author of the first anti-Semitic best-seller, entitled *The Victory of Jewry over Germany* (1879), and the man normally given credit for coining the term *anti-Semitism*.[5] Marr was among the most important of those who derided Christian hostility to Jews and instead emphasized racial themes, what he believed the Jewish race did in the real world. Eugen Dühring (1833–1921), a prominent economist and social theorist in Germany, similarly, offered his readers a somewhat more sophisticated if also virulently racist, pagan anti-Semitism, rejecting Christianity because of its roots in Judaism, and offering in its stead an anti-Marxist "German socialism."[6]

[5] Cf. Moshe Zimmermann, *Wilhelm Marr: The Patriarch of Anti-Semitism* (New York, 1986).
[6] Cf. Jacob Katz, *From Prejudice to Destruction: Anti-Semitism, 1700–1933* (Cambridge, Mass, 1980), 265 ff.

The rise of modern, racist anti-Semitism was Europe-wide, but German-speaking theorists and activists, like Dühring and Marr, are normally given credit for being the leaders or the pacesetters of the new anti-Semitism of the 1870s and 1880s, just as the anti-Semitic movements in German-speaking Europe set the tone for those in other countries. In part this Europe-wide reputation of Germans derived from the enormous prestige of the new German Reich, just unified in 1870–1 under Bismarck's leadership. German intellectuals in particular enjoyed wide prestige; even a middle-brow journalist like Marr benefited from the reputation of German-speaking scientists, academics, and artists both in the new Reich and in the Austro-Hungarian Empire. Germans seemed well on their way to becoming the dominant people in Europe, much as the French had been for the preceding two centuries.

Many Germans, from nearly all walks of life, some who enjoyed much greater prestige and respectability than either Marr or Dühring, expressed their concern about the new role of Jews in German life. Heinrich von Treitschke (1834–96), an extremely popular and influential historian, wrote a number of articles in the late 1870s and early 1880s about what he considered to be the unfortunate influence of Jews in German culture, and those articles were the source of very wide comment and often emotional controversy in 1879–80.[7] Treitschke's concerns were in fact nationalistic and cultural rather than racial: He accepted Jewish civil equality, refused support for the political anti-Semites of the day, praised a number of Jews in German history, and did not believe in racial determinism. But he believed that the rise of the Jews in Germany had gone far enough. He granted that Jews had formerly been useful to Germany, but he argued that they were now becoming destructive. He found many in Germany who agreed with him. The slogan "The Jews are our misfortune!" became associated with his name, and many university students, following – and, indeed, going much beyond – his lead, took up the new cause of anti-Semitism. That slogan, which derived from Heine's quip about it being a "misfortune" (*Unglück*) to be Jewish, was later made even more notorious by the Nazis.

Concurrently, Adolf Stöcker (1835–1909), the chaplain to the court of the German emperor, began an ambitious public campaign against the ravages of modern capitalism in Germany. His Christian-social position was epitomized in the slogan "The social question is the Jewish Question." In other words, the Jewish spirit, or character, was responsible for the greed, corruption, and exploitation that so characterized the Germany of his day. Jews had, he charged, succeeded in "jewifying" Germany, in drawing it away from its Germanic-Christian roots. The famous composer

[7] Cf. Walter Boehlich, ed., *Der Berliner Antisemitisimusstreit* (Frankfurt am Main, 1965).

Richard Wagner republished in the 1870s an earlier broadside, *Jews in Music*, asserting that Jews, lacking true roots in any European culture, could never become genuinely creative artists. Their interest in art, Wagner maintained, had only to do with the money they could make from it.

In the capital of the German Reich the anti-Semitic "Berlin Movement" gained international attention in the early 1880s. It represented an attempt to bring together previously antipathetic parties or hostile social groups around a program of anti-Semitic legislation. Young activists circulated the Anti-Semites' Petition, which by late 1880 had gathered over a quarter of a million signatures, ten thousand in Berlin alone. The petition charged that an "alien tribe" had rapidly gained domination over the "Aryan race" in Germany since the unification of the country (in 1871), and it called for a number of measures to reverse that domination. These included the limitation of Jewish immigration into Germany, the exclusion of Jews from positions of high governmental or political authority, a special census to keep track of Jews, and the prohibition of Jewish teachers in primary schools.[8]

The petition was presented to Bismarck in the following year. Although he later let it be known that he did not approve of anti-Semitism, he made no immediate public response to the petition. He was at this point moving to the right and was willing, at least for a short time, to use the anti-Semites against the left in Germany. In his immediate entourage, moreover, were a number of figures who were explicitly hostile to the Jews. But Bismarck soon recognized that the anti-Semitic movement of the 1880s was less impressive than many had at first thought. Some of the leaders of the Berlin Movement were socially conservative, whereas others were not. Some spoke for the Junkers (Germany's ruling aristocratic class, the class from which Bismarck came); others spoke for the peasants, and yet others for the lower-middle class. Some were practical and moderate; others, fanatical and revolutionary. Some were racists (such as Marr and Dühring); others, such as Treitschke and Stöcker, explicitly rejected racism – indeed, Treitschke refused to sign the petition. Such differences led to violent disagreements within the ranks of the anti-Semites and to schism after schism in their various organizations and parties.

In spite of the sudden attention they attracted in the 1880s, Germany's anti-Semites were notable failures in the political arena. They never received more than 5 percent of the vote in national elections, and that 5 percent represented a fractured and confused body of voters. Many Germans were repelled by the demagogy of prominent anti-Semitic activists. Others, initially attracted by what they believed were the genuinely re-

[8] Cf. Paul Massing, *Rehearsal for Destruction* (New York, 1967; first published, 1949); Richard S. Levy, *The Downfall of the Anti-Semitic Political Parties in Imperial Germany* (New Haven, Conn., 1975).

forming elements in anti-Semitic agitation, were finally disillusioned by the low moral tone of many anti-Semitic leaders, by the numbers of them who were implicated in scandals – bribery, blackmail, embezzlement, and paternity suits. Not one of the various anti-Semitic bills introduced into the Reichstag from the 1880s to 1914 was passed or even had a remote chance of being passed. Marr, the "patriarch" of the anti-Semites, renounced his earlier anti-Semitic writings in the late 1880s. He summed up the opinion of many who had been initially attracted to the Berlin Movement by remarking that the anti-Semites were worse than the Jews.[9]

Anti-Semitic agitation in German-speaking Austria in the 1880s developed into a stronger, more violent movement. The discredit of liberalism in Austria among the common people was greater than it was in Bismarck's Reich, the rise of the Jews was more spectacular, and the two, liberalism and the Jews, were more closely linked in the public mind. Similarly, German national identity was a more threatened and paranoiac affair in Austria than in the German Reich. Various nationalities were demanding an end to German domination, and Jewish influence in public life had assumed greater dimensions in Austria. Treitschke, who so effectively expressed the German sense of being threatened culturally inside the German Reich, viewed the situation of Austrian Germans with utter horror, as being "unspeakably corrupted by Semitism."[10]

The Jewish population of Austria-Hungary was many times larger than that of the German Reich and in many areas far more dense. The crownland, or province, of Galicia contained the largest population of Jews in Europe outside the Russian Pale of Settlement, both absolutely and relatively (810,000, or 11 percent of the total population of Galicia, by the turn of the century).[11] In the German Reich as a whole there were around 500,000 Jews, about 1 percent of the population, as contrasted with 1.3 million Jews in the Austrian half of the Dual Monarchy, approximately 5 percent of the total. Although there were pockets of urban, middle-class affluence in Galicia, on the whole the Jews of that province were widely considered the poorest, least educated, most economically backward, and most religiously orthodox of any major area, including the Russian Pale.

The Jews of Austria-Hungary received civil equality in 1867, which meant that the impoverished Jews of Galicia and other areas in the east could legally move about, and they did so in great numbers, many of them to the capital, Vienna. However, the largest migration of Jews to the capital came from other regions, especially from western areas of the

[9] Zimmermann, *Patriarch*, 103.

[10] Quoted in Geoffry Field, *Evangelist of Race: The Germanic Vision of Houston Stewart Chamberlain* (New York, 1980), 144.

[11] Marsha L. Rozenblit, *The Jews of Vienna, 1867–1914: Assimilation and Identity* (Albany, N.Y., 1983), 32.

empire. In 1860 Vienna's Jewish population had numbered 6,000. By 1870 the figure had risen to 40,000, by 1910 175,000,[12] about 9 percent of the total population of the city, thus an increase of about thirty times in less than half a century. For the citizens of Vienna the rise of the Jews was a most striking, palpable matter.

That non-Jews in the capital of Austria had a sense of being overwhelmed by a Jewish "invasion" is at any rate easy to understand, particularly because Jews tended to choose certain occupations from which non-Jews were often consequently driven out, when they did not leave simply of their own volition. Those occupations were ones that were highly visible and particularly associated with modern liberalism. Nearly all banks in the capital, and indeed in the Dual Monarchy as a whole, were owned by Jews, as were many of the most important newspapers, especially those of mass circulation. Similarly, the presence of Jews in medicine and the law, although not so overwhelming as in finance and journalism, was still much disproportionate to the overall numbers of Jews in Austria. Both the absolute and relative numbers of Jewish doctors and lawyers continued to rise until World War I.

Anti-Semitism arrived in Austria, after the crash of 1873, with an explosive force, making the disturbances in Germany seem mild and law-abiding by comparison. Charges in Germany that Jews were responsible for the crash had to be considered in the light of abundant evidence that many non-Jews were also involved. But in Austria the capitalist financiers, the stockjobbers, the builders of railroads, those responsible for the bankruptcies of artisans and small retailers, the deceivers of the small investors were undeniably to a large extent of Jewish background. Even more than in Germany, anti-Semitism mixed with anticapitalism in Austria, and that mixture explains to an important degree its greater appeal. Such radical-democratic or populist anti-Semitism found its most successful exponent in the person of Georg Ritter von Schönerer (1842–1921). He captured the attention of the nation in a way that no single anti-Semitic politician in Germany came close to doing. Even the *Neue Freie Presse*, a Jewish-owned and -operated newspaper of considerable prestige in Austria, described him as the "man of the hour."[13]

Von Schönerer has been described as a "sincere" anti-Semite, as distinguished from those who used anti-Semitism cynically, without any heartfelt hatred for Jews, as a way of manipulating the masses and avoiding real change. Such "insincere" anti-Semitism was common in the German Conservative Party, for example. Von Schönerer's concern for the German peasants, artisans, and shopkeepers was manifestly heartfelt. His sincerity

---

[12] Ibid., 18; Alexander Whiteside, *The Socialism of Fools: Georg Ritter von Schönerer and Austrian Pan Germanism* (Berkeley, Calif., 1975), 17.
[13] Whiteside, *Socialism of Fools*, 75–6.

also verged on fanaticism, and he waged his war against the rise of the Jews in Austria in an increasingly intemperate way. But his fanaticism matched the popular mood in Austria in the early 1880s. The so-called *Reformvereine* (reform organizations), which were especially numerous in Vienna, brought together rowdy, violence-prone artisans and workers itching for a fight. Their economic and social grievances found expression in a shockingly vulgar, even obscene Jew-hatred. Posters, figurines, cartoons, and jingles portrayed thick-lipped, large-nosed Jews in various undignified guises, often hanging from gallows.

Von Schönerer himself, although of respectable background, soon cast respectability to the winds. In word and in deed, he became ever more coarse and brutal. He gave leadership to a wave of efforts to hound Jews out of democratic-radical caucuses, student fraternities, and various other social and political organizations. He became a hero not only to the non-Jewish lower classes but also to non-Jewish university students, who felt threatened by the influx of Jews into Austrian universities. He addressed large crowds who ardently chanted, "It's the Jews' fault!"[14]

Yet his anti-Semitic movement also failed in its goals. An important part of the explanation for that failure lies in his own sincerity, for von Schönerer was more radically and genuinely racist than was the great mass of his followers in Austria. Similarly, his hatred for the Catholic Church and his admiration for Prussia were not shared by the Austrian masses. His speeches grew ever more wild and irresponsible, as did his actions. He provoked endless factionalism within the ranks of his followers, and he was repeatedly challenged to duels by those he insulted and defamed. In 1888, after he broke into the editorial offices of an offending Jewish-owned newspaper and broke up the presses, he was stripped both of his parliamentary immunity and of his right to serve as an elected official. A jail sentence followed. As a convict, he automatically lost his title of nobility. His Pan-German movement ("pan-German" since he wanted to unite all Germans into one Reich) fell into confusion and disarray, hounded by the authorities and denounced by respectable opinion.

Eastern Jews and western Jews

There were, by the late nineteenth century, huge differences between the Jews in the advanced, industrialized countries like Germany, France, or the United States and those, at the time often referred to collectively as *Ostjuden* (German for "eastern Jews") in tsarist Russia (which at this time included most of historic Poland), Romania, and parts of the Austro-

[14] Ibid., 87.

Hungarian Empire, particularly Galicia. Western European Jews spoke the languages of the countries in which they resided; Ostjuden spoke Yiddish. In eastern Europe, too, tens of thousands of Jews emerged as a prosperous, progressive bourgeoisie by the end of the nineteenth century, often taking up Polish or Russian as the language spoken at home, but the numbers of impoverished traditional and Yiddish-speaking Ostjuden were much greater. The great majority of these millions in eastern Europe were often pushed to the edge of survival.[15]

In spite of their poverty, one may also speak of a rise of Ostjuden in one important sense: Eastern Europe was where the population of Jews grew most rapidly, where it was the largest to begin with, and where the major part of Jewish population growth elsewhere originated, through immigration. The ranks of the Ostjuden grew at a remarkable rate for most of the century, far more rapidly than the numbers of Jews in the West, and also more rapidly than the non-Jewish, mostly Slavic peoples among whom they lived. The reasons for these differences in fecundity are obscure,[16] but an important if not always adequately recognized point is that the degrading poverty of the Jews in eastern Europe derived from this population explosion in the context of backward economies in early stages of industrialization, not simply from the hostility, undeniable as that sometimes was, of those who ruled over the Jews.

The economies of the countries of eastern Europe were unable to absorb this extraordinary increase in numbers of Jews. At the same time, the governments and non-Jewish peoples of the area were deeply uncertain whether they even wished to absorb the Jews. They were inclined to fear that the rapidly increasing Jews would eventually dominate them. The inability of traditional or sluggish economies to absorb a rapidly expanding population has become, of course, a familiar syndrome in many areas of the world, well into the twentieth century. The attending miseries of the Ostjuden and the peoples of the non-European world have many parallels. Also similar is the tendency to offer simplistic, moralizing, and self-serving explanations for those miseries.

Related to the population explosion, and no doubt partly a cause of it, was the disintegration of traditional Jewish society in eastern Europe. Young people were inclined to pick up and leave not only because of demographic pressures but because they no longer identified with traditional Jewish values. Even more broadly and palpably, many of them had come to resent existing Jewish authorities. As one historian has com-

---

[15] Cf. Jack Wertheimer, *Unwelcome Strangers: East European Jews in Imperial Germany* (Oxford, 1987); Trude Maurer, *Ostjuden in Deutschland, 1918–1933* (Hamburg, 1986); Steven Aschheim, *Brothers and Strangers: The Eastern European Jew in Germany and German Jewish Consciousness, 1800–1923* (Madison, Wis., 1982).
[16] Cf. Paul Ritterband, ed., *Modern Jewish Fertility* (Leiden, 1981).

mented, "The rich and the poor, the traditionalists and the enlightened, all shared a sense of distaste and distrust of their putative leaders."[17] As Jews broke free of the controls of tradition and established authority, they were perceived by many as "out of control," not only because they joined revolutionary movements, as hundreds of thousands of them eventually did, but because they became part of the milling masses of Russia's burgeoning cities, where non-Jews, too, usually of peasant background, flocked, having broken free from their own traditional societies.

In much of eastern Europe, Gentile employers would not hire Jews; they were not considered desirable employees, both for objective reasons and out of prejudice ("fantasy"). Many Jews themselves did not want to work for Gentiles and resisted taking up certain trades, either for religious reasons (for example, dietary regulations and prohibitions against Sabbath labor), or because of certain powerful cultural values, themselves linked to religious traditions (a disinclination to take up heavy manual labor, such as mining, for example, which was matched by a widespread belief by employers – Jewish employers no less than Gentile – that Jews were physically unsuited to engage in such work). Jews therefore gravitated to the needle trades and other light industries rather than to mining or work in steel factories.

These complications were in turn linked to tsarist regulations that limited the kinds of economic activity Jews were allowed to undertake and that restricted, or attempted to direct, where they could move in Russia in search of a better life. These many factors encouraged the emigration of hundreds of thousands, finally of millions, of Jews out of eastern Europe in the late nineteenth and early twentieth centuries. Most of them finally found their way to the Americas, especially to the United States. A smaller number settled in western and central Europe, and even smaller numbers made their way to Palestine.

The departure of these throngs of impoverished Jews from eastern Europe, one of the most extensive movements of population in modern times, had decidedly unfavorable implications for relations between Jews and Gentiles in the rest of Europe, as well as in America. Jews from eastern Europe had been arriving in relatively moderate numbers in western Europe for much of the nineteenth century, but by the late 1870s and early 1880s the numbers of immigrants began a rapid rise. This population movement, coinciding as it did with the depressed economic conditions of the 1880s, acted almost everywhere as an intensifier or a

---

[17] Michael Stanislawski, "The Transformation of Traditional Jewish Authority in Russian Jewry: The First Stage," in David Berger, ed., *The Legacy of Jewish Migration: 1881 and Its Impact* (New York, 1983), 28.

catalyst for tensions of many sorts – economic, social, cultural, political
– that had been building for some time.

The shift of the *Fin de Siècle*, 1890–1914

The Three Affairs occurred within a fifteen-year period, from just before
the turn of the century to the eve of World War I. The span of years
from the 1890s to 1914 have often been seen by historians as having a
certain unity to them, a common spirit, although the exact contours differ
from country to country, as do the rubrics used – the Wilhelmian period
in Germany (after Wilhelm II, who dominated the German political scene
after he forced Bismarck to retire in 1890), the *Belle Epoque* (beautiful
epoch) in France, the Edwardian era in England (after Edward VII, who
took over after Victoria's long reign), the Progressive Era in the United
States. Behind the many differences of the various countries certain important similarities, helpful in understanding the Three Affairs and in
various ways related to the rise of the Jews, can still be discerned.

Probably the most widely discussed of these similarities, and one that
bears most tangibly upon the Three Affairs, was the disenchantment with
the prevailing liberalism of the fifties, sixties, and early seventies. This
disenchantment had begun to emerge in the depression years of the 1870s
and 1880s, but by the 1890s antiliberal and antirational trends assumed
a much greater importance. From nearly all quarters, in fact from both
non-Jews and Jews themselves, came searing critiques of what was now
considered the shallow optimism of the midcentury, of the uncritical belief
in progress, science, and technology. No less searing critiques were directed at the often corrupt practices of liberals in power. Intertwined
with such critiques were fears for the future, a sense that society was in
decay.

International relations between 1890 and 1914 assumed forms that suggested as well a relative lack of rational control, of an increasingly reckless
competition, and of nations driven by forces their leaders could scarcely
control – the increasingly clamorous masses; the new, yellow journalism;
the alliance systems that were formed in response to militarism, popular
nationalism, and imperialism. Many scholars have seen Germany as the
key troublemaker and also as the country that was most ominously driven
by internal troubles and contradictions.

Germans, only recently unified into a national state, yearned for their
"place in the sun." Those yearnings naturally worried Germany's neighbors and led to growing tensions with them. Germany suffered from
important internal tensions as well. In 1890, with Bismarck's departure,

the German Social Democratic Party was allowed to regain the legal status denied it after 1878. From 1890 to 1914 the party grew with great speed, threatening to take over Germany in the not too distant future. This prospect, with its intimations of a proletarian dictatorship and the so-cialization of the means of production, understandably alarmed Germany's ruling elite and its property-owning classes.

The period between 1890 and 1914 saw a gradual diplomatic rap-prochement of France, Russia, and Great Britain, resulting in what Ger-many's leaders had long feared: "encirclement" by enemy powers. German leaders and the country's privileged classes persuaded them-selves that they faced enemies of growing power both internally and externally. The efforts by Germany's ruling elites to counter these per-ceived threats, even to exaggerate them in order to mobilize support for the status quo, set the tone of the Wilhelmian period in Germany, and by extension, of Europe as a whole from 1890 to 1914. France and Russia were also haunted by fears of both internal and external threats.

In some respects, however, there seemed to be grounds for optimism. The Great Depression in Europe eased, after a final plunge in the early 1890s, and thereafter most European economies showed renewed dy-namism and rising productivity. However, not all shared in the new prosperity. Small producers in particular, often harder hit by the depres-sion of the 1880s than were large firms, felt ever more beleaguered. The trends toward concentration continued: from boutique to department store, from workshop to factory, from family farm to concentrated agri-cultural units producing for national and international markets. Moreover, Germany's unusual economic dynamism and demographic fecundity from the mid-1890s on generated many problems, the growth of the socialist labor movement being only one of them. The Imperial Reich seemed unable or unwilling to deal with these problems imaginatively. Germany's relatively rapid growth made her neighbors increasingly nervous. Their concerns found focus in the new emperor: Wilhelm's erratic leadership, his intemperate pronouncements and saber-rattling, were part of a general picture of German aggressiveness that drove Germany's neighbors, France, Russia, and finally Great Britain, to combine forces against it. That combination only intensified German paranoia and belligerence. It was a vicious cycle that would culminate in general war.

It would be natural to assume that anti-Semitism in Germany was on the rise between 1890 and 1914, that the external and internal pressures, the rising tribalistic and paranoiac nationalism in the country, would inevitably turn against the Jews. Some historians have spoken of a "gath-ering storm" of anti-Semitism. However, after the turn of the century anti-Semitic sentiment became fractured and confused in Germany, as well as in many other countries. Jews themselves joined in the mood of aggressive nationalism, while the anti-Semitic parties in Germany, after the excitements of the early 1880s, weakened, and by the eve of the war had collapsed. Anti-Semites in Germany as well as other countries were absorbed into more respectable right-wing movements, generally of a moderately conservative nature, if also moderately anti-Semitic. Historians speak of a dormant period for political anti-Semitism in Germany from the mid-1890s until 1914, although some have argued that hatred of Jews merely went underground, or "sunk in," assuming forms other than overtly political, most notably cultural and social.[18] Nevertheless, many Germans, both Jews and non-Jews, took satisfaction that their country was calm in the years that many other countries, including France and Russia, were torn by violent expressions of anti-Semitism.

In Austria, German-speaking but different from the German Reich, overt forms of anti-Semitism continued to be important. After the collapse of von Schönerer's movement, political anti-Semitism, as embodied in the Christian social movement under the leadership of Karl Lueger (1844–1910), achieved its greatest prewar success. Just when the Dreyfus Affair was raging in France and anti-Jewish sentiment in Russia was about to explode in pogroms, Lueger was enjoying enormous popularity in Vienna. He had finally become mayor of the city after being repeatedly rejected because of his anti-Semitic demagogy (Emperor Franz Joseph long refused to accept such a man as the mayor of the imperial capital). Lueger offered a program of municipal reform, or what was called "municipal socialism," and he promised to limit what he denounced as the overweening power of Jews in the capital.

Hitler would later describe both von Schönerer and Lueger as models, yet Lueger's anti-Semitism was of a peculiar nature, significantly different from Hitler's. It has been termed insincere because it lacked the racist fanaticism of the sort expressed by Dühring, von Schönerer, or Hitler. In spite of his attacks on the role of Jews in Austria, Lueger maintained Jewish friendships and eventually, after noisy confrontations, worked out compromises with powerful Jewish financiers in order to get some of his public welfare measures introduced. Although he dismissed some Jews from municipal employment and harassed Jewish peddlers, in truth he and his Christian social movement caused only superficial damage to the material fortunes of Jews in Vienna (the impact of Lueger and his movement on the Jewish psyche, much more difficult to measure, is another matter). Indeed, the period when he was mayor coincides with what has been called the golden age of Viennese Jewry, and Jews continued to move into the city at much the same rate as before. Nevertheless, his brand of demagogic politics, his cynical exploitation of resentments against

[18] Levy, *Downfall*, 1–7.

the Jews to mobilize the masses, may be seen as a typical expression of the period, as well as the most successful use of anti-Semitism as a political device in the world immediately preceding the war. Still, one might certainly question if anti-Semitism was the key to his success and popularity.[19]

Lueger's efforts to help the common people through municipal socialism and his attack on liberal principles and practices had parallels in many countries in the same years. The power of the central state grew in nearly all countries of Europe in the generation before 1914, and Europe's states began to intervene in the economy in an "illiberal" way, seeking to regulate the economic relations of its citizens through taxation and social-welfare measures. This power was in part in response to the growing centralization of industry, the size and power of economic concentrations, which required state regulation. The numbers of state employees increased, and the size of the armies expanded. State-sponsored education was extended to previously untouched elements of the population, providing a newly literate or at least semiliterate audience for the burgeoning popular press. That press began to sell copies in wholly unprecedented numbers, making profit from advertisements rather than from purchase price. Many newspapers now attracted readers through crude sensationalism, typically playing upon war scares, espionage, colonial adventures, and government corruption. Such newspapers played a key role in all of the Three Affairs.

Trends that put new kinds of power in the hands of political and economic leaders tended to increase the appeal and plausibility of long-standing charges, now taken up by the popular press, that powerbrokers or moneymen were working behind the scenes. Popular orators as different as William Jennings Bryan in the United States and Karl Lueger in Vienna charged that the common people were being "crucified" by financial magnates. These magnates were often identified as Jews, particularly in continental Europe but also, if to a significantly smaller degree, in Great Britain and the United States.

A Europe-wide body of opinion, cutting across class lines, focused on what was perceived as Jewish ruthlessness and immorality in the search of profit. It was often asserted, and much discussed in the press, that the brutal Boer War (1899–1902) was manipulated to benefit wealthy Jews.[20] The repression of an uprising in Romania in 1907, in the course of which thousands of starving and desperate Romanian peasants were slaughtered,

[19] Cf. Richard S. Geehr, *Karl Lueger, Mayor of Fin de Siècle Vienna* (Detroit, 1990).
[20] Colin Holmes, *Anti-Semitism in British Society: 1876–1939* (New York, 1979), 13; Stephen Koss, *The Pro-Boers* (Chicago, 1972).

was widely described as protecting Jewish interests.[21] International prostitution rings, termed white slavery at the time, were commonly believed
to be in the hands of Jews.[22]

Involvement of Jews in these matters was not only plausible but real
enough, and in the case of white slavery was a concern of Jewish leaders
throughout the world, who recognized it as a special Jewish problem.
However, the whole story in all of these cases was more ambiguous than
anti-Semites were willing to believe. Still, whether merely plausible or
objectively verifiable, the idea of Jewish manipulation of important events,
of vast and malevolent Jewish power over the destiny of Europe's peoples,
often greatly excited the general public of Europe and America. In the
Belle Epoque the Jewish Question, apparently dying down in Germany,
came to center stage in many other countries. The Three Anti-Semitic
Affairs were among the most dramatic expressions of this development.

The issue of Jewish involvement in world affairs at this time, and the
more general phenomenon of the rise of the Jews, may be said to come
down to the question, in its classic formulation: Were modern times good
or bad for the Jews? There is a converse question: Were the Jews good
or bad for modern times? If ever questions have resisted being answered
with a simple yes or no, it was these, for the evidence is extraordinarily
difficult to interpret. Whether or not there was a "gathering storm" or a
"rising tide" of anti-Semitism may have to do with deceptive imagery.
The contours of European opinion between 1890 and 1914 do not comfortably fit into the metaphor of a "storm" or a "tide." In each country,
behind the surface phenomena of trials, demonstrations, and riots, were
not only structural trends toward greater tribalism and rejection of modern
times but also concurrent trends that indicated a continued rise of the
Jews and a growing acceptance of it by non-Jews, a broader recognition
of a legitimate position for Jews in the states and societies of modern
Europe and America. Philo-Semitism of a modern sort also appeared in
the nineteenth century, but because it did not become a "problem" in
the way that anti-Semitism did it has been studied far less.[23] At any rate,
the development of hostile attitudes to Jews looked very different in 1914
than it did after 1945. Those attitudes require a most careful examination,
one that tries not to project back onto the prewar years the attitudes and
conclusions of later, much more bitter and disabused generations.

[21] Cf. Philip Gabriel Eidelberg, *The Great Rumanian Peasant Revolt of 1907: Origins of a Modern Jacquerie* (Leiden, The Netherlands, 1974).
[22] Edward J. Bristow, *Prostitution and Prejudice: The Jewish Fight Against White Slavery, 1870–1939* (Oxford, 1983).
[23] This matter will be further explored in the conclusion of Chapter 4.

3

Earlier anti-Semitic affairs

The Dreyfus, Beilis, and Frank affairs were preceded by a number of others in the nineteenth century, before the rise of modern mass politics. The earlier affairs, too, were colorful and bizarre almost beyond belief but remain little known.

Of course, popular uprisings in Europe against the Jews, "affairs" of a different sort, dot the centuries from the Middle Ages through the French Revolution. The Crusades are famous examples of great popular excitements that also entailed violent attacks on Jews in Europe, undertaken before the crusaders left for the Holy Land. During the outbreaks of plague in the late Middle Ages, Jews were accused of poisoning wells in order to spread the disease among Christians. At other times Jews were accused of "desecrating the Host," that is, stealing communion wafers after the Eucharist ceremony and spitting or urinating upon them, revealing an ineradicable hatred of Christ and Christians. Perhaps the most pervasive charge, one that remained most stubbornly in the minds of the great mass of Christians, was that Jews used Christian blood for their rituals. Particularly at Easter season, coinciding with the Jews' celebration of Passover, the charge was made that Jews ritually murdered Christian children and mixed their blood into matzot.

Although the charge seems straight out of the Dark Ages, accusations of ritual murder by Jews continued to crop up well into modern times, especially in central and eastern Europe. One scholar has identified over twenty of them in the two or three decades before World War I.[1] Mendel Beilis was charged with murdering a Christian boy for ritual purposes, as late as 1911. Many ritual murder or "blood libel"[2] trials were held in the nineteenth and early twentieth centuries, particularly in Russia,[3] and several of them became affairs of a sort. Two deserve brief consideration as providing useful and revealing background for the Three Affairs: the Damascus Affair (1840) and the Tisza-eszlár Affair (1882).

---

[1] Zosa Szajkowski, "The Impact of the Beiliss Case on Central and Western Europe," *American Academy for Jewish Research, Proceedings*, vol. 31, 1963, 198.
[2] The charge of ritual murder has sometimes been called the "blood libel," although the term has been confused and debased, much like "anti-Semite."
[3] Cf. Salo W. Baron, *The Russian Jew Under Tsars and Soviets* (New York, 1987), 28–9.

The Damascus Affair and the power of international Jewry

Both Jews and Christians were protected minorities (*dhimmis*) under Ottoman rule. Insofar as Jews faced Muslim persecution it was typically for blasphemy or apostasy (converting to Islam and then back to Judaism), not for ritual murder. Christians in Muslim lands, themselves a vulnerable minority, were hardly in a position to persecute Jews, and until the nineteenth century they did not much borrow from European Christian charges against the Jews. However, in the course of the nineteenth century, as European influence grew in areas of Muslim rule, the charge of ritual murder began to appear with growing regularity.

The Jews of Syria in the nineteenth century could normally rely on protection from their Muslim overlords, at least in comparison with the riot-plagued Jews in neighboring Iraq. Nevertheless, relations between Jews and Arab Christians, a much larger and more conspicuous minority than the Jews in Syria, remained tense. Syrian Christians were receptive to the anti-Semitic notions brought into the country by French traders and missionaries.[4]

In early February 1840 in Damascus, an Italian Capuchin friar, Father Tomaso, disappeared without a trace, along with his personal servant. In the confusion that followed, his fellow monks spread the charge that the Jews had murdered the two for ritual purposes. This was not a wholly unprecedented charge in this area, even in the first part of the century, but the international attention it finally received certainly was. A number of factors came together to make the accusation of ritual murder in this case stand out from previous and subsequent charges, both in its immediate notoriety and its long-range historical influence. Indeed, the Damascus case is one of the generally recognized signposts of modern Jewish history.

After the disappearance of Father Tomaso, a Jewish barber was arrested by the governor, Sharif Pasha, in his investigation of the case. The barber confessed to the crime and named seven leaders of the Jewish community in Damascus who had, he claimed, organized the murder of the monk. In the arrests that followed, a number of other Jews also confessed to the murder. News of the murder and the confessions spread throughout the Levant. Many Muslims as well as Christians came to believe that Jews had in fact committed a ritual murder. In Damascus the Jewish community suffered mob violence, and in other parts of Syria there were reprisals against Jews.

It was later revealed that these confessions were exacted under duress,

---

[4] Cf. Norman A. Stillman, *The Jews of Arab Lands* (Philadelphia, 1979), 104–5.

in some cases under brutal torture or the threat of it. But the initial reports that the accused had confessed seem to have persuaded many observers, no doubt some of whom were quite ready to believe in Jewish guilt and who then allowed themselves to be overwhelmed with indignation about it. They subsequently found it difficult to back down as new information emerged that put the guilt of the Jews into doubt. This was a pattern that would operate time after time in the anti-Semitic affairs of the nineteenth and early twentieth centuries.

Furthermore, an initially sincere belief in the guilt of the accused, in the Damascus Affair and in subsequent ones, was particularly important in the case of the authorities, not all of whose representatives were corrupt or necessarily driven by anti-Semitism. The governor's apparently genuine belief that the Jews were guilty justified torture in his eyes. It also prompted him to arrest sixty-three Jewish children in order to force their parents to divulge the secret of where the Jewish community had hidden the blood of the murdered monk and his servant. Other authorities were later genuinely persuaded that Dreyfus had sold secrets to the Germans or that Frank had murdered Mary Phagan.

A further important development in the case was the support given by the French consul in Damascus to the ritual murder charges. The French government, in turn, supported its representative in Damascus. To the modern reader this support must appear surprising, and it was the cause of much puzzled comment at the time, for France was considered a leader of the enlightened nations of the world. The French Revolution had given civil equality to the Jews of France in 1791, and the armies of the revolution had emancipated the Jews in much of the rest of Europe. In the reactionary period following 1815, when France's European empire was dissolved, some of the legal rights of Jews outside France had been reduced, but the situation of Jews inside France by 1840 constituted an ideal for aspiring modern Jews in the rest of Europe. France was the homeland of humanity and toleration; in no European country did Jews have a better legal position. Had the Russian government supported the charge of ritual murder, there would have been less surprise, but for the French to do so persuaded many that the Jews in Damascus must be guilty.

Why should France take such a stance in regard to the ritual murder charges? The answer appears to be that France's leaders at that time believed it was in the long-range interest of their country to do so, whatever the truth of the charges against the unfortunate Jews. At this time France was supporting Muhammad Ali Pasha, the Ottoman governor of Egypt who had turned both Egypt and Syria into a semi-independent principality, with only nominal recognition of Ottoman authority. Great Britain and other European powers opposed the expansion of French power in the area. The ritual murder charges, which might otherwise have passed unnoticed in Europe, gained general attention because of the rivalry of Europe's great powers in the Middle East.

One must doubt that many in the French government at this time actually believed that the Jews in Damascus had committed a ritual murder. Nevertheless, responsible officials in the French government were willing to exploit the passions that gripped the area in order to consolidate French influence. The French consul went further: He supported a press campaign, in France itself, against the Jews of Damascus and Jews in general.[5] Of course, other nations, hostile to France, saw the affair as an opportunity to embarrass the French and to weaken their influence in the Levant if the charges against the Jews could be exposed as false. Ironically, Metternich, the archreactionary minister in Austria, denounced the ritual murder charges, as did the leaders of Great Britain.

How much a disinterested concern for justice, to say nothing of a genuine sympathy for Jewish suffering, played a role in these denunciations is not easy to determine, but obviously there is no more impassioned partisan of justice than someone who personally stands to benefit from it. Nevertheless, the United States, which had little to gain from the matter, one way or the other, also lodged a protest in favor of the accused and against the very idea of ritual murder. Many influential aristocrats in Europe in the early nineteenth century had formed friendships with wealthy Jews and were also financially dependent upon them. Metternich had established close relations with the Jewish financier Solomon Rothschild, and he had taken measures to improve conditions for Jews in Austria, even if he rejected the idea of full civil equality for them as a liberal or even dangerously radical notion. Similarly, friendships between wealthy Jews and the English aristocracy were common, but that did not necessarily mean that those aristocrats supported civil equality for Jews in general.[6]

The Damascus Affair has been described as a turning point in modern Jewish history because of the role that leading Jews in France played, a role that had far-flung and sometimes unforeseen implications. French Jews were among the strongest exponents of the modern notion that the traditional, or "religious," nationalism of the Jews was outmoded, that Jews both could and should become full citizens of modern nations. As full citizens, Jews could be as patriotic as any other people. Their religion should be a private matter, one that did not stand in the way of their duties as citizens. But with the developments in Damascus, French Jews found to their dismay that the leaders of their adopted country were

---

[5] Bernard Lewis, *The Jews of Islam* (Princeton, N.J.), 156.
[6] Cecil Roth, *A History of the Jews in England* (Oxford, 1964), 242 ff.

willing to give support to an ugly anti-Semitic libel in order to forward French international ambitions. French Jews found it necessary to oppose their government, in turn opposing what many in the country perceived as French interests.

Mere opposition to government policy was the stuff of French parliamentary life at the time and in itself not particularly remarkable or difficult. What was remarkable and difficult was the necessity of cooperating with France's enemies in order to rescue the Jews in Damascus. Adolphe Crémieux (1796–1880), a Jew and a prominent French politician, openly cooperated with Jewish leaders in Great Britain and Austria, countries considered to be France's enemies. Partly through exploiting the pressures exerted by those enemy countries, Jewish leaders in France were successful in obtaining the release of the Jewish prisoners in Damascus. Simultaneously, Muhammad Ali was forced to abandon Damascus and the rest of Syria-Palestine, which were restored to full Ottoman sovereignty. The sultan met with a delegation of European Jews, including Crémieux and Moses Montefiore of Great Britain, and issued an official denunciation of the charge of ritual murder by Jews.[7]

Thus the dilemma – and a troubling precedent: A victory for the Jews was perceived by many French patriots as a defeat for France, a defeat in which French Jews had collaborated with France's enemies. It might be countered, and indeed was at the time, that this was not a defeat for "true" France, the protector of liberty and justice, but many in France felt that their side had lost this particular contest to Jewish interests, to an internationally linked group of powerful Jews. It is revealing that Montefiore was received, on his return to England, as a national hero, while Crémieux was treated by some Frenchmen as a traitor.[8]

Anti-Semites, and even some Europeans who were not particularly hostile to Jews, saw in the Damascus Affair evidence of a central contradiction in the ideal of Jewish emancipation: A Jewish nation remained; Jews, no matter in which country they lived and in spite of their protestations of a modern-style patriotism, still held the interests of their Jewish brethren to be higher than those of their adopted countries. Indeed, Jewish observers themselves generally hailed the Damascus case as a great victory for Jews, as a Jewish historian later wrote, "not only because of its triumphant issue, but because it was the starting point of a new solidarity between the Jews of various countries."[9]

What was hailed as a new solidarity of Jews by such observers appeared as the reaffirmation or reemergence of a very old and ominous one to other observers. For them Jews remained, as they had been for centuries, a peculiar nation spread throughout the nations of Europe. But now, in

[7] Lewis, *Jews of Islam*, 157.
[8] Roth, *History*, 258–9.
[9] Cecil Roth, ed., *Essays in Jewish History by Lucien Wolfe* (London, 1934), 322.

sharp and troubling contrast to the past, that peculiar nation was able to exercise great power within those nations. Even more ominous was the spreading belief that wealthy and prominent Jews like the Rothschilds, Crémieux, or Montefiore were part of a covert international network with steadily growing power in the highest councils of Europe's states. It was a natural step from such beliefs to the panicked conviction in the latter part of the century that Jews were surreptitiously taking over in Europe, that a secret Jewish power was everywhere and nearly omnipotent.

Belief in international Jewish power was strengthened by a number of developments in the following two decades, particularly the Jewish response to the so-called Mortara Affair in 1858, having to do with the kidnapping in Italy of a six-year-old Jewish child from the home of his parents by the papal guard. The details of that affair need not detain us here; the important point for our concerns is that in order to respond more effectively to charges against Jews throughout the world, a formal International Israelitic Alliance (usually known by its French name, Alliance Israélite Universelle) was formed in Paris in 1860, with Crémieux as its president.

The founders of the Alliance emphasized their intention to defend Jewish honor, oppose prejudice, and strive toward civil emancipation of Jews everywhere. Concurrently, the new organization spoke of the need to improve the moral and intellectual condition of the Jews, especially in areas less fortunate than France. It took up as its slogan the rabbinic injunction "All Israel is responsible, one for the other." In England an Anglo-Jewish Association was formed, with similar goals. Many anti-Semites believed that the French Alliance was a front for the world Jewish government, exercising far-reaching clandestine power in the councils of Europe.

The issue of Jewish power is central to the Three Anti-Semitic Affairs. There are few more prickly issues than that of the international power of Jews in modern times, whether one is speaking of the 1860s or the 1980s. It would be fatuous and of little use to conclude that the truth about Jewish power lies somewhere between anti-Semitic fantasies of Jewish omnipotence and the claims by Jewish apologists that Jews have been utterly powerless, whether internationally or within in the various countries inhabited by Jews.

Obviously, the issue of the power of the Jews is linked to the rise of the Jews and must be considered in its historical evolution and in its contrasting national forms. In international relations individual Jews and Jewish organizations came to exercise undeniable influence in specific instances. The Damascus Affair is one of the more famous; another is the Berlin Congress of 1878, when Romania was forced, much against its will, to grant civil equality to its Jews. Even better known is the Paris Peace Conference of 1919, when protections for Jewish national minorities were incorporated into the constitutions of several new states – again often in the face of vehement opposition by the leaders of those states. There are even more striking examples in the decade before World War I, central to the Three Anti-Semitic Affairs, of the exercise of power by individual Jews and Jewish organizations to protect Jews and to forward Jewish interests in the world.

Against such cases must be posed many others, when the influence of individual Jews and Jewish organizations was minimal. Even when they did their utmost to exert pressure and when issues of vital interest to them were at stake, they proved impotent. But there was enough truth to concerns and complaints about Jewish power in a wide range of specific instances to assure that many people, not only a lunatic fringe, firmly believed in it. Individual Jews engaged in corrupt practices, and Jewish organizations were not above offering bribes or exerting behind-the-scenes pressure in the name of protecting Jews and Jewish interests. Moreover, there was enough secrecy surrounding the actions of Jewish organizations and powerful Jews, especially the Rothschilds, to nurture elaborate fantasies about the clandestine actions and designs of Jews throughout the world.

The background to Tiszaeszlár: The Jews in Hungary

Hungary in the nineteenth century may be seen as a revealing example of a country where Jewish power rose with remarkable rapidity. Indeed, the rise of the Jews in the Hungarian half of the Dual Monarchy, or Austro-Hungarian Empire, was even more noteworthy than it was in Austria, where von Schönerer's and Lueger's denunciation of it had caused such a sensation. In Hungary, at any rate, another influential anti-Semitic affair occurred in 1882–3, at Tiszaeszlár, a village on the Tisza River, some hundred miles northeast of Budapest.

Hungary is usually perceived as part of an eastern European cultural area, and since the treatment of Jews in eastern Europe was notoriously bad in the nineteenth century, it is easily assumed that Jews in Hungary faced the same degree of hostility and legal discrimination as Jews in Romania, Poland or Russia. But that would be a mistaken assumption, for Jews in Hungary in the second half of the nineteenth century encountered, on the whole, an even more hospitable environment than in western Europe, including France or Great Britain.

This environment is all the more remarkable because the number of Jews in Hungary and their rate of increase in the course of the nineteenth century were much greater than anywhere in western Europe. From less than 1 percent of the population for most of the eighteenth century, the

The Russian Pale of Settlement

proportion of Jews in the country steadily rose: 2 percent in the first decades of the nineteenth century, 4 percent by midcentury, 5 percent at the turn of the century. By 1910 there were 911,000 Jews in Hungary, out of a total population of twenty-one million.[10] Expressed in other terms,

[10] *Hungarian Jewry Before and After the Persecutions* (Budapest, 1949), 25 ff.; cited in

between 1787 and 1910 the overall population of Hungary grew 125 percent, whereas the number of Jews in the country grew 1,021 percent.[11] There seems little question that Hungary experienced the largest relative increase in Jewish population through immigration of any country in the world in the nineteenth and early twentieth centuries. The Jewish population in France for the same period increased only two or three times, only slightly more than the rise of the non-Jewish population. Even the massive increase, absolute and relative, of Jews in the United States hovered, at its highest points, between 1 and 2 percent of the population, as compared with 5 percent in Hungary.

These figures still do not tell the entire story in that a large percentage of Jewish immigrants moved to the capital. The Jewish population of Budapest toward the end of the century surged to around 200,000, close to a quarter of the population of the city (732,000 total) and the largest population of Jews in any capital city of Europe. Lueger once referred to it as "Judapest," and the term stuck. In Paris, a city with a considerably larger total population than Budapest (circa 2.7 million in 1900), Jews numbered between 30,000 and 40,000, about one percent of the total.[12]

What might be termed the Jewish presence in Budapest overshadowed even that 25 percent. Jews could exercise a potentially decisive influence in elections since, as a relatively affluent population, they constituted about half of those in the capital who were qualified to vote. Similarly, in national elections, where only 5 percent of Hungary's population had the vote, Jews played a role wholly disproportionate to their own 5 percent of the total population, both as qualified voters and, more subtly, as those who provided money, advice, and organizational support to parliamentary candidates.

Thus, not only Jewish population increase but the rise of the Jews in a more general way was nowhere in modern times more remarkable than in Hungary. It was remarkable not only in terms of the tangible or easily measurable aspects of that rise – disproportionately increasing population, per capita income, educational levels, numbers of Jews in high political, military, and judicial positions – but also in terms of the generally favorable attitude of the ruling orders in Hungary to that rise. Hungary stands as an instructive counterargument for those who maintain that the absolute number of Jews or the proportion of Jews to non-Jews in any given area or even the rise of the Jews as an overall phenomenon represents a decisive stimulus to anti-Semitism. The Hungarian experience suggests how much

Randolph L. Braham, *The Politics of Genocide: The Holocaust in Hungary*, vol. 1 (New York, 1981), 2.

[11] Randolph L. Braham, ed., *Hungarian-Jewish Studies* (New York, 1966), 62.

[12] B. R. Mitchell, *European Historical Statistics, 1750–1975* (New York, 1981), 86–9.

more tangled are the causes of Jew-hatred than mere numbers; it reveals in particular how culture and history can subtly but substantially alter the influence of material determinants. It similarly offers a revealing example of the intricate interplay of fantasy and reality.

Throughout the nineteenth century Hungary remained an attractive destination for Jews, and the ruling elite of the country welcomed large numbers of Jews as did no other. It would overstate the case to term the ruling Magyar upper classes in Hungary philo-Semitic or to describe the country as a haven for masses of oppressed Jews from Russia, as the United States would later become. Indeed, the sovereign disdain that many of the Magyar nobility felt for the great mass of Ostjuden was scarcely distinguishable from the feelings of the ruling elites elsewhere in Europe. Even the willingness of the Magyar upper orders to work closely with Jews in specific areas, for example, to let Jews handle their economic affairs, was not significantly different from the attitudes of the upper orders in much of eastern Europe.

What was different may appear a nuance, but it was finally an important one: The Magyar ruling class was inclined to accept Jews who magyarized, that is, who embraced Magyar language and culture, as potentially "real" members of the nation, not as permanent outsiders whose race or religion categorically precluded their ever becoming adequately Magyar. Such an inclination was less significant among the Polish, Russian, Romanian, or even German elites in their respective countries. Acceptance of accultured Jews by the ruling elite may even have been stronger in Hungary than in France, since in France the tendency to "integral" nationalism, to a linkage of race, religion, culture, and nation, found wide support, especially but not exclusively on the traditionalist right.

A related point is that Magyar nationalism focused more on cultural, as distinguished from racial or religious, matters; those Jews who adopted Magyar culture were acceptable in ways that Jews who embraced German culture in Germany or German-speaking Austria ultimately were not, since the racial issue loomed larger in those areas, especially by the last quarter of the century. Similarly, since Catholic religion was so integrally a part of Polish national identity, it was difficult for Poles to accept non-Catholics as genuine Poles, whether they were German Protestants, followers of Russian Orthodoxy, or Jews. Religious and racial intolerance were present in Hungary also, but the ruling elites by the latter half of the nineteenth century come across as subtly more tolerant than their counterparts in most other countries of Europe in relation to accultured Jews. It must be reemphasized that these were nuances, not stark contrasts; social barriers persisted for Jews, even when political and economic barriers had fallen. Still, the nuances of Magyar–Jewish relationships came

to have long-range significance in the unusual ability of Hungary to assimilate large numbers of Jews, to accept them as useful members of the
Magyar nation.

Several factors played an obvious role in the adoption of this peculiar
attitude on the part of the Magyar elite. One is that both Catholic and
Protestant faiths were significantly represented among the ruling orders
of Hungary, reducing the attractions of unitary nationalism based on
religious identity. Probably far more important, however, was the status
of the Magyars as a minority in the lands over which they ruled. They
were especially concerned about their numerical weakness in an epoch
of nascent nationalism in eastern Europe. There was a fairly numerous
Magyar peasantry, but much of the rural lower class in territories claimed
by Hungary was Slavic and Romanian, whereas the urban middle class
was predominantly German and Jewish. Magyar nationalists, such as Lajos
Kossuth, were haunted by the remark of Johann Herder, the extremely
influential German theorist of nationalism, that Magyars might eventually
disappear, swallowed up by the Slavic and Germanic peoples that surrounded them.[13]

This Magyar fear of disappearing through absorption by more rapidly
reproducing peoples, which many contemporaries described as verging
on an obsession, led government authorities in Hungary, particularly in
the second half of the nineteenth century, to launch a concerted, sometimes brutal effort to magyarize the population.[14] But those authorities
often encountered stubborn resistance. Therefore, any non-Magyars who
willingly took up Magyar language and culture were viewed as valuable
allies.

Of the groups that did magyarize during the nineteenth century, the
Jews were important in terms of sheer numbers but even more so because
magyarized Jews contributed more powerfully than other groups to the
modernization of the Magyar nation, to its economic development, scientific progress, and international stature. A significant proportion of the
Jews of Hungary embraced a Magyar cultural identity with genuine enthusiasm. Such Jews accepted, often in a most intransigent way, the
prevalent nineteenth-century notion that there were "historic" peoples,
such as the Germans, Poles, and Magyars, and "unhistoric" peoples, such
as the Slovaks, Romanians, or Ukrainians, who should "disappear." The
unhistoric peoples, so the argument went, had not developed a culture
worth preserving; in order to enter modern civilization they needed to
abandon their native language and culture and take up a historic one.
(Whether the Jews in Hungary should also disappear as Jews was a more

[13] William L. Langer, *Political and Social Upheaval: 1832–1852* (New York, 1969), 271–2.
[14] Cf. R. W. Seton-Watson, *Racial Problems in Hungary* (New York, 1972; first published,
1908).

tangled issue, especially in terms of how complete that disappearance should be.)

Jews came to be perceived as a vanguard for Magyar culture and Magyar domination. In the process they sometimes earned for themselves a special enmity from the "unhistoric" peoples who resisted magyarization, refused to disappear, and resented being dealt with as inferior. Such resentments assumed even larger dimensions in the relations of German-speaking Jews with "unhistoric" peoples elsewhere in the Dual Monarchy, since German-speaking Jews were even more notorious as crusaders for the superiority of German culture. Thus, paradoxically, Jews in central Europe, who would later suffer so much at the hands of racists, were themselves often perceived as racist defenders of Magyar and German superiority.

A remarkable number of the major artists, poets, and authors in the Magyar language in the nineteenth and twentieth centuries were of Jewish background. The accomplishments of Jewish-Magyar scientists were possibly even more impressive, and certainly better known and appreciated by the rest of the world.[15] Again, we are speaking of a nuance, since in nearly every country of Europe, particularly in German-speaking areas, accultured Jews made major contributions to the arts and sciences, but their contribution stands out in Hungary more than elsewhere.

Yet another aspect of the Hungarian scene that made for a warmer welcome to Jews was the peculiar nature of liberalism in the country. Whereas in most western countries liberal ideas were identified with the bourgeoisie or the middle classes, in Hungary those ideas were forwarded by intellectuals from the nobility, a class that was relatively more numerous than elsewhere. Such men saw liberal, modernizing reform as necessary to the survival of their country and as a necessary element of a national assertion in the modern world. However, they were not themselves bourgeois in style and habits, and they did not engage in commerce and industry.

There were certainly liberal, reforming nobles in France and Great Britain, but their numbers were small in relation to liberals of middle-class origin. In Hungary the non-noble allies of the reforming nobility were overwhelmingly Jews who, more than was the case with the native bourgeoisie of other countries, embraced the cultural style of the nobility and gentry. Again, an absorption by the upper classes of the native bourgeoisie was a common enough phenomenon in other countries, as for example the much-discussed "junkerization" of the German bourgeoisie, but in Hungary it was particularly notable in the case of the Jews.

---

[15] William O. McCagg, Jr., *Jewish Nobles and Geniuses in Modern Hungary* (New York, 1972).

Their highest aspiration was to be like the haughty Magyar nobility and gentry, even if they did retain certain bourgeois traits having to do, for example, with financial discretion and regular work habits. The peculiar nature of Hungarian liberalism tended to diminish not only tension between Jew and non-Jew but class tension as well, at least class tension between middle class and upper class.

A final reason that might be mentioned for the relative weakness in Hungary of anti-Jewish sentiment, especially of the modern racial sort that was emerging with such force in Germany and Austria, was that Hungary's native, non-Jewish middle and lower-middle class was small, and it was, of course, from that element of society (artisans, clerks, minor officials, shopkeepers) that the political anti-Semites in Germany and Austria in the 1870s and 1880s recruited most effectively. Insofar as there was a non-Jewish middle and lower-middle class in Hungary, it tended to be German in origin, "native" only in that it had been in the country since the eighteenth century, when Empress Maria-Theresa had invited German settlers into Hungary to help remedy the ravages of Turkish occupation. Interestingly, Hungarian anti-Semites in the late 1870s were hurt to some degree by the accusation that they were introducing a Germanic, racist (and thus foreign) ideology into Hungary.

These aspects of the Hungarian scene make it initially puzzling that Hungary should be the site of a major anti-Semitic affair, one involving a charge of ritual murder at that. But such apparent incongruities are to be found in each of the Three Affairs. There were, to be sure, very few anti-Semitic politicians in Hungary in the 1860s and 1870s, But, as has been noted, the 1860s and early 1870s were not years of major successes for anti-Semitic politicians anywhere in Europe. The late 1870s and early 1880s saw a distinct change in mood, with significant anti-Semitic agitation in German-speaking Europe, which influenced central and eastern Europe, where a number of changing conditions inside each country favored it.

The 1880s also saw a vastly increased movement of Jews out of eastern Europe, out of the lands bordering on Hungary. In Russia in 1881, Tsar Alexander II was assassinated by revolutionaries, and among his assassins were Jews. Although their role in the assassination was not a major one, Jewish terrorists had figured prominently in a number of notorious attacks on government officials in the years immediately previous to the murder of the tsar, and the role of Jews in the revolutionary movement was much discussed at the time. Pogroms, or anti-Jewish riots, broke out following the assassination, particularly in the Ukraine. For many observers, including influential ones in the government, the riots confirmed what they had long been asserting: that the liberalizing reforms under Alexander II in the 1860s and 1870s had helped to produce masses of Jews who were "out of control"; the reforms had unleashed what those observers considered the predatory and destructive proclivities of Jews, the very proclivities that since at least the time of Nicholas I in the early nineteenth century had been a special worry of the authorities in Russia. Now, it was claimed, the Russian masses were striking back at the Jewish "destroyers."

In order to rectify what had gone wrong in the preceding two decades of liberal experimentation, the government of Alexander III introduced new controls on Russia's Jewish population, avowedly in order to bring that population back into line and to protect the rest of the population from the alleged predations of the rising numbers of Jews – indeed, to protect the Jews themselves from the rising indignation of the Russian people. In practice these controls, proclaimed as necessary for social peace, threatened the economic well-being of Jews, when economic depression and demographic explosion had already worsened their condition. After 1881 many Jews could see no future in Russia.

It is revealing to note in the context of the emigrations of the 1880s that the Jews of Galicia, the large Austrian province bordering Russian Poland to the north and Hungary to the south, up the river from Tisza-eszlár, too, began leaving in record numbers. Yet Galician Jews, under Austrian jurisdiction, enjoyed full civil equality, suffered no pogroms, and experienced little or no persecution by government authorities. In fact, the rising numbers of Jews leaving both Russia and Galicia predated the assassination of the tsar by a decade. Social, economic and demographic factors, linked to new opportunities for emigration (the "push" and the "pull") were more important than political persecution.[16] The same may be said for Romania, where hostility to and persecution of the Jews was at least as pervasive as in Russia.

Although the greater part of the Jews leaving Russia, Galicia, and Romania made their way to the New World, for many of them Hungary, where Jews had been granted full civil equality in 1867 and where there were economic opportunities for Jews, was an attractive destination. It was, of course, also close, whereas the New World was distant and for many a frightening prospect. As noted, Jews had been moving into Hungary since the early part of the century. At first they came from the western, mostly German-speaking parts of the Habsburg Empire. But by the 1880s migration out of Russia and of neighboring Galicia began to replace the earlier patterns.

[16] Cf. Elyohu Cherikover, ed., *Geshikhte fun der yidisher arbeter bavegung in der fareyniker shtatn*, vol. 1 (New York, 1943–5), 39; Jonathan Frankel, *Prophecy and Politics: Socialism, Nationalism, and the Russian Jews* (Cambridge, 1981), 50; Simon Kusnets, "The Immigration of Russian Jews to the United States: Background and Structure," *Perspectives in American History*, vol. 10, 1975, 35–124.

The first waves of Jewish immigrants in the early nineteenth century were relatively modern in their habits. They took up Magyar language and culture with relative ease. The next waves were more backward, poorer, religiously more orthodox, and more resistant to assimilation. Within Hungary there developed a replication of the tensions between Jews of German origin and Ostjuden that were so prominent in Germany, in Austria, and eventually in the United States. In all three areas a central reason for that tension was the belief by German Jews that the Ostjuden would revive or intensify anti-Jewish feelings that had been steadily dwindling.

In Hungary these fears were especially strong, since the overall and relative numbers of Jews arriving in the country much exceeded those arriving and staying in any western European country. True enough, the rise of the Jews in Hungary, however dramatic, had heretofore been more willingly accepted by the country's ruling elite than in any other country. However, there were limits to how long the process of assimilation could go on, both at the upper and lower ends of society.

By the late 1870s Jewish predominance in the economic and professional life of Hungary had already reached an extraordinary level. As one Jewish historian has put it, "within a few decades, the Jews of Hungary achieved a formidable, if not commanding, position in the country's economic, financial, and cultural life."[17] Grumbling began to be heard on the part of non-Jewish Hungarians who had previously remained silent, especially as wealthy Jews began to buy up, at a very rapid rate, land previously held by the gentry and aristocracy. In Hungary, thus, it was members of the upper classes, rather than the lower-middle class, that set the tone of the anti-Semitic agitation in these years, even if the greater part of the Hungarian upper classes remained favorably inclined to the participation of Jews in the life of the nation.

When the Ostjuden threatened to pour into the country after the tsar's assassination, even Hungarians who had actively defended a Jewish presence as beneficial to the country began to express reservations. Back in the 1840s, in the debates concerning Jewish emancipation, Count István Széchenyi, a prominent statesman and reforming, liberal aristocrat, had quipped that other, larger countries might be able to absorb large numbers of Jews, since such countries were "lakes" into which a bottle of Jewish "ink" could easily disappear, but the same amount of Jewish ink would spoil the Magyar "soup."[18] While his arguments did not prevail, by the 1880s the metaphor of Jewish ink ruining the Magyar soup took

---

[17] Braham, *Politics of Genocide*, 2.
[18] George Barany, "Magyar-Jew or Jewish-Magyar," *Canadian-American Slavic Studies*, vol. 8, 1974, 1; Jacob Katz, *From Prejudice to Destruction: Anti-Semitism, 1700–1933* (Cambridge, Mass., 1980), 234.

on a new meaning and appeal. Petitions from the northern counties began arriving in the capital, protesting "the inundation of Jewish immigrants from Russia"; residents in those counties, it was charged, were suffering from the ever-increasing number of poverty-striken Jews who "settle with the intention of enriching themselves but without making the slightest sacrifice to acquire Hungarian citizenship."[19] In short, the reasons for accepting earlier immigrants as "useful" did not hold in regard to these refugees from Russia.

In spite of his early warnings about the dangers of Jewish immigration, Széchenyi does not qualify as an anti-Semite. Indeed, his concern with the Jewish Question was not major. The first important anti-Semite in Hungarian history was Győző Istóczy, one of the more enigmatic agitators to appear in Europe in the 1870s. Istóczy's early life and personality hardly suggest the makings of a racist bigot. He was of Catholic background, a member of the landed gentry, well-educated, widely traveled, an excellent athlete, a "friendly, well-mannered young man who moved with facility and grace in social circles"[20] and who was successful in his career as a lawyer and public servant in the late 1860s and early 1870s. In these years his political views were liberal, which naturally entailed an acceptance of Jewish emancipation and a belief that Jews could be useful additions to the Hungarian nation.

What turned Istóczy so single-mindedly against the Jews is not entirely clear. By his own account, which appears too simplistic and monocausal, it was because of his experience with Jews in a complicated series of trials surrounding the auction of an estate, during which a large number of them conspired in false testimony against him.[21] He eventually won the case and was cleared of the charges that the Jews allegedly concocted against him, but the experience apparently transformed his attitude to Jews. He was subsequently elected as a deputy for the Liberal Party in Hungary, and in a debate in the Hungarian parliament in April 1875 about granting citizenship to foreign Jews living in Hungary, he broke into an anti-Semitic tirade. Revealingly, his words were greeted with surprise, catcalls, and laughter. The prime minister proudly dismissed his remarks by stating that there was no Jewish Question in Hungary, in sharp contrast to the countries on its borders both to the east and the west.

Istóczy's attacks on Jews took on texture and scope by the late 1870s, but he remained on the fringe of Hungarian politics. He began to seek out contacts with the anti-Semitic agitators in Austria and Germany, al-

[19] Cited in Andrew Handler, *An Early Blueprint for Zionism: Győző Istóczy's Political Anti-Semitism* (Boulder, Colo., 1989), 76.
[20] Andrew Handler, *Dori: The Life and Times of Theodor Herzl in Budapest, 1860–1878* (Tuscaloosa, Ala., 1984), 108.
[21] Handler, *Dori*, 109.

though, unlike many of them, his hostility to Jews was expressed in cultural rather than explicitly racial terms. Also unlike German-speaking anti-Semites, he developed a program for solving the Jewish Question that had strikingly proto-Zionist elements to it. He argued that it was unreasonable to believe that the Jews, who had resisted assimilation for millennia, could suddenly become genuinely Hungarian. Their ultimate and strongest attachments would always be to the Jewish people and the Jewish nation. They should therefore be encouraged to move to Palestine, where they would find kindred Semitic peoples in the Arabs and might, with their many talents, even be welcomed by the sultan. Istóczy's attitude to the Jews, much like that of Marr, remained a disorienting mix of admiration and distaste, broad-mindedness and narrow resentment. Even in attacking them, however, he did not describe them as vermin or call for their physical destruction – or for any form of physical violence against them[22] – as did figures like Dühring.

The charge of ritual murder

In Easter season 1882 a fourteen-year-old servant girl, Eszter Solymosi, who lived in the village of Tiszaeszlár, disappeared without a trace. Rumors began to circulate that she had been the victim of a ritual murder. Istóczy's anti-Semitic agitation had not really been characterized, up to this point, by such primitive charges against the Jews, but he and other anti-Semites apparently saw in the case as a welcome opportunity to gain national attention. For some time the authorities refused to give the slightest credence to the claims by Eszter's mother and others in the area that there had been a ritual murder. Even the word of the Catholic priest in Tiszaeszlár, who came to believe the rumors, was not sufficient to cause the authorities to change their minds especially since Eszter's body had not been found.

Istóczy and his followers in Hungary denounced what they described as an unfeeling response by the authorities to the pleas of a despairing mother. It was another example, they claimed, of how Jews in Hungary enjoyed special governmental protection, how the Jews had wormed their way into the legal establishment and prevented justice from being done whenever it threatened their image or interests.

News from Tiszaeszlár soon turned these "unfeeling" authorities around, indeed, drew the astonished attention of the entire nation: The two sons of the town's synagogue sexton came forward with stories, full of graphic detail, of how their father and several other Jews had murdered

---

[22] Handler, *Early Blueprint for Zionism*, 79.

Eszter in the synagogue of Tiszaeszlár and collected her blood. Contrary to initial suspicions, these stories were apparently not the result of torture or threats of it from overzealous and bigoted local officials. Just why the two boys came forward with the lurid accounts they did remains a mystery. A family feud may have been the stimulus, a desire for revenge against an overbearing father and, in the case of the older boy, Móric Scharf, a desire to be free of the confines of his Jewish birth. At the trial he testified that he often read the anti-Semitic press, and in it were predictions that the Jews were to be driven from Hungary. Conceivably, he hoped to avoid that or some worse fate.[23] (In 1882, it should be noted, a new wave of pogroms rolled over neighboring Russia.)

The younger boy, Samu, was the first to "confess." However, he was just a month short of five years old, and his story may simply have been the product of childish fantasies, derived from tales of ritual murder by Christian neighbors with whom he had frequent contact. He quickly found that he could get a great deal of attention by telling people in the village how his father, older brother (that is, Móric), and other Jews kidnapped Eszter, washed her body ritually, and then "cut" her for her blood. His brother, fourteen years old, was a more credible witness, although his version denied that he had anything to do with the murder. He reported that, looking through the keyhole of the synagogue door, he had seen his father, in the company of several ritual slaughterers, tie Eszter to a chair, cut her throat, and collect her blood.[24]

Móric's story seemed to collapse when, on June 18, a corpse was finally found floating downriver. The body was badly decomposed and not easily recognizable as Eszter's, but on it were the clothes Eszter had been wearing when she had mysteriously disappeared some seventy-nine days earlier. There were no discernible cuts on her throat. Thus many concluded that Móric's testimony was disproved. However, the matter was not settled, for Eszter's mother adamantly denied that this was the body of her daughter. Others who had known Eszter intimately, including her aunt, also stated that this could not possibly be her body. Their objections received support from local physicians. After an examination of the corpse, they concluded that it had been in the water for only a short time, less than a week, although death had occurred some months before. They also concluded that the body was that of a much older woman than Eszter, someone who had engaged in a great deal of sexual activity before she had died (Eszter, at fourteen, was assumed to have been a virgin).

A sensational meaning to these puzzling conclusions was soon forthcoming: The boatmen who had found the body confessed that it had been

---

[23] Paul Nathan, *Der Process von Tisza-Eszlar: Ein Antisemitisches Culturbild* (Berlin, 1892), 229–41.

[24] Andrew Handler, *Blood Libel at Tiszaeszlar* (New York, 1980), 44 ff.

given to them by Jews, later identified as from Tiszaeszlár, who had brought it to the riverside in a wagon. For those who had all along believed in the ritual murder charge, the explanation seemed obvious. Eszter's murderers had searched high and low for a corpse that could plausibly be substituted for hers, which because of the incriminating cuts on it had been securely hidden. At last they had found one. Aided in their search by the wealthy and powerful Jews of Budapest, who had taken an interest in the case, the Jews of Tiszaeszlár had come up with the body of a Jewish prostitute who had died some time before and who was approximately Eszter's size. They had then tried to pass it off as Eszter's by putting her clothes on it and by bribing the boatmen to say that they had found it in the water.

By this time the Tiszaeszlár case had begun to emerge as a genuine affair. It had attracted international attention, and the trial of the Jews accused of the murder, finally set for June 1883, attracted reporters from most countries of Europe and even from the Americas. Inside Hungary the case began to take on the dimensions of a major confrontation between Jews and non-Jews, one that was not really about ritual murder but rather about the prominence and power of Jews in Hungarian national life.

For some, the Tiszaeszlár case was perceived as a weapon against the Jews, a way of embarrassing them. For such people, how Eszter had died was of minor importance. They did not necessarily believe that Jews actually engaged in ritual murder, but they were willing to see the Jews charged with such a heinous crime as a way of discrediting Judaism and blackening the reputation of Jews generally. One journalist offered the "real story," certainly a more plausible one: Eszter had made disparaging remarks to the Jews, and a quarrel had ensued in which she had been hit and fatally injured. The efforts to cover up this accidental death had caused the Jews to blunder into actions that made it appear they had committed a ritual murder. Once that charge had been leveled, powerful Jews in Budapest had become involved, taking an active part in the ensuing cover-up.[25] Apparently the investigating magistrate, József Bary, although himself anti-Semitic, believed that Eszter's death was simply a criminal case, and he was angry when others tried to make a ritual murder case of it.[26]

The local Jewish lawyer in Tiszaeszlár who was initially engaged to defend the accused Jews soon proved himself out of his depth. More important, however, the leaders of the Jewish community in Budapest who had organized to fight the case were deeply concerned to counteract as much as possible the impression, spread by Istóczy and others, that

[25] Ibid., 74 ff.
[26] Handler, *Early Blueprint for Zionism*, 178.

this was a matter of Jewish versus non-Jewish interests. It must be understood, they believed, that the real issue was justice for the accused and a fight against bigotry and medieval superstition. In looking for a non-Jew who could effectively present these issues, they found an ideal candidate in Károly Eötvös, who quickly consented to take the case.

He was of Calvinist gentry background and had been active in politics since the 1840s. He had been a parliamentary deputy, cabinet minister, and newspaper editor and was now a leader of the Independence Party, the second largest party in the Hungarian parliament. Eötvös's patriotism and overall character were beyond reproach. The anti-Semites would be hard-put to portray him as a tool of Jewish interests or as a man who had been bought by Jewish money. (It is of no little significance that in each of the anti-Semitic affairs examined in this book, a prominent Gentile lawyer agreed to defend the Jews accused of various crimes. In each of the affairs, the role of Gentile defenders in a larger sense, whether as journalists, politicians, or even within the police and military, was of central importance. In none of the great affairs was the issue merely Jew versus non-Jew.)

Eötvös's expertise as a lawyer, as well as his wide contacts with the political establishment in Hungary, helped to unravel many of the mysteries of the case.[27] Also decisive were the efforts of what would now be called the "investigative reporter" Miksa Szabolcsi, who discovered and publicized how Bary had browbeaten the boatmen in order to get the incriminating confessions he wanted from them. The evidence was less clear-cut in regard to Bary's relations with Móric Scharf. Bary did not elicit the boy's story initially, but he may have coached him afterward, in order to make his story as credible and consistent as possible when he was called to testify. When he first came forward with his testimony, Móric was taken from his family and lodged with the authorities for his own protection. That seemed an appropriate step, since he was openly and repeatedly threatened with violence by members of his family and other members of the Jewish community in Tiszaeszlár, who not surprisingly did all they could to get him to change his story. But Bary then apparently took advantage of his custody of the boy.

Bary was dismissed and reprimanded by the government for his handling of the investigation before the case went to trial. Eötvös was able to get a new autopsy performed on the body, one that cast doubt on many of the findings of the first one. However, the issue of the corpse became tangled to a ludicrous degree. Medical experts argued endlessly over its age, as evidenced by the condition of its joints, for example. All of them

[27] His three-volume *A Nagy Per* (Budapest, 1904) is a major source for the trial and the affair more generally.

were at a loss to explain how one of the ribs they had so carefully examined turned out to be that of a suckling calf. By careful cross-examination Eötvös was able to discredit the testimony of Móric Scharf. He demonstrated that it was impossible to see, from the keyhole in the door, the area of the synagogue where the fourteen-year-old described the murder as having taken place.

Eötvös had a powerful if surprising ally in the trial: Ede Szeyffert, the prosecuting attorney. From the very first day, Szeyffert (a non-Jew, also, whose name suggests a Germanic origin) openly complained that he had been obliged to take up a ridiculous case. His concluding remarks were barely distinguishable in tone and conclusions from those of the defense. There was, then, hardly a trial in the sense normally understood. His attitude outraged many in the audience, who often hooted loudly and applauded the interjections of Istóczy that the prosecution was not doing its job.

The trial in truth became a circus and a farce. Many observers faulted the presiding judge for failing to exercise adequate control over the unruly crowd in the courtroom, or even over the tone of the formal proceedings. One of the defendants, in cross-examining Móric, a procedure that was permissible under Hungarian law, spit in his face. Other defendants, including Móric's father, repeatedly threatened him with violence in open courtroom if he persisted in his testimony. Both Eötvös and Szeyffert finally found it necessary to travel in the company of an armed guard. Outraged charges were made that Szeyffert and Eötvös had entered into an unholy conspiracy in the service of the Jews to free the ritual murderers. The people of Hungary, at the prey of Jews, were being left unrepresented at this trial, it was further charged, since after Bary's dismissal no one had even made an effort to assemble and present evidence against the accused. (How Bary might have handled the case is difficult to say; he hated Istóczy and did not believe in the ritual murder charge, but he believed that the Jews of Tiszaeszlár were "without exception uncultured, unwashed persons, living in moral and bodily filth, Yiddish-speaking and evil-looking religious fanatics who harbor a burning hatred for Christians."[28])

The final verdict of the three presiding judges was "not proven," rather than "not guilty," an ambiguous judgment that encouraged doubts to linger. In the audience could be heard muffled curses and angry weeping.[29] Many of those who had come to the trial had not gotten the satisfaction they had expected. Immediately following the trial, there was widespread rioting in Hungary: Jews were assaulted on the street, Jewish

---

[28] Quoted in Handler, *Early Blueprint for Zionism*, 67.
[29] Handler, *Blood Libel*, 156

stores looted, and synagogues defaced. Anti-Semites, publicly lamenting that the "murdering Jews" of Tiszaeszlár had gone free and that the trial was a mockery, discovered a significantly larger audience for their propaganda than had been the case in Hungary before the trial. Even relatively moderate voices, such as the clerical *Magyar Allam*, lamented that "unfortunately, Hungary has reached the point where its prosperity is unconditionally dependent upon compromise and transaction with Jewish interests."[30] Other voices loudly complained that Jews now had a stranglehold on the central institutions of the Hungarian state. They would protect their own, with lies, bribery, and intimidation if necessary, and non-Jews had no chance against them.

In October 1883 Istóczy founded the National Anti-Semitic Party, with a platform that called for major reforms, including loosening and counterbalancing the powerful role of Jews in Hungary's political, economic, and cultural life; regulation of licenses to sell alcoholic beverages, designed to prevent Jews from owning taverns; a prohibition of civil marriages between Jews and Gentiles; and measures to stem the influx of Jews into Hungary.[31] In 1883 his party won thirteen seats to the Hungarian parliament.

Yet this flare-up of hostility to Jews in Hungary had no important sequel, at least not before World War I. In the long run, Istóczy was even less successful politically than the anti-Semites in Germany and Austria. His movement collapsed only a few years after it started. None of his proposals was passed in parliament or even had a remote chance of success. Unlike the situation in Germany, where Bismarck was willing, at least for a short time, to exploit anti-Semitism for his own purposes and where the Conservative Party toyed with anti-Semitism in its party program, in Hungary the authorities and recognized leaders spoke up quickly and forthrightly against Jew-hatred. The minister of culture characteristically remarked that "anti-Semitism serves only as a pretext to undermine the foundations of the social order. . . . [Riots] begin with Herschko or Itzig [characteristic Jewish names in Hungary] and lead to Prince Esterhazy."[32]

Remarks of this sort were also made in both Germany and Austria, but they seemed to reflect a less firm consensus about the dangers of anti-Semitism, and clearly the ruling orders in those countries were more reticent to accept a major Jewish role in their state and society. The rise of the Jews in Hungary continued without significant reversal, particularly in the upper ranks of society. The 1890s did see a revival of anti-Jewish political activity in the Catholic People's Party, which, like Lueger's Chris-

---

[30] Ibid., 172.
[31] Ibid., 178.
[32] Quoted in Nathaniel Katzburg, *'Antishemiut Be-Hungaria, 1867–1964* (Tel Aviv, 1969), 170.

tian Social Party, attacked liberalism and socialism as Jewish or alien imports. But throughout the prewar period, the interests and power of Jews in Budapest were not seriously challenged. Such may be said to have been true in Vienna as well, in spite of Lueger's victories. Yet the situation in Budapest was significantly different. In 1896, in an act full of symbolism, the Hungarian parliament passed a law that placed the Jewish faith on an equal level with the Christian.[33] Instead of a Lueger, Budapest elected a Jewish mayor, Adam Vazsonyi. For such reasons, there were still many Hungarians, both Jews and non-Jews, who maintained that there was no Jewish Question in Hungary, and no rising tide of anti-Semitism, whatever might be happening elsewhere in Europe.

[33] Hugh Coleman, ed., *The Jews of Czechoslovakia* (Philadelphia, 1968), 77.

4

France before the Dreyfus Affair

Jews, vomited from the ghettoes of Europe, are now installed as the masters of the historic houses that evoke the most glorious moments of ancient France. . . . Jews are the most powerful agents of disorder the world has ever seen. (Edouard Drumont)

The Republic has governed in the interest of the Jews. . . . It is . . . the Republic, which by raising Jewish power to new heights . . . has stirred up wishes for revenge. (Arthur Mayer)

Jews are possessed by millenarian dreams inherited from the depths of Asia. . . . In whatever sphere he works the Jew carries with him the taste for destruction, the thirst to dominate, the need to pursue an ideal, whether precise or confused. (Joseph Caillaux)

Behind every fortune lies a crime. (Balzac)

The evolution of French Jewry in the nineteenth century

As we have seen, France was the first European country to award full civil equality to Jews. Throughout the early nineteenth century the legal position of Jews in France was widely envied by Jews in other countries. And not only the legal position: In much of central and eastern Europe, the common expression "to live like God in France" summed it up; France was idealized as a secular paradise of fine food, intellectual sophistication, polished manners, and *joie de vivre*.

In the 1870s and early 1880s the waves of popular hostility that Jews experienced in central and eastern Europe had only weak counterparts in France. Efforts were made to set up anti-Semitic organizations in those years, but they enjoyed little success. Throughout the century France was no stranger to popular uprisings or to harsh social and economic conflict. The country experienced a number of bloody episodes, most notably in the revolutionary upheavals of 1848 and again in 1871 following upon the humiliating defeat in late 1870 in the Franco-Prussian War. Yet in none of these were Jews important leaders, and in none of them were Jews prominently attacked as being responsible for France's troubles. Similarly, the depression of the mid-1870s and 1880s had a smaller and less dramatic impact in France than in most of the rest of Europe, and its less serious effects were only rarely blamed on France's Jews.

These remarks are not meant to suggest that there was no anti-Semitism in France in the early and middle years of the century. The Damascus Affair was, of course, an example of it. Nor was there a shortage of French theorists of anti-Semitism and other forms of racism.[1] But "scientific" racism in these years remained a theory that attracted only a few isolated intellectuals. Anti-Semitism and modern racism more generally did not become part of French political life in the same way that it did in German-speaking Europe of the late 1870s and 1880s. A more diffuse xenophobia, on the other hand, remained deeply rooted. Its most virulent expressions, however, were not directed against Jews but against Italians, who, at over three hundred thousand by the turn of the century, were the most numerous of aliens residing in the country. They suffered repeated attacks in the 1890s, "rising at times to what could be described as pogroms."[2]

The transformation of the condition of the Jews in France into a prosperous bourgeoisie paralleled that in Hungary or Germany, but France's significantly smaller Jewish population made the rise of the Jews less noticeable and less threatening, a point that observers in Germany, like Treitschke, or in Hungary, like Széchenyi, had emphasized. Large areas of France counted no Jews at all. The total population of French Jews, approximately seventy-five thousand toward the end of the century and concentrated largely in Paris and the northeastern departments, grew at a rate that was a little faster than the French population as a whole, which stood at thirty-nine million in the 1890s, but was nothing like the extraordinary explosion in the numbers, absolute and relative, of Jews in eastern and central Europe in the course of the same hundred years. The percentage of Jews in France toward the end of the century ranged from 0.1 to 0.2 percent of the total population.[3]

France's total Jewish population was less than one-tenth that of Germany, one-fiftieth that of Hungary. In Russia's western regions Jews were about one hundred times more numerous in relation to the Gentile population than in France. Even The Netherlands' Jewish population was larger than France's, and Great Britain's was about twice as large. Had France's Jews wanted to maintain a strictly separate identity, as they clearly did not, such an identity would have been far more difficult than in eastern Europe, simply because Jews in France were overwhelmed by

[1] Cf. Jacob Katz, *From Prejudice to Destruction: Anti-Semitism, 1700–1933* (Cambridge, Mass., 1980), 107–144; Léon Poliakov, *The History of Anti-Semitism*, vol. 3, (New York, 1975).
[2] Eugen Weber, *France: Fin de Siècle* (Cambridge, Mass., 1986), 135.
[3] Patrick Gérard, *Les Juifs de France de 1789 à 1860* (Paris, 1976), 105–14; Katz, *Prejudice*, 120.

the sheer numbers of Gentiles.[4] France's Jews did little to preserve that more subtle variety of separate social existence and cultural consciousness typical of German-speaking Jews.

The allures of assimilation in France and the pressures to conform culturally, what might be termed the "push and pull" that they felt, were greater not only because of the prestige and hospitality of French civilization, as compared to the cultures of central and eastern Europe, but also because French cultural style was highly "integral." That is, in France cultural pluralism was severely discouraged; there was only one "permissible" cultural style. Paris stood as the unquestioned center of French life, not only politically and administratively but in nearly every other sense, and its spirit massively dominated France's cultural life. The cultural pluralism of a country like the United States was simply not acceptable in France; the belief expounded by influential Americans by the early twentieth century that each immigrant group had a special "gift" or contribution to make to U.S. culture found no parallel in France.

Insofar as an independent Jewish identity remained for French Jews, it was a most elusive matter. French Jews themselves found it difficult to arrive at a commonly agreed upon description of what their Jewishness involved. Many of them had social contacts in Jewish charitable organizations, contacts that linked to a sense of a special Jewish virtue in charity, but French Jews were not united in feeling that they faced, as Jews, a pervasive outside hostility from the rest of French society or, more important, from the state. They did not think of themselves, in other words, as Jews in the sense that Jean-Paul Sartre later made famous, as people whose only unity consisted in knowing that they were hated by anti-Semites.[5] Their internal divisions, along lines of social class and political fidelity, appeared to most French Jews to be more significant than divisions they felt in relation to non-Jews in France. In this sense, many contended that there was no Jewish community in France, in the way that one could speak of such a community in Germany, Austria-Hungary, or Russia. One assimilated French Jew remarked, in words full of symbolism, that although he and his family belonged to Jewish organizations of various sorts, his uncle was "incapable of reciting Kaddish by his father's coffin, as I was myself incapable of reciting it by his. My father, who would have thought it dishonorable to have had me baptized, would have thought it stupid to have me fast at Yom Kippur."[6]

[4] Cf. Michael Marrus, *The Politics of Assimilation: The French Community at the Time of the Dreyfus Affair* (Oxford, 1971), 29, for further statistics.

[5] Jean-Paul Sartre, *Anti-Semite and Jew* (New York, 1967); first French edition, *Réflections sur la question juive* (Paris, 1946.)

[6] Quoted in Stephen Wilson, *Ideology and Experience: Anti-Semitism in France at the Time of the Dreyfus Affair* (East Brunswick, N.J., 1982), 695.

By the fifth and sixth decades of the century French Jews began to enter the liberal professions in impressive numbers, although still small in total as compared to Hungary or even to Germany. French Jews also began to reach the middle and upper echelons of the government, again, in smaller absolute numbers than in Austria-Hungary but still disproportionately large in relation to the Jewish population of France. By the 1880s French Jews began to make a notable appearance in highly fashionable circles. One contemporary wrote, "today [1885], the barons of Israel represent luxury... charity... the arts... the smart set... fashion's latest style."[7]

Even the military in France by the 1870s and 1880s enrolled a surprisingly large number of Jewish officers (the figure of three hundred was often mentioned by the early 1890s, of whom ten were generals),[8] whereas in Germany the officer corps was one area where Jews were strictly kept out, as they were in Russia, except as medical officers. Indeed, in spite of the reputation of the French army as a haven for right-wing nationalists and monarchists, the Jewish percentage among regular officers was consistently at around 3 percent, from the 1860s to the eve of World War I. With Jews constituting between 0.1 and 0.2 percent of the total population in those years, that meant an overrepresentation of between thirty and sixty times.[9] Jews no doubt encountered prejudice in the ranks of the French military, but such figures suggest that those Jews who desired a career in the French military – and they can hardly have been very large in number – did not face overwhelming obstacles. On the contrary, as will be seen, many spokesmen for the Jews in France claimed that the military was unusually open and just in its treatment of Jews.

Jews came from eastern Europe to France in small numbers during the 1870s and 1880s. There was a more significant influx of Jews, around ten thousand, out of Alsace and Lorraine, mostly to Paris, after those provinces were annexed to Germany in 1871. Resentments were directed at the new arrivals by elements of the Parisian population; nevertheless, these Jews, who had grown up as French citizens, were, after all, leaving the newly expanded German Empire in order to remain in France. They were patriots who preferred France to Germany and were thus less likely to incur resentment than those of foreign origin. Non-Jews who lived in

---

[7] Alexandre Hepp, *Paris tout nu* (Paris, 1885), 169; quoted in Weber, *France: Fin de Siècle*, 131.

[8] Cf. Jean-Denis Bredin, *The Affair: The Case of Alfred Dreyfus* (New York, 1986), 21; first French edition, *L'Affaire* (Paris, 1983).

[9] Doris Bensimon-Donath, *Sociodémographie des Juifs de France et d'Algérie* (Paris, 1976), 166 ff.; Rabi, *Anatomie du Judaisme français* (Paris, 1962), 67; David Cohen, *La Promotion des Juifs en France à l'époque du Second Empire*, vol. 2, (Aix, 1980) 420; Weber, *France: Fin de Siècle*, 133.

the annexed provinces also moved into a now truncated France in fair numbers.

In the early 1890s, before the outbreak of the Dreyfus Affair, rising numbers of eastern European Jews began to arrive in Paris, settling in a number of immigrant neighborhoods, particularly the so-called *Pletzl* ("little plaza," in Yiddish),[10] but their numbers, not much more than ten thousand, were insignificant compared to those arriving in other capitals at the same time. Predictably, these eastern European Jews were not well received in Paris. Unlike the Jews from Alsace and Lorraine, they were decidedly alien in speech, manner, and political fidelities. They were also poorer, of a lower social class, less skilled, and less educated. Many of them brought along radical political ideas out of Russia, alarming those French citizens who were already much concerned about the rise of revolutionary socialism in the country.

Most French middle-class Jews, those who had been citizens since the Revolution, were at least as contemptuous of Yiddish-speaking Jews from the east as were acculturated Hungarian or German Jews. The tendency by Jews themselves to denigrate both traditional Jewish identity and the newer Jewish ideologies (such as Bundist socialism or Zionism) was especially prominent in France, above all among the richest and most upwardly mobile. Charles Péguy, a Catholic man of letters who had many cordial contacts with Jews and who has been termed a philo-Semite, commented that anti-Semitic feelings were to be found among three-quarters of the French Jewish upper bourgeoisie, among half of the Jewish middle bourgeoisie, and among one-third of the Jewish petty bourgeoisie.[11]

Julien Benda, a prominent French intellectual of Jewish background, described the Ostjuden as avaricious and inflexible, "blind preservers of a set of customs that have lost their meaning." Bernard Lazare, who would become a leading Dreyfusard and who was also of Jewish background, earlier made a distinction between "Jews" (the Ostjuden) and "Israelites" (western, assimilated Jews). He, as a Frenchman of long standing, felt nothing in common with the former; they were "predatory Tartars, coarse and dirty. . . . Everywhere, up to the present time, the Jew has been an unsociable being. . . . The Jewish nation is small and miserable, . . . demoralized and corrupted by an unjustifiable pride."[12]

Prominent and highly successful Jews like the eminent sociologist Emile Durkheim or the man of letters Daniel Halévy freely spoke of the "defects"

---

[10] Cf. Nancy L. Green, *The Pletzl of Paris: Jewish Immigrant Workers in the "Belle Epoque"* (New York, 1986).

[11] Wilson, *Ideology*, 707.

[12] Quoted in Lazare Prajs, *Péguy et Israël* (Paris, 1970), 48–9; cf. Marrus, *Assimilation*, 61, 170.

and "tainted idiosyncrasies" of their "race."[13] When newspapers associated with Jewish organizations began to publish articles that openly celebrated the successes of French Jews, a number of those Jews objected. They wanted recognition as successful Frenchmen, not specifically as Jews.[14] These points are worth recording, not only because they give a more concrete sense of what integral nationalism came to mean for Jews in France but also because Captain Alfred Dreyfus was a member of a wealthy, upwardly mobile family of the French Jewish bourgeoisie, one that had left Alsace after the Franco-Prussian war, and that much emphasized French patriotism and French cultural identity, while playing down its Jewishness.

In the early part of the nineteenth century, conversions to Christianity were fairly common in France, as they were in central Europe.[15] But even those French Jews who did not convert to Christianity still typically expressed a sense of relief at being free of the confinements of traditional belief. Daniel Halévy wrote, "How happy I am to have left that hell, to have escaped from Judaism."[16] Solomon Reinach similarly complained: "At a time when the progress of science and consciousness has done everything to bring men together, the ritualism of the Jews isolates them. . . . It gives credit to the deceitful idea that the Jews are strangers among nations."[17] Reinach went on to make the point, which was straight out of Kant and later used by German anti-Semites, that ritualism was a sign of backwardness, not an aspect of true religiosity. Of course, non-Jews, especially former Catholics, expressed equally forceful opinions about their relief in abandoning traditional Christianity. This was an age of triumphant secularism and rationalism.

French Jews excelled in the realm of the intellect, a matter of no little significance in a country where intellectuals enjoyed a special prestige. Jewish intellectuals were by no means so numerous or so visible in Paris as they were in Berlin, Vienna, or Budapest, but in Paris, too, they made notable contributions in most of the sciences and the arts, especially in the newer disciplines, such as sociology. At the *lycées* (the French elite secondary schools), Jewish students were represented well beyond their relative numbers, and especially among those at the top, the prizewinners. Although not incurring the kinds of resentments that similar performances did in Vienna or Berlin, Jewish intellectual success was noticed by non-Jews. One alumnus of the lycées recalled:

[13] Wilson, *Ideology*, 707.
[14] Marrus, *Assimilation*, 122 ff.
[15] Katz, *Prejudice*, 406.
[16] Marrus, *Assimilation*, 40.
[17] Ibid., 60.

... the Jewish boys topped the list. They understood all the problems, handed in the best compositions, and collected most of the prizes at the end of the year. There was no vying with them; they were far ahead of us, and even offered to coach us during recreation hours. Math, languages, literature, everything seemed their forte.[18]

The Third Republic and the Jews

From the ruins of the Second Empire, the Third Republic emerged gradually and uncertainly in the early 1870s. Although Jews had little to do with its founding, it was to prove a favorable environment for Jewish aspirations in the subsequent decades. A republican constitution was accepted by the national assembly, after much indecision, in 1875. The republican form of government was at first not popular with most French people, especially in the countryside, where monarchist sympathies prevailed. But a monarchy was not established because, after years of quarreling, the rival monarchist factions could not overcome their differences. A republic with a conservative constitution was, in the words of one French statesman, finally acceptable as the form of government that divided the French the least. Still, most monarchists continued to consider the republic a temporary expedient, until the monarchy could be reestablished, and the constitution was transparently designed to ease such a transition, when the time came.

These political struggles of 1871–5 worked themselves out with little reference to the Jews, whose civil equality was not at issue in the debates concerning the new constitution. Nor were Jews so clearly identified with the liberal left as was the case in Germany or Austria-Hungary, where Jewish politicians held leading positions in the dominant liberal parties, where Jewish financial contributions were often extremely significant, and where Jewish voters in a few areas, particularly the capital cities, had come to constitute a powerful liberal voting bloc.

At the same time, the upward mobility of French Jews in the 1870s and 1880s was faster and more visible than it ever had been. Also, the tendency of Jews in France to identify with what a noted French scholar has termed the "party of movement," as distinguished from the "party of order," became ever more pronounced with the Third Republic.[19] In the 1870s and 1880s many French Jews supported the so-called Opportunist Party, headed by Léon Gambetta. This support was primarily as advisers,

---

[18] Wilson, *Ideology*, 406.
[19] François Goguel, *La Politique des partis sous la IIIe République* (Paris, 1958).

as behind-the-scene financial supporters, and as government appointees, not as elected political leaders. As voters, of course, their numbers were too small and too scattered to be of real significance, even in Paris, where the largest concentration of Jews in France was to be found (about forty thousand of the seventy thousand in France as a whole). For the most part French Jews resisted identifying themselves as a voting bloc, just as they shunned the idea that they were a community with identifiable common interests.

Gambetta had been a fiery radical and intransigent nationalist in 1870 and 1871, but in the following years he moved toward the political center (thus the term *Opportunist*). In so doing he earned the gratitude of those who yearned for an end to the unrest of the preceding years, who hoped for national and social reconciliation. Those Jews who rallied to Gambetta's banners were mostly of the propertied French bourgeoisie; they found him attractive in large part because he seemed to promise social stability. He was an effective opponent of socialist and anarchist demands, yet he avoided reactionary extremes. The French right, and the "party of order" more generally, being traditionalist, monarchist, and Catholic, was perceived by most French Jews as hostile to their aspirations, although a select few of extremely rich Jews, such as the Rothschilds, continued to move in right-wing circles, as did small numbers of Jewish artists and intellectuals.

To the dismay of the monarchists, the Third Republic, a mere temporary expedient in their minds, slowly began to win popular support. Similarly, republicans gradually displaced the older monarchist and Bonapartist cadres in the civil service and government bureaucracy. This displacement entailed a change in social class as well, from aristocrats to bourgeoisie, and in religion from Catholic to Protestant or nonbeliever – or Jew. In short, a new governing class began to come to power in France. Many monarchists in the French civil service retired to their country estates in disgust or disgruntlement. Some monarchists, however, turned to the one major area of employment by the state that remained open to them, the army – a development of no small importance in the Dreyfus Affair.

The rise of the Jews and the dilemmas of modernism

The growing political importance of middle-class Jews in the new republican establishment was a different matter from the older connections that the Rothschilds and other Jewish financiers had established with the kings and emperors in the earlier part of the century. But as the republic grew in popular support in the late 1870s and early 1880s, its enemies professed to see a connection between the long-standing power of the Rothschilds and that of the newly important Jews among the Opportunists, mostly nouveaux riches. Those inclined to believe in conspiracies complained with rising bad temper about the "Jewish Syndicate," a purported clandestine organization that they claimed worked behind the cover of the Alliance Israélite Universelle. Enemies of the Republic were similarly inclined to see rising Jewish power in terms of a growing – and menacing – foreign influence inside France. Jewish immigrants from Germany were particularly resented, at a time when the new German Reich loomed as a continuing major threat to France.

Fantasies aside, the Rothschilds had undeniably built up an imposing financial empire in France, Germany, Austria, and Great Britain. Nowhere was the rise of the Jews throughout Europe more visible, more widely discussed by the great public, non-Jewish and Jewish, than in the case of the Rothschild family. Their spectacular rise in France and their unmistakable German origin – the first generation spoke a thickly accented, somewhat comical French – made them a perfect symbol for those who harbored paranoiac visions of a foreign threat.

Much of what the Rothschilds accomplished, and the way that they accomplished it, was in truth concealed from public view. They made a near fetish of privacy, secrecy, and keeping their power within the family. But they also eagerly sought out public honors and titles of nobility. The Rothschilds' purchase of the Hôtel Talleyrand, overlooking the Place de la Concorde in Paris, was for some an unbearable symbol of foreign, Jewish money, a Jewish rise to power and bogus respectability, pushing aside the older, genuinely French elites, in the very center of the capital of France. It is also true that the Alliance Israélite Universelle sometimes did operate clandestinely. The fantasy of anti-Semites in France concerning Jewish secretiveness was based on a real secretiveness of some highly placed and influential Jews. What anti-Semites suspected in this regard was not so much a fantasy as a malicious exaggeration.

There was equally an element of exaggeration in the visions of the triumph of money, linked to new economic forces in France. At least compared to Germany and the United States, where such developments were dramatic and sweeping, France's rate of economic growth was more gradual and less disruptive of its society. However, this gradual rate of growth entailed another kind of concern. The French began to worry that, lacking the economic dynamism of other countries, they were being left behind. From its position as the second industrial power in Europe early in the century, France dropped to fourth place, passed by both Germany and Russia by the eve of World War I. The deceleration of France's economy in the 1880s, from a 1.6 percent growth rate in the previous decade to 0.6 percent, alarmed many French patriots; the country's poor export performance was due in large part to the ravages of foreign competition, German and U.S. prominently.[20] French population growth also lagged behind nearly all other European countries, finally an even greater source of anxiety than industrial stagnation. The French became increasingly possessed by fears of decline, of decadence and impending national dissolution.

France was rich in natural resources and enjoyed an unusually well balanced economy, but much more of its population than that of Great Britain or Germany continued to live in the countryside and in small towns, remaining attached to premodern, small-scale production, with an emphasis on handicrafts and items of luxury and artistry, not on heavy industry or factory production. Frenchmen typically took pride in quality production – high fashion, perfumes, fine wines, objets d'art – in contrast to the mass-produced goods that were ever more typical of the United States or Germany. Small towns and villages, independent peasants and artisans, rather than industrial cities and rootless masses – such, at any rate, was the republican ideal. The survival of the Third Republic from 1875 to 1914 undeniably had something to do with these persisting social and economic realities, for the "little man" in France increasingly supported the Republic rather than a return of the monarchy.

But this was an age in which the little man was everywhere under attack, and the middle and lower-middle classes in France, although perhaps less immediately threatened than in other countries, saw many dangers on the horizon. Industrialization and modernization produced many tensions within Germany, but rapid economic growth also resulted in greater material comfort and a stronger country militarily. The stresses and strains of modern life in Germany were smoothed over, though hardly resolved, by the country's series of military victories and by indications that Germany was moving into a period of preeminence in Europe.

France's humiliating defeat by Prussia in 1870–1 supported the potent symbolism of a rising Germany and a declining France. France's centuries-old antagonist England was also outstripping it in material wealth and military power. Across the seas, the United States represented another kind of vague threat, not in any direct military sense but rather as a new and powerful model, one that many in France found repellent: "Americanization" became a kind of dirty word for the French right, and indeed for many cultured French citizens of whatever political persuasion. It conjured up images of shoddy mass production, a shallow, homogenized mass culture, and mediocre, corrupt political leaders. That was the case in spite of a parallel sense among French republicans of identification

---

[20] François Caron, *An Economic History of Modern France* (New York, 1979), 105–12.

with the United States (in 1885–6 the Statue of Liberty was presented to the American republic). But that identification was due in part to the United States being the only other major power of the day that was not monarchical.

In short, France's less dynamic economy, linked to its slower population growth, although easing the disorientation and shock of change, tended in the long run to feed the anxiety felt by many of its more sensitive, thoughtful, and nationalistic citizens that their country was falling behind – and, of special concern, falling behind its bustling, saber-rattling neighbor to the northeast.

The political crises and scandals of the 1880s

A key question for such citizens was whether the new republic could lead France effectively in such troubled, dangerous times. Many on the right did not believe so, and they were doubly distressed to see the republicans gain in popular support. Their belief that the republican form of state could not really compete was buttressed by a series of scandals in the 1880s, a number of which involved Jews in prominent roles. The stability of the French republic was also put into question by the divisive political crises in the 1880s and early 1890s, before the Dreyfus Affair itself. France was, in one historian's words, in a state of "endless crisis."[21]

One such crisis involved Jews only indirectly but powerfully nonetheless. From 1879 to 1886 a highly controversial body of legislation, known as the Ferry Laws, was introduced. The laws sought to establish secular control over primary education and to expand the scope of that education, consistent with liberal-secularist goals throughout Europe. In removing primary education from the control of Catholic Church, the Ferry Laws were designed to modernize the countryside, "liberating" the minds of the peasants, so to speak, by providing them with a secular-republican education, again in conformity with liberal-democratic principles throughout the continent.

Although the agitation over these laws did not quite assume the dimensions of Bismarck's more famous *Kulturkampf*, which so divided Germans a few years earlier, the issues and political forces involved were broadly similar. One such similarity was that French Jews, like German Jews, were among the most ardent and articulate supporters of the notion of removing public education from the control of the Catholic Church. French Catholics, as an overwhelming majority that fancied themselves the "true" French, were not particularly concerned about the principle

---

[21] Weber, *France: Fin de Siècle*, 105 ff.

of minority rights; being Catholic was in their minds part of French integral nationalism. On the other hand, the German Catholic minority, facing a Protestant majority, was concerned about minority rights, and eventually, after the Kulturkampf agitation calmed down, German Jews and German Catholics came to recognize, however shakily, common interests in that regard. Moreover, in Germany the issue of modernizing education and putting it under state control took on a Lutheran, and thus still a Christian, aura, whereas in France the supporters of the Ferry Laws were often explicitly anti-Christian, militantly secular, and vehemently anticlerical. Since French Jews were allied with determined enemies of organized religion, they could be presented more plausibly as both anti-Christian and antireligious.

French Catholics, believing that France, long a Catholic nation, should remain one, naturally began to feel besieged under the Third Republic. It was, they believed, increasingly dominated by atheists, secularists, Protestants, and Jews, all of whom had set out to de-Christianize France. There were elements of exaggeration and overdramatization in that belief but, again, it cannot really be termed a fantasy. Many of the leaders of the Third Republic had explicitly set out to combat the Catholic Church, which they considered a dangerous, unyielding, and conniving enemy, one that poisoned the minds of the country's youth. These were real struggles, involving real issues that had quite concrete implications in the real world – jobs, political power, popular support.

Traditional Catholics, for their part, regarded the parliamentary republic as one of unbridled corruption, of quarrelsome, petty, venal, and recklessly ambitious politicians. These were vices, they believed, that were endemic to the republican form. The U.S. republic of these years, similarly plagued by corruption and scandal, served as a negative model for them. Even recognizing the exaggeration in those charges, any student of the Third Republic must recognize an element of truth in them.[22] More disputable, although also corresponding to reality in a number of notorious cases, was the belief of traditional Catholics that the Republic's leaders were in the pay of Jews. A related belief was that the Jews were illicitly gaining high political office, buying positions of power in the state and military. A story circulated, of very doubtful authenticity but still indicative of what some French Catholics feared, that at a banquet given by the Rothschilds, Gambetta, "heated by wine," had said that "the priest is the past, the Jew is the future." It was further rumored that at Gambetta's death in 1882 "the prefectures of 47 out of 80 departments were

---

[22] Cf. Theodore Zeldin, *France, 1848–1945*, vol. 1 (Oxford, 1973), esp. Chap. 19, "The Politicians of the Third Republic."

in the hands of Jews."[23] Fifteen years later the Union nationale, a Catholic organization in France, claimed that there were 49 Jewish prefects and subprefects, and 19 Jews in the Conseil d'état.[24] These figures are all highly doubtful and may be seen as examples of how facts and figures were manipulated to suit partisan purposes. Yet there is little doubt that Jews, who represented around one-tenth of 1 percent of the total population, were strongly overrepresented in these areas. And in a state as centralized as that of France such positions in the high administration no doubt represented considerable influence. It is also beyond question that Catholics had good reason to feel pushed aside by a new political class, within which were many Jews. The distinguished historian of France, D. W. Brogan, wrote of the situation in the 1880s:

> In certain parts of the administration, it was rare to find a practising Catholic in a position of power. A Jewish prefect could, with impunity, observe Passover, but a prefect who was openly zealous in the observation of Easter might find himself under violent attack from a paper like the *Lanterne*, whose main stock in trade was anti-clerical scurrility and whose editor was a Jew, the great "priest-eater," Eugène Mayer.[25]

Even some Jewish testimony of these years speaks of how French Jews believed the future belonged to them; as a superior people that had long been suppressed they had a "destiny" to assume greater power, a "right to rule." Julien Benda, for example, wrote that among the editors of *La Revue Blanche*, "there were certain magnates, financiers rather than literary men, with whom the belief in the superiority of their race and the natural subjection of those who did not belong to it, were visibly sovereign." Non-Jews like Emile Zola or André Gide reported much the same impressions in regard to many Jews they encountered, among them Léon Blum, who would later become the first Jewish premier of France and who would surround himself with a number of Jewish advisers.[26] Leaders of the Alliance Israélite Universelle warned its members against "arrogance" yet still implicitly accepted, often in the social-Darwinian language current at the time, the notion of Jewish superiority.[27]

As was the case in Germany and Austria in the 1870s, the financial scandals of the 1880s in France undeniably involved Jewish culprits, many

[23] Egal Feldmann, *The Dreyfus Affair and the American Conscience* (Detroit, 1981), 136–7.
[24] Wilson, *Ideology*, 396.
[25] Denis W. Brogan, *The Development of Modern France, 1870–1939*, vol. 1 (New York, 1966) 276.
[26] Wilson, *Ideology*, 410.
[27] Marrus, *Assimilation*, 16–17.

of whom were of German, Austrian, or Polish background. One of the most famous and influential of the scandals involved the Union générale, a bank that Catholic financiers had established with the explicit goal of allowing Catholic investors to avoid the Jewish and Protestant institutions that so dominated finance in France. After a promising beginning, the new enterprise collapsed in 1882, ruining many small Catholic investors. It was widely believed that the Union générale had been done in by the Rothschilds, with whom it was for a time in fierce competition.[28] Mass-circulation newspapers exploited the issue, and, not surprisingly, the directors of the bank were quick to blame the Jews in order to cover up their own mismanagement. Few doubted that the Rothschilds, as others in high finance, could be ruthless when necessary. Indeed, criticism of the Rothschilds within the Jewish community often exceeded criticism by non-Jews. The episode found novelistic treatment in a number of books in the 1880s and 1890s, among which was Zola's novel *L'Argent* (Money), giving even wider exposure to the idea, already well established, of con-spiratorial, relentlessly expanding Jewish financial power.[29]

Zola was France's most famous novelist at this time, and he was within a few years to be a leading defender of Alfred Dreyfus. He became a hero to Jews and was widely believed by anti-Semites to be in their pay. That such a man shared the widespread apprehensions of the period about the rise of Jewish power, particularly in the form of money, suggests how much that sort of anti-Jewish hostility cut across the political spectrum. Zola was a man of the left, not a backward-looking monarchist, and his negative remarks about Jews complemented those of many on the left in France. Even Friedrich Engels, who on other occasions marveled at the positive contributions made by Jews to the socialist movement throughout Europe, was unfavorably impressed by the activities of Jewish financiers in France. He commented: "I begin to understand French anti-Semitism when I see how many Jews of Polish origin and German names intrude themselves everywhere."[30] Lucien Wolf, the Anglo-Jewish activist, noted for his efforts on behalf of Russian Jewry, similarly observed how the "obnoxiousness of [the] Jewish element" of the French bourgeoisie was "accentuated" by the German origin of a number of its prominent members.[31]

It is no doubt true that many in France were inclined to blame Jews for problems concerning which Jews had no responsibility, to make scape-

---

[28] Jeannine Verdès-Leroux, *Scandale financier et antisémitisme catholique: le krach de l'Union générale* (Paris, 1969); Brogan, *France*, vol. 1, 171.
[29] Robert Byrnes, *Anti-Semitism in Modern France* (New Brunswick, N.J., 1950), 102, 109.
[30] Quoted in Robert S. Wistrich, *Socialism and the Jews: The Dialectics of Emancipation in Germany and Austria-Hungary* (East Brunswick, N.J., 1984), 34.
[31] Cecil Roth, ed., *Essays in Jewish History by Lucien Wolf* (London, 1934), 449.

goats of Jews, and thus to ignore the extent to which those problems had broader and deeper roots.[32] Nevertheless, that such foreign observers, including Jews like Wolf, also blamed them points to problems that were more than mere fantasies of anti-Semites. That the great majority of law-abiding Jews in France, who had nothing to do with high finance or political scandals, were drawn into a net of suspicion underlines the per-plexities and predicaments they faced in this land of liberty, equality, and fraternity.

Nascent political anti-Semitism: the Boulangists

These various resentments began to coalesce in France by the late 1880s. According to one historian, it was with the Boulangist movement of those years that the "mobilizing power and . . . revolutionary force" of popular anti-Semitism began to be realized.[33] In a more general way those who believed that the Republic could never bring France back to unity and glory looked to a Man on Horseback. A strongman could give new di-rection and authority, heal France's wounds, and vanquish its enemies. After the revolutions of 1789 and 1848, just such men, Napoleon and then his nephew, Napoleon III, had overthrown the first and second republics and introduced authoritarian regimes. By the late 1880s General Georges Boulanger (1837–91) seemed to some in France to be a possible savior, a new Napoleon.

He did resemble the two Napoleons but was also different from them in revealing ways. He had at first been a protégé of Gambetta's Oppor-tunists, and he had, after being appointed minister of war in January 1886, introduced a number of well-conceived reforms, including better food, more comfortable barracks, and new weapons. He won a dazzling pop-ularity with the common people through military parades and patriotic speeches that emphasized the need to stiffen France's backbone, to stand up to the Germans. Indeed, the breadth of his appeal, as he began to stake out an independent political position (he was dismissed as minister of war in the spring of 1887 and began to run for parliament on his own a year later), was impressive. He attracted workers and shopkeepers who had been up to that point followers of the Radical Party (that is, the republican left), yet he also won the support of wealthy conservatives, most notably the monarchists.[34] His campaign shook up established po-

---

[32] Cf. Wilson, *Ideology*, passim.
[33] Zeev Sternhell, "The Roots of Popular Anti-Semitism in the Third Republic," in Frances Malino and Bernard Wasserman, eds., *The Jews in Modern France* (Hanover, N.H., 1985), 103.
[34] William D. Irvine, *The Boulanger Affair Reconsidered: Royalism, Boulangism, and the Origins of the Radical Right in France* (Oxford, 1989).

litical patterns and fidelities. In many areas the older notables of rural France, who represented an "old-fashioned political style of personal influence and aristocratic prestige,"[35] lost influence in competition with the Boulangists. Although he repeatedly proclaimed his attachment to republican principles and institutions, Boulanger accepted funds from the monarchists and the Bonapartists. Indeed, in spite of the threat he and his movement seemed to present to older elites, monarchists in many rural areas not only supported him financially but worked with him organizationally as well.[36] He retained an American political adviser and used "American" methods, or what has been called, in the French terminology of the day, political "burlesque" – songs, poems, broadsheets, raucous demonstrations.[37] Most historians since have termed these methods simply modern, but some have detected protofascist elements in them. Undoubtedly, in the way that General Boulanger was able, through public pageantry and ambiguous rhetoric, to put together an improbable alliance of old elites and a volatile, resentful populace, he may be said to resemble Mussolini or Hitler. Obvious parallels may be found as well in the way that those elites, after initial aversion, came to believe that Boulanger and his movement could be manipulated for their purposes.

Historians have disputed, however, the importance of anti-Semitism in the Boulangist movement.[38] It was rumored that he had promised he would "get rid of the Jews," the many public officials who had been appointed by Gambetta and the Opportunists, if he were to come to power. These Jews, he is supposed to have said, were a major source of the problems currently afflicting France. However, such rumors were almost certainly spread by the anti-Semites in Boulanger's entourage and did not reflect his personal views. He was not an anti-Semite and did not disguise his distaste for some of the more prominent French anti-Semites of the day, even though he was willing to accept their support.[39] Several Jews were prominent in the Boulangist movement and were personal friends of Boulanger. He never used anti-Semitism as a political device in his speeches and campaigns, whatever he was rumored to have said privately.[40]

Still, there definitely were a number of anti-Semites among leading

[35] Patrick H. Hutton, "Popular Boulangism and the Advent of Mass Politics in France," *The Journal of Contemporary History*, vol. 11, 1976, 92; cited in Michael Burns, *Rural Society and French Politics: Boulangism and the Dreyfus Affair, 1886–1900* (Princeton, N.J., 1984), 59.

[36] Irvine, *Boulanger Affair Reconsidered*, passim.

[37] Burns, *Rural Society*, 8.

[38] Compare the accounts in Sternhell, "Roots"; Wilson, *Ideology*; Burns, *Rural Society*; Irvine, *Boulanger Affair Reconsidered*; and Philip G. Nord, *Paris Shopkeepers and the Politics of Resentment* (Princeton, N.J., 1986).

[39] Sternhell, "Roots," 104.

[40] Burns, *Rural Society*, 21, 114.

Boulangists, and many of them would be active in the anti-Semitic movement that emerged from the Dreyfus Affair a decade later. Their greatest successes, revealingly, both at the time of the Boulangist agitation in 1889–90 and a decade later, were in the Paris region and particularly among the shopkeepers and small merchants of the capital. It was in such strata that the encroachments of economic modernization were particularly apparent. There, too, the threat of modernism in a more general sense was the subject of open discussion and agitation.

Since the 1860s Paris had witnessed extensive changes; the shape of the twentieth-century city dates to that period. Many of the older *quartiers* were demolished in order to build the spacious *grands boulevards* and the new railway stations. These changes not only forced many center-city residents to the suburbs but changed economic relationships and transformed the patterns of economic activity within the city. Department stores (*grands magasins*) became prominent, offering a most unwelcome competition to many small merchants.

Small shopkeepers suffered in the depressed 1880s; many went bankrupt. But the new department stores prospered and expanded. "Shopkeepers watched once prosperous businesses wither as, not a hundred feet away, boulevard boutiques and department stores did a booming trade."[41] A smaller proportion of department stores were owned by Jews in Paris than in the major cities of central Europe, but enough were so owned to make anti-Semitic charges appear justified. Those charges blended into a more general belief that "outsiders," non-Parisians, were bringing a ruinous competition to the city. "Foreigners, cosmopolitans and Jews were infiltrating the world of commerce from every side. . . . They took over the street as they had *grand commerce* and the commission house."[42]

The complaints ranged far beyond charges of destructive competition, however. Organizations representing small business (*petits commerçants*) drew a picture of an invasion of mass-produced, shoddy merchandise; of a new architecture, inhuman in scale, of which the detested Eiffel Tower came to serve as a symbol; of faceless crowds in the boulevards. Spokesmen for small business even attributed the moral decline of the day to the frenzied atmosphere within the department stores, which encouraged kleptomania and an unhealthy mixing of the sexes. Quality merchandise, handwork, and artistry were being driven from Paris, they claimed. The charm and calm of the old quartiers, the very heart of Paris, could not survive.

Shopkeepers harbored hopes that Boulanger would come to their rescue

[41] Nord, *Shopkeepers*, 191.
[42] Ibid.

by revising the constitution and introducing legislation that would protect the little man and save the soul of the capital. In the course of the 1880s owners of small businesses had come to feel neglected or even abandoned by the Radical Party. At the same time, they began to sense a new hostility to them on the part of the working class, increasingly organized into militant, collectivist trade unions and parties. Leading Opportunists had dismissed this petite bourgeoisie as "incompetent" and doomed to disappear from the modern scene. Members of that class thus felt threatened from large-scale production and from organized labor, from above and below.

But it would be facile to dismiss the shopkeepers of Paris as people who had lost a grip on reality, who were acting irrationally and were willing to throw themselves into the hands of reactionary demagogues who offered anti-Semitic nostrums. Parisian shopkeepers were undoubtedly attracted to anti-Semitism, but they were not consumed by it. They had been, it must be remembered, up to this point among the staunchest supporters of the Republic and believers in the ideals of the revolution, liberty, equality, and fraternity. They did not readily join the ranks of those on the right, whom they had heretofore considered their worst enemies. The Boulangist movement did not present itself to them as reactionary but rather as progressive in important ways. Shopkeepers attacked contemporary economic developments in the "progressive" language of Radical republicanism: The department stores represented a "new feudalism," a new and dangerous concentration of wealth and power. These monstrosities threatened to ruin the little man, the small property owner who was the mainstay of republican democracy and an egalitarian society. The new factories and the new collectivist organizations of the working class also posed a threat because of their concentration of power, because of the way they undermined self-sufficiency and independence. Such ideals were as central to American democracy of the time as they were to the republican shopkeepers of Paris.

The Old Order of kings, nobles, and privileged orders did not much attract these shopkeepers, who continued to believe in an open society, upward mobility, equality before the law, and free, republican institutions. They were unquestionably afflicted by a xenophobic fear of menacing "outsiders"; however, anti-Semitism, at least in the form that attracted them, was fed not only from xenophobia but also from the Radical hatred of privilege and concentrated power. Jews represented to them either the fabulously rich and privileged or the newly rich owners of factories and department stores, ruinous to the little man and threatening to the future of the republic.

The racism of central Europe, of a Marr or a Dühring, had relatively little popular appeal in France, although it had certainly begun to gain greater visibility in the 1880s. Nor did the charge, common in central and eastern Europe, that Jews were the leaders or inspirers of collectivist socialism gain much credence in France at this time. Eastern European Jews in Paris had begun to make themselves felt as peddlers (unwelcome competitors, to be sure, vulnerable to charges of introducing cheap and shoddy merchandise), but their numbers were still too small to present a major problem. All of these issues had potential, but as yet that potential in France had been realized much less than in central Europe. They had not been effectively tied together and widely propagated through a racist ideology that could make the Rothschilds, the Jewish department store or factory owner, the peddler, and the revolutionary socialist all part of a single threat, the threat of the destructive Jewish race. Similarly, it had not become what the Germans termed an *Integrationsideologie*, an ideology capable of powerfully uniting previously hostile social and political groups, rich and poor, right and left.

These words are not meant to suggest that even in German-speaking central Europe such an ideology had reached a coherent and widely effective form, but the process was definitely further advanced there. Boulangism, whatever its ambiguous anti-Semitic content, at first appeared to have potential as such an ideology, but after his initial successes Boulanger proved a great disappointment, and the movement collapsed ignominiously. The anti-Semitic organizations that had begun to form in the ranks of the Boulangists also fell apart. Boulanger, in exile, committed suicide at the grave of his mistress. The republican establishment, so suddenly threatened by the wave of Boulangist agitation in 1889–90, breathed a sigh of relief.

Some have seen the Boulangist movement as a rehearsal for the anti-Semitic movement of the late 1890s in France,[43] but others have pointed to crucial differences between the Boulangists and the Anti-Dreyfusards, differences in leadership, in following, and in ideology.[44] Although a number of Boulangists did become Anti-Dreyfusards, a large number also became defenders of Dreyfus. The workers who voted in such surprising numbers for Boulanger in 1889 moved, after the movement collapsed, not to the right but to the left, into the ranks of the socialists. The Parisian shopkeepers, too, by no means moved directly into the camp of the reactionaries, although they undoubtedly were more tempted to do so.

Perhaps most instructive was the evolution of opinion among monarchists. Until the 1880s Jewish issues had remained of peripheral interest to them. The traditional forms of anti-Jewish disdain were certainly present, but such feelings were not important enough to find expression in

[43] Zeev Sternhell, *La Droite révolutionnaire, 1885–1914: les origines françaises du fascisme* (Paris, 1978).
[44] Nord, *Shopkeepers*.

the monarchist party program. Monarchist opinion until the mid-1880s was perhaps even less influenced by modern racist theory than was the opinion of the center and left in France; monarchists expressed themselves in a disconcertingly diverse way about Jews. The same writer might make slighting references to Jewish traits while defending Jews against such charges as ritual murder. Another might bitterly denounce Jewish financiers or war profiteers while expressing disgust at the pogroms in Russia.[45] In short, the specter of "the Jew," or the threat of the Jewish race, simply did not speak to most monarchist leaders.

The competing pretenders to the French throne openly denounced anti-Semitism; the Count of Paris ostentatiously donated 500 francs toward the establishment of a Jewish school. The reticence of the monarchists to ally openly with racist anti-Semites was undoubtedly in part based on a fear of losing the large contributions made to the monarchist party coffers by Alphonse de Rothschild and Maurice de Hirsch, but the social radicalism of many anti-Semites also genuinely repelled those on the French right. It is noteworthy that even when some monarchists began to give more serious consideration to racial anti-Semitism as a political device, they did so, much like the leaders of the German Conservative Party, in a calculated, "insincere" fashion (as in Germany, too, a number of prominent French monarchists had Jewish wives). Interestingly, once the royalists could define anti-Semitism as directed against a race, and not against a religion or a rich caste, they seemed to have less difficulty in accepting it. Yet even during the Dreyfus Affair that acceptance was slow and directly linked to their growing appreciation of how Jew-hatred might be turned against the republic and linked to the conservative cause.[46]

At any rate, from the standpoint of the Opportunists, and their Jewish supporters, the collapse of the Boulangists meant that the Republic had survived another storm. Jews could more confidently reaffirm their long-standing beliefs that anti-Semitism had no staying power in France. Non-Jewish republicans in France, as well, took pride that the backward-looking bigotry of central European racists had failed to gain the support of the French nation.

The Assumptionists

Anti-Jewish, antimodern feelings were building in other areas, outside Paris, and they found other champions. A Catholic and rural counteroffensive against the secular republic was underway in these years, one

---

[45] Irvine, *Boulanger Affair Reconsidered*, 167–9.
[46] Ibid., 169–71.

self-consciously distinct from developments in Paris and the larger cities of France. Since the middle of the century, the Catholic Church had railed against a broad range of modern ideas. This Catholic offensive was part of the reason that Bismarck had undertaken his Kulturkampf. As late as 1885 the Papal encyclical *Immortale Dei* declared that "equal toleration of all religions," a central tenet of French republicanism, "is the same thing as atheism." Toleration of religious pluralism was commonly denounced among Catholic spokesmen in France as "Americanism," yet another way that the United States constituted a bad example.

The Ferry Laws became a special concern of the recently created Assumptionist Order. In addition, its members took upon themselves, much as the Jesuits and Dominicans had done in the past, the task of combating Jewish influence. In a statement that graphically reflected the order's viewpoint, an Assumptionist leader declared that God had allowed the modern Church to suffer like Christ Himself, "to be betrayed, sold, jeered at, beaten, covered with spittle, and crucified by the Jews."[47]

The Assumptionists published a newspaper, *La Croix* (The Cross), that aggressively forwarded Catholic-traditionalist ideas but was edited and marketed in a distinctly modern way, seeking to reach the Catholic masses by new means.[48] *La Croix* was only one of many mass-circulation newspapers that appeared in France in the 1880s, and many of them propagated anti-Semitic imagery of one sort or another, however diffuse and contradictory.[49] Particularly in the rural, more backward areas of France, Catholics who had not regularly read a newspaper now got their information from *La Croix*. Many parish priests considered it to be the last word on developments in France. The Assumptionists contributed to the tendency of many devout French Catholics in these years to retreat into an intellectual and cultural ghetto. Such tendencies in turn meshed with a resurgent popular fundamentalism among French Catholics of the late nineteenth century. They showed a renewed interest in miracles, prophesies, and relics. This was a time, for example, when the Lourdes cult flourished.[50]

Yet, again, most Jewish observers in the 1880s were not particularly alarmed over the activities of *La Croix* and the Catholic fundamentalists. French Jews dismissed anti-Semitism, whether religious or racial, as alien to the modern French spirit. Jew-hatred seemed endemic in Russia, the bastion of backwardness, and still strong in Germany and Austria. But in France, so the reasoning went, anti-Semitism was harbored only by a few

---

[47] Quoted in Wilson, *Ideology*, 554.
[48] Cf. Pierre Sorlin, *"La Croix" et les juifs (1880–1899): contribution à l'histoire de l'antisémitisme contemporaine* (Paris, 1967).
[49] Cf. Sternhell, *Droite révolutionnaire*, 217.
[50] Wilson, *Ideology*, 557.

reactionaries, whose numbers and power were dwindling, by fanatical Catholics, whose activities were being curbed by the state, or by the ignorant mob, which was gradually disappearing through education and a rising standard of living. Time was on the side both of the Jews and of enlightenment, reason, and justice.

Both Boulangism and the agitation of the Assumptionist Order have been widely accepted by modern historians as signs of an awakening of previously passive, traditionalist elements of the population, even though *La Croix* paradoxically forwarded monarchism and traditionalism. Both helped to draw the French peasantry out of its political apathy and isolation, its reliance on the leadership of local elites or notables. There is little doubt that their "marked repugnance against the Boulangist adventure" impelled many peasants to vote for the Republic for the first time in 1888.[51] This alteration in rural voting patterns was but another manifestation of the prorepublican drift of French politics in the 1880s, a drift all the more remarkable in light of the rural depression of those years.

Although these prorepublican votes constituted evidence of a political awakening among France's rural population toward greater assertiveness and self-reliance, that was a long and gradual process.[52] Even the Dreyfus Affair did not engage most of France's peasant population, and the implication, found in many histories, that the agitation of the Assumptionists played an important role in the Affair is highly questionable. The Assumptionists represented a certain provincial mentality of the time, but in Paris they attracted almost no following. More broadly, anti-Semitism among peasants throughout Europe, whether in France or in Russia, remains a relatively ill-understood phenomenon, especially in terms of how it translated into action, into political activity. As a modern racist ideology it had little appeal or meaning to peasants.

In examining evidence of growing tensions between Jews and non-Jews in the 1880s, of structural or impersonal forces that tended to turn the two against one another, one further major development at this time is worthy of mention. In 1891, France signed an accord with Russia, bringing to an end the Republic's long period of diplomatic isolation following the Franco-Prussian war. By 1894 the accord had developed into a full military pact, the beginning of the "encirclement" that Germany so dreaded.

This alliance between democratic, republican France and autocratic, tsarist Russia was an anomaly. Some contemporaries believed it could not last, but most French welcomed it as substantially advancing national

[51] Burns, *Rural Society*, 8.
[52] Ibid. Burns presents a most complex and many-sided picture, where the survival of traditionalist patterns mixed into the "awakened" attitudes of the peasants.

security. However, the left in France, above all the socialists, remained skeptical about an alliance with such a reactionary power. French Jews, too, expressed reservations, especially since the early 1890s marked yet another wave of oppressive measures by the tsarist government against its Jewish population. To a degree, these contrasting reactions were a replay of the Damascus Affair, and anti-Semites naturally accused French Jews of putting the welfare of Jews in other countries over the national security of France.

Anti-Semitic ideology and movement: Toussenel, Barrès, Drumont

If the Boulangist episode and the anti-Semitic agitation associated with it may be considered notable failures, and if anti-Semitic ideology exercised less popular appeal in France than in central Europe, it is also true that the ideology of modern Jew-hatred was maturing and becoming attuned to special French sensibilities in the years immediately preceding Dreyfus's arrest. The explosive popular appeal of anti-Semitism by the end of the 1890s, and even more the extent to which anti-Semitic imagery seems to have been accepted by a wide range of educated people in France in those years, must be understood not only in terms of the kinds of economic, social, and religious developments so far mentioned, but also in the productions of a number of theorists, men whose ideas in certain ways stand out in relation to the anti-Semites of central and eastern Europe.

As early as the 1840s a flood of both theoretical and polemical works aimed at exposing the Rothschilds and denouncing all they symbolized had appeared in France. One of these, reprinted in the 1880s, is worth attention, for it exercised an obvious influence on the most prominent anti-Semites of those years. Alphonse de Toussenel (1803–55), a follower of Charles Fourier, developed what might be termed an aristocratic and aesthetic variety of socialism. Like a number of left-wing activists of the 1840s, he turned to anti-Semitism after 1848 (Marr in Germany was another, as was Wagner). His many books on nature and wildlife enjoyed a great popularity throughout the century; he was called the "Balzac of the natural world." His writings seemed to inspire the French as the writings of John Muir inspired Americans. Toussenel evoked with considerable power the fear that his beautiful homeland, *la belle France*, was being irreparably spoiled, ravaged by railroads, ugly, smoking factories, and characterless industrial cities. Unlike Muir, however, Toussenel saw the destruction of pristine nature as primarily the work of foreigners, to a large degree Jews, men who had contempt for the common people, no feeling for the land, no deep roots in the country, and who were consumed by the egoistic pursuit of profit.

In his book *The Jews, Kings of the Epoch* (first published in 1845) Toussenel lamented the role of Jews in France in terms that were based on long-standing perceptions of Jews, even on Jewish self-perception, dating back to ancient times. His description of contemporary Jews might even be considered an early version of the kinds of descriptions later common among Zionists, who believed Jews in *galut* (in exile from the land of Israel) were inevitably "perverse" and "false." Toussenel portrayed the Jews as a people long divorced from the land, who had lost a feeling for nature, who had little love for or even interest in natural beauty. For thousands of years, he observed, Jews had not worked the land or hunted in the forests. Instead, they had cooped themselves up in dank, airless rooms, poring over talmudic tomes, and in those very works was to be found a fundamental suspicion of the natural world. The livelihood of Jews for thousands of years was similarly not one that involved the world of soil, open air, animals, forests, and mountains. Rather, it was a crowded urban world of money, profit, calculation, and financial enterprise. In modern times Jewish capitalists were ravaging the countryside, polluting the natural world, ruining the honest, hard-working artisan and peasant, all in the service of capital accumulation, greed, and profit. Modern railways, financed by Jews, were violating the pristine fields and pastures; factories were fouling the air. Jewish nouveaux riches became ever richer and more powerful, while France and simple French people were being ruined.

Toussenel's portrayal of Jews was not based on biological racism but rather on historical-cultural factors. He also bitterly attacked French Protestant capitalists, especially the "foreign" ones based in Geneva. As he put it, even the English and Dutch "who profess the same contempt as does the Jew for the laws of justice and the rights of the workers" were also "Jews."[53] Similarly, Toussenel was talking about real issues, however questionable his presentation of them, not fantasies, in the way, for example, that the charge that Jews need Christian blood for their religious ceremonies is a fantasy. Nevertheless, Toussenel's ideas meshed comfortably with, and inevitably gave support to, those who argued that Aryans were at home in nature whereas the Semites were "unnatural," locked into messianic visions and alien ideals designed to destroy the peoples among whom they lived. Moreover, in combining anticapitalist, antibourgeois themes with those of tradition, of an aesthetic preference for traditional production of artisans and for the beauties of the precapitalist natural world, Toussenel's writings spoke to both right and left and

---

[53] Poliakov, *History of Anti-Semitism*, vol. 3, 371.

contributed to an emerging "new right," or "revolutionary right," in France at the end of the nineteenth century. This kind of aesthetic anti-Semitism would be a key characteristic of that new right.

If the quality of thought in Toussenel may be described as superior to that of a Marr or even a Dühring, the case for a first-rate intellect, one finely attuned to aesthetic issues and sensitive to the social injustices of the day, can be made even more persuasively in the example of Maurice Barrès (1862–1923), a novelist and poet who was a leading Boulangist and who would become a leading Anti-Dreyfusard and theorist of the revolutionary right. His graceful, lyrical prose and the penetration of his intellect earned almost universal admiration, and a place in the Académie Française. Some indication of his stature may be gained from the comment in the memoirs of Léon Blum, who in the early 1890s, before he became involved in a major way in socialist politics, was a kind of literary dandy in Paris. He wrote: "For me Barrès was not only the master but the guide; we formed a school around him, almost a court." Blum, significantly, approached Barrès at the beginning of the Dreyfus Affair, absolutely convinced that his "master" would support Dreyfus. Barrès demurred, remarking that the case was too uncertain, and when faced with such uncertainty he relied upon "the national instinct."[54]

Barrès, like Toussenel, is interesting not only because of the subtlety of his intellect and his socialist sympathies but because his anti-Semitism was focused on real issues and rarely, if ever, partook of the more fantastic ravings of the radical wings of the anti-Semitic movement, whether racist or religious. Even the racism that came to play an ever-larger role in his thought was a relatively subtle matter; it, too, was more cultural-historical than biological or genetic. He was able to have Jewish friends and admirers like Blum and even to conclude, during World War I, that the Jews were part of a legitimate family of French people[55] – a conclusion that he had questioned in the 1890s, and, of course, a conclusion that biological racists could never accept since they saw Jewish traits not only as alien but also as unchangeable.

Indeed, the cultural-historical "racism" that Barrès expressed as the appropriate basis for French nationalism had something remotely in common with the notion of *Yiddishkayt* among eastern European Jews at this time. That is, this kind of Jewish nationalism mixed with socialism, also later facilely dismissed as racism, emphasized the special qualities of Jews that had emerged out of centuries of historical experience, qualities that Gentiles lacked and that it would be nearly impossible for them to acquire. So Barrès argued that the "real" French must have deep roots in France;

[54] Léon Blum, *Souvenirs sur l'Affaire* (Paris, 1929, 1981), 83; Bredin, *Affair*, 197.
[55] Stephen Schuker, "The Origins of the 'Jewish Problem' in the Later Third Republic," in Malino and Wasserstein, *Jews in Modern France*, 152.

one did not become French overnight or even in a generation. An even more revealing comparison might be with the Zionist Revisionist movement. The ultranationalism and denigration of Arab culture articulated by its leader, Vladimir Jabotinsky (1880–1940, thus of Blum's generation), was not, as an Israeli scholar has emphasized, "racial but *cultural*."[56] It is a distinction that Arabs did not find particularly appealing, any more than French Jews were inclined to look with sympathetic understanding upon Barrès's exclusion of them from the national community in France.

The Boulangist excitements helped to interest Barrès in anti-Semitism, which he openly described as attractive because it might bind together left and right, the oppressed lower classes and the privileged upper classes. In Boulangism, he reasoned, was hope for a national reconciliation of a much divided French people. Such reasoning found an ever-widening circle of adherents on the right, as they wrestled with the unpalatable necessity of reconciling themselves with modern mass society. But Barrès linked his sense of the unbridgeable foreignness of Jews with attention to real issues. In complaining, for example, that the numbers of Jews in the republican government "infinitely exceeded" what they would have been if proportionate to the Jewish population of France, he was referring to a reality that both Jews and philo-Semites openly recognized – indeed, some took pride in it.

Such observers were naturally less willing to accept his claim that Jewish money was regularly used to obtain government appointments and other privileges, and, of course, they could only angrily reject his reckless charge that the Republic was "enslaved" by the "Semites."[57] But the point is not that Barrès's beliefs were strictly accurate, or generous, or free of exaggeration but rather that he was addressing real issues. Similarly, his ability to evoke even more powerfully and extensively than had Toussenel the concerns of traditional French people regarding the turn that modern French life was taking, how that turn benefited Jews, attached as they were to commerce and industry, but hurt those in traditional occupations, built upon undeniably real trends. Factories were real, department stores were real, railroads were real, the decline of quality artisanal production and the appearance of shoddy mass-produced goods – all of these were realities in France at the end of the nineteenth century, realities that deeply concerned many who were not anti-Semites.

Factories, railroads, and department stores – modern trends generally – were not uniquely "Semitic" in inspiration, of course, and neither Toussenel or Barrès claimed that they were. But Jews were disproportionately involved in them and benefited from them more than those in traditional

[56] Robert Wistrich, *Hitler's Apocalypse: Jews and the Nazi Legacy* (New York, 1985), 252.
[57] Sternhell, "Roots," 108.

occupations. "France for the French!" – a slogan coined by Barrès and widely used by the new right in France – spoke to real issues in a country where the issue of foreign penetration was constantly in the press and where the number of foreigners had risen from 400,000 in 1851 to 1.3 million in 1891 and would continue to rise steadily into the twentieth century.[58]

Not only did the subtlety and coherence of Barrès's view of the world put it into another class than that of the crude, social-Darwinistic racism and demagogy of many central European anti-Semites, but his brilliance and personal success as a writer stood in sharp contrast to the personal failures and mediocrity of men like Marr and others in the German anti-Semitic movement. Nor did his tone, ugly as it sounds in retrospect, approach the fanaticism of von Schönerer or the cynical demagogy of Lueger.

To be sure, crude demagogues and men who discovered new careers in anti-Semitism after having failed repeatedly in others were to be found in France. The most famous of them was Edouard Drumont (1844–1917), who in 1886 published *La France juive* (Jewish France). It became a runaway best-seller, going through a hundred printings in one year, over one hundred thousand copies, and continued to sell well into the twentieth century.[59] It finally outsold Marr's pamphlet of 1879, the first anti-Semitic best-seller, by a wide margin. It constituted, indeed, one of the best-selling books in the history of French publishing before World War I.

The sudden popularity of this work, paralleling the rise of the Boulangist movement, would seem to cast doubt on the stubborn optimism of French Jews about their position in France. It would also seem to indicate that tens of thousands in the country were ready to move beyond the vague prejudices and unconnected, unfocused imagery of the past to embrace a modern ideology of anti-Semitism. Yet the meaning of Drumont's success is more difficult to evaluate than might at first seem the case. It was a peculiarly French and even more a Parisian phenomenon, and comparisons with Marr's best-seller, although obvious and appropriate, can also be misleading. If the political anti-Semitism of Germany and Austria was a "socialism of fools" or a "bundle of contradictions," as it was so often described, Drumont's work was even more confused and foolish.

In it was a scissors-and-paste anti-Semitism, assembled with almost comical defiance of consistency and judiciousness. *La France juive* was a two-volume work, with many of the trappings of scholarship, but Drumont was anything but a serious scholar, nor could his scribblings be compared

---

[58] Wilson, *Ideology*, 292.
[59] Ibid., 35.

to those of Toussenel (from whom he borrowed amply) or other, more talented and respectable writers like Barrès and Wagner. Drumont's volumes were an ill-digested, credulous, derivative, journalistic compendium. Only one consideration seemed to interest him: to include anything and everything negative that might be said about the Jews, the more outrageous the better, even if one account implicitly contradicted the next. Accounts of ritual murder out of the Middle Ages found their place next to factual (if still credulous) examinations of Jewish political and economic power. Drumont borrowed from premodern and modern, right-wing and left-wing, Catholic and secular, the relatively serious and factual along with the ludicrous and absurd – a potpourri of anti-Semitic anecdotes, legends, rumors, and heavy-handed jokes.

One theme was pervasive, almost monomaniacal: the Jewish conspiracy, the operation of the Jewish Syndicate behind the scenes. Drumont traced, back into French history, the machinations of Jews to take over France. Again, the charges he made ranged from the possible and plausible, as in the case of the purported destruction of the Union générale by the Rothschilds, to the utterly ridiculous, as when he described Napoleon's takeover as the result of a plot by Jews that backfired when Napoleon turned on them.

Some observers dismissed Drumont's anti-Semitic writings as lacking in seriousness. Without a doubt many of Drumont's thousands of readers in Paris and in France's major cities, where the overwhelming majority of copies were sold, viewed his pages as little more than light entertainment, a *jeu d'esprit* from which no real ideology of anti-Semitism or coherent program in regard to Jews was to be derived. He was widely suspected of being interested in making money through light if outrageous entertainment, by pandering to popular prejudice and the voracious taste for scandal that characterized French journalism of the day. Even sophisticated readers – Jews themselves – seemed to find private delight in this assortment of often bizarre diatribes against the Jews. Doubts about Drumont's sincerity were buttressed by his earlier employment by Jewish publishers; his praise of them when he was in their pay was as unbounded as was his vitriol for Jews in general afterward.[60] The man was a so-far failed literary entrepreneur, many concluded, who had at last found something that would sell. Leading monarchists dismissed *La France juive* as sensationalistic trash, touching upon "a few serious grievances" but unleashing "a lot of evil passions" in pursuit of journalistic profit.[61]

Whatever the truth of these assertions, getting Drumont's measure

[60] Frederick Busi, *The Pope of Antisemitism: The Career and Legacy of Edouard-Adolphe Drumont* (Lanham, 1986), 35.
[61] Irvine, *Boulanger Affair Reconsidered*, 168.

turns out to be an unexpectedly difficult task. He was a strangely emotional and credulous man, shy and lonesome, on the one hand, brash and pop-ulist, on the other, with an array of beliefs and attachments that defy easy categorization. He counted among his closest friends and admirers an implausible range of characters, from semicriminal brawlers to distin-guished artists, writers, and political figures, such as Georges Bernanos (mildy anti-Semitic), Edgar Dégas (increasingly inclined to vehement anti-Semitism),[62] Benoit Malon (a labor leader who retained the pre-Marxian hostility to Jews), and Victor Hugo (mildly philo-Semitic; he had, inter-estingly, headed a committee of public protest against the pogroms in Russia in 1881).[63] Jean Jaurès, the revered socialist leader and later prom-inent among the defenders of Alfred Dreyfus, admired Drumont for his dogged uncovering of corruption in the government, and the unlikely pair for a while exchanged compliments.[64] A spokesman for an organization of shopkeepers in Paris confidently referred to "the indisputable good faith of the anti-Semitic polemicist" (his comment came as Drumont was being sued for libel after he had accused a parliamentary deputy of taking a bribe from the Rothschilds in order to pass legislation beneficial to the Bank of France[65]).

Perhaps Drumont's most surprising admirer was Theodore Herzl, who was in Paris in the early 1890s as foreign correspondent for the *Neue Freie Presse* of Vienna. He wrote in his diary: "I owe Drumont much for my present freedom of conception, because he is an artist."[66] The ad-miration was mutual: When Herzl's *Judenstaat* ("Jewish State," his de-scription of a future national state for Jews) appeared in 1896, it received what Herzl himself described as a "highly flattering" review in a paper edited by Drumont.[67] Herzl had earlier been a regular visitor to the literary salon of Alphonse Daudet, another Jew-baiting intellectual – one who accepted Herzl as a charming, "exceptional" Jew, as was Marcel Proust – and had met Drumont there.[68]

Drumont was much admired by the petite bourgeoisie of Paris, and to that degree comparisons with Marr, who so powerfully appealed to the German *Mittelstand*, seem apt. Before publishing *La France juive*, Dru-mont had written *Mon vieux Paris* (My Old Paris). While not the record-

[62] Cf. Linda Nochlin, "Dégas and the Dreyfus Affair: Portrait of the Artist as an Anti-Semite," in Norman L. Kleeblatt, ed., *The Dreyfus Affair: Art, Truth, and Justice* (Berkeley, Calif., 1987), 96–116.

[63] Bredin, *The Affair*, 554. Cf. also Busi, *Pope of Anti-Semitism*.

[64] Cf. Harvey Goldberg, *The Life of Jean Jaurès* (Madison, Wis., 1962), 209 ff.

[65] Nord, *Shopkeepers*, 387.

[66] Carl E. Schorske, *Fin-de-Siècle Vienna, Politics and Culture* (New York, 1980), 157.

[67] Quoted in Conor Cruise O'Brien, *The Siege: The Saga of Israel and Zionism* (New York, 1986), 667.

[68] Ernst Pawel, *The Labrynth of Exile: A Life of Theodor Herzl* (New York, 1989), 164, 176–7.

breaking success of the anti-Semitic work, it touched on many of the same points. Its central theme was a lamentation over the passing of the old Paris, its destruction through railroad stations and department stores, faceless crowds, iron and steel – terms that were nearly identical to those that appeared in the journals of the shopkeeper organizations.

In fact, Drumont, for all his rantings in *La France juive*, was also concerned about real changes. In his subsequent political and journalistic career, he was quick to deny that he attacked Jews out of religious bigotry. He insisted that he was concerned with real economic and social issues, that it was the Semitic race, not Judaism, that he detested and blamed for France's misfortunes. Drumont intoned, "the dream of the Semite, . . . his obsession, has always been to reduce the Aryan to servitude."[69]

If Drumont's writings may be seen both as a sign of the growth of modern anti-Semitism in France and as an important vehicle through which an anti-Semitic ideology was beginning to take roots in French society, one might expect that he would be able to turn his sudden literary success into more concrete directions, into an anti-Semitic movement with a political program. He certainly tried to do so. He become involved in the organization of an anti-Semitic league in 1890, associated with the Boulangists, but, as noted, it collapsed within a year. When he ran for a parliamentary seat in 1890 he was overwhelmingly defeated.[70]

The cause of these defeats is not entirely clear, but at least part of the reason seems to have been that Drumont simply lacked talent as a politician. That was the conclusion of the other anti-Semitic activists with whom he worked. But there were others associated with him whose talents in the street and at the tribune were more notable. Prominent among them was the Marquis de Morès, a man who may well qualify as the best example of a protofascist, of a prewar Mussolini or Hitler, of any politician in the Belle Epoque. De Morès worked diligently if without much success among working-class organizations, often disbursing funds to them.[71] His greatest success was in attracting the owners of small businesses in Paris. In a notorious episode he accused the Jewish meat firm, Dreyfus Frères, in April 1892, of selling rotten meat to the army. He was sued and found guilty of libel. Nevertheless, the butchers of the La Villette slaughterhouse welcomed this embarrassment of a powerful business competitor. In September they presented de Morès with a "saber of honor."[72]

Not only had the butchers begun to feel competitive pressure from Jewish firms, but they claimed to be offended by the practices, increasingly present in Paris by the early 1890s, of kosher butchering (*shehita*).

[69] Wilson, *Ideology*, 509–10.
[70] Busi, *Pope of Anti-Semitism*, 93 ff.
[71] Nord, *Shopkeepers*, 381.
[72] Ibid., 382.

The La Villette butchers denounced this practice as unnecessarily cruel, which Jewish butchers forcefully denied. Efforts to get the city authorities to outlaw ritual slaughter did not succeed. In a number of cases the La Villette butchers intervened to put animals to a speedy death that were dying according to Jewish ritual practices.[73] De Morès, at any rate, became a hero to the butchers, and he gradually gathered around him an armed bodyguard of young toughs from La Villette, complete with uniforms and arm bands.

Yet in spite of this devoted following among a part of the Parisian petite bourgeoisie (and it must be said that the La Villette butchers were a distinct subgroup, with their own peculiar traditions), de Morès was only slightly more successful in elections than was Drumont. Both lost badly in 1890. However, Drumont's good fortune with *La France juive* had encouraged him to establish the newspaper *La Libre Parole* (Free Speech), to which de Morès was a frequent contributor. Although not quite so gross in style or vulgar in content as the yellow journalism that was growing up throughout Europe and America in these years, Drumont's paper was full of wild stories and libelous accusations. Such journalism was less risky in France than in other countries because of the extremely lax press laws of the Third Republic. One charge that appeared in a number of articles in *La Libre Parole*, and that caused a particular sensation, was that the army was filled with incompetent and even treasonous officers, often Jews. This accusation took on considerable significance in the genesis of the Dreyfus Affair in 1894, but it was also the cause of a most revealing episode in 1892, to be described below.

Drumont showed undeniable talent as a muckraking journalist, and *La Libre Parole* had a field day with the Panama Scandal of 1888–92. In that period Drumont was able to expand his readership, and profits, considerably. Investigation into the activities of the Panama Company revealed widespread bribery of parliamentary officials to assure support of loans to continue work on the canal, work that had been slowed by endless technical and administrative difficulties. Here was a strikingly modern project that involved large amounts of French capital and threatened national prestige – and Jewish agents were deeply involved. The intermediaries between the Panama Company and parliament were almost exclusively Jews, with German names and backgrounds, some of whom tried to blackmail one another. One of those being blackmailed then committed suicide, but not before providing Drumont with a list of members of parliament who had been bribed.[74]

---

[73] Ibid., 381–2.
[74] Cf. Byrnes, *Anti-Semitism*, 331; Lavaillant, "La Génèse de l'antisémitisme sous la troisième République," *Revue des études juives*, vol. 53, 1907, 97; cited in Hannah Arendt, *The Origins of Totalitarianism* (New York, 1963), 96.

As in Germany in 1873 and as in the collapse of the Union générale, thousands of small investors lost their savings in the Panama fiasco. "The Panama scandal was a Republican debacle. Over a hundred deputies, senators, ministers, and ex-ministers were implicated in the company's dishonest and demeaning shenanigans."[75] A trial in 1893 was widely believed to be a whitewash. The accused escaped punishment through bribery and behind-the-scenes machinations, or so it was widely believed. The Panama scandal seemed almost designed to confirm the long-standing charges of the French right, and of Drumont's newspaper in particular, that the republic was in the clutches of corrupt and unscrupulous Jews who cared nothing for France and who were contributing to the country's weakness, its inability to keep up with other modern nations, its failures and humiliations.

A gathering storm of anti-Semitism?

The above account of the 1880s and early 1890s, culminating with Drumont's remarkable successes, would seem to offer much concrete evidence for a gathering storm of anti-Semitism in France on the eve of the Dreyfus Affair. The traditionalist right in France, as well as important elements of the population that had previously voted on the left, felt under attack, and Jews were believed to be prominent among their attackers. On the other hand, organized anti-Semitism, or anti-Semitism as a modern political movement, was unable to get off the ground, even to the limited degree that it had in Germany and Austria in the same period. Foreign visitors to France, like Herzl, were impressed with the differences between France and central Europe in terms of Jewish integration in state and society. French Jews themselves constantly emphasized how little popular appeal anti-Semitism had in France and how much better off French Jews were than the Jews of nearly any other country of the world.

Some even claimed that a significant degree of philo-Semitism existed in France, and there is little question that philo-Semitic sentiments played a role in French life, sentiments that went farther than merely welcoming Jews to modern civilization, praising their contributions to it – and expecting them to disappear. Nineteenth-century admiration of Jews is a large and neglected topic, but mention must be made of at least such works as Theodore Vibert's *La Race sémitique*,[76] the writings of Péguy, and George Eliot's *Daniel Deronda*, completed in the late 1870s. One author has judged Eliot's work, which was widely read outside England,

[75] Weber, *France: Fin de Siècle*, 113.
[76] Wilson, *Ideology*, 464.

to be "probably the most influential novel of the nineteenth century" in terms of its practical effects (in particular, in spreading sympathy for Jews among the British ruling elite).[77] Similarly, Ernst Renan, an enormously influential author in France, began to make philo-Semitic pronouncements in the 1890s, partly to counter what he realized were the ugly uses being made of his earlier, ambiguously anti-Semitic writings.

The "gathering storm" of anti-Semitic agitation in the late 1880s and early 1890s in France remained moderate in tone, "moderate" at least in the somewhat dubious sense that most anti-Semites condemned violence and recognized the rights of Jews as human beings, if not as citizens of modern nation-states. Nearly all French anti-Semites argued that immigration into France by Jews should be limited by law, but that was hardly a radical proposal. It was one that in various forms would be adopted by many countries, including the United States (not exclusively for Jews, of course, but for all immigrants). The more general notion of somehow "controlling" Jews already in France also found widespread support. Drumont's (and Herzl's) friend Daudet, a prominent monarchist, stated the matter as follows:

> Kept under close surveillance by a power as clear-sighted as the monarchy, the Jews would be tolerable and almost acceptable. . . . To persecute Israel would be unwise and odious. But to lay down guidelines limiting Jewish activity, particularly in the political sphere, would be a good thing, and a benefit that the Jews themselves would quickly appreciate. . . . Many intelligent and prudent Jews are beginning themselves to feel the need for order, for an order which puts them cordially but firmly in their place.[78]

Similarly, writers for the Assumptionists' *La Croix* called for prohibition of Jews in the army, the financial world, education, and the courts of law, areas where they would be "in command of Christians." But, those same writers concluded, once such measures were in place, "let us leave the Jews alone and not persecute them as in the Middle Ages." Charles Maurras, along with Barrès one of France's leading right-wing intellectuals, wrote in 1898, at the height of the popular passions over the Dreyfus Affair, that "care should be taken not to pass a law against the Jews which persecutes them, that is to say, which injures them as human beings."[79]

The moderate tone in these pronouncements was the prevalent one nearly everywhere in Europe at this time. Even depriving Jews of civil equality was by no means accepted as appropriate by all anti-Semites of the day. Treitschke and Stöcker in Germany opposed such steps, for

[77] Paul Johnson, *A History of the Jews* (New York, 1987), 378.
[78] Quoted in Wilson, *Ideology*, 672–3.
[79] Ibid., 673, 679.

example. In both Germany and France proposals of a more radical nature were certainly made. On a number of occasions Drumont and journalists associated with him launched into tirades that described Jews as vermin that should be exterminated,[80] but such outbursts were widely condemned. Inflated rhetoric, at any rate, was by no means the exclusive preserve of the anti-Semites; workers on strike in France referred to employers as "lice" and coined slogans that called for putting them to death.[81] People without power typically resort to verbal excess, to calls for violence that do not always reflect genuinely violent intent. Indeed, although the parallel is of course not exact, the Jews of eastern Europe, certainly among the least inclined to violence of Europe's peoples, nevertheless excelled in a humor of exaggerated threats and insults, often with imagery that described opponents as vermin.

Suggestions that violent action be taken against Jews found a much less general acceptance than the more moderate proposals mentioned above, and even they seem to have had distinctly limited appeal. Legislation to deprive Jews of civil equality had not even a remote chance of being passed in the French parliament. The idea of expelling the Jews was widely rejected as impractical, quite aside from humanitarian considerations. Suggestions that heavy taxation should be levied on large concentrations of Jewish wealth were often made but also consistently and forcefully rejected since they were seen as an attack on property, smacking of socialism. Again, their chances of being passed by the French parliament were remote.

It is indicative of the fundamental moderation of many such anti-Semites that their concrete proposals were forwarded as necessary to maintain social peace; if something moderate and sensible were not done to remedy the Jewish problem, to counter a too rapid rise of the Jews, they argued, a violent outburst could soon be expected. Marr had made a similar point, and it was a central assertion of officials in Russia.

There was nothing like a consensus about what should be done about the "problem" of French Jews, even among the minority that believed there was a problem in need of political remedy. The political situation in France might be usefully presented in terms of two large, opposing clusters: one that was republican, secular, left-wing, modernist, and on balance friendly to modern Jews; another that was monarchist, Catholic, right-wing, anti-modernist, and thus not friendly to modern Jews. The word "cluster" is chosen because these were hardly coherent or without major internal contradictions. In bewildering ways the two intertwined, and individuals moved from one cluster to another or, more typically,

---

[80] Busi, *Pope of Anti-Semitism*, 97.
[81] Cf. Susanna Barrows, *Distorting Mirrors: Visions of the Crowd in Late Nineteenth-Century France* (New Haven, Conn., 1981), 193.

felt themselves drawn in different directions simultaneously. One of the reasons that the Dreyfus Affair is of such interest is that it exerted powerful pressure on these clusters to "shape up," to become internally more consistent and ideologically coherent. The French, or at least important minorities among them, were obliged to think about things that they had ignored before, to decide where they really stood, where their most fundamental commitments lay. It was a most arduous and painful process, producing many surprises.

What might have happened in France if Dreyfus had not been arrested in 1894 for espionage, if that historical accident had not occurred? Might the forces of republicanism have prevailed with more ease and less drama than they eventually did? How much were broad, impersonal forces pushing in the direction of a decisive republican victory, whatever the accidents, the surface occurrences? In the light of these questions, the story of another kind of historical accident, one that occurred shortly before Dreyfus's arrest, is revealing and further underlines the dubiousness of the gathering storm argument.

The articles in Drumont's *La Libre Parole* about treasonous activities in the army, with direct accusations of Jewish officers, challenging as they did the honor of the officers in question, led to a number of duels. (Again, it is of some symbolic significance that in France Jews were widely considered worthy opponents in a duel. In central and eastern Europe, they were often not deemed *satisfaktionsfähig*, "capable of giving satisfaction" to a person of rank whose honor had been put in question.) In 1892 the Marquis de Morès, who had written a number of such articles, was challenged by a Jewish officer, Captain Armand Mayer. De Morès was a veteran of many duels, and this one ended in the death of the young Jewish officer.

By 1892 the anti-Semitic movement, hardly a great success up to that point, was in total disarray, and Captain Mayer's death further discredited it. The French public reacted with revulsion and indignation. Denunciations poured out from nearly all quarters against Drumont, de Morès, *La Libre Parole*, and the anti-Semitism they had cultivated. Commentator after commentator, left-wing and right-wing, lamented that such a duel had occurred, that the French nation should be so divided, and, most of all, that officers of the French army should be subjected to aspersions by low scandal-mongers and thugs like Drumont and de Morès. Even Drumont and de Morès appeared contrite: Drumont openly regretted the death of "such an honorable man" and de Morès joined him in expressing his chagrin over the death of "this honorable man."[82]

A great funeral cortège was arranged for Captain Mayer, with full

[82] Pawel, *Exile*, 169–70.

military honors, attended by the largest crowd that Paris had seen since the death of Gambetta, a decade before. The grand rabbi of France, Zadoc Kahn, eloquently addressed those assembled at the grave. It appeared that the whole French nation was being led by a rabbi in heartfelt mourning over the death of a Jewish officer of the French army at the hands of universally detested anti-Semite. It seemed, indeed, to some of the more sanguine like a final nail in the coffin of an already dead anti-Semitic movement in France.

French Jews felt, in this great outpouring of sympathy, yet further evidence in support of their trust in the tolerance and decency of the average French citizen, in what the grand rabbi termed "the unifying force of French opinion." Even more, French Jews were inclined to view the army, in whose ranks Captain Mayer had proudly served, as a "magnificent example of toleration." It was a "single family" of Frenchmen, Jews and non-Jews, in the widely applauded words of the grand rabbi.[83]

At this same period, that is, the early 1890s, Jews in Germany and Austria were finding themselves excluded from fraternities and social clubs, they were dropping away from leadership positions of the liberal parties, and they were encountering a rising racist fanaticism in the Pan-German movements. Of course, at no time, even in the earlier liberal period, had German Jews entered into the military, the judiciary, and other high government offices. Anyone who would have described the Prussian military establishment as a single family with the rest of the nation or as magnificently tolerant would have been considered a lunatic. French Jews did indeed appear to be living in a significantly different world, and one steadily, in spite of some unpleasant contretemps, changing in their favor.

That impression was further reinforced by something much more substantial than a massively attended funeral. The parliamentary elections of 1893 were believed to register a final, definitive victory of the Opportunist republic over the antirepublican and anti-Semitic reactionaries. Only seventy-six candidates of the right were elected. Four years earlier, the conservatives and Boulangists had won 210 seats in the Assembly. The governing coalition of republican parties, after the elections of 1893, constituted approximately 280 deputies, a coalition that was becoming more anxious about the extreme left than about the extreme right since the 1893 elections had also seen a dramatic increase in votes for the socialists (from 90,000 in 1889 to 600,000 in 1893). The socialists now counted 50 deputies, while the Radicals (immediately to the right of the socialists) counted 143.[84] The long-range leftward drift of French politics

---

[83] Marrus, *The Politics of Assimilation*, 197–201.
[84] Statistics from Bredin, *The Affair*, 39.

since the mid-1870s continued, contrary to the rightward drift of politics in Germany or Russia from the 1870s to 1890s.

Whatever the contrasting potentials of the situation in France, toward greater hostility to Jews or away from it, we know that another historical accident, the arrest of Alfred Dreyfus, suddenly tapped the potential toward an increase in openly expressed anti-Semitic hatred. What might have been should not be ignored, but what was must draw our attention, for the events following Dreyfus's arrest seemed to change everything, to put all earlier confidence and optimism of French Jews into question – and indeed to transform the issue of anti-Semitism in the modern world.

5

The Dreyfus Affair,
more than a trial

Dreyfus has become . . . the most famous name since . . . Napoleon. (Charles Péguy)

I was only an artillery officer, whom a tragic error prevented from pursuing his normal career. Dreyfus the symbol . . . is not me. (Alfred Dreyfus)[1]

I will defend 36 million Catholics against 70,000 [Jewish] tyrants. . . . I am for the persecuted against oppressors, . . . against the sectarian and cosmopolitan oligarchy. (Gaston Pollonais)[2]

Contrasting interpretations of the Affair

A hundred years after the Dreyfus Affair we no doubt find it easier than did contemporaries to accept that both Anti-Dreyfusards and Dreyfusards were in important ways morally flawed. But a few of Dreyfus's contemporaries were not blind to the ambiguities of the Affair. One of them wrote that Dreyfus's accusers and defenders were simply "two rival gangs of charlatans, squabbling for recognition by the rabble."[3] That states the matter too brutally, although it is also refreshingly free of the cant that has characterized so many accounts of the Affair. A recent historian has stated that "nothing is more striking than the [moral] similarity . . . of the Dreyfusards and Anti-Dreyfusards."[4] That judgment, too, may overstate the similarities between the two, but it may be seen as an appropriate corrective to the confident tone of moral superiority assumed by most Dreyfusards and accepted by later generations as wholly justified.[5]

Historians of the Dreyfus Affair, even some of the most respected of

---

[1] Quoted in Stephen Wilson, *Ideology and Experience: Anti-Semitism in France at the Time of the Dreyfus Affair* (East Brunswick, N.J., 1982), opening page.
[2] Quoted in Michael Marrus, *The Politics of Assimilation: A Study of the French Jewish Community at the Time of the Dreyfus Affair* (Oxford, 1971), 230.
[3] Georges Sorel, *La Révolution dreyfusienne* (Paris, 1911), 70–1; cf. Hannah Arendt, *The Origins of Totalitarianism* (New York, 1963), 108.
[4] Douglas Johnson, *France and the Dreyfus Affair* (New York, 1966), 212.
[5] Popular histories of the Jews have erred most notably in these regards. Cf. Howard Fast, *The Jews, Story of a People* (New York, 1982), 339; Nathan Ausubel, *A Pictoral History of the Jewish People* (New York, 1953), 158. Both present as an indisputable fact that there was a plot to frame Dreyfus. Fast implicates the Jesuits, again, in tones that suggest there is no doubt of their role.

them, but especially popular historians, have not been immune to the often subtle tug of political persuasion or seeing things from an ethnic perspective. Scholars whose political fidelities lie on the left, for example, have been tempted to concentrate on the villainy of the Anti-Dreyfusards. Jewish historians, especially those who wrote at the time of the Affair, have perceived a more central role for anti-Semitism and Gentile villainy, whereas non-Jewish students of the Affair have tended to question such perceptions, although on both sides a wide range of opinion is to be found.[6]

The following account strives for greater balance, for if there were a number of dishonest scoundrels and morally weak individuals among Dreyfus's accusers, there were also scrupulously honest, "heroic" Anti-Dreyfusards who made decisive discoveries and who revealed the errors and forgeries upon which the case against Dreyfus was based. Heroes and villains, in other words, were to be found on both sides. We will also find heroes and villains, similarly and often disconcertingly placed, in the Beilis and Frank affairs.

The background to Dreyfus's arrest

The beginnings of the Dreyfus Affair are to be found in the year 1894, although the case did not assume major dimensions until four years later. In 1894 officers of the French military intelligence concluded that some-one was selling military secrets to the military attaché at the German Embassy in Paris. This was a time of spy mania; France's newspapers were filled with rumors and accusations, and a number of espionage cases had already drawn the attention of Paris's sensationalist tabloids, of which Drumont's *La Libre Parole* was but one of many. Nationalist paranoia about the danger posed by Germany had reached unparalleled levels, partly because the recently concluded alliance between France and Russia had increased tension with Germany. The new alliance had also tempo-rarily increased French vulnerability, since it made necessary a major reformulation of military plans and mobilization orders.

Officers of military intelligence recovered a document that came to be known as the *bordereau*, the "list" of military secrets for sale. From evidence within the document, those officers concluded that the traitor had to be on the General Staff, or at least had to have easy access to its inner workings and those of the Ministry of War. These were most trou-bling and potentially embarrassing conclusions: A traitor was working

---

[6] Examples of these various historians are in subsequent notes. The issue of a characteristi-cally Jewish, or "Semitic," interpretation of the Affair became an issue among Dreyfus's defenders, as is described below.

within the very inner councils of the nation's army. By a convoluted and still somewhat obscure process, the officers in charge of investigating the matter persuaded themselves that they had discovered the culprit, Captain Alfred Dreyfus.

Dreyfus was a candidate officer on the General Staff, and, the reasoning went, he was one of a small number who had access to the kinds of information listed on the bordereau. Of that small number, he was the only one whose handwriting resembled that on the bordereau. In fact, to an untrained eye the resemblance between his handwriting and that of the bordereau is striking. A number of those who jumped to conclusions about his guilt seem to have done so mostly on the basis of that resemblance, linked to his position as candidate officer on the General Staff. However, handwriting experts called in on the matter differed with one another concerning whether Dreyfus was the author of the document. Further drawing attention to him was a collection of obscure and inconclusive documents (to this day we are not completely certain what all of them were) assembled by military intelligence, one of which contained references to a traitor with the initial *D*.

This evidence was thin and inconsistent, a problem common in proving guilt in espionage, where secrecy is pervasive and evidence usually destroyed. Still, in retrospect the evidence seems scarcely strong enough to prove the grave charge of treason against a French officer, especially one who had no obvious motive and an excellent record. Can one conclude, then, that the intelligence officers in charge decided to accuse Dreyfus primarily because he was a Jew? Was the anti-Semitic temper in Paris, or in the army, at this time such that they easily jumped to the conclusion that this Jewish officer must be guilty? Did they, moreover, conspire to convict an innocent man, on the basis of flimsy evidence – or with evidence they forged to strengthen the case – because of their hatred for Jews?

Anti-Semitism was at a low ebb in 1894, as we have seen. The anti-Semites had lost badly in the elections since 1890, and the funeral of Captain Mayer in 1892 had deeply discredited those who had charged Jewish officers with being spies. But the first major history of the Affair, written by Joseph Reinach, himself Jewish and a leading Dreyfusard, provides a lurid picture of the role of conspiratorial, reactionary anti-Semites in the military.[7] The most popular account of the Affair in English, by Nicholas Halasz, also Jewish, followed Reinach's lead in describing Dreyfus's arrest as unquestionably motivated by anti-Semitism.[8] Spirited

---

[7] Joseph Reinach, *Histoire de l'Affaire Dreyfus*, 7 vols. (Paris, 1901–11).
[8] Nicholas Halasz, *Captain Dreyfus: The Story of a Mass Hysteria* (New York, 1955), 18, 29. Halasz writes of those who first accused Dreyfus: "They went down the Ds [on a list of possible officers] and came to a halt at the name of Dreyfus. In their immense relief,

dissents have subsequently appeared.[9] They have complained that the accounts of writers like Reinach and Halasz are too polemical, one-sided, and, most important, in attributing a primary role to anti-Semitism, are simply not supported by the evidence.[10]

Such divisions existed even at the time of the Affair, and were then explicitly attributed to differences in ethnic perceptions. Fernand Labori, Alfred Dreyfus's own lawyer and a non-Jew, denounced Reinach's history as "biased . . . , written in bad faith, . . . strictly Semitic in inspiration. . . . well suited to mislead future historians. . . . " Labori published, in collaboration with Georges Picquart (another non-Jew, one who played a key role in exonerating Dreyfus), a long list of errors, false accusations, and questionable interpretations in Reinach's work.[11] Léon Blum, himself Jewish, also dissented from Reinach's views, agreeing that anti-Semitism had not played a major role in Dreyfus's arrest.[12]

There appears to be an emerging consensus among professional historians, whatever their political or ethnic background, that at least initially suspicion was not directed at Dreyfus because he was Jewish, even if anti-Semitism later came to play a key role.[13] It is at any rate nearly impossible to determine with certainty what it was that motivated each of Dreyfus's initial accusers. It is similarly impossible to be certain that

they found no words. Each read the other's thought, 'It was the Jew!' " Halasz offers no documentation for these conclusions, nor any clue as to how he knew what these men were thinking and feeling.

[9] Another popular account by a Jewish historian – perhaps the most widely read of any of the authors here mentioned – offers a more balanced account: "The arrest, trial, conviction, and sentencing of Captain Alfred Dreyfus . . . was not a deliberate plot to frame an innocent man. It was the outcome of reasonable suspicion acted on by dislike, some circumstantial evidence and instinctive prejudice." Barbara W. Tuchman, *The Proud Tower: A Portrait of the World Before the War, 1890–1914* (New York, 1966), 173.

[10] Cf. Johnson, *France*; Guy Chapman, *The Dreyfus Case: A Reassessment* (London, 1955); Allan Mitchell, "The Xenophobic Style: French Counter-espionage and the Emergence of the Dreyfus Affair," *Journal of Modern History*, vol. 52, no. 3, Sept. 1980, 414–25. The most recent, and in nearly all ways the most satisfactory history of the Affair is Jean-Denis Bredin's *The Affair: The Case of Alfred Dreyfus* (New York, 1986; French edition, 1983). He is sharply critical of Reinach's lack of balanced judgment in certain areas; cf. p. 58.

[11] Bredin, *Affair*, 466.

[12] Paula E. Hyman, "The French Community from Emancipation to the Dreyfus Affair," in Norman Kleeblatt, ed., *The Dreyfus Affair: Art, Truth, and Justice* (Berkeley, Calif., 1987), 31. To avoid possible misunderstanding, it should be stressed that the point here is not that ethnic background has blinded or currently blinds various observers, whether scholars or not, to the truth. The point is rather that the ethnicity of the observer, like the political persuasion of the observer, can sometimes work subtly on both perception and reasoning. The issue arises again in subsequent chapters, particularly in terms of shifting Jewish and Gentile perceptions of the nature of anti-Semitism in Russia and in the United States.

[13] Cf. Benjamin F. Martin, "The Dreyfus Affair and the Corruption of the French Legal System," in Kleeblatt, *Dreyfus Affair*, 38.

the anti-Semitic climate of opinion by the early 1890s influenced the decision to charge Dreyfus and later to convict him.

Alfred Dreyfus's unpopularity with his fellow officers is certain. However, his manifest abilities as an officer and his single-minded devotion to his career had so far won him regular promotions and support from his superiors. French military authorities under the Republic had clearly and repeatedly articulated the policy that religious and racial background was to have no effect on an officer's career. Was Dreyfus's lack of popularity due to his Jewishness? Or was it rather because he was, as even his defenders recognized, stiff, distant, inclined to brag about his money, and something of a grind?

His personal qualities aside, one might ask if Dreyfus, as a Jew, had a genuine option of becoming intimately friendly with the other officers. Most of them were Catholics, and many were *postards*, that is, graduates of an elite Jesuit preparatory school. They were urbane, disciplined, and courteous Frenchmen, but they came mostly from conservative, often aristocratic backgrounds, where suspicion of Jews, as well as of Protestants, freethinkers, and foreigners was almost instinctual. And the Jesuit teachers of these Catholic officers apparently had a well-deserved reputation of being unfriendly to Jews. The salaries of French officers were meager, and many of them came from families of modest means, in which they were taught to disdain great wealth, especially when it came in the form of new money. There were also, it should be noted, however, a number of Protestant officers among those with whom Dreyfus worked, and there were freethinking, lapsed Catholics, largely indifferent to the faith of their forefathers, much as Dreyfus was to his.

Alfred Dreyfus was a rich man, a member of a successful family of industrialists. He had married the daughter of a wealthy diamond merchant. If he had been a Protestant, a non-believer, the son of an Italian immigrant, or even a wealthy Catholic nouveau riche, he might also have encountered suspicion and resentment from Catholic officers, particularly given his reclusive personality, his customary attitude of distant superiority, his inclination to brag about his wealth.

Among those who were guilty of peremptory and injudicious accusations against Dreyfus, and who then became entangled in a web of falsehood and criminal deceptions, were Protestants, free-thinkers, and firm supporters of the Republic, men who had no history of anti-Semitic belief or action. Among those who urged caution and who eventually came to his defense were traditional Catholics, monarchists, and postards, some of whom were openly anti-Semitic. Anti-Semites like Drumont asserted that a Jewish heritage inclined individual Jews to criminal or otherwise morally weak action; some historians since, while waxing indignant about such assertions, have been willing to accept kindred ones in the case of the Catholic officers in Dreyfus's entourage.[14] A sensitivity to the tug of ethnic factors no doubt can help us to understand a climate in which actions occur, but a careful examination of the evidence in this case underlines how important it is for historians, no less than officers of military intelligence, to avoid jumping to conclusions, to proceed without double standards, and most of all not to lose sight of the wide range of individual personalities that comprise all ethnic and religious groups.[15]

Even if Catholic officers had offered their friendship, and a few did, Dreyfus was not a particularly sociable sort. He was a loner, even among Jews, and a single-minded, spit-and-polish, strictly-by-the-book kind of officer, little interested in bonhomie and after-hours comradeship or even in the social climbing that so absorbed many other wealthy French Jews of the day. He later reproached himself, in his memoirs, with being cold and haughty in his relations with his fellow officers. Other Jews, with different personalities, blended in amiably with French military men. As noted in the previous chapter, among the approximately three hundred Jewish officers in the French army, ten had risen to the rank of general, a number nearly as remarkable as that of Jewish generals in Austria-Hungary, where the Jewish population was something like fifty times larger. Even the widespread belief at the time, apparently spread by Drumont, that Dreyfus was the first Jew to serve on the General Staff was false; Colonel Abraham Samuel had served on the intelligence branch of the General Staff throughout the 1870s, retiring honorably in 1880.[16]

At this very time the commandant of Paris, General Saussier, was on intimate personal terms with a Jewish former army officer, Maurice Weil. The general was, it should be noted, "a notorious homosexual, [who] had become or pretended to be the lover of the lovely Mme Weil,"[17] and in this case, too, anti-Semites suspected espionage.[18] Such suspicions aside, there is little question that Maurice Weil, was "a man of extremely dubious reputation,"[19] one whose personal vices corresponded to anti-Semitic fantasies about Jews in general. He had earlier been forced out of the army because he had been caught cheating at the races. Yet he retained many friends and connections in the world of Jewish finance and politics.

Alfred Dreyfus's personal qualities eventually became the subject of much unfavorable commentary, even among those who believed him innocent. Although he demonstrated great physical and psychic tenacity,

---

[14] Cf. Halasz, *Captain Dreyfus*; Fast, *The Jews*; Ausubel, *Pictorial History*.

[15] For a stimulating exploration of this theme in a totally different context, see Robert Kelley, *The Cultural Pattern in American Politics* (New York, 1979).

[16] Eugen Weber, *France: Fin de Siècle* (Cambridge, Mass., 1986), 133.

[17] Bredin, *Affair*, 508–9.

[18] Michael Marrus, *The Politics of Assimilation: A Study of the French Jewish Community at the Time of the Dreyfus Affair* (Oxford, 1971), 41; Johnson, *France*, 51.

[19] Bredin, *Affair*, 66.

he did not show the heroic qualities that many believed he should have. His moral horizons at times appeared disappointingly limited; they were those of a painfully ordinary member of the provincial bourgeoisie, not of a crusader for Truth and Justice. His manners, speech, even the tonalities of his voice, struck many observers as gauche or false. He was an easy man to mock – and to hate. Anyone who reads Dreyfus's memoirs or his letters to his wife can hardly avoid the sense of reading a bad novel, filled with mawkish and self-congratulatory passages. By his account, the members of his family were, with monotonous and one-dimensional consistency, paragons, one and all. He wrote of how he was "strong in my pure and immaculate conscience." He and his wife were "two pure and honest hearts, two hearts whose thoughts have only been for our beloved country, for France."[20]

Dreyfus stubbornly refused to accept the mantle of Jewish martyr. To the very end he resisted believing that anti-Semitism had played a role in his arrest, a tendency shared by his wife.[21] His accusers in the military were not anti-Semites, both the Dreyfuses insisted; they were honorable men who were simply mistaken about what he had done. He scrupulously avoided, during his ordeal, reference to his Jewish background. He similarly refused to identify his fate or his suffering with that of the Jewish people. This was a personal tragedy, period.

When Dreyfus was arrested, most of the officers who knew him were not much inclined to rally to his defense, certainly not out of personal friendship or admiration for him. Unlike nearly all other up-and-coming officers, he had no friendly superior officer, no *patron*, who was concerned to look after his interests, nor had he apparently made an effort to acquire one. It was simply not in his character to do so. In the military trials that were held to decide his fate in the following years, the animosity of some of his fellow officers in testimony against Dreyfus apparently came as a surprise to him. It is entirely plausible that some of them found it psychologically satisfying that this man, whom they perceived as a rich, bragging, and arrogant Jewish parvenu, should be brought so low. They seemed particularly to resent his boasts that his money allowed him to "pay for" more women than they could. One officer later claimed that Dreyfus's many sexual liaisons in the Parisian demimonde constituted one of many signs of his low moral character – "the adulterous husband is a potential traitor."[22]

Dreyfus's faith in his superior officers was no doubt tragically ill placed, especially as the Affair developed. One must marvel at his apparent in-

[20] Ibid., 7–8.
[21] Egal Feldman, *The Dreyfus Affair and the American Conscience, 1895–1906* (Detroit, 1981), 88–9.
[22] Bredin, *Affair*, 72–3.

sensitivity to how vulnerable he was, when the newspapers of the capital had been filled with flagrant accusations of treachery by Jewish officers. Yet, looking only at the immediate issue of his arrest, his instincts may not have been so far off. After all, insofar as concrete evidence is available, anti-Semitic prejudice does not seem to have played a primary or decisive role among those officers who concluded he was the culprit. Much more significant seem to have been the considerations already mentioned: the spy mania, the desperate concern to root out the traitor in the inner councils of army, Dreyfus's status as one of a very few possible suspects, the similarity of his handwriting to that on the bordereau, and the "D" documents.

The agents of military intelligence were humiliated by the existence of a spy and even more humiliated that they could not discover who he was. Under tremendous pressure, they jumped to conclusions that turned out to be tragically unfair. A few of them then became involved in an ever more tangled web, attempting to justify their initial imprudence, finally violating the law, altering evidence, and simply lying. Among those so involved were a few who may be suspected of anti-Semitism. On the other hand, there were others concerning whom such suspicions are not justified. But none of them showed the moral strength to admit initial mistakes or to accept the responsibility for jumping to false conclusions. Their moral culpability must be placed primarily in such realms and not in their being overwhelmed by hatred of Jews. Rather than face the consequences of bad decisions, they preferred to see an innocent man convicted, and they concocted stories about how the security of the nation would be deeply threatened by a further investigation of the case.

If Dreyfus had not been a Jew, especially if he had been a more typical and a more widely liked officer, Jewish or non-Jewish, with an influential patron, it is a fair guess that those who decided to move against him would have exercised more caution in their initial decisions. In other words, their desire, if Dreyfus had been well liked and had enjoyed powerful connections, not to believe him guilty might have led to a more judicious scrutiny of the evidence, which could well have made them hesitate, avoiding the fatal process whereby one investigator stimulated another, each unwilling to back off for fear of appearing insufficiently vigorous, often persuading one another by their apparent confidence that they had found the guilty man. Dreyfus's Jewishness alone, it seems reasonable to conclude, was not a decisive factor.

This lamentable process snowballed once the highest army officials, most notably the minister of war, General Mercier, publicly announced that Dreyfus was guilty beyond a doubt. Once such a statement, which we can now recognize as profoundly irresponsible, had been made by someone of the highest authority in the army, the habits of discipline, respect for authority, and solidarity within the ranks of the military came powerfully into play, often drawing in honest men who were not aware of the poor decisions, moral weakness, and deceptions of their colleagues and superiors. But no evidence has ever emerged of an anti-Semitic plot against Dreyfus by intelligence officers, especially not of a premeditated effort to convict someone they knew from the beginning to be innocent. Alfred Dreyfus was not the victim of a "conspiracy of aristocratic officers against the Jewish outsider,"[23] as many came to believe at the time and as many histories to this day present the matter.[24]

Ironically, the very personal qualities that made Dreyfus unpopular and vulnerable tended to weaken the case against him. It made little sense that a rich man would sell secrets to the Germans for the paltry sums involved. Why should a man like Alfred Dreyfus, who had since boyhood wanted to be a French officer, and who was, to a fault, dedicated to his work, betray his country? The question of motive was undoubtedly the weakest part of the prosecution's case, and it bothered a number of those who drew up the indictment against him. A few speculated that Dreyfus may have harbored a grudge against the army, since he had once received unfair marks from an anti-Semitic instructor at the Ecole de Guerre (a graduate school for officers). However, that episode was exceptional in Dreyfus's career and did not significantly affect his advancement or, apparently, his confidence in his superiors. All who knew him agreed that he was inclined to unquestioning respect for those above him, not to harboring grudges. It was a common mentality among military men, and it was the very trait that led many of Dreyfus's fellow officers to believe him guilty, since General Mercier had said he was.

Other investigating officers considered Dreyfus's family background suspect, since his brothers chose to stay in Alsace and become German citizens when that province was taken from France in 1871. Members of his immediate family were "Germans," citizens of the enemy nation. The charge that Jews had international fidelities, that they remained outsiders who never became genuine patriots in any country, no doubt lurked in the background. Yet there were many non-Jewish Alsatians in the army, many whose families remained in Alsace rather than move to France to avoid becoming German citizens. In fact, the director of military intelligence, Colonel Jean Sandherr, a man directly responsible for Dreyfus's arrest, was an Alsatian with family still in Alsace. It was common for Alsatians to work in intelligence because of their knowledge of German.

---

[23] Norman Stone, *Europe Transformed, 1878–1919* (Cambridge, Mass., 1984), 21–2.
[24] This issue has been most carefully studied by Marcel Thomas, *L'Affaire sans Dreyfus* (Paris, 1961), 114 ff. See also, Bredin, *Affaire*, 532.

Reactions to the arrest of Dreyfus

Dreyfus, shocked and bewildered, was arrested and thrown into a cell of the Cherche-Midi Prison in Paris. The irony was too much: Alfred Dreyfus, the French superpatriot, accused of being a spy for Germany! Agents searched his house and those of his relatives, without finding further incriminating evidence. His wife was advised to say nothing to anyone. She was warned that war with Germany threatened if details of this case became known. Furthermore, the warnings went, anything she might say or do could damage her husband's interests. Upon his arrest, Dreyfus was informed that an ironclad case against him existed. He was offered a revolver and the honorable way out: suicide. He refused and ardently insisted on his innocence, protesting that a terrible mistake had been made. Nevertheless, his arresting officers later reported that he "acted guilty," and one of his jailers testified that Dreyfus confessed to the crime, in a moment of weakness.

Dreyfus's arrest and the charges against him were leaked to the popular press, most significantly to *La Libre Parole* of Edouard Drumont. From then on, any drawing back on the part of Dreyfus's accusers was certain to be denounced as the result of Jewish pressure or Jewish bribery. Drumont had been discredited over the duel between de Morès and Captain Mayer. Now he had an opportunity for revenge, to prove that he had been right all along about Jews in the army, and he jumped at the chance.

Turning from the predictable response by Drumont and the anti-Semites, initial reactions in general to the news of Dreyfus's arrest were not what might, with hindsight, be expected. Even among those who had little use for Drumont, most concluded that a guilty man had been caught. Neither did French Jews immediately rally to Dreyfus's defense. Even Theodore Herzl, who would later attribute his conversion to Zionism to the Dreyfus Affair, at first accepted that Dreyfus was guilty. Similarly, the great majority of middle-class Jews in France were not inclined to accuse the army of anti-Semitism, certainly not publicly.

French Jews may not have assumed as readily as other French citizens that Dreyfus was guilty, but they were in general confident that he would get a fair trial from his military peers. Even if they entertained inner doubts, they were happy to let other, non-Jews take the lead. They were most careful to avoid provocative statements, above all statements that might seem to denigrate the army or encourage disruptive dissent. The so-called *volonté de paix*, or desire for peace and quiet, was strong among French Jews; that was one of the reasons that they were partial to the moderate Opportunists. Few wanted to get mixed up in this matter; few wanted a protracted controversy about a Jewish traitor. Moreover, most French Jews were themselves ardent, deeply emotional French patriots; they were as much alarmed as other Frenchman about the threat from Germany and the infiltration of spies into the French army. They were French versions of the ardently *Kaisertreu* (true to the Kaiser) Jews in Germany, Austria, and Hungary.

Drumont followed up aggressively on the opportunities now opened to him. He charged that "all Jews" (*toute la juiverie*) were lining up in defense of Dreyfus – quite the opposite of what was occurring – and solemnly warned his readers that Dreyfus, rich Jew that he was, would finally escape punishment, even though he had "admitted everything." The Panama scandal, in which a number of Jews who were guilty of bribery and other crimes had escaped justice, was still fresh in the public's mind. A large number of observers expressed concern that a rich man like Dreyfus might also somehow escape justice.

Long before Dreyfus's official trial, he was tried and convicted in the popular press, often on the basis of rumor, conjecture, and the most astonishing sort of misinformation. Those few who urged that judgment should be suspended until adequate and reliable evidence could be obtained were drowned out by those who were vehemently convinced of Dreyfus's guilt and filled with indignation about it. One could hardly imagine a better example of how the popular press may pose a danger to legal justice or, again, of how people typically believe what they want to believe, finding it impossible to suspend judgment until all evidence is in.

The trial

The military trial was held in December 1894. The evidence presented against Dreyfus in the courtroom was not strong. On the other hand, it was not so flimsy as some histories would have one believe, and in the course of the proceedings a few new wrinkles to the case made it easier to believe in Dreyfus's guilt. What is often not mentioned in accounts of the trial is that appeals to anti-Semitic prejudice were not made by the prosecution. The army had a weak case, but the prosecution did not try to bolster it by aspersions about Dreyfus's racial or religious background, by asserting that Jews were naturally treacherous. Such aspersions would almost certainly have been sharply condemned if they had been made. The issue was undeniably lurking in the background, but it was not an explicit one in the trial.

The bordereau was the main piece of material evidence presented in the courtroom, and it hardly established guilt beyond a reasonable doubt.

Doubts about the handwriting persisted since the handwriting experts disagreed so sharply. Other difficulties, aside from the obvious one of motive, were also pointed out by the defense. The author of the bordereau alluded to secrets to which Dreyfus would not normally have had access. The document ended by noting that the author was "going on maneuvers," which did not seem to apply to Dreyfus at the relevant period.

The prosecution freely recognized the inconclusiveness of each individual piece of evidence but maintained that linking the bordereau to the other evidence (all, admittedly, bits and pieces) resulted in an impressive indictment, since there were too many pieces that fit together for all to be accidental. Time and again, Dreyfus was shown to have been in places where he might have gathered information listed on the bordereau, far too often for mere coincidence, the prosecution insisted. Dreyfus's status as candidate officer gave him access to an unusually wide variety of information, and his fellow officers testified to his curiosity about details, his tendency to come back to the office when others were at lunch, his habit of taking documents home.

Still, most observers at the trial, including those representing the army, thought it was going well for the defense, that there was a good chance for acquittal.[25] That opinion was shaken by an unexpected occurrence toward the end of the proceedings. Commandant Hubert Henry, an intelligence officer who had already testified, was again called to the witness stand. This second testimony was by far the most dramatic and incriminating of any offered in the open courtroom. Pointing his finger at Dreyfus, Henry blurted out, "The traitor, there he is!" Henry reported that a highly reliable "secret informer" had identified Dreyfus as a spy for Germany. But Henry refused to provide the informer's name or any further information, citing the need for intelligence officers to protect their sources.[26]

Henry was a respected officer. He was a member of the Legion of Honor, known as a simple, solid soldier, a man of the people who had worked his way up through the ranks. He was asked by the prosecution to repeat carefully what he had reported and to swear on his honor that Dreyfus was the treasonous officer. Lifting his hand, and looking toward the picture of Christ hanging on the wall, he spoke in a firm, confident voice, "I swear to it." He impressed those in the courtroom and the judges with his "total sincerity."[27] Subsequent revelations would do much to undermine Henry's reputation, but at this point his weaknesses of character were apparent to few if any observers.

On the last day of the trial, the judges were given a secret, sealed

[25] Bredin, *Affair*, 94.
[26] Johnson, *France*, 29.
[27] Bredin, *Affair*, 94.

dossier sent by the minister of war, General Mercier. At least three
documents in this dossier seemed to point to Dreyfus as the spy. The
dossier was in fact not thick, as certain accounts would later have it, nor
was there anything in it, as later was widely believed, that contained
comments by Kaiser Wilhelm himself identifying Dreyfus as a spy for
Germany. If such a document had existed, it would have been top secret
since it would have threatened to dishonor the German emperor. Just
such a case of threatened imperial honor had been the immediate cause
of the Franco-Prussian War of 1870–1.

The defense was not allowed to see or even learn of the existence of
this dossier during the trial. For the judges to receive evidence in this
fashion was in flagrant contradiction of French law and established legal
procedures, whether in civil or military court. But these considerations
were brushed aside with the argument that public knowledge of the
documents in the dossier might threaten war with Germany and undermine the position of secret agents in the field.

If Dreyfus's lawyers had been given a chance to look at this secret
dossier, possibly they could have discredited the documents in it. The
judges, in their private examination of the documents, found nothing
problematic or contradictory. Indeed, it appears that some of them considered this dossier to contain the conclusive material evidence that was
still lacking in the open courtroom, although it is likely that they had
already made up their minds by this point, especially after Henry's
testimony.[28]

They were apparently not concerned that in considering evidence in
this way they were violating the law and were not allowing Dreyfus to
have a fair trial. They were persuaded that considerations of French
security justified such blatantly illegal procedures. However, there is no
more evidence at this point than before that prejudice against him specifically as a Jew played a role in their deliberations. Sentiment in the
streets and in the popular press was another matter.

Dreyfus was found guilty by a unanimous vote of the military judges
and sentenced to life imprisonment on Devil's Island. It was decided as
well that he was to undergo public degradation (the famous ceremony
that Herzl, as a foreign journalist, personally attended, which consisted
of breaking Dreyfus's sword and ripping off his insignia). Outside the
courtyard, while the ceremony of degradation was taking place, a mob
chanted "Death to the Jews!" Throughout France there seems to have
been a general sense of satisfaction that a rich man, and a Jew at that,
had been caught in the net of military justice – a less corruptible form
than civil justice, it was widely believed.

[28] Ibid., 96.

Jean Jaurès, the popular socialist leader and later prominent defender of Dreyfus, expressed a widespread regret that the death penalty had not been applied in this case. He believed that the "light treatment" of Dreyfus was either due to the solidarity of military officers or to the "enormous Jewish pressure, which has been far from ineffective."[29] Isadore Singer, a prominent Jewish figure, suggested that Dreyfus should be subjected to the "pitiless penal code of Moses," death by stoning, with the grand rabbi of France casting the first stone.[30]

The smoldering Dreyfus case

There was not yet a Dreyfus Affair, properly speaking, for almost no one of any prominence yet doubted Dreyfus's guilt. In the eyes of the overwhelming majority of French people, a traitor had been caught and properly punished. Nor can one speak of a rejuvenated anti-Semitic movement in 1894 because of Dreyfus's crime, for in spite of the press coverage and the milling crowds, the excitement proved temporary and without apparent repercussions. Within a few months, popular attention moved away from Dreyfus, who was left to rot in Devil's Island. Only Dreyfus's brother, Mathieu, and a small number of others, including members of the family of his wife, refused to accept the verdict. Those who knew Alfred well simply could not believe him capable of such a crime. But other prominent Frenchmen, including many who would later become ardent defenders of Dreyfus, were happy to see the case fade from public view. Mathieu later bitterly observed that from the moment his brother was convicted, "not one hand was extended[;] . . . every door was closed[;] . . . those who knew us avoided us. . . . We were the plague-stricken."[31]

Mathieu and the small band of those who worked with him persisted in spite of their pariah status. At first they remained away from the public eye – indeed, worked much as anti-Semites believed the Jewish Syndicate worked: behind the scenes, with money and personal contacts. Anti-Semitic fantasies aside, Mathieu had little choice, and if he had not used his money as he did, his brother might never have been freed. Still, such methods were also preferred by most Jews in France, especially the wealthy Jewish bourgeoisie. In spite of the brave words of the grand rabbi at the time of the Mayer trial, many Jews in France, and in other western countries like Germany, Great Britain, and even the United States, were more comfortable working quietly with men of position and power than with agitating in the streets. They replicated, in a sense, the activities of

[29] Harvey Goldberg, *The Life of Jean Jaurès* (Madison, Wis., 1962), 132.
[30] Marrus, *Assimilation*, 213.
[31] Michael Burns, "The Dreyfus Family," in Kleeblatt, *Dreyfus Affair*, 149.

the premodern *shtadlan*, the delegate of the Jewish community who intervened quietly with the authorities in times of trouble, often with bribes, and tried at all costs to avoid public scrutiny and mass excitement.

Such methods are also to be identified with the political liberalism of the day, where major decisions were in the hands of wealthy notables, and active participation by the broad masses of the population was neither sought nor desired. To agitate among the common people was the kind of thing done at this time by the extreme left, by the Boulangists, by the demagogues – and by the anti-Semites. Liberals, and undoubtedly Jewish liberals more than non-Jewish, were much attached to proper procedures and respect for properly constituted authority in the Republic. In a broader sense, the French state, and French law, had long been the most reliable defender of the rights of Jews as citizens; "the quiet pressure and personal influence employed by Mathieu...was a compelling habit formed across generations by a Jewish family of Alsatian origin whose security, from the time of the Emancipation to the Affair, had depended upon the state."[32] Similarly, the association of wealthy Jews with Gambetta's Opportunists was characteristically behind the scenes, mostly involved with financial support and appointments to high office; open political agitation was avoided.

Mathieu similarly preferred to avoid a *cause célèbre*, public excitements and mass demonstrations, with all the implied likelihood of extralegal violence. Of course, he did not want his brother's case to fall into oblivion, but like many Jews, and wealthy ones most of all, he was more inclined to consider the masses the natural enemy of the Jews rather than their friend; that was certainly the historical pattern in Alsace. Thus, he and Alfred's in-laws often acted in a way that many observers found "guilty," as they would have acted in protecting a guilty man. Hannah Arendt has stated the matter with characteristic bluntness: "In trying to save an innocent man they employed the very methods usually adopted in the case of a guilty one."[33]

These ostensibly prudent methods entailed their own risks, however. For example, in meeting with Chief of Intelligence Sandherr, Mathieu stressed his determination to use his "entire fortune" in his brother's behalf. That was an ambiguous and incautious remark, one that Sandherr chose to interpret as an offer of a bribe. He subsequently took Mathieu to court with charges to that effect.[34] The ensuing trial served to reinforce

[32] Ibid.
[33] Arendt, *Origins*, 105. Michael Burns, in his slightly hagiographic article "The Dreyfus Family," 148–9, strongly objects to Arendt's tone and choice of words in this matter, but he accepts the basic account of Mathieu as defensive, full of faith in the French state, and committed to working in the proper channels.
[34] Bredin, *Affair*, 90–1.

the widespread belief that Jewish money was being used in an attempt to free the traitor Alfred Dreyfus. (At the time he took Mathieu to court, Sandherr was almost certainly implicated in an effort to cover up the irregularities associated with Dreyfus's arrest and trial. He died in 1895, before the Affair erupted, and thus never faced cross-examination for his conduct. No doubt, with him died the possibility of solving many of the mysteries of the Affair.)

As Mathieu's frustrations grew, and particularly as he became disillusioned with the legal system and the proper channels, he slowly began to accept the idea of a more public agitation. From the beginning he was willing to use French newspapers to keep his brother's case in the public eye, but, again, given the often well founded suspicions concerning the role of Jewish money in journalism in the 1890s, his efforts in this regard simply gave rise to further suspicions. No doubt, some of the expedients he resorted to were questionable, even offensive. Many honest people, even those who began to have doubts about Dreyfus's guilt, wanted absolutely nothing to do with Mathieu, with Alfred's in-laws, or with anyone who was known to have contacts with them. Any association with these rich and secretive Jews was assumed to be dangerous to an honest person's reputation.

Those who believed Dreyfus guilty often cultivated a plausible image of themselves as the honest and incorruptible party. They would have nothing to do with the Jewish money that was so lavishly being used to win support for the traitor, as it had been used to get the Panama swindlers off the hook. Those who feared that the Jewish Syndicate, through tenacious effort, was finally beginning to have an effect in the Dreyfus case saw their fears confirmed, when, in mid-1895, several prominent public figures in France began to express doubts about Dreyfus's guilt and about the legality of the trial procedures. For a number of observers, and not only paranoiac anti-Semites, the expression of such doubts by such figures constituted alarming proof that Jewish money was being effectively used to pressure and bribe people of influence, or to mislead them even when they were honest. Many who would later join the Dreyfusard camp were genuinely concerned at this point that foul play on Dreyfus's behalf was afoot.

It was widely rumored that the Dreyfus family was trying to set up a "patsy" (*un homme de paille*, literally a "straw man"), another army officer who could be blamed for the treason of which Alfred Dreyfus was guilty. A number of politicians, ever fishing for issues to forward their careers, began to perceive the political potential of a charge that the minister of war had engaged in a conspiracy to convict an innocent man. Those honestly convinced of Dreyfus's guilt were seriously concerned about the political appetites of such men, the great harm that their ambitions might pose to France's national interests. Again, such concerns were by no means limited to anti-Semites. Many steeled themselves against believing any new evidence that might seem to exonerate Dreyfus, for they believed such evidence was merely being fabricated by Jewish money.

The role of Georges Picquart

Early in the next year (1896), after Sandherr's death, a new head of military intelligence, Colonel Georges Picquart, was appointed. Like many officers he had been puzzled by Dreyfus's supposed espionage. He was finally persuaded of Dreyfus's guilt but uncomfortable about the meagerness of the evidence. He was further alarmed by indications that military secrets were continuing to flow into the German embassy. His suspicions came to center on a certain Commandant Esterhazy, and, in comparing Esterhazy's handwriting with that of the bordereau, Picquart was struck by the strong resemblance.

Esterhazy's record was remarkable: a string of gambling debts, dubious liaisons, mistresses, and shady business deals. In short, this was the kind of man, as Alfred Dreyfus was not, who might well try to sell military secrets to extricate himself from financial embarrassments. Ironically, one device that Esterhazy had so far used to help pay off his debts was to act as a second to Jews who were seeking to protect their honor in duels. One such instance earned Esterhazy 10,000 francs.[35] But the ironies ran much deeper: Esterhazy was an intimate friend of the aforementioned Maurice Weil, a genuine example of a corrupt Jew, who peddled influence in high places and was able to present Esterhazy as a friend of the Jews. Esterhazy himself had claimed that he was treated as a pariah in certain social circles because of his service to Jewish duelists. The grand rabbi described him as an "unfortunate fellow, who appeared to be suffering for having defended the Jews,"[36] and thus Esterhazy was able to milk the Jewish community further for funds. He was also in contact with Drumont and *La Libre Parole*, working both sides of the fence.[37] Because of Esterhazy's intimate contacts with Jews, many who first believed he was falsely accused of Dreyfus's crimes later concluded that he had been, after all, always in the pay of the Jews; he was a "poor devil" who finally consented to be the "straw man," in return for enough money to clear him of his debts.

Georges Picquart was a traditional military officer, a conservative, a Catholic from Alsace, a postard, and distinctly unsympathetic to Jews.

[35] Arendt, *Origins*, 104.
[36] Bredin, *Affair*, 156.
[37] Ibid., 122–3.

He could be offered as a perfect example of a traditional anti-Semite, that is, someone whose background and cultural values naturally led to disdain for Jews but who otherwise had little in common with Drumont or de Morès, the modern, populist anti-Semitic demagogues of the day. He had been Alfred Dreyfus's teacher at General Staff training and had not liked him. In witnessing Dreyfus's public degradation after the trial, the tearing off of his insignia, Picquart had maliciously observed, "Just like a Jew. Even now he is calculating how much money he lost when he went to the tailor." Picquart was further of the opinion that "there is not a Jew who doesn't have a few convicts in his family."[38]

When he began his investigations, Picquart was much concerned about being tricked, about being set up by what he considered the cunning and devious Jews who were working for the Dreyfus family. He had been specifically warned by his superior officer about the machinations of the Dreyfus family against Dreyfus's conviction. Indeed, many of those who knew Picquart and his attitudes toward Jews could only explain his apparent change of mind concerning Dreyfus's guilt as the result of Jewish bribery or of his having fallen into the kind of Jewish trap that he was so concerned to avoid. Their suspicions were heightened by what they considered his unseemly zeal in building a case against Esterhazy, during which he overran his authority and violated the law. They became all the more suspicious because of leaks of classified information to the Dreyfusard camp that they believed only Picquart could have provided.

Picquart became a pivotal figure in the Dreyfus Affair, but he remains an enigmatic character. Some observers have presented him as the real hero, "a noble and serenely beautiful character."[39] That is a tempting conclusion, especially for those who conceive the Affair as a matter of heroes and villains, virtue and vice. But subsequent idealization of Picquart at times assumed ludicrous and wholly misinformed dimensions, especially in light of his personal aversion for Dreyfus. The *Yiddishes Tageblatt* intoned that "all along, outside of his family, Dreyfus had a friend, not a Jew, whose belief in him, whose love for him never faltered. . . . History will write that the true hero of the Dreyfus case is not Dreyfus at all but Picquart."[40]

Picquart's courage is not in question. Without his efforts (efforts that threatened to ruin his career and that may have put his life in danger) Dreyfus would have likely remained forgotten and mostly unmourned on Devil's Island. But a close analysis of Picquart's moves and apparent motives makes it difficult to describe him as unequivocally heroic. He was haughty, secretive, priggish, on occasion duplicitous and insubor-

---

[38] Ibid., 337; Reinach, *Histoire*, vol. 4, 256 ff.
[39] Halasz, *Captain Dreyfus*, 6.
[40] Quoted in Feldman, *The Dreyfus Affair and the American Conscience*, 117.

dinate. Such qualities may be natural to someone doing the kind of work he did. Secretiveness and duplicity were very likely necessary in dealing with the hostility he encountered from his superiors when he began to suggest that Dreyfus was innocent and that Esterhazy was the author of the bordereau. However, his actions were not always consistent with the picture of him as risking all in the name of justice. Not surprisingly, he struggled to protect himself, and in the process he may have been unable to make a decision, or perhaps he was simply confused. Undoubtedly, one of the most unappreciated factors in the Dreyfus Affair was plain confusion, in both Dreyfus's defenders and accusers. Ambition and honesty may have warred in Picquart's breast; he apparently decided to make a real fight of it when he concluded that his career was in deep trouble and could no longer be saved by silence.[41]

The Dreyfusards later maintained, as have historians sympathetic to them, that Picquart's superiors acted with a guilty conscience, that they knew Dreyfus was innocent and Esterhazy guilty, and that they did everything possible to prevent the truth from being discovered. But there is little evidence upon which to base such sweeping accusations. Picquart's superiors were unquestionably appalled at the implications for the honor and standing of the army if Dreyfus were found innocent. Even more appalling in their eyes was the prospect of the ambitious and opportunistic politicians among the Dreyfusards using the issue to forward their careers. But some of Picquart's superiors also genuinely doubted the purity of his motives. They finally consented, after much initial resistance, to have him charge Esterhazy with espionage, but they adamantly refused to accept Picquart's conclusion that Esterhazy's guilt meant Dreyfus's innocence.

Picquart's persistence caused them to take action against him. He was sent away from Paris on various missions, finally to North Africa, to a dangerous war zone. His insubordination, illegal activities, and apparent administrative inadequacies provided them with an excuse for such moves. In April 1897 Picquart wrote out a last will and testament, describing the reasons for his belief in Dreyfus's innocence and Esterhazy's guilt, with instructions that, in the event of his death, this information should be handed over to the president of the Republic. In June Picquart met with an old friend and lawyer and verbally revealed to him his findings.

Other important developments in the Affair were also under way. As information about Esterhazy began to circulate, many observers concluded that the Jewish Syndicate had finally found its "patsy." They

[41] Cf. Johnson, *France,* for a perceptive exploration of this issue. Arendt, *Origins,* 109, describes "Picquard" [*sic*] as "no hero and certainly no martyr" but rather "that common type of citizen . . . who in the hour of danger (but not a minute before) stands up to defend his country in the same unquestioning way that he discharges his daily duties."

reached such conclusions especially after the the so-called Uhlan letter was published in the popular press. In it Esterhazy revealed himself as a man who secretly detested the French. He wrote, "I would not hurt a puppy, but I would have a hundred thousand Frenchmen killed with pleasure."[42] The Anti-Dreyfusards believed the letter to be a forgery; it was evidence of a conspiracy that, in planting false information, was attempting to blacken Esterhazy's reputation. Esterhazy himself assumed the role of outraged innocent, demanding that he be brought to trial, so that he could demolish the ugly rumors and false charges that had been circulated about him. Such hardly seemed the stance of a guilty man.

Many jumped to conclusions about Esterhazy. They assumed his guilt on the basis of disclosures that were as unreliable and flimsy as those on which Dreyfus had been charged, if not more so. Esterhazy's financial difficulties provided a plausible motive, but experts finally declared that his handwriting did not match that on the bordereau. Similarly, it was not clear how he could have obtained information concerning matters mentioned in it, nor was he "going on maneuvers." In short, many who expressed outrage at the way Dreyfus had been railroaded seemed just as willing to railroad Esterhazy. The Dreyfusards wanted to believe Esterhazy guilty, just as others wanted to believe Dreyfus guilty. Such pressing desires were more important than carefully assembled evidence.

Picquart's superiors in the military were among those who suspected that he had sold out to the Dreyfus family. Nearly the opposite was the case: Supporters of Dreyfus were repeatedly frustrated by Picquart's stubborn and principled refusal to have anything at all to do with the Dreyfus family, by his reticence to cooperate actively with the now gathering Dreyfusard forces. He did not trust them. Moreover, he did not like them.

Picquart's superiors also concluded that the case put together by Picquart against Esterhazy was weak, so weak that they agreed to try him. They were confident that the trial would deliver a crushing blow to the Dreyfusards. His court-martial, on January 10, 1898, resulted in a speedy verdict of "not guilty." He was enthusiastically greeted by crowds outside the courtroom, almost as a national hero, an innocent man saved from the ruthless machinations of Jews and others who sought to undermine the army. Once again the army had prevailed.

The Affair erupts: Zola's *J'Accuse!*

After Esterhazy's trial many Dreyfusards fell into discouragement and depression. A daring, even reckless act was soon to change that mood.

---

[42] Bredin, *Affair*, 222.

On January 13, three days after Esterhazy's trial ended, Emile Zola published his *J'Accuse!* (I Accuse), destined to be one of the most famous manifestoes in modern European history. Zola pulled out the stops: He accused ministers of war and prominent members of the General Staff of having conspired to convict an innocent man through false evidence and an illegal trial, later suppressing evidence that revealed his innocence. Zola similarly charged the judges in both Dreyfus's and Esterhazy's trials of having knowingly violated the law in order to convict an innocent man and of having followed orders to acquit a guilty one. He made these charges without being able to prove them and on the basis of much reckless guesswork. We can now see that some of his charges were both untrue and unjust. Still, he breathed life back into the case, and many have justified his recklessness in terms of that accomplishment.[43]

Zola was France's most famous writer at this time. He was more than a writer of popular novels; he had also become a public figure, a symbol. For the Catholic right wing in France, Zola personified the modern trends that so offended traditional, religious sensibilities. His highly successful and lucrative novels were considered sensationalist, tawdry, even obscene, certainly lower in moral tone than Drumont's works. They were, in short, for traditionalists in France typical products of the debased, secular culture that had grown up under the Republic, the "slut" (*la gueuse*). Children in conservative families were taught to call their potties Zolas.

Unsophisticated, archconservative Catholics and fearful, provincial petits bourgeois were not Zola's only detractors. The leaders of the most prestigious cultural institutions in France, the academies, the Conservatoire, the Beaux-Arts, massively mobilized against the Dreyfusards after the publication of *J'Accuse!*, as did a great number of France's most respected and best-selling novelists, playwrights, and journalists.[44] No matter what Zola actually said in this manifesto, no matter how persuasive his arguments might have been to an objective observer, few in France were able to read words from this particular novelist in an open and dispassionate spirit. Even many of his supporters in this enterprise had little respect for him as an artist or as a man, and many of them also harbored reservations about specific charges he made. What impressed them was who his enemies were, who it was that he was taking on. These supporters came largely from intellectual and artistic avant-gardes, and from certain academic disciplines, especially sociologists, philosophers, and historians.

Zola obviously knew that many of his charges were reckless and po-

---

[43] Ibid., 245 ff.

[44] Arno J. Mayer, *The Persistence of the Old Regime: Europe to the Great War* (New York, 1981), 222.

tentially libelous. He knew they could not be proved in a court of law. A number of lawyers, approached about defending him in impending court action, declined the honor. The president of the French Bar, Henri du Buit, said that he would be willing to defend Zola in court only if he entered a plea of insanity.[45] But it seems clear enough that Zola's goal was not to win a case in court. Rather, it was to put life back into the case against the army, and in that goal he certainly succeeded, well beyond what he intended. In the process he persuaded many who had so far remained uninvolved that the Dreyfusards were reckless destroyers and irresponsible slanderers, out to make political mileage by attacking prominent military men and undermining the army, unconcerned that in the process they were jeopardizing the nation.

Zola has often been portrayed as a shining hero of the Dreyfus Affair, a crusader for truth, justice, and toleration, a courageous humanist and opponent of anti-Semitism. A century later he remains a symbol for many Jews of the unflinching upholder of justice.[46] Zola's courage, like that of Picquart, is undeniable, but closer examination reveals details about him, as about Picquart, that diminish the heroic image. His works were full of crude racial determinism, including those that by later standards would be considered flagrantly anti-Semitic. His novel *L'Argent* had portrayed Jewish financial conspiracies in bringing down the Union générale. In it he wrote: "It is indeed Jewry as a whole, that stubborn and cold-blooded conqueror, marching toward the sovereign kingship of the world's nations, that it has bought, one by one, with its omnipotent gold."[47] In *La Débacle* (1892), describing the scene of France's defeat in the Franco-Prussian War, he described a "whole crowd of low, preying Jews [who] followed in the wake of the invasion."[48]

Like many French intellectuals, right and left, Zola was alarmed by the rapid rise of Jews in France, not only in its economic but even more in its cultural life. His main concern in composing *J'Accuse!* was not to express sympathy for Jews or even to fight for justice on their behalf; it was rather to counter what he believed were reactionary, Jesuit, and militarist conspiracies, concerning which he harbored fantasies that were strikingly akin to those harbored by Drumont in regard to the Jewish Syndicate. Just as it was sufficient, for many in France, to learn that Zola was supporting Dreyfus for them to decide to join the Anti-Dreyfusards, so it was with Zola: He had only to see who Dreyfus's enemies were in

---

[45] Bredin, *Affair*, 258.
[46] Cf. Norman Podhoretz, "J'accuse," *Commentary*, vol. 74, no. 3, Sept. 1982, 21–31.
[47] *L'Argent* (Paris, n.d.), 483; as cited in Pierre Birnbaum, "Anti-Semitism and Anticapitalism in Modern France," in Frances Malino and Bernard Wasserman, eds., *The Jews in Modern France* (Hanover, N.H.), 215.
[48] Quoted in Wilson, *Ideology*, 475.

order to come to Dreyfus's aid. The man, Dreyfus, was decidedly a secondary consideration. Dreyfus, the Jew, was even less important.

To make these points is not to suggest that Drumont and Zola were morally, artistically, or intellectually equivalent. Yet Zola's motives and methods have been praised by people who knew only part of the story or have assumed things about him that are not justified. Zola's true motivations have led more than one scholar to suggest that the Dreyfus Affair was not, in the deepest sense, about Jews and anti-Semitism, but rather about the struggle of right and left in France.[49]

Zola's charges and his subsequent trial, in which he was found guilty of libel, pulled thousands into the Affair who had so far remained uninvolved. Anti-Jewish riots spread throughout France, to some seventy towns and cities; mobs screamed "Death to the Jews" and attacked synagogues, Jewish shops, and Jews on the streets. The police often seemed ineffective, perhaps even in sympathy with the rioters, a situation right out of Russia. In Algeria, where historically anti-Semitism had been much stronger and where anti-Semitic riots had already broken out in early 1897, violence was more serious, although nowhere did it cause deaths on the scale of the pogroms in Russia in 1881 (or of those that would come in Russia from 1903 to 1906).[50]

In the following weeks and months anti-Jewish boycotts were organized, and the anti-Semitic leagues sprang back to life, gaining an unprecedented following. The belief of Mathieu and other Jewish leaders that sensational publicity could be dangerous was now painfully confirmed. To the easily excited, France appeared to be on the edge of a full-fledged popular uprising against the Jews. In short, Zola not only succeeded in putting life back into the campaign to free Dreyfus, but even more powerfully revived the previously unsuccessful anti-Semitic movement of the late 1880s and early 1890s. A liberal non-Jew who had worked for a quiet and procedurally proper release of Dreyfus wrote of Zola's initiative: "What a blunder! The era of stupidity is about to begin."[51]

He was not entirely wrong. The years 1898–1900 may be considered the high point of prewar anti-Semitism in France, the point at which an anti-Semitic ideology and movement seemed to have its greatest appeal, while Jewish upward mobility and Gentile toleration of it seemed to be coming to an end. In this regard, if not in others, Herzl's perception of the Affair as epoch making seemed justified. But Zola's initiative and the reactions to it also helped to make an organized movement of the Dreyfusard cause. In the long run, that transformation may be considered an

---

[49] Cf. Eugen Weber, in Kleeblatt, *The Dreyfus Affair*, xxv–xxviii.
[50] Cf. Wilson, *Ideology*, 734.
[51] Bredin, *Affair*, 252.

even more important development than the mobilization of the Anti-Dreyfusards.

A key element in the awakening of pro-Dreyfus sentiment was the involvement, finally in a major way, of the forces of republican moderation, the political middle-of-the road. Again, they were drawn into the Affair not so much because of outrage at the injustice of Dreyfus's conviction (they had had plenty of time to express such outrage) but because they worried about public order and about the possibility of revolutionary violence from the antirepublican right, possibly a military coup d'état. They also perceived an opportunity to discredit the traditionalist right in France because of its association with such flagrant injustice.

The earlier hesitations of moderate republicans had been based on their concern that the Dreyfusard cause challenged the integrity of one of the French republic's most sacred institutions, the army, at a time not only of threatening war from Germany, but of a newly threatening "internal war," that is, class conflict, anarchist outrages, working-class strikes and demonstrations, and proclamations by the socialists in favor of violent revolution. The ugly head of the *classes dangereuses*, the dangerous lower classes, was rising again, as in 1793–4, 1848, and 1871. A strong army was viewed by much of the moderate, republican bourgeoisie as the ultimate bulwark against a new and seemingly more ominous effort at social revolution.

However, with the Dreyfus Affair, at least after Zola's entry into it, popular agitation was assuming a right-wing rather than a left-wing complexion, and it appeared that the right, not the left, was on the point of challenging the existing political system. Probably no element of the French bourgeoisie was more concerned about social unrest than were the Jews of that class. No group was more inclined to respect *la chose jugée*, decisions made by the legally constituted authorities. Those French middle-class Jews who doubted whether Dreyfus was guilty faced a painful dilemma. They now suspected that the republican establishment, to which many of them had been close, was willing to back away from its liberal principles, its commitment to justice and equal treatment of all citizens, in the name of public order. Yet even some Jews were willing to entertain the reasoning that the sacrifice of one Jew might be necessary to save France from both external and internal threats. Only when Dreyfus's innocence became overwhelmingly clear did significant numbers of the Jewish bourgeoisie openly rally, in the company of the non-Jewish bourgeoisie, to the Dreyfusard cause.

A key consideration for many bourgeois Jews was fear of the anticapitalism of anti-Semites like Drumont. They were relieved to be able to present the Dreyfusard cause as one that favored social stability, that was not radical or disruptive, and that was not a "Jewish issue," but one that concerned the nation as a whole. As one conservative, non-Jewish commentator, the editor of the influential *Le Figaro*, had earlier put it: "I call on people to recognize, with me, that anti-Semitism is the most dangerous form of socialism, that it is, in reality and above all, a campaign against the moneyed classes."[52] Such fears had played a role in Germany and Austria, but generally the socially conservative there were more inclined to see in it a welcome expression of antiliberal sentiment.

In all three anti-Semitic affairs the Jewish communities in France, Russia, and the United States bitterly quarreled among themselves about the appropriate response. Their divisions reflected both generational differences and differences of social class. In turn, differences of social class usually meant, in France and the United States, older residents, assimilated, liberal, and middle class versus newer residents, mostly eastern European, poorer and more inclined to radicalism or socialism. The future premier, Léon Blum, a militant Dreyfusard and something of an angry young man in the 1890s – and thus not typical of the French bourgeoisie in his opinions – expressed deep contempt for what he believed was the cowardice of his class in regard to the Dreyfus Affair.[53] Established organizations like the Alliance Israélite Universelle, the supposed front for the Jewish Syndicate, did not become involved in it, nor did any leading Jewish organizations. Grand Rabbi Zadoc Kahn established a secret organization of Jews to aid Dreyfus, but it was not of great importance, and, predictably, when discovered was denounced as yet further evidence of Jewish conspiracies.[54]

Other camps hesitated as well. The socialist left, while divided on this as on so many other issues, did not rally immediately to Dreyfus's cause. In the opinion of one scholar, the socialists remained indifferent to the Affair until it seemed that they were losing control of the streets to right-wing radicals.[55] As late as February 1898, the time of Zola's trial, French Marxists expressed their suspicion that Jews were using the Dreyfus case to rehabilitate themselves after the scandals they had suffered in the previous decade. One Marxist writer warned about the Jewish bourgeoisie:

---

[52] Marrus, *Assimilation*, 203–4; Wilson, *Ideology*, 326, contests the degree of Jewish pusillanimity as described by Marrus. The issue is, of course, a central one; it comes up in nearly every country. We will see similar charges, articulated by Jews themselves, made against the Russian and U.S. bourgeoisie, in the Beilis and Frank cases. And in the issue of how much Jews fought back against the Nazis it becomes a central if somewhat different issue.

[53] Léon Blum, *Souvenirs sur l'Affaire* (Paris, 1982), 151; Bredin, *Affair*, 527.

[54] Paula Hyman, "The French Community from Emancipation to the Dreyfus Case," in Kleeblatt, *Dreyfus Affair*, 31–2.

[55] Zeev Sternhell, "The Roots of Popular Anti-Semitism in the Third Republic," in Frances Malino and Bernard Wasserstein, *The Jews of Modern France* (Hanover, N.H., 1985), 120.

If they can show that one of their number has been the victim of a miscarriage of justice through pressure of public prejudice, they will seek, through the rehabilitation of this individual of their class . . . the indirect rehabilitation of all the Jews and Jew-lovers among the Panama men. They will wash away all the filth of Israel in this fountain.[56]

This comment strikingly recalls the situation in Austria, where Jewish Marxists stubbornly resisted speaking out against anti-Semitism, since they had observed how Jewish liberals cynically used charges of anti-Semitism to mask capitalist corruption.[57] The reticence of French Marxists to become involved in the Affair also underlines how tentative and often confused were the initial responses to it in the left. Hostility to Dreyfus was not restricted to the antirepublican political right, nor were openly expressed doubts about his guilt restricted to the prorepublican left. As the examples of Picquart and Zola illustrate, many who did not like Jews finally made decisive contributions to Dreyfus's eventual freedom, whereas a number of Jews and long-standing opponents of anti-Semitism were reticent to see his case reopened.

Further developments in the course of the year 1898 added powerfully both to the drama and the ironies of the case. It was discovered that Commandant Henry, whose testimony had played such an important role in Dreyfus's trial, had committed forgery in an effort to cinch the case against Dreyfus. The discovery was made by an unlikely figure, Captain Louis Cuignet, who was a personal friend of Henry and a firm believer in Dreyfus's guilt but, like Picquart, believed in telling the truth, whatever the consequences. Even more ironic, the discovery had come in the course of an investigation initiated by the new minister of war, Godefroy Cavaignac, also a firm believer in Dreyfus's guilt, in order to dispel all lingering doubts about that guilt. Cuignet was appalled at his discoveries, as was his superior officer, but both agreed to inform Cavaignac, and all three made their findings public. The cover-ups and illegal procedures of the past were now at an end. The probity of men like Picquart and Cuignet, right-wing military men generally hostile to Jews, was decisive in the liberation of Alfred Dreyfus. (Cavaignac continued to assert that he believed Dreyfus guilty, in spite of the new evidence, and he continued to believe it his special mission to destroy the power of the Jewish Syndicate.)

Arrested and put into jail, Henry confessed to his forgeries and committed suicide by cutting his throat. Anti-Dreyfusards suspected that the

[56] Quoted in Wilson, *Ideology*, 335.
[57] Cf. Robert S. Wistrich, *Socialism and the Jews: The Dilemmas of Assimilation in Germany and Austria-Hungary* (East Brunswick, N.J., 1982), 225 ff.

Jewish Syndicate had gotten to him, that it was not a case of suicide. Some Dreyfusards believed that since Henry had known too much about how Dreyfus was framed, he had been killed on the orders of the General Staff. (The razor with which his throat had been cut was inexplicably closed, and he had had a mysterious visitor, never identified, shortly before his death.) Henry, like Esterhazy, became a folk hero, a simple soldier doing his utmost for the fatherland. A subscription was established to help support his widow and orphaned children. Contributions poured in from all over France, often accompanied by venomous anti-Semitic letters.[58]

Esterhazy fled to England. Once established there, he confessed that he was the author of the bordereau. However, he maintained that he had written it under the secret direction of the now deceased Sandherr, as part of an involved and highly secret counterespionage ploy. He had taken subsequent "undisciplined" actions, he insisted, on the orders of the General Staff. Again, the more stubborn Anti-Dreyfusards merely concluded that even Esterhazy, the man they had earlier lionized, had finally sold out to the Jews, had been paid off to confess to crimes of which he was not guilty. Such suspicions were fed by Esterhazy's report that he had earlier been offered 600,000 francs by Jews if he would declare himself the author of the bordereau.[59]

The triumph of the Dreyfusards

By the autumn of 1898 the Dreyfusards were in a state of high alert and excitement, not only because they feared a right-wing coup but also because they were confident that the case against Dreyfus was disintegrating beyond repair. Many of them shared Zola's belief in a conspiracy, what the socialist leader Jaurès denounced as a "Jesuitical-militaristic cabal." Again, believers in conspiracy continually failed to discover concrete evidence to support it[60] – nor has any appeared in the following century as more and more documents have become available. Still, among many Dreyfusards the fantasy of a syndicate of military men and Jesuits hardened into an article of faith, comparable to the fantasy among Anti-Dreyfusards about the Jewish Syndicate.

This belief in a plot by the Jesuits and the military extended far beyond the specific accusations made by Zola. Among the Dreyfusards there were unquestionably those who suffered from paranoiac intolerance, roughly

[58] There is a fascinating study of these in Robert Louis Hoffmann, *More Than a Trial: The Struggle over Captain Dreyfus* (New York, 1980).
[59] Bredin, *Affair*, 325 ff.
[60] Cf. Johnson, *France*, 144.

comparable to, if somewhat less extensive and blindly malicious than, that of Drumont and his sympathizers. The anticlericals among the Dreyfusards often expressed themselves in bigoted ways, with words intended to insult, wound, and inflame. Louis Lévy, for example, writing for the Jewish newspaper *l'Univers Israélite*, conjured up a vast Jesuit conspiracy against the Republic. In imagery worthy of Drumont, he wrote, "a black crow has planted its talons into the head of the French rooster and has begun to peck its eyes out." The Jesuits were unprincipled plotters, he asserted, willing to stoop to any device: "The odors of the vestry mix their rancid perfume with the smell of the sewer."[61]

Lévy's writings may be seen as an exact fulfillment of Marxist warnings concerning how Jews would try to use the Affair for their own purposes. Lévy charged that all the recent events that had reflected badly on the Jews of France – the collapse of the Union générale, the Panama scandal, the Dreyfus Affair – were somehow linked to Jesuit plotting. Joseph Reinach, the first historian of the Affair, also believed in an extensive Jesuit conspiracy. And just as anti-Semites were inclined to see the Rothschilds as the evil geniuses behind the Jewish Syndicate, so Reinach and other Dreyfusards believed that Father du Lac, the confessor to many postards, played a key role in Jesuit plotting against the Republic.[62]

These fantasies aside, the Dreyfusards found solid evidence of malfeasance: the irregular court procedure, Henry's forgeries, the army's bogus claims that war might ensue if the contents of the secret dossier became public. There was also Esterhazy's confession, for what it was worth, about Sandherr's plotting. In short, just as anti-Semites found much in Jewish behavior to nourish their anti-Semitic fantasies, so French Dreyfusards found much in the behavior of the military that buttressed their own fantasies concerning a conspiracy. And both let their fantasies lead them to conclusions not supported by the evidence.

In spite of the sensational revelations concerning the case that continued to surface in late 1898 and early 1899, most of the Anti- Dreyfusards were still not dissuaded from their belief in Dreyfus's guilt. No doubt for many of them the issue remained – and would always remain, whether or not they could admit it to themselves – who it was that was defending Dreyfus, not the actual evidence in the case. Still, much of the evidence one way or the other remained in doubt. Not only bigots gravitated to the Anti-Dreyfusards; a number of fair-minded people did, too, especially in the earlier stages of the Affair. On the other hand, amazingly contorted reasoning began to appear in a few right-wing circles. One argument was that to rehabilitate Dreyfus, *whether or not he was innocent*, would deeply

---

[61] H. R. Kedward, *The Dreyfus Affair, Catalyst for Tensions in French Society* (London, 1965), 56, 61, 63.
[62] Ibid., 84.

undermine the army – and implicitly the principles of authority – and could not be allowed because the survival of the nation was at stake. Some even spoke approvingly of Henry's "patriotic forgery." Dreyfus's actual guilt or innocence, in the eyes of such observers, became an insignificant detail when weighed against the prospects that so horrified them: a ruined homeland, irresponsible and corrupt politicians triumphant, a France whose military was discredited and defamed, vulnerable to a second humiliating invasion by a triumphant Germany.

The autumn and winter of 1898–9 were filled with passionate debate and complex, confused maneuvers, including an ill-organized, somewhat pathetic attempted coup in February 1899 by the Anti-Dreyfusard League of Patriots. That was as far as the rumored right-wing coup d'état ever got, and the military had little or nothing to do with it. In June a new trial was ordered for Dreyfus, and a new parliamentary coalition, behind a "ministry of republican defense," brought the Dreyfusards to power. The new coalition set out to combat vigorously the reactionary, antirepublican forces in the army and the Church and more generally to move against the antirepublican, anti-Semitic movement that had spread so rapidly since Zola's manifesto.

Dreyfus was granted a retrial at Rennes in August and early September 1899. The Dreyfusards were confident of vindication, but he was again found guilty by a military tribunal. This trial and its verdict have often been portrayed as astonishing, even farcical. The proceedings certainly did have some odd aspects. For example, the judges voted five to two against Dreyfus, yet alluded to "extenuating circumstances" that were not explained. But the trial was not simply a farce, and it did not surprise some of the more careful observers at the time. The military judges, with one exception, were widely recognized to be honest and unprejudiced. The prosecution's case, while much weakened by the confessions of Esterhazy and Henry, was reasonably coherent and was fortified by new evidence, including further testimony that Dreyfus had confessed. Even more abundantly and cogently than at the first trial, the prosecution showed that wherever there had been known leaks of information, Dreyfus had been in a position where he might have been responsible for them. The pattern of this evidence was so overwhelming, it was argued, that it simply could not be the result of mere coincidence.[63] Moreover, Dreyfus's lawyers, bitterly divided by personal antipathies, were not at their best. The defense only called twenty witnesses, whereas the prosecution called seventy.[64]

By this time most of those who had taken an interest in the trial had

[63] Johnson, *France*, 175.
[64] Bredin, *Affair*, 401–3.

so committed themselves to one camp or another that what was proved or disproved in court was not going to change their minds. The Dreyfusards professed to be stunned and outraged at the verdict. The Anti-Dreyfusards were jubilant. In September, shortly after the trial, the president of the republic granted Dreyfus a pardon. For complex legal reasons, Dreyfus was obliged to petition for the pardon, with the implication that he had done something that required pardoning. He finally accepted that path, unable to face the possibility of returning to prison. Some of his supporters were bitterly disappointed; in their eyes he had dishonored their cause. Similarly, Anti-Dreyfusards could claim that he had implicitly recognized his guilt.

In part these matters came down to a matter of timing; Dreyfus would soon be fully exonerated, although not without lingering ambiguities. In 1906, after yet another full examination of the case had clarified many remaining mysteries, the previous judgments against Dreyfus were annulled, and he was reintegrated into the army with a promotion. He was also awarded the Legion of Honor. In a formal ceremony meant to erase his horrible humiliation twelve years earlier, Dreyfus was restored to his military honors, with crowds now shouting, "Long live Dreyfus! Long live the Republic!"[65]

In the same year Picquart – General Picquart – became minister of war. The year 1906 also marked an impressive electoral victory for the left.[66] The republican left, finding solidarity in the Dreyfusard movement, proved after all to be much more powerful than the anti-Semitic, anti-republican, Anti-Dreyfusard right. The acceptance by French citizenry of the Republic, an acceptance that had steadily grown in spite of ups and downs, was now more secure than ever.

What may be termed an ultimate sign of success was that the mob, that is, those members of society prone to violence and vandalism on the streets, which had so ardently rallied to the Anti-Dreyfusards in 1898, had begun to attack and abuse those same Anti-Dreyfusards in the latter stages of the Affair.[67] Another sign of "success" was that the Dreyfusards were willing to use the force of public opinion, now on their side, to exert improper pressure on judicial authorities.[68] In years to come that victory of the left in France, however flawed, would loom large. France seemed to many observers, in spite of all the excitement in 1898–9, a tolerant country, one where Jews could rely both on the state and on the people, in contrast to the situation in Germany, Austria, or Russia. Anti-Semitism had raised its ugly head, yet it had been decisively defeated by a repub-

[65] Ibid., 485.
[66] Ibid., 476.
[67] Arendt, *Origins*, 108.
[68] Martin, "The Corruption of the French Legal System," 45.

lican state and movement that enjoyed broad popular support. Indeed, Jews and non-Jews were brought closer together, so some argued, through a common fight for decency and toleration.

A "Dreyfusian revolution"?

Obviously, such conclusions have not found universal assent by subsequent generations, looking back from the perspective of the violent waves of anti-Semitism that broke out at the end of World War I, the widespread if more "cold" anti-Semitism of the 1930s, and, of course, the Holocaust. Many have questioned whether it is appropriate to speak of a "Dreyfusian revolution," in the sense of a decisive, long-term victory of the forces opposed to anti-Semitism. Others have suggested that anti-Semitism was not defeated but simply went underground. May we then speak of a gathering storm of anti-Semitism in France prior to 1914 as well as in central and eastern Europe?

The issue is by no means easily resolved. By 1906 anti-Semitic activists of the 1880s and 1890s in France recognized that they had lost another battle, if not the war. Some of them lost heart or restrained themselves in public. A number of their leaders died in the immediate prewar years and did not find successors. The Church, the monarchists in the military, the anti-Semitic popular press, the anti-Semitic leagues were all unmistakably chastened by the Affair. Public expressions of anti-Semitism visibly receded; no anti-Semitic riots, demonstrations, or boycotts occurred in France in the remaining years before the war; and the anti-Semitic press fell on hard times. That the anti-Semitic movement of 1898–1900 could collapse so rapidly suggests that Jew-hatred, in itself and not pulled along by other issues, lacked significant roots, self-generating substance, or broad popular appeal.

Insofar as anti-Semitism survived in France and in German-speaking central Europe it was mostly as part of larger conservative movements, not as self-standing anti-Semitic movements. In France the new right's claims to speak for the nation were successfully contested by a new generation of establishment conservatives, such as Raymond Poincaré. As the historian of the shopkeeper movement in Paris has written, "extremist protest gave way to conservative reintegration."[69] Representatives of big business and moderate liberals, people who had earlier dismissed the distress of the small shopkeepers as unworthy of serious attention, now showed a new sympathy for them. Anti-Semitism undoubtedly remained

---

[69] Philip G. Nord, *Paris Shopkeepers and the Politics of Resentment* (Princeton, N.J., 1986), 477.

in the ranks of such establishment conservatives, but it was a cooler sentiment, not a central concern of theirs. It was significantly different from the ardent, radical, populist variety of Drumont and de Morès.

Recent scholarship has also shown rather conclusively that the Dreyfus Affair has been overdramatized, its long-range significance exaggerated. Its immediate impact throughout France was less extensive than once believed. Captain Dreyfus's story has been too tempting, too appealing to the popular, vulgarizing kind of historian, and too appealing to various political agendas, such as those Zionist interpretations of modern history that emphasize European decadence, ineradicable Jew-hatred, Jewish self-hatred and inauthenticity, and the need for Jews to leave Europe. Intellectuals have been especially drawn to the story; it has been hard for them to accept that most people in France, who were not intellectuals, in spite of the unusual prestige of intellectualism in parts of the country, were not as drawn to the Affair as much as they. Recent studies have shown how little the peasantry and the population of small towns, still a majority of the population of France, were touched by the Affair.[70]

Similarly, Jewish immigration to France did not decline in response to the Affair. It actually increased in 1898, at the height of the Affair,[71] although the numbers of Jews moving into France from the 1880s onward were far smaller than those moving into other countries. Parallel observations have been made about the continuing influx of Jews into Vienna during the years of Karl Lueger, the city's immensely popular anti-Semitic mayor.[72] In short, the sweep of political anti-Semitism appears to have been shallow in comparison to that of developments in the economy and society of Europe in these years. It might even be questioned if a single event like the Dreyfus Affair, whatever Herzl's testimony, could persuade great masses of Jews that the land of liberty, fraternity, and equality had somehow changed irrevocably.

As noted at the close of the previous chapter, the elections of 1893 already registered what seemed a definitive victory of the Opportunist republicans over the monarchists. One scholar has argued that those elections presaged the political and social alignments that came together in the Affair. The elections of 1898 and 1906 did no more than establish beyond doubt an already overwhelming republican majority.[73] Again, one can easily question how much the Dreyfus Affair as such exercised a fundamental effect, one way or another, on these deeper shifts.

The victory of the Dreyfusards, whether "revolutionary" or not, was a morally flawed one, for the republicans who came to power are best

---

[70] Cf. ibid.; Burns, *Rural Society.*
[71] Cf. Green, *Pletzl,* 28–9.
[72] Cf. Geehr, *"I Decide,"* 323.
[73] Bredin, *Affair,* 521.

described as enemies of the anti-Semites, rather than of anti-Semitism, and hardly friends of the Jews. Moreover, many Dreyfusards harbored what might easily be termed anti-Semitic doubts about the rise of the Jews, especially about how far it would go: What were the limits of Jewish success in a country like France, where they remained less than two-tenths of 1 percent of the total population? That such concerns existed in the ranks of the Dreyfusards again underlines the point that apprehension about the rise of the Jews was not limited to reactionaries, to people who were insecure or personal failures, or to those threatened by modern trends whose minds were overcome by fantasies about the Jews. It also underlines the ambiguities of the Affair.

Bigotry was not decisively defeated by the Dreyfusards in part because in their own ranks were many bigots, Jewish and non-Jewish. Nor was a respect for truth, come what may and unsullied by political calculation, particularly notable among leading Dreyfusards; many of them were quite willing to believe that the justice of their cause made it acceptable to bend the rules – an "end justifies the means" perspective that is finally difficult to distinguish from that forwarded by those who spoke of Henry's "patriotic forgery."[74] Once in power, the Dreyfusards proved themselves scarcely less prone to duplicity and illicit manipulation of the legal system than had the Anti-Dreyfusards. Waldeck-Rousseau, the Dreyfusard premier during Dreyfus's retrial at Rennes, secretly contacted the prefect in that district and instructed him to pressure the military prosecutor, even the judges, to arrive at a not-guilty verdict.[75]

An irony that remains little appreciated has by now been amply stressed: the often central role of honesty and respect for truth among right-wing, often anti-Semitic people in France. The ideals of Truth and Justice, claimed by the left, were not without their power among those who spoke of competing claims of Discipline and Authority. They could not ignore the dishonesty and opportunism of some of Dreyfus's accusers, but they did not find it easy to join Dreyfus's defenders, who were also dishonest and opportunistic.

The victory of the Dreyfusards was also soured by quarreling within their ranks, of a personal but also a more ideological nature. The depth of hostility among those who worked to free Alfred Dreyfus was symbolized at the final hearing, where he was fully exonerated: Mathieu Dreyfus offered Picquart his hand, and Picquart refused it. Picquart made no secret of his belief, even at this date, that the Dreyfus family was scheming and pusillanimous, unwilling to take a clear and courageous

---

[74] Cf. Martin, "The corruption of the French Legal System," 43.
[75] Bredin, *Affair*, 396.

stand in denouncing the bad faith of those who had arrested and railroaded Alfred.[76]

Historically better known are the reflections on the Affair of Charles Péguy, the Catholic poet and man of letters who was among the earliest of the Dreyfusards. He was an interesting example of a philo-Semite in these years, one who received Jewish financial support but who was anything but a tool of the Jews.[77] He became bitterly disillusioned with the moral qualities of the Dreyfusard camp. His reflections on the Affair in *Notre Jeunesse* (Our Youth), published in 1910, eloquently denounced the move from *mystique*, the selfless idealism of the initial, lonely crusaders for truth and justice, to *politique*, the cynical calculations of politicians and careerists concerning advantages they might derive from the Affair.

Péguy was also offended by the anti-Catholic demagogy of many in the Dreyfusard camp, especially in the Radical Party, and by the anti-Catholic legislation that accompanied the political victory of the Dreyfusards. Even the socialist Jaurès, who in moral terms stood head-and-shoulders above most parliamentary deputies of the day, finally earned Péguy's vitriolic contempt. When Jaurès was assassinated by a right-wing fanatic on the eve of World War I, Péguy was recorded to have let out a "shout of savage exultation."[78] Péguy's own psychic development after the Affair, before he would die on the battlefields of World War I, was feverish and often bizarre, marked by bitter quarrels with former friends and colleagues and growing, all-consuming patriotism.

What most embittered men like Péguy and Picquart was the nature of the final amnesty granted by the government, since it entailed letting men like General Mercier go scot-free (he was minister of war at the time of Dreyfus's arrest and deeply implicated in the irregularities of the arrest and conviction). Mercier's real crimes were thus implicitly equated with the "crimes" of Dreyfus and Picquart. All these crimes were to be equally "forgotten" in the general amnesty legislation that was overwhelmingly approved by both houses of the French legislature and was clearly supported by the population at large. Undoubtedly in terms of healing the wounds in French society, of calming political passions, such an amnesty was politically astute. The general population seemed rapidly to lose interest in the Affair, and in anti-Semitism, after the amnesty. But in terms of justice and truth, the legislation was a travesty.

---

[76] Ibid., 467–8, 476.
[77] Cf. Lazare Prajs, *Péguy et Israël* (Paris, 1970); Marjorie Villiers, *Charles Péguy, a Study in Integrity* (London, 1965); Hans A. Schmitt, *Charles Péguy, the Decline of an Idealist* (Baton Rouge, 1967)
[78] Goldberg, *Jaurès*, 566.

The Affair marked certain changes in France, rather than being a cause of them. Modern mass politics was more firmly established, and notable politics coming to an end. The older rule of committees of local notables and elected intermediaries, corresponding to nineteenth-century liberal ideals, began to give way to new pressure groups and organized interests: the press, various leagues (such as the League of the Rights of Man, or the League of Patriots), trade unions, professional and business organizations. These and many others now began to regard themselves as more active, central participants in public life and to exert powerful pressure on parliament and other institutions of state.[79]

Developments in the year 1906, marking Dreyfus's full exoneration and the overwhelming victory at the polls of republicanism in France, stood in stark contrast to developments in that same year in Russia, France's ally. And whatever the corruptions of the political establishment in France, they also stand in rather stark contrast to those of the political elite in Russia. Members of that elite would, within a few years, undertake actions against an innocent Jew that, in conscious and calculating injustice, exceeded anything undertaken by members of the French military. It is to that unhappy country that we must now turn.

[79] Cf. Madeleine Rebérioux, *La République radicale* (Paris, 1975), 40 ff.

6

Beyond the Pale; Russia and the Jews, 1890–1914

[Russian Jews] never seem for an instant to lose the consciousness that they are a race apart. It is in their walk, in their sidelong glance, in the carriage of their sloping shoulders, in the curious gesture of the uplifted palm. (Harold Frederick, 1892)[1]

We felt joy and pride in our newness: we eat and rejoice, while all Jews fast and cry. (A member of the Jewish Bund, in Vilna on the Day of Atonement)[2]

The scribblers here [in the United States] try to persuade the reader that the shtetl was a paradise full of saints. So comes along someone from the very place and says "stuff and nonsense!" They'll excommunicate you. . . . (Isaac Bashevis Singer, from *Lost in America*)

The Jewish Question in Russia

To move from France to Russia offers some instructive contrasts on the Jewish Question. Many of the questions asked in the previous chapters about France – the interplay of reality versus fantasy or the gathering storm thesis – take on a different and revealing cast in regard to Russia. France was a country with strong democratic traditions, a republic after 1875, and widely considered the epitome of a modern western country, while Russia remained an autocracy and the most backward of the major European powers, although it began to industrialize rapidly by the last decades of the nineteenth century. While the Third Republic was more internally secure than ever with the resolution of the Dreyfus Affair, tsarist autocracy, which had always been characterized by a paranoiac style, felt more insecure than ever before – and with good reason, for it was increasingly challenged by its enemies, internal and external, especially after the turn of the century.

Even more conspicuously different, the number of Jews in Russia was roughly a hundred times that of France. Unlike French Jews, by the late nineteenth century only a small minority of Jews in Russia had moved

---

[1] Harold Frederick, *The New Exodus: Israel in Russia* (London, 1892), 79–80.
[2] Ezra Mendelsohn, *Class Struggles in the Pale: The Formative Years of the Jewish Workers' Movement in Tsarist Russia* (Cambridge, 1970), 153.

into the status of comfortable, assimilated middle-class citizens. Russia's Jews were often referred to as a stubborn, compact mass. Most of them remained, by their own image of themselves, "a people apart," not only in religion but in language, dress, culture, and economic activity. They were a self-consciously separate nation within the Russian fold: They were not "Russians," and most resisted the idea of ever becoming Russians. Even those Jews, the so-called *maskilim* ("enlightened ones"), who looked to a modernizing reform of Jewish communities did not accept the idea of blending into Russian society, unlike their counterparts in France or Germany.

Whether or not Russian Jews constituted a distinct state within a state, that is, more than a separate nationality under the tsar, became an increasingly explosive issue. In 1868 a Jewish convert to Christianity, Jacob Brafman, charged that the *kahillot* (roughly, Jewish parliaments, dating from the days of the Polish Commonwealth) continued to exist clandestinely after they had been abolished by Nicholas I in 1844. They had established firm contact, he claimed, with Jewish organizations in the West, such as the Alliance Israélite Universelle.[3] Brafman's charges were believed by many influential officials and blended into related beliefs about international Jewish political power. Such officials worried especially that Jewish connections, the clandestine political power of Jews, were used by Jewish financiers to forward the economic success of Jews in Russia.

Even when modern industry and secularism began to affect an important minority of them, Russia's Jews responded in ways that were quite different from what Jews were doing in France, reflecting the peculiar history, culture, and socioeconomic composition of Russian Jewry. Perhaps least appreciated of all, Russian Jewry was riven by the stresses and strains of extraordinarily rapid population growth, in the context of a backward economy and society.

A recent popular volume, viewing the relations of Jew and non-Jew in Russia from a Jewish standpoint, has referred to a "century of ambivalence."[4] That ambivalence was felt on both sides. The authorities in Russia found Jewish issues incomparably more vexing, seemingly insoluble, in the forty-odd years before 1914, than did the authorities of France and indeed of most other countries. Russian officials resorted to what must be termed idiosyncratic, inconsistent, even self-defeating measures in dealing with the Jewish Question.

[3] Steven J. Zipperstein, *The Jews of Odessa: A Cultural History, 1794–1881* (Stanford, Calif., 1985), 115.
[4] Zvi Gitelman, *A Century of Ambivalence: The Jews of Russia and the Soviet Union* (New York, 1988).

However, tsarist authorities were in truth not so consistently malevolent in regard to their Jewish subjects as has often been believed; in
certain areas, for example, Odessa, and in certain periods, particularly
the late 1850s and early 1860s, officials and Jewish subjects got along
quite harmoniously.[5] But even if the tsars and their ministers had been
consistently enlightened, benevolent, and competent – hardly the case –
they would have had to wrestle with major problems, real problems,
perhaps insoluble problems, in finding a workable path of development
and an acceptably harmonious relationship for both Jewish and non-Jewish
subjects.

For many years, the most influential histories of Jews in Russia were
written by Jews for whom the brutal oppression and irrationality of the
tsarist authorities was patent, often because of personal experience. Scholarly efforts to view the Jewish Question in a more balanced fashion,
considering the dilemmas of the tsars and their ministers, have only
recently begun to be written, offering some interesting reinterpretations
of tsarist policy, particularly in the direction of questioning the role of
religious-based anti-Semitism and looking instead at palpable social and
economic frictions, understandable political dilemmas.[6] Similarly, many
of the persistent confusions, exaggerations, and myths about the pre-1914
experience of Jews in Russia have only recently been subject to careful
scholarly critique.[7]

From such studies emerge the conclusion that even efficient, modernized states like France, Prussia, or Great Britain would almost certainly
also have been sorely taxed by the dimension of the problems faced in
Russia. The undeniable failures of tsarist policy must be evaluated in that
light. In France, it might be said, it was finally possible to ignore the
Jews since there were so few of them and since most of them blended so
well, so enthusiastically, into Gentile society. Anti-Semitic excitements
like the Dreyfus Affair therefore lacked broad appeal or staying power.
In Russia, however, it was not possible to forget about the Jews; they
numbered in the millions, and their status was a major issue, one of
growing importance, one that would not go away and that simply could
not be ignored.

Tsarist policy in regard to the Jews developed in the course of the
nineteenth century into an ever more hopeless farrago. "No one . . . could

---

[5] Cf. Zipperstein, *Jews of Odessa*.
[6] For a useful discussion of these historiographical trends, see John Doyle Klier, *Russia Gathers Her Jews: The Origins of the "Jewish Question" in Russia, 1772–1825* (Dekalb, Ill., 1986), xii–xix.
[7] See, for example, the articles in David Berger, ed., *The Legacy of Jewish Migration: 1881 and Its Impact* (New York, 1983).

make sense of the mounds of self-contradictory laws and regulations regarding Jewish autonomy in Russia."[8] Tsarist officials failed to pursue a coherent set of policies in regard to their Jewish subjects, and they often expressed their frustration, despair even, in trying to overcome "the quiet Jewish obstinacy"[9] in opposition to governmental policies. It was an obstinacy that became distinctly less quiet in the generation before the war. One may speak of a competition between negative and positive images concerning Jews in Russia as in the rest of Europe and America, but negative images prevailed and grew in Russia, almost certainly more than in the great majority of other countries.

A factor that further deeply affected the peculiar relationship of Jew and non-Jew in Russia was that the Jews in the country were a conquered people. They had not emigrated to Russia, looking for a better life but rather had been incorporated into the Russian Empire, with the partitions of Poland in the late eighteenth century. And that empire had in the immediately preceding centuries strictly forbidden Jews to reside in it. The official state religion, Russian Orthodoxy, had been at times fanatically – murderously – preoccupied with stamping out "judaizing" heresies, that is, beliefs that denied the divinity of Christ.

Throughout the nineteenth century, most Jews in the Russian Empire remained deeply suspicious of their conquerors, uneasy about the motives of the tsar's officials in regard to them, even while outwardly proclaiming their submission and fidelity to the Russian autocrat. When measures were introduced by the government that appeared benevolent, as for example when state schools were opened to Jews in the first part of the century, the wholly justified suspicion remained that an underlying motive in opening the schools, aside from the officially proclaimed one of making useful citizens of Jews, was to win young Jews away from their ancestral religion.

In other regards, efforts to integrate Jews appeared more unequivocally threatening. Jews were told that they must bear the same burdens as the rest of the population, and the so-called *rekrutchina* was applied to them, the forced recruiting of Jewish youths for twenty-five years of military service, often accomplished by brutal "kidnappers" (*khappers*, Jews hired by Jewish communal authorities to round up Jewish recruits). Previously, Jews had not been required to render military service, and this forced draft of Jews evoked a special horror within Jewish communities. It remained a bitter memory, long after it was abolished in midcentury.[10]

---

[8] Michael Stanislawski, "The Transformation of Traditional Authority in Russian Jewry: The First Stage," in Berger, *Legacy of Jewish Migration*, 24.
[9] Salo W. Baron, *The Russian Jew under Tsars and Soviets* (New York, 1987), 102.
[10] Cf. Michael Stanislawski, *Tsar Nicholas I and the Jews: The Transformation of Jewish Society in Russia, 1824–1855* (Philadelphia, 1983).

Bitterness also long remained within Jewish communities between the poor, whose children were "kidnapped," and the rich who could arrange for their children to be exempt from the rekrutchina, usually by substituting the children of the poor. On this issue, as in a widening range of others, class conflict grew within the Jewish communities of the Pale in the course of the nineteenth century. "The antagonisms that resulted from the conscription experience . . . were of an entirely new order, for now it was Jew oppressing Jew."[11]

The suspicion between tsarist authorities and Jewish subjects was not only mutual; it was part of a vicious cycle. The tsar's advisers were of a divided mind about how "useful" the Jews might ever become to the state. On the one hand, they welcomed and sought to encourage Jewish enterprise, education, and economic diversification. On the other, they viewed most Jews as inclined to parasitical activities and feared that Jews would exploit and corrupt the common people or would join hands with powerful Jews elsewhere to undermine Mother Russia. Partly because of such apprehensions, the Jews were legally confined to a so-called Pale of Settlement, comprising for the most part the area in which they had long resided under Polish dominion, before Poland was incorporated into Russia. The Pale was thus a vast territory, approximately the size of France and Spain combined, spreading from the Baltic to the Black seas, but not including the historic heartland of Russia, especially not its major cities, St. Petersburg and Moscow.

The rise of the Jews in the nineteenth century took on particularly threatening dimensions in the Russian Empire, culminating in what might be termed a Jewish offensive, inside and outside Russia, against the autocratic rule of the tsars. In spite of the movement of millions out of Russia from the 1870s onward, the population of Jews inside Russia continued to mushroom, and massive internal migration, from the north to the less densely populated south, preceded and then paralleled emigration to other countries. The extraordinary fecundity of Jews in Russia during most of the nineteenth century was the source of wide comment and alarm. Karl Marx's notorious quip that this "dirtiest of all races" was "breeding like lice"[12] was not uncommon in both tone and content.

As noted, scholars are still struggling to understand the dynamics of this Jewish population explosion. The statistics they must work with are not adequate or reliable, but it appears that the overall rate of population growth for Jews in Russia in the sixty-year period from 1820 to 1880 was about 150 percent, while the non-Jewish population increased only 87 percent. Even more remarkable was the Jewish increase

---

[11] Stanislawski, "Transformation of Traditional Authority," 26.
[12] Edmund Silberner, *Sozialisten zur Judenfrage* (Berlin, 1962), 128.

in the southwest of Russia, where anti-Semitism would make its most violent appearance in the late nineteenth and early twentieth centuries: From approximately 3 percent of the population in 1844, Jews came to make up around 9 percent by the turn of the century. During the period from 1844 to the eve of the war, the Jewish increase in the southern provinces was nearly 850 percent; the non-Jewish, 265 percent. In Congress Poland (that part of Poland that came under Russian domination after the Congress of Vienna), from 1816 to 1913, the Jewish population grew 822 percent; the non-Jewish, 381 percent; the Jewish percentage of the total rose from 7.8 percent to 15 percent.[13] Even these percentages do not adequately indicate the impact of Jewish population growth in many regions since Jews moved mostly into newer urban areas; they did not spread evenly throughout the country. And those new urban areas were the most turbulent in Russia, in terms not only of violence against Jews but against other minorities as well. Similarly, there was a marked increase in industrial violence and crime in the street in the new cities of the south.

These internal migrations were significantly different from immigration into other countries. Jews moving west, out of Russia, were inclined to accept a new nationality, a new language, a new culture, and were less likely over the long run to be perceived by the native population as irredeemably foreign, whatever the initial hostilities. But Jews who remained in Russia were part of a typically tight-knit long-existing language and culture, a vibrant, well-populated world of its own, in which the attractions of assimilation were relatively minor.

Similarly, Jews moving west tended to see the countries into which they were moving as culturally superior to Russian culture and even to their own Yiddish culture, a perception that made assimilation to western cultures more attractive to them. But Jews who remained in the Russian Empire overwhelmingly retained their Yiddish culture and language, and usually did not learn to speak Russian or other Slavic tongues, such as Polish, Ukrainian, and Byelo-Russian, with proficiency, reflecting in part their sense that Slavic culture was both alien and inferior. There were important exceptions to this rule, especially as the century progressed and in the newer, more open cities like Odessa, but russifying Jews were always unimportant compared to, say, germanizing or magyarizing Jews outside of Russia. A notable exception was the experience of the Jews of Odessa, which for most of the middle years of the century was almost "American" in terms of the openness of the city, its Jews' rapid upward mobility, their harmonious relationships with government officials, their

---

[13] Baron, *Russian Jew*, 63–4.

active participation in local government, and their abandonment of many of the practices of orthodox Judaism.[14]

The strength of anti-Semitism in Russia, however, cannot be simply attributed to the rapid growth and movement of the Jewish population. In Budapest, where the rate of Jewish population growth was more rapid than in many cities of Russia, anti-Semitism remained relatively weak, especially among the ruling elite. The deeper issue revolved around the degree to which Jews, whatever their numbers, were perceived as "destructive," rather than "useful."

Anti-Semitism was so tenacious and pervasive in Russia, especially from the 1880s onward, because of the fear that Jews threatened vital Russian interests and values. This fear, although it gave rise to exaggerated, even preposterous fantasies about Jews, was stimulated and nurtured, as in France and other countries, by real factors. Such fearfulness blended into a larger paranoiac Russian psyche, related to the existence of an array of by no means imaginary enemies surrounding Russia. For many Russians, their country's Jewish population appeared a rapidly growing, intractable, foreign, and increasingly hostile body. The uncontrolled and apparently uncontrollable rise of such a population was a distinctly more threatening development than the rise of Jews in other countries.

This fear in Russia seems to have been most pervasive among those who had embraced certain Russian nationalist ideals. For Slavophiles, men who believed in a special Russian nature and destiny, the traditional, religiously based antipathy to Jews was powerfully blended into a secular one: More and more the Jews came to symbolize for them the threat of an alien and decadent West, of a destructive modernism, one that would undermine their hopes and dreams for Russia. Traditional Jews were objectionable enough to such Russian nationalists, but at least such Jews were politically passive. But as hundreds of thousands of Jews began to abandon, to one degree or another, their traditional ways, when they began to embrace western-style liberalism or socialism, when they became wealthy and important in the Russian economy, they appeared ever more menacing.

Anti-Jewish racism as such, or anti-Semitism in its strictly etymological sense, was relatively weak in Russia, if growing visibly by the eve of World War I. Attacks on Jews borrowed more from religious themes than was the case in the West, where even a Drumont denied religious hostility to Jews. Well into the twentieth century one often encountered in Russia the charge that Jews "killed Christ" or that they used Christian blood for their ceremonies, the kind of charge that was by that time rare and widely discredited in western Europe and the United States. Jewish converts to

---

[14] Cf. Zipperstein, *Odessa*, passim.

Christianity encountered less opposition in government than was the case in many German-speaking areas at this time, although they may have been accepted simply because they were so few. Several such converts became notorious for their cooperation with the tsarist regime in persecuting Jews, indeed in offering "expert" support for such charges as ritual murder by Jews or, as in the above-mentioned case of Brafman, in supporting other kinds of charges of Jewish conspiracy.

Fears about the incursions of modernism afflicted a larger part of Russia's ruling elite and many more of her most influential ministers than was the case in the West. The rise of the Jews in countries on Russia's western borders was a kind of warning for such men. A rise in Russia comparable to the rise of Jews in Hungary, for example, was a development that Russian nationalists regarded with horror, to be prevented at all costs. They argued that Russians and other Slavic peoples who were predominantly peasant, such as the Poles, Byelo-Russians, and Ukrainians, could not compete with Jews. The simple and generous Slavic peasant was no match for the wily, avaricious Jew. The greater number of Jews in Russia made the likelihood of their domination over the Slavs all the greater. Even those who might grant that Jews were not "destructive" in the most direct sense of the word still feared Jewish domination. Jews might well be good for the economy, but they posed a dire, if more subtle and indirect threat to the cultural independence and identity of Slavic and other peasant peoples.

In countries to the west of Russia, a blending of Jewish and non-Jewish values and cultures could be discussed and entertained by many non-Jews, especially because the Jewish contribution would necessarily be small – and more important, because it was obvious that Jews were taking up Gentile ways incomparably more than Gentiles were taking up Jewish ways. A Jewish presence was less a concern in Germany, France, or Hungary, where Jews became perfect Germans, Frenchmen, or Magyars, than in Russia, where Jews were much less likely to embrace a Russian identity. Moreover, Russian nationalists concluded that most Jews did not want to blend or to compromise; they wanted to take over and control. And even if Jews in Russia might actually be inclined to compromise, their large numbers would almost necessarily entail a compromise with a much larger Jewish component than Russian nationalists were willing to entertain.

In Germany, with its mere 1 percent of Jews, Treitschke expressed a demand that Jews become more "purely" German than they were. He registered horror at the already "jewified" (*verjudet*) German culture in Austria. His voice was opposed by influential others, such as that of Theodor Mommsen, who saw a useful and stimulating role for Jews in the formation of a new German national identity. Voices like those of

Mommsen were rare in Russia, if they existed at all, and even Mommsen believed that Jews should eventually disappear into the new German amalgam, and not remain a permanently separate group in it. He, too, considered Jewish influence to be "destructive," but beneficially so, since some destruction was a prerequisite to the amalgamation of a new national character.

As we have seen, the issue of Jewish aspirations to power, the Jewish "right to rule," was one that even in France was taken seriously by men as different as Drumont, Zola, and Gide. It should not be surprising that Russian nationalists, facing a Jewish population a hundred times as large in an undeveloped, peasant country, were obsessed with it. They maintained that the peasants would fall under the rule of the Jews and would inevitably be undermined morally by their contact with them. In the eyes of such nationalists, the peasants – unsophisticated in money matters, illiterate, and generous – borrowed money from Jews and eventually lost their lands to them. Jews offered the peasants both cheap credit and cheap vodka, encouraging and exploiting their tendencies to drunkenness and improvidence. Even when the role of Jews was not painted in such black colors, Russian nationalists feared that Russians were no match for Jews in a modern, liberal, and competitive society. Russian conservatives similarly feared that Jews introduced foreign ideas that were ruinous to Mother Russia and the peculiar Russian personality.

As in France, there were obvious elements of exaggeration and falsification in these interlocking images. Detailed studies have not supported the charge that peasant drunkenness and indebtedness were markedly higher where Jews were involved in the liquor trade,[15] and other charges, such as large-scale Jewish expropriation of peasant land, can only be accepted with qualifications. However, those interrelated images provided a most plausible and gripping nexus – indeed, an appalling specter – for many Russian nationalists. Moreover, the images corresponded to reality often enough that those who were not anti-Semitic, even many Jews themselves, registered similar complaints. In short, the issue was, again, not pure fantasy but an exaggeration of reality.

Arnold White, an English journalist and member of Parliament, who had on occasion represented the Jewish philanthropist Baron de Hirsch and who had spent much time dealing with Russian officialdom, vividly communicated the extent of Russian nationalist fears: He predicted that if Russia were to "fling down the barriers to Jewish emancipation, not five years would pass before Russia would be Jewish. In ten years every place of importance in the empire would be filled by a Jew."[16] One

[15] Ibid., 76–7.
[16] Quoted in Isadore Singer, *Russia at the Bar of the American People: A Memorial of Kishinef* (New York, 1904), 153.

conservative Russian nationalist warned that "the Jewish force is extraordinary, almost superhuman."[17] The reactionary minister and tutor of Tsar
Nicholas II, Konstantin Pobedonostsev (1827–1907), with whom White
had much contact, openly defended Russia's discriminatory policies by
asserting that Jews were natively more intelligent, more aggressive, and
more inclined to seek an education than was the mass of the Russian
population.[18] For him, government control of Jewish activities had a quality of *noblesse oblige* to it. The peasants needed paternalistic protection
by the state or else they would become in effect slaves of the Jews. A
western-style society, with its atomistic individualism and its free competition would lead to the ruin of the peasants, and to the rule of the
Jews in Russia. (It was he who, in a much-quoted quip, purportedly
concluded that the Jewish Question in Russia would be solved by the
conversion of one-third of the Jews, by the emigration of another third,
and by the death of the remaining third.)

Such paranoiac views were typical of but not limited to the reactionary
right. Among more moderate, liberally minded members of the ruling
class there seemed to be a consensus that Jewish character was inherently
more competitive than and alien to Russian national character. In such
quarters, too, one heard repeatedly that the gullible, generous peasant,
as well as the easy-going average Russian in the towns and cities, could
not successfully compete with the shrewd and hard-driving Jew.[19] Indeed,
the same was said about other nationalities in Russia that had traditions
of hard work, commerce, and dealing with money, such as the Germans,
Greeks, and Armenians. But the Jews, because of their large population
and because they resisted assimilation more than other nationalities, were
seen as the main threat.

Even on the socialist and liberal left in Russia, where by the turn of
the century anti-Semitism was perceived as a reactionary device and
denounced as such, the notion that Russia's Jews were "unchangeably
foreign," economically threatening, and morally destructive to the non-
Jewish population popped up with arresting frequency.[20] There was, in
short, a rather widespread consensus in Russia that Jews were a separate,

[17] Maurice Samuel, *Blood Accusation* (New York, 1966), 88.
[18] Baron, *Russian Jew*, 53.
[19] Cf. Michael Davitt, *Within the Pale: The True Story of Anti-Semitic Persecution in Russia*
(New York, 1903), passim. Davitt was a correspondent for the Hearst papers and conducted
interviews throughout Russia following the Kishinev pogroms in 1903.
[20] Cf. the article by Tugan-Baranowsky (professor of political economy at St. Petersburg),
"Anti-Semitism in Contemporary Russia," *Monthly Review*, Jan. 1904; included in Singer,
Russia at the Bar, 224 ff. Tugan-Baranowsky, typical of many liberals, emphasized that
the peasants were in fact friendly to the Jews, seeing them as economically useful in the
village economy; it was, rather, the middle and upper classes that felt threatened and that
increasingly took up anti-Semitic agitation.

somehow superior race, stubbornly resisting assimilation, and steadily working to dominate those among whom they lived.

The crisis of late nineteenth-century Russia

The anti-Jewish rioting after Alexander II's assassination in 1881 and the rising tide of impoverished and desperate Jews out of Russia and other parts of eastern Europe intensified the anti-Semitism of the 1880s and 1890s in central and western Europe, but inside Russia the mid- to late 1880s were relatively calm, marked by repression and vigilance by the government over popular agitation. These years saw the beginnings of what would develop into a period of rapid industrial growth in Russia in the 1890s, financed by investments from the West as well as by "squeezing" peasant savings inside Russia. That growth fed popular agitations of a sort that had only just begun to be felt in 1881. An industrial proletariat, most of it with one foot still in the village, concentrated in a few burgeoning industrial areas and increasingly rebellious, assumed a new importance. The peasantry, too, became once again restive.

The conditions in the new industrial centers were, as one historian has commented, "fantastically overcrowded, unhygienic, and squalid."[21] Many revolutionaries who had looked to an oppressed and restive peasantry to overthrow tsarism and introduce a humane, rational regime now turned to the industrial proletariat to perform that redeeming mission for Russia. They thus moved from Russian populist (*narodnik*) theories to those of western Marxists, from a "romantic" theory to a "scientific" one.

Although tsarist authorities had attributed the pogroms of 1881 to peasant anger over Jewish exploitation, the riots of that year began not in the peasant villages but overwhelmingly in large towns or middle-sized market cities where rapid growth and large-scale Jewish immigration had recently occurred. Peasants rioted in 1881 only after they had heard about riots in nearby urban areas and apparently hoped to share in the booty. Villages that were distant from such areas, even those with significant Jewish settlements, were almost entirely free of rioting.[22] Evidence suggests, moreover, that the riots were spontaneous, not encouraged or planned by the central authorities, as many Jews at the time believed and as many historians have subsequently asserted.

However, "spontaneous" is a slippery term, and one that in this context may have unwarranted connotations, since those who blamed the riots

[21] Lionel Kochan and Richard Abraham, *The Making of Modern Russia* (New York, 1963), 229.

[22] Michael Aronson, "Geographical and Socioeconomic Factors in the 1881 Anti-Jewish Pogroms in Russia," *The Russian Review*, vol. 39, no. 1, Jan. 1980, 19–20.

on Jewish exploitation referred to them as "spontaneous outbursts" of the people against their Jewish exploiters. There is some evidence of organized efforts by a shady organization of reactionary, anti-Semitic nobles to encourage attacks on Jews. Similarly, some business competitors of the Jews opportunistically encouraged the roving bands of unemployed to attack Jewish shops.[23] Undoubtedly, in a few instances local officials helped to spread the rumors that the tsar wanted the Jews to be punished, and at times the local forces of order were suspiciously slow in repressing the riots. There were even some reports that police officers mixed with the rioters, but mostly the instances of delay seem to have been the result of uncertainty rather than any preconceived plan.[24] With over two hundred pogroms in southern Russia, there was considerable variety in their origins and in the shape they took, allowing many observers, then and subsequently, to speculate freely and according to their own agendas about the "real" causes of them as a whole.

It is clear that Alexander III and his advisers, quite the opposite of having planned the uprisings, were surprised by them. Alexander was personally shocked by the bloodshed and at first firmly believed that the riots were part of a general attack on the government by what he termed anarchists, the same revolutionaries who had assassinated his father.[25] He called for a "careful investigation" since "someone must have had a hand in instigating the people against the Jews."[26] Throughout the nineteenth century the officers of the tsar, however unsympathetic they may have been to Russia's new Jewish subjects, had usually repressed popular violence against them. To encourage violent lawlessness would have been entirely out of character for a government that so feared the tendencies to uncontrolled, anarchic violence of the lower orders. There is little evidence of a change of policy in 1881, at least not from the central government. Even many normally well informed Jewish observers at the time were firmly convinced that the revolutionary socialists, not the government, had provoked the pogroms.[27]

But those conclusions were also unjustified since revolutionaries in Russia were also caught unawares by the riots. Some of them tried to exploit the unrest once it had started, going so far as to applaud the attacks of the people on their Jewish exploiters. In August 1881, for example, the executive committee of the People's Will issued a proclamation that announced:

[23] Ibid., 23.
[24] Jonathan Frankel, *Prophecy and Politics: Socialism, Nationalism, and the Russian Jews, 1862–1917* (Cambridge, 1981), 53.
[25] Aronson, "Geographical and Socioeconomic Factors," 25.
[26] Baron, *Russian Jew*, 45.
[27] Frankel, *Prophecy and Politics*, 52.

The people in the Ukraine suffer most of all from the Jews. Who takes the land, the woods, and the taverns from out of your hands? The Jews. From whom does the peasant, often with tears in his eyes, have to beg permission to get to his own field? The Jews. Wherever you look, wherever you go – the Jews are everywhere.[28]

Yet such efforts to turn popular passions against the Jews came only after the riots had started; they were not the root cause of them, nor did this particular proclamation reflect a widespread conviction among members of the People's Will. The origins of the riots had much less to do with conspiracies, whether by the authorities, by revolutionaries, or by secret anti-Semitic organizations, than with disruptive shifts in Russia's economy and society.

The riots were spontaneous in that they would not have occurred without genuine social tensions, themselves the product of unprecedented change in Russia. That change involved Jewish population growth and the movement of Jews into new arenas, geographically, socially, and economically. Many Jewish observers, especially among the younger, socialistically inclined, saw the riots as provoked by Jewish exploitation and the growing wealth of Jews: "We were convinced," one of them wrote, "that all the Jews were swindlers." Even those who viewed the Jewish situation with sympathy, such as the noted Marxist, Pavel Akselrod, himself Jewish, noted that "however great the poverty and deprivation . . . of the Jewish masses, . . . the fact remains that, taken overall, some half of them function as a non-productive element, sitting astride the neck of the lower classes in Russia."[29] And as an American sociologist has recently commented, however poor Russian Jews of that period appear, they were on the whole "decidedly better off than the surrounding population,"[30] which made them the object of envy and resentment.

In the spring of 1881 there were large numbers of Great Russian emigrant workers in the southwestern regions of Russia, where the most important riots occurred. Many had been thrown out of work in the industrial crisis and depression in St. Petersburg and Moscow in 1880–1, and they had moved from these cities to the south in desperate search of employment. Some of them were recorded to have committed minor illegal acts in order to get arrested since in jail they would at least be fed. Such people, outsiders in the communities to which they had moved, desperate, brutalized, and often on the edge of starvation, were obviously

[28] Quoted in ibid., 98.
[29] Ibid., 52, 105.
[30] Stephen Steinberg, *The Ethnic Myth: Race, Ethnicity, and Class in America* (New York, 1981), 97.

prone to looting and rioting, especially since the local police forces were overwhelmed with the task of maintaining order in cities that were growing uncontrollably. Among the Jewish population, similar phenomena were not unknown in this period. In 1886, for example, more than two hundred poverty-stricken Jewish artisans in Vitebsk threatened violence unless they were given work or assistance from charity. "Even if you arrest us," they said, "we won't lose anything; then at least we will be in warm rooms and be given bread, which we lack now."[31]

The more simplistic Marxists of the time were inclined to fit such violence into a pattern of capitalist–proletarian class conflict and to see a redemptive mission in it. But in truth that violence was characterized by a random, unideological quality, turning in directions that are difficult to fit into preconceived Marxist patterns – or into preconceived notions about the anti-Semitic motives of those who engaged in violence. Some of the looting and vandalism no doubt served the purpose of challenging tsarist authority and of giving support to demands for a more humane and rational society, but lower-class violence was by no means all so "conscious" or rationally directed as that. As Lenin would later formulate the issue, providing a more sophisticated Marxist perspective, the "spontaneity" (*stikhinost'*) of the proletariat in rebelling against its condition could be "purely destructive" if not properly guided by revolutionary leaders with "consciousness" (*soznanie*), by men who "knew better."[32]

Members of the ruling orders spoke in similar terms: Prince Mirsky commented, in a conversation with Empress Alexandra, that "it is the intellectual class that makes history everywhere, while the masses are merely an elemental power; today they massacre the revolutionary intellectuals, tomorrow they may loot the Czar's palaces."[33] Such opinions much resembled the long-standing belief of the tsars and their officials since at least the time of the bloody Pugachev revolt in the eighteenth century that they were sitting on a volcano, that the "dark" masses were forever prone to wild, destructive, and brutal outbursts, and that constant vigilance by the authorities was absolutely necessary. A recent historian has graphically expressed a slightly different but still related perspective; she notes that workers could join socialist parties and fight for a world of justice and humanity, but they also could "loot, brawl, break machinery, beat up intellectuals and Jews, and rape women from the old upper classes."[34] Many Russian revolutionaries, from the 1870s on, accepted that "popular excesses" – often, they acknowledged, of a shocking brutality

[31] Mendelsohn, *Class Struggles*, 27–8.
[32] Cf. Alfred G. Mayer, *Leninism* (New York, 1963), 43.
[33] Abraham Yarmolinsky, ed. and transl., *The Memoirs of Count Witte* (Garden City, N.Y., 1921), 190.
[34] Sheila Fitzpatrick, *The Russian Revolution* (Oxford, 1982), 6.

and irrationality – were an unavoidable aspect of a revolutionary uprising of the people.[35]

Whether it was a focused anti-tsarism, anticapitalism, or anti-Semitism that motivated such men, as distinguished from simple, undifferentiated anger, material distress, and brutal resentment, may certainly be questioned. Again, even Jewish workers by the early 1880s were "beating up the industrialists, breaking looms, striking, struggling," as one of them proudly put it.[36] The Jewish socialist Arbeter Bund (Workers' Union), proclaiming that Jews must "fight back," must end their millennia-old passivity, was not always able to "guide," in the Leninist sense, the anger and resentments of starving and overworked Jewish proletarians. This was the beginning of a process even more impressive among Jewish workers than among non-Jewish: Passivity and fatalism were being shaken off. Jewish suffering was no longer accepted as God's will; rather, it was something that Jews could fight against and change. But such changes did not proceed smoothly, and working-class leaders, whether Jewish or non-Jewish, could not maintain a firm control over the working masses.

As in western Europe, the new techniques of production and distribution, linked to precipitous population growth, not only created a new proletariat but undermined the position of traditional industries and handicrafts, resulting in sometimes explosive tension within both the working and the middle classes. Inevitably, ethnic differences were mixed into these tensions. Jewish employers at times used the more pliant and less class-conscious Christian workers as strikebreakers against their Jewish employees, even filling the Christian workers' heads with stories of how Jewish workers hated them. Jewish socialists found it necessary to implore Jewish workers to refrain from violent retaliation against Christian scabs. In Bielsk Jewish workers organized special "terrorist squads" (*shrekotriaden*), often composed of semicriminal elements, against both employers and strikebreakers.[37] Christian hoodlums were similarly organized by the so-called Black Hundreds to terrorize Jewish workers, finally achieving, from 1903 to 1906, a level of horror and bloodshed that exceeded anything even dreamed of by these earlier Jewish terrorist squads.

By the turn of the century, local officials and the secret police began to mix into these conflicts. The secret police at times collaborated with the Jewish underworld and with Jewish employers. At Dvinsk, the Jewish owners of Zaks's match works employed gangsters and pimps, with the support of the secret police, to attack striking workers. In Warsaw, in an episode that was widely reported in the European press of the day, followers of the Bund rioted for three days in 1905, in what was called a

[35] Frankel, *Prophecy and Politics*, 99–101.
[36] Mendelsohn, *Class Struggles*, 28.
[37] Ibid., 99–104.

"pimp pogrom" (*Alphonsenpogrom*). Jewish pimps and the Jewish underworld in Warsaw had also engaged in strikebreaking and other anti-worker activity; Jewish workers, in retaliation, broke into houses of prostitution, smashing windows and furniture, knifing both pimps and prostitutes, and throwing them out of the windows. The government did not intervene in any consistent or effective way, in this pogrom as in so many others, and the rioting stopped only when the leadership of the Bund was able to regain control over the rioters. Some eight deaths and over a hundred injured were counted at the end of this Jewish riot, or "pogrom."[38]

Most of the rapidly growing cities in European Russia, especially in the Pale of Settlement, were populated by ethnic groups that were different from the surrounding majority peasant populations, which were mostly Slavic (Great Russian, Byelo-Russian, Polish, and Ukrainian). Germans and Jews were among the most successful of those urban minority groups in taking advantage of the new economic opportunities, and the Jews were not only the most numerous of such minorities but also the most vulnerable, especially after the assassination of the tsar by revolutionaries who were identified as Jews. As in western Europe, modern, racist anti-Semitism linked to nationalism seems to have been most pronounced in those urban areas where elements of the Jewish and Gentile middle classes found themselves in harsh competition. Violence between Jew and peasant in the countryside, so much the concern of the authorities, seems to have been of a different quality, less systematic or ideological, and more sporadic.

By the turn of the century, in response to popular rumblings throughout Russia, parties and other political organizations had begun to form, still embryonic by western standards but drawing to them important elements of Russia's population. The most important of these organizations were the (liberal) Constitutional Democratic Party, the (Marxist) Russian Social Democratic Workers' Party, and the (peasant-populist) Socialist Revolutionary Party. Until 1914 the Jewish Bund, variously and precariously allied with the Social Democratic Workers' Party, became in many ways the most impressive of all these organizations.

Tsarist ministers repeatedly complained that the Jews were particularly prone to joining revolutionary socialist movements, a complaint made as well by Jewish employers. Several ministers also charged that the Jews were extraordinarily successful as capitalists, as exploiters of others' labor. And there was much truth to both of these assertions. Not all Jews, or even a majority of them became socialists, but young Jews did flock in

---

[38] Edward J. Bristow, *Prostitution and Politics: The Jewish Fight Against White Slavery, 1870–1939* (Oxford, 1983), 58–62.

disproportionately high numbers to socialist and revolutionary organizations. Jewish activists at the time took pride in that fact, while lamenting the prominent role of Jewish capitalists, and it has been amply affirmed by later historians.[39] The Zionist activist Chaim Weizmann despairingly wrote:

> The larger part of the contemporary younger generation is anti-Zionist, not from a desire to assimilate, as in Western Europe, but through revolutionary conviction. . . . Almost all those now being victimized in the entire Social Democratic movement are Jews, and their number grows every day.[40]

The proclivity of Jews, or an important minority of them, throughout Europe for revolutionary socialism had many roots, but in Russia an undeniably important one was that, especially after the educational reforms and new opportunities of the 1860s and 1870s, there were more university-educated Jews than the Russian economy could absorb, a problem that was exacerbated, from the 1880s on, by renewed restrictions on Jews in government service.[41] In 1889 the Ministry of Justice submitted a special report to the tsar, warning that the legal profession was being "flooded with Jews" and that their peculiar traits were tarnishing the reputation of the bar. The tsar approved measures to limit Jewish lawyers accepted to the Russian bar.[42]

The problem of a "Jewish flood" in certain occupations existed even in Germany, with a Jewish population one-tenth that of Russia's and with a larger job market for the university educated. In Germany, too, many educated Jews, especially lawyers and journalists, found attractive careers in the social democratic movement.[43] But Jews in Russia inevitably felt themselves, much more than in Germany or any western European country, to be hated and hounded outsiders, and thus the attractions of revolutionary doctrines were all the greater. Socialist internationalism offered an attractive answer for an important minority of Jews to the issue of what kind of a cultural "compromise" could emerge out of a blending of Russian and Jewish traditions.

Jews were even more disproportionately represented in capitalist enterprise than in socialist activism, at least certain kinds of such enterprise. As noted above, the attitudes of tsarist authorities to Jewish entrepreneurs

---

[39] Cf. Robert S. Wistrich, *Revolutionary Jews from Marx to Trotsky* (New York, 1976); idem, *Socialism and the Jews: The Dilemmas of Assimilation in Germany and Austria-Hungary* (East Brunswick, N.J., 1983).

[40] Yehuda Reinharz, *Chaim Weizmann, the Making of a Zionist Leader* (Oxford, 1985), 152.

[41] Mendelsohn, *Class Struggles*, 29.

[42] Cf. Samuel Kucherov, "Jews in the Russian Bar," in Jacob Frumkin et al., eds., *Russian Jewry* (New York, 1966), 220–2.

[43] Wistrich, *Socialism*, 81; J. P. Nettl, *Rosa Luxemburg* (Oxford, 1969), 262–7.

were more ambiguous than to socialists. Many of the most successful Jewish capitalists remained at least outwardly loyal to tsarism and naturally hostile to socialism. They were encouraged by Russian authorities, with erratic swings from minister to minister, to play a "useful" role in Russia's effort to keep up with the West.

However, the great mass of Russian Jews, while increasingly urbanized and not as a whole the very poorest of the poor, were not strongly present in primary production or in the introduction of the most advanced techniques of production. "Almost invariably, the larger and more modernized the factory, the fewer the number of Jewish workers employed."[44] This fundamental economic reality worked in the long run against prosperity for the Jewish masses inside Russia, at a time when their aspirations began to climb. It was yet another structural factor, along with the increase in Jewish population, that was finally more important than the anti-Semitism of individual tsars or their ministers in producing poverty and despair among Jews. But oppression by the authorities and the legal disabilities were more visible than structural factors; they were something that could be fought. It was the combination of subjective factors (the actions of individual tsars and their ministers) and structural change unfavorable to millions of Jews that made Jewish life in Russia ever more intolerable and that led Jews themselves to search for solutions to the Jewish Question with a rising urgency – emigration, assimilation (an unrealistic or unappealing option to the great mass of Jews), or violent revolution.

The proclivities of a visible minority of Russian Jewry to revolutionary socialism or to capitalist enterprise were, of course, only part of the story. Even Jews who were abandoning old ways held on to elements of their tradition, and many, perhaps most, Russian Jews remained strongly attached to the old ways and to religious orthodoxy. Traditional Jews, respectful of established authorities, Jewish and non-Jewish, resisted change and were locked into what would later be termed a culture of poverty. In a related way, they continued to view their miseries, material and otherwise, as God-given, certainly not to be changed by political activity, as either the Bundists or the Zionists urged. Such Jews were as hostile to socialist and liberal activism as were the ministers of the tsar. Orthodox rabbis were notorious for cooperating with the police in ferreting out Jewish socialist and union activists, a cooperation that may be seen as yet another aspect of the growing class conflict within Jewish communities.[45]

But in balance, the liberal-to-socialist left exercised a powerful and growing attraction for those Jews who in one way or another had begun to enter the modern world, even if pushed unwillingly into it. As in

[44] Mendelsohn, *Class Struggles*, 23.
[45] Ibid., 106–7.

France, the left was friendly territory, at least in comparison to the territory of the Russian conservatives and nationalists. The program of the left in Russia promised civil equality for Jews, and its leaders denounced anti-Semitism. It was no accident that the authorities, and the Russian right more generally, were ever more inclined to bunch liberals, socialists, intellectuals, and Jews into one hated category.

Russian anti-Semitism and the counteroffensive of the Jews

While a few advisers to the tsar continued to forward the idea of making useful citizens of Russia's millions of Jews, in the long run tsarist officials worked in a contrary direction – to encourage large numbers of them to leave the country. Especially under Alexander III (1881–94) and Nicholas II (1894–1917), tsarist authorities grew ever more suspicious of their Jewish subjects. The suspicion on the part of those authorities was even more pronounced in regard to Jews outside Russia, who were believed, especially after the turn of the century, to be in close, conspiratorial contact with their brethren inside the country.

A comparison with other monarchies in Europe gives some sense of how different things were in Russia. It is hard to imagine any Russian tsar, even Alexander II, the great "liberal" reformer of the 1860s and 1870s, openly and repeatedly expressing the kind of gratitude that the Emperor Franz Joseph of Austria-Hungary did for "his" Jews, whom he regarded as unusually loyal and among the most useful of his subjects in modernizing his realm. Even the concerns of the Hungarian Count Széchenyi in the 1840s about Jews spoiling the Hungarian soup did not prevent a massive entry of Jews into government service and into the political elite of that country, nor did it much limit the fairly extensive intermarriage of wealthy Jews with the Magyar nobility. By the late nineteenth century the usefulness of Jews to the Magyar nation was widely accepted by its elite.

These trends had few parallels in Russia. It is true that certain classes of Jews that were specifically designated as useful (merchants of the first guild, university graduates, skilled artisans, for example) continued to enjoy wide privileges. Wealthy Jews, the Jewish "magnates," most of whom had laid the foundation of their fortunes in the liberal years of Alexander II, continued to have access to the tsar's ministers, including the most reactionary of them. Still, the legendarily wealthy Jewish magnates in Russia, the Brodskys, Ginzburgs, or Poliakovs, some of whom were decorated and honored by the government and who even acquired titles of nobility, did not hobnob with Nicholas II and his court in the way that their counterparts in Germany did with Bismarck or Wilhelm II or, to cite an even more conspicuous example, the way certain wealthy English Jews did with Edward VII of England. Disdain for Jews was common among the ruling aristocracy of all European countries, but it was especially pronounced in the court of Nicholas II – and in Nicholas himself.

The tsar and his ministers saw the hand of the Jews not only in revolutionary activity but also in Russia's foreign policy disasters, most notably the Russo-Japanese War of 1904–5. And increasingly Jews, both inside and outside Russia, were themselves inclined to view Nicholas II and most of his ministers as devious, implacable enemies. The great Jewish historian Simon Dubnov, in describing this period, declared that "Russian Jewry has developed an irreconcilable hatred for the despotic regime. . . ."[46]

There had always been distrust, but after 1890, and especially after 1903, these already tense relationships deteriorated steadily. The tsar's ministers, many Jews believed, were trying to turn Russia's social and economic tensions against them, and to make scapegoats of them for Russia's foreign-policy disasters. An escalating underground "war" (the word was used on both sides) between Jews and tsarist authorities developed in the generation before World War I. It broke repeatedly into violence, in pogroms against the Jews, on the one hand, and in assassinations of government officials and revolutionary violence by Jews, on the other.

The regulations drawn up after the pogroms in 1881, called the May Laws because they were drawn up in May 1882, were expressly designed to keep Russia's Jews "under control" after the disruptive period of liberal reform in the 1860s and 1870s. During that period, according to conservative observers in Russia, Jews had extended their ownership of land dangerously and had begun to overwhelm Russia's schools and universities, especially in medicine and the law. A special concern of the Laws, reflecting the paternalistic opinion of their authors, was to prevent Jews from exploiting the peasantry. The Laws thus decreed that Jews were to be moved out of the villages, and they were forbidden to buy further land.

Earlier in the century, efforts had been made to settle Jews on the land, particularly in the less densely populated southern territories of the Pale. Although some ten to twenty thousand Jews took up agriculture (the father of Leon Trotsky, a future leader of Soviet Russia, was one such Jewish peasant), these efforts to transform unskilled and "useless" Jews into productive peasants were a failure. Most of Russia's millions of Jews,

[46] Quoted in Frankel, *Prophecy and Politics*, 137.

it was concluded, were both physically and psychologically unsuited for arduous manual labor, an argument forwarded by Jews themselves as much as by non-Jews, although it is by no means clear that the government provided the Jewish settlers with the means by which they might realistically have succeeded. Those most hostile to the Jews further argued that even when settled on the land, Jews would not work it with their hands; they inevitably resorted to their skills in handling money, their notorious craftiness, to get others to do the work for them, to exploit the labor of others.

The May Laws in one sense merely reinforced an existing demographic trend in both Russia and the West, and everywhere among Jews more than any others, to move from the countryside to the new, rapidly expanding urban centers. Those centers could not properly absorb the Jewish population moving into them. A 1907 study analyzing the Russian census of the same year concluded that approximately three-quarters of the Jews in Russia lived in urban areas by the end of the century.[47] Given the dimensions of the population increase among Jews, May Laws or no May Laws, there would have been overcrowding in the urban centers of Russia. No such laws existed in the United States, yet nearly catastrophic urban overcrowding of Jews occurred there as well, especially in New York. Similar problems developed in London.

It is not often recognized, in any case, that a full and consistent implementation of the May Laws was repeatedly postponed in the decade following their introduction. Moreover, they did not apply in Congress Poland, a large area of particularly dense Jewish settlement. As with the pogroms of 1881, simplistically described as the key stimulus for the emigration of Jews in the 1880s, so with the May Laws: They were less the source of urban ills than was the population increase of the time, linked to the disruptive effects of rapid economic development, trade, and unemployment cycles. But also like the pogroms, the May Laws were more palpable, satisfying targets for criticism than impersonal economic forces or demographic expansion.

It would be wrong, however, to suggest that the May Laws were without major harmful effect. The Laws, not to mention the earlier accumulation of special legislation affecting the Jews, were by the turn of the century deeply resented and widely denounced as ill-conceived by both Jews and non-Jews. The Laws may be seen as the perfect symbol of the perplexity, bungling, and plain confusion of the tsar's officials about what was to be done about Russia's Jewish population.

Even those Russian conservatives and nationalists who believed in the

---

[47] Israel Rubinow, "The Economic Condition of Jews in Russia," *Bulletin of the Bureau of Labor*, no. 72 (Washington, D.C., 1907), 487–583; cited in Steinberg, *Ethnic Myth*, 94.

need to keep the Jews under control came to recognize that the Laws simply did not work. Jews succeeded in circumventing them on a massive scale (for example, by leasing land through proxies, by remaining in the villages "temporarily," by bribing officials, and by illegally moving out of the Pale of Settlement). An American diplomatic observer remarked in the early 1890s that the Laws "have heretofore been so loosely and lightly observed as practically to be inoperative."[48]

Time after time recommendations were made by various committees and ministers to amend or revoke the May Laws, which in the first place had been conceived as temporary until better ones could be drawn up. But they remained in effect until 1917, largely because Nicholas II himself repeatedly blocked any change of them, at times referring to an "inner voice" that guided him in resisting reform.[49]

Bribery on the part of Jews seeking to evade the multitude of special laws concerning them became a way of life in many areas. Millions of rubles a year moved into the pockets of officials who had authority over Jews. Many conscientious police officials and members of the judiciary came to consider the Jews a troublesome and corrupt people, forever importuning the authorities with petitions, protests, and bribes. The courts were crowded with Jewish criminals and litigants, quite aside from those arrested for revolutionary activity, incurring the ire of overworked officials. The governor of the province of Bessarabia, a liberal noble who was widely recognized as friendly to the Jews and who openly criticized the May Laws, commented in his memoirs, in words that strikingly recall those of Istóczy in Hungary, that the judges he encountered in the province in 1904

> unanimously declared that not a single lawsuit, criminal or civil, can be properly conducted if the interests of the Jews are involved. In civil suits... [the Jews arrange] fictitious deals and contracts, ... concealment of property, and usury... hidden in legal guise. Criminal cases... afford the Jews a chance to fill the court with false witnesses set against one another.[50]

Matters were not made any easier, he remarked, by the notorious vehemence of the Jewish petitioners. They were not, at least not in this area, a passive and fatalistic people. The governor, Prince S. D. Urussov, was struck by their wild gesticulations (especially the women) – "so that

[48] Gary Dean Best, *To Free a People: American Jewish Leaders and the Jewish Problem in Eastern Europe, 1890–1914* (Westport, Conn., 1982), 27.

[49] H. H. Fischer, *Out of My Past: Memoirs of Count Kokovtsev* (Stanford, Calif., 1935), 164; Alexander B. Tager, *The Decay of Czarism: The Beiliss Trial* (Philadelphia, 1935), 14; Baron, *The Russian Jew*, 61.

[50] Prince Serge Dmitriyevich Urussov, *Memoirs of a Russian Governor: The Kishinev Pogrom* (New York, 1908; reprinted, 1970), 73–4.

one had to back away from them" – and their shrill demands for immediate action.[51] But Urussov sympathized with the frustrations that provoked the vehement demands of these petitioners. The conservative, anti-Semitic editor V. V. Shulgin complained that the May Laws and other restrictions on Jews "are offensive to us and we strongly desire to get rid of them. They are full of nonsense and contradictions . . . ; the Police of the Pale of Settlement live on Jewish bribery on account of Jewish restrictions."[52]

The Russian police force was required to devote a major part of its energies to enforcing the myriad of often contradictory regulations that applied to the Jews. Jews themselves naturally were tempted to evade laws that they considered grossly unfair, indeed that in some cases made it nearly impossible for them to earn an honest living. Since many ordinary Jews in Russia were obliged to become "criminals" in order to survive, the attitude of many other Jews to the law in a more general way inevitably became evasive or even contemptuous. Jews gained a reputation of being inveterate liars and dissimulators when dealing with the authorities. A Yiddish-language paper in the United States wrote that even after leaving Russia and dealing with American or German authorities, "Our Jews love to get tangled up with dishonest answers," or they get themselves into trouble by offering bribes to officials unaccustomed to receiving them.[53]

This contempt for the law in Russia helps to explain the large population of Jewish criminals in the more familiar sense of the word (that is, thieves, pimps, arsonists, con-men, smugglers), especially in the rapidly growing cities of the south, like Odessa or Kishinev, where the Jewish population was large (in those two it was close to half of the total population), and where Jews often faced desperate poverty as well. Thus the May Laws over the years contributed in a major way to corruption, ethnic tension, and other mischief in Russian life for both non-Jews and Jews. Urussov remarked how he

> frequently observed that the hatred of the police officials toward the Jewish population is partly due to the worries, annoyances, complaints, explanations, mistakes, and responsibilities which constantly fall to the members of the police in consequence of the senseless and ineffective legislation concerning the Jews.[54]

Periodic and unpredictable crackdowns made the situation all the more unbearable. In 1891 thousands of Jews, many of whom had established a relatively comfortable existence, were abruptly ordered to leave Moscow

[51] Ibid., 24–5.
[52] Samuel, *Blood Accusation*, 245.
[53] Ibid., 44.
[54] Urussov, *Kishinev*, 32.

and return to the Pale. (It is typical of the difficulties of dealing with the documents of the period that some sources place the numbers of Jews expelled at less than two thousand, others twenty times that number. Some deny that there was any brutality in applying the orders; others maintain it was commonplace and sometimes shocking.[55]) Similar administrative edicts followed for the Jewish population of other major cities outside of the Pale, including St. Petersburg and Kharkov, causing much misery. In 1896 the state set up a liquor monopoly, depriving thousands of Jews of lucrative occupations either as wholesale liquor merchants or as innkeepers. In many areas up to this time, the liquor trade had been vital to Jewish economic survival. In the villages of Zhitomir province, for example, 73.7 percent of the Jews earned a living by leasing distilleries and selling the product at inns.[56]

Since early in the century the role of Jews in contributing to peasant drunkenness had been a concern of the authorities. Charges that Jews corrupted the peasants through the sale of alcohol were made throughout eastern and central Europe at the time, more often by liberal reformers than by conservative officials. Not surprisingly, after the establishment of the state liquor monopoly many Jews continued to produce and smuggle contraband alcohol, further swelling the ranks of Jewish criminals who found it necessary to bribe local officials to survive. Smuggling, not only of alcohol, was another recognized Jewish vice that the tsarist authorities had tried, mostly in vain, to stamp out by means of special laws that prohibited Jews from living close to the borders.

After the turn of the century, the tide of terroristic acts again rose, and terrorists succeeded in killing a remarkable number of Russian high officials, prominent among them figures who were known for their hostility to the Jews, including the minister of interior, Vyacheslav Plehve; Grand Duke Sergei, the governor general of Moscow; and Prime Minister Peter Stolypin. Many minor officials, especially policemen, were shot down by terrorists. The role of Jews in these assassinations was unquestionably more important than it had been two decades before. "There was a procession of pale, thin, and often Jewish students to the gallows and to Siberia, after spectacular trials."[57]

The much-discussed role of individual Jews in these assassinations deeply impressed the tsar and his officials. The assassins did not claim to speak for or somehow represent the Jewish population of Russia, and the Marxist organizations, including the Jewish Bund, explicitly rejected terrorism. But such distinctions little impressed those whose suspicion of Jews was already so deep-rooted. In any case, many Jews in Russia only

[55] Baron, *Russian Jew*, 357–8.
[56] Mendelsohn, *Class Struggles*, 2.
[57] Norman Stone, *Europe Transformed, 1878–1919* (Cambridge, Mass., 1984), 214.

feebly disguised their satisfaction at the violent deaths of notoriously anti-Semitic officials. On several occasions those deaths were cause for open celebration in the streets by Jews. In 1902, when Hirsh Lekert, a Jewish shoemaker, was unsuccessful in assassinating Vilna's repressive governor general and was hanged, it was cause for Jewish mourning and the elevation of Lekert to the status of Jewish martyr. Ironically, the terrorists who killed Plehve were part of an organization he had himself help set up, headed by his "secret assistant," Yevno Azeff, a Jew who was chief of the Socialist Revolutionaries' terrorist wing.[58] Stolypin's Jewish assassin was, similarly, a double agent for the police.

The paradoxes of modernization in Russia; the Kishinev pogrom

The diplomatic alliance with France that developed in the early 1890s was supplemented by a large movement of investment capital from France into Russia. Investors, businessmen, and various technical experts from other western countries, prominently Germany, Great Britain, and Belgium, also took an interest in Russia. Foreign investment in Russia soared, from 98 million rubles in 1880 to 215 million in 1890 and to 911 million by the turn of the century.[59] Unavoidably, Russia's leaders began to feel a new dependence on western good will, and in turn western governments exploited that feeling as a form of leverage in dealing with the Russian government.

Jews inside Russia, whether revolutionary socialists or legalistic liberals, were not slow to realize that this was a potentially powerful weapon to be used in their underground war with the tsars. They seized every opportunity to embarrass and expose Russian officialdom. There were many such opportunities. Similarly, Jews outside of Russia, in attempting to aid their beleaguered coreligionists inside the country, did their best to publicize the various malfeasances of Russian officials and to mobilize public opinion in their own countries against tsarist policies. Such was the case especially in countries, such as Germany and Austria-Hungary, that considered Russia to be a potential enemy in war. Even in allied or more friendly countries, such as France or Great Britain, the left was quick to denounce Russia's reactionary internal policies. In the United States, at this point mostly uninvolved in European power politics, many prominent figures actively protested the anti-Jewish stance of the Russian government.[60]

[58] Conor Cruise O'Brien, *The Siege: The Saga of Israel and Zionism* (New York, 1986), 99.
[59] Kochan and Abraham, *Making of Modern Russia*, 227.
[60] For detailed account, see Best, *To Free a People*.

The pogroms of the early twentieth century were the most notorious of the alleged misdeeds of the tsar and his ministers, and the most notorious of them occurred in April 1903 in the city of Kishinev, the capital of the province of Bessarabia (modern Moldavian S.S.R., the region bordering on Romania to the west and the Black Sea to the south). Indeed, this pogrom might be described as the most widely publicized and denounced act of anti-Semitic violence in Europe before 1914. It is now recognized as the first of ever-rising waves of pogroms in Russia, over six hundred that rolled over the country from 1903 to 1906.

The Kishinev pogrom merits careful attention not merely for what it actually was but even more for what it came to symbolize. In bloodshed and destruction to property it exceeded any single previous pogrom in modern times: Forty-five Jews were reported killed, over five hundred injured (apparently including rapes), and approximately fifteen hundred homes and shops were pillaged or vandalized. The Kishinev pogrom was thus responsible for more deaths and injuries in a few days than the hundreds of riots in early 1881.

Jewish sources initially reported over seven hundred dead, a figure that was denounced by Russian officials as typical of Jewish exaggeration and plain falsification. Hyperbole and mendacity do seem to have been a problem on both sides, since the first official news releases denied that there had been any pogrom at all. But as even a friendly American reporter recognized, some of the atrocities initially reported were exaggerated or simply did not occur, and some Jews made false claims in hopes of getting relief money from western Europe and America.[61] On the other hand, rapes were almost certainly underreported, since by traditional Jewish law a wife who is raped must be divorced by her husband. Similarly, a raped unmarried woman is no longer eligible for marriage by an observant Jew. The Jews of Kishinev and Odessa were widely known as the least observant in Russia, so it is difficult to know just how relevant these traditional laws were, but there is little question that rapes were held in special horror and underreported.

The Kishinev pogrom is revealingly understood not only as an expression of the rising social, economic, and ethnic tensions of the period but as part of the underground warfare between tsarist officialdom and the Jews. Exaggerations and indignant denials in the press were part of a publicity war, of a battle to gain the favor of international public opinion. It may seem the height of paradox to describe a pogrom as marking a rising Jewish combativeness. Yet the Kishinev pogrom, in terms of what it symbolized and especially what Jews made of it, became just that.

Kishinev was prominent among the cities that had grown rapidly in the

---

[61] Davitt, *Within the Pale*, 240–1.

preceding decades; like many of them, it had an ethnically mixed population. Some fifty thousand Jews lived there by the eve of the pogrom, close to half of the population. Contemporary accounts of the relations of Jews and non-Jews in the city differ markedly. Some observers claimed that relations were mostly harmonious, that the majority population, made up of Moldavians (ethnically and linguistically close to the Romanians), was easy-going and tolerant, not inclined to ethnic and religious fanaticism. Part of the explanation for this harmony, so it was maintained, was that the social separatism and religious intolerance of the Jews themselves was less prominent here than in other parts of Russia. But the contemporary Jewish historian Dubnov dismissed the non-Jewish population as living in "gloom and crude superstition";[62] non-Jews harbored resentments against the Jews, who constituted a large proportion of the wealthy and professional classes of the city. The Moldavians of the city, numbering slightly more than fifty thousand, were described by some as especially prone to Jew-hatred and barbaric violence.[63] Neighboring Romania had a reputation for being the most anti-Semitic nation in Europe. Ethnic Russians, who held most of the posts of authority in the city, numbered only around ten thousand.

Such contrasting perceptions characterized many contemporary descriptions of the relations of Jews and non-Jews in the rest of Russia. What various observers "saw" derived not only from the enormous variety of conditions in Russia but also from where those observers stood in the propaganda war between the Jews and the regime. Russian conservatives, who wished to emphasize that the Jews were hated for good reason, naturally pointed to the growing social and economic tensions of the time, the rapidly growing wealth of the Jews and their exploitation of the rest of the population. They similarly rejected the assertion of Jewish observers like Dubnov that the hatred was based on religious superstition, on baseless fantasies about Jews, or on government manipulation of popular superstition. Indeed, many Russian officials steadfastly maintained that without government protection, which included the May Laws, there was a rising danger that Russia's Jews would be massacred in great numbers by the resentful lower classes, whether urban or rural.

In contrast, other observers, especially those of liberal persuasion, denied the importance of social and economic resentments against the Jews. Particularly in the countryside, so these observers maintained, the peasants lived mostly in harmony with their Jewish neighbors, even welcomed them as useful elements in the rural economy, since Jews marketed

---

[62] Simon Dubnov, *History of the Jews: From the Congress of Vienna to the Emergence of Hitler*, vol. 5, (New York, 1973; first English edition, 1920), 717. Dubnov says nothing about Jewish attitudes toward Gentiles, religious or not, in Kishinev.
[63] Davitt, *Within the Pale*, 93.

the peasants' produce and brought to the isolated peasant villages commodities they would otherwise lack. According to this interpretation, attacks on Jews occurred only when the credulous peasants were egged on and misled by malevolent agitators, who were often aided and abetted by tsarist officials. Some liberals denied any particular peasant hostility toward Jews; modern racist hostility, at any rate, did not reflect the mentality of the peasantry.

Support for these contrasting interpretations, but with important qualifications, can be found in a careful examination of the Kishinev pogrom. Significantly, Kishinev had been relatively calm in 1881, when anti-Jewish riots had broken out elsewhere in Russia. In the following two decades, the city underwent a transformation, as tens of thousands of new residents, Jews and non-Jews, arrived there. Such rapid population changes are conducive to civil strife in almost any environment. Violent attacks on Jews had since ancient times been stimulated by a rapid increase in Jewish numbers or power.

However, it is far from clear in this instance that the economic role of the Jews in the city was universally or even widely resented. The popular and respected mayor of the city, Karl Schmidt, who had been in office since the 1880s, openly attributed the city's prosperity to its Jews. He noted that in the 1870s the city had been an isolated outpost, "on a level with the average Turkish town." Schmidt maintained that the city owed its rapid rise and prosperity almost entirely to the Jews. He informed an American reporter that "they built up its commerce, organized its banks, developed its general business, and made it the handsome, thriving city it is today."[64]

But these accomplishments, if they were reliably described by Schmidt, undoubtedly generated envy and resentment in some quarters. Nor was Schmidt's openly philo-Semitic attitude to the Jews shared by others in authority, whether in Kishinev or in Bessarabia generally. In the early 1890s there had been a notable incident involving one of the police chiefs in the city, who had been too greedy in collecting Jewish bribes. When the Jews finally tried to resist, he retaliated with fury, applying the May Laws in full severity, as was being done at this time, at any rate, in a number of other cities in the north.[65] The official directly above that police chief, the vice-governor, Ustrugov, let it be known that he considered the Jews of the region to be a "plague."[66]

It was at about this time (1894) that Pavolachi Krushevan, a virulently anti-Semitic journalist, arrived in Kishinev. He established a newspaper, the *Bessarebetz*, which began a scurrilous campaign against the Jews of

[64] Ibid.
[65] Ibid., 96.
[66] Urussov, *Kishinev*, 12–17.

the region, denouncing them both as corrupt businessmen and as socialist agitators. Such charges were common enough in the Russian conservative press, but Krushevan's attacks were unusually venomous and unbridled. It is tempting to conclude that Krushevan was taking cues from Drumont in France, who by 1894 was the object of interested comment throughout Europe. Dreyfus's arrest had occurred early in this year as well; it was an event that naturally concerned France's new ally, Russia. Krushevan, like Drumont, had previously written a popular work of local color,[67] and like Drumont he seemed possessed both by fears of Jewish power and by a belief that greedy Jewish capitalists were destroying sacred local traditions. Krushevan was ostensibly following Drumont's lead as well in introducing, along with modern racist themes, a grab-bag of accusations against the Jews, many medieval in origin, such as the charge of ritual murder.

There were, on the other hand, some revealing differences in the situations of the two. Even at the height of his success, Drumont remained an outsider, a fringe agitator attacking the republican powers-that-be. Krushevan established friendly contacts with the officials of the area and received financial support from them. Some officials, including the vice-governor, Ustrugov, wrote columns for his newspaper. Drumont's journal was an example of the flourishing popular Parisian press of the time, but it was merely one of many. Krushevan's was the only paper of any significance in Kishinev, with a circulation of around twenty thousand. It was delivered to the offices and libraries of the educated, ruling elite, the police officials, army officers, and high church officials.

A U.S. reporter marveled, in observing the quality of the anti-Semitic press in Russia, that "among educated and enlightened Russians one finds anti-Semites who are not one whit less rancorous than the ignorant and benighted mujik [peasant]."[68] Prince Urussov, who would become governor after the pogrom, also expressed dismay at the bigotry to be found among the privileged and educated classes, but he denied that the peasants of the region were hostile to the Jews. Indeed, in his tours of the countryside he found the peasantry either overwhelmingly supportive or without decided opinions about the Jews.[69]

Much like Drumont and the leaders of the Ligue antisémitique, Krushevan tried to gain readers and followers among the middle and lower-middle classes, as well as among the ruling elite. One of his first press campaigns focused on the many Jews who served as municipal employees,

---

[67] Krushevan's work *Bessarabia* seems to have had something in common with Drumont's *Mon Vieux Paris*; cf. Urussov, *Kishinev*, 10.

[68] Davitt, *Within the Pale*, 117.

[69] Urussov, *Kishinev*, 162.

and he succeeded in having many of them dismissed, to be replaced by Christians. Such efforts paralleled not only those of Drumont but those of Lueger in Vienna. Krushevan also succeeded in attracting an especially ardent following among non-Jewish physicians in the city, who were alarmed over the Jewish "takeover" of the medical profession.[70]

In the political arena, Krushevan's activities closely paralleled those of Drumont and de Morès. He organized various anti-Semitic societies in Kishinev. It is tempting to conclude that Krushevan studied the methods of the French Ligue antisémitique in the anti-Semitic riots of 1898. However, not having to worry about police intervention, he had a much simpler task. Almost all observers credit Krushevan with organizing the rioters of 1903. He and his co-workers openly recruited them, to a large degree from the villages around the city. But he also brought in Macedonian and Albanian thugs from afar, armed them all with iron bars, and even provided them with addresses of Jews in the city.[71]

In one regard, Krushevan's organized efforts, benefiting as they did from government benevolence if not open cooperation, appear to have been substantially different from those of the Ligue antisémitique. De Morès made a genuine and substantial contact with a productive element of the Parisian common people, the La Villette butchers, as did Drumont with other elements of the commercial petite bourgeoisie. The Kishinev pogrom has not benefited from the kind of in-depth studies that have been devoted to the French riots of 1898, but the evidence suggests that Krushevan's contacts, aside from those with government officials, were rather with the rabble of Kishinev and surrounding villages, joined by a few seminary students. At any rate, he was not "rousing the masses" so much as organizing and arming outsiders and a marginal riff-raff that did not number more than a couple of hundred. He spread rumors, similar to those of 1881, that a "punishment" of the Jews would be favored by the tsar and not opposed by the local authorities. Also similar to the situation in 1881, others began opportunistically to join in once the riots were under way, since the forces of order were not intervening, and it thus appeared that the rumors were true.

But the participation of those opportunists still did not constitute a popular uprising, and accounts by some Jews in Kishinev of massive popular approval of the violence – even of women and children merrily joining in[72] – may have been hyperbole by those seeking to influence international opinion. A few of these accounts paralleled, with striking and suspicious similarity in certain ghoulish details, stories of the Chmiel-

---

[70] Davitt, *Within the Pale*, 96 ff; Singer, *Russia at the Bar*, 3 ff.
[71] Singer, *Russia at the Bar*, Davit, *Within the Pale*, and Urussov, *Kishinev* – in many ways quite different in tone – agree on these details.
[72] Cf. Singer, *Russia at the Bar*, 13 ff.

nicki massacres of Jews in the seventeenth century. No doubt the shock concerning what happened, which was horrifying enough, and the failure of significant numbers of non-Jews to come to the aid of the Jews further inclined Jewish observers to sweeping condemnations and sensationalism. But many of the more lurid accounts by Jewish witnesses, as we will see, were put into serious doubt by later investigations.

Krushevan ruthlessly exploited genuine tensions in the city (a city that had grown very rapidly and that ostensibly lacked the degree of community and stability that a more long-established and homogeneous city might have had), but one must wonder if he could turn large numbers of established residents into the kinds of monsters who drove nails into people's eyes, disemboweled their pregnant victims, or forced fathers to watch the rape of their wives and daughters. It is plausible that the non-Jewish poor could be made to envy and resent the Jewish rich, and it is likely that Christian middle-class competitors to the Jews, such as doctors, also felt envy and resentment. All accounts emphasize that Christian merchants in Kishinev as elsewhere in Russia feared Jewish competition and that Jews were generally more successful in business. The purported rapacious business practices of Jews were widely denounced.[73] But it can be doubted if the drunken, rampaging mobs in Kishinev were in any fair sense representative of the city's population. The mobs consisted overwhelmingly of young males (certainly the three hundred or so who were later arrested were)[74] – mostly outsiders, unknown in the areas they attacked. Their inhibitions were dissolved not only by drink and the urgings of Khrushevan but by their character as outsiders and by their sense that no legal authority would oppose them. In short, they were not "the people," nor was this a popular uprising.

The feeble response of the authorities was of decisive importance in this pogrom, as in those of 1881. The reasons for this inactivity remain unclear, but there is little doubt that the police forces in Kishinev were woefully understaffed. Police recruits were insufficiently trained, poorly paid, and generally held in low regard by the populace.[75] The situation in the army was even worse; its officers disliked becoming involved in civil disorders, and its recruits were raw and unreliable.

The initial failure to repress the disorders may have been the result of confusion because of ambiguous orders; it may alternatively have reflected covert sympathy by the police and army for the rioters – or a mixture of these, since there was much variety in the response of the forces of order

---

[73] Davitt, *Pale*, 116.

[74] Singer, *Russia at the Bar*, 273.

[75] Cf. Neil Wasserman, "Regular Police in Tsarist Russia, 1900–1914," *The Russian Review*, vol. 44, 1985, 45–68; Shlomo Lambroza, "The Tsarist Government and the Pogroms of 1903–6," *Modern Judaism*, vol. 7, no. 3, Oct. 1987, 292.

in various parts of the city. At any rate, when the mobs perceived that the authorities in some areas of the city were passive, the rumors about the tsar's desire to see the Jews "punished" seemed justified. The rioters became more brazen, and some bystanders began to join in. Once the police and army began to intervene consistently and energetically, the rioting ceased almost at once, suggesting that such a response initially might have prevented the entire tragedy.

Immediately following the pogrom, accusations were made that it had been instigated by the minister of interior, Vyacheslav Plehve, allegedly fulfilling the desires of the tsar. These accusations have found their way into a number of the classic accounts by Jewish historians of the period, Dubnov's and Greenberg's in particular, and they were for many years uncritically accepted.[76] Greenberg stated flatly that "There is no doubt whatsoever that Minister of the Interior Plehve was the instigator of the pogrom."[77] Even recently an otherwise well-informed writer identifies Plehve as the minister who "fomented the Kishinev pogrom," without providing documentation, presumably because Plehve's role is so well known as not to require it.[78] However, as in 1881, the available evidence does not support charges of direct complicity by officials in St. Petersburg. Rather, one finds confusion, incompetence, and purely local complicity.[79]

It was no secret that Plehve by 1903 considered the Jews to be enemies of the regime. He angrily told a Jewish delegation from Odessa that "the Jews in southern Russia constitute ninety percent . . . of all revolutionaries."[80] But he did not directly foment the pogrom. (As noted, Plehve would be assassinated in the following year by a Jewish terrorist. Krushevan, too, would be shot down by a Jewish assassin in the same year, though he survived.[81]) In truth, not even all local officials supported Krushevan's efforts, and some, for example, Mayor Schmidt, were strongly opposed to them. Schmidt in particular insisted that the rioters were not natives of the city, that they were a criminal band brought in by Krushevan.[82] The provincial governor at the time of the riots, von

---

[76] Cf. Wasserman, "Regular Police," and Lambroza, "Tsarist Government," for a discussion of the historiography of this issue.

[77] Louis Greenberg, *The Jews in Russia: The Struggle for Emancipation*, vol. 2 (New Haven, Conn., 1965), 51. Greenberg states that Prince Urussov finally came to agree concerning Plehve's culpability. However, the pages cited by Greenberg from Urussov's *Kishinev* (81–2) do not support that conclusion. Instead, Urussov states that local officials tried to please Plehve; they did not receive orders directly from him.

[78] Bernard Avishai, *The Tragedy of Zionism* (New York, 1985), 63.

[79] One of the most recent and amply documented studies is Lambroza, "Tsarist Government," 287–96.

[80] Baron, *Russian Jew*, 56.

[81] The case would be handled by Gruzenberg, who would later become one of Beilis's lawyers. Cf. Samuel, *Blood Accusation*, 177

[82] Singer, *Russia at the Bar*, 254.

Raaben, was not an anti-Semite, but he was lazy, inefficient, and pleasure seeking; he handed most of his duties over to subordinates, including the openly anti-Semitic vice-governor, Ustrugov. Von Raaben was dismissed in disgrace immediately after the pogrom, and his replacement as governor, Prince Serge Urussov, was known as a moderate liberal and philo-Semite. Urussov was familiar with the ruling circles in St. Petersburg and later commented that Plehve was "too shrewd and experienced to adopt such an expedient" (that is, fomenting a pogrom) in his fight against the Jews,[83] particularly because he was aware of the damage an anti-Semitic riot would do to Russia's international standing.

Urussov, who had privileged access to governmental files, found no evidence of complicity in the riots on the part of any higher officials, although he suspected that the secret police may have played a role; he did not have the same access to their records. Such suspicions were widely shared. Plehve often met western observers and usually impressed them favorably. Even Lucien Wolf, the noted Anglo-Jewish journalist and intransigent critic of Russia's policies at this time, met with Plehve in 1903 and afterward commented favorably on his personal geniality and openness. Plehve emphasized to Wolf that he considered himself a moderate conservative and that he opposed the extreme reactionary, anti-Semitic party in Russia. He noted that as a student in Warsaw University he had personally acted as a peacemaker between his Roman Catholic and Jewish fellow students, adding "to call me an anti-Semite is *une véritable ironie.*"[84]

Pogroms continued after Plehve's death, when he was followed as minister of interior by Prince Sviatopolk-Mirsky (1904–5) and Sergei Witte (1905–6), both of whom were widely recognized as opponents of anti-Semitism. They openly criticized the May Laws and established good working relations with Jewish leaders. In short, popular disorders, whether anti-Jewish or anti-tsarist, were not something that Russian ministers were likely to foment, nor could they easily stop them once they started.

Nonetheless, those who have accused Plehve have not been entirely off the mark even if his responsibility is not direct or easily established. He had one face for one audience, as his angry accusations in meeting the delegation of Odessa Jews demonstrate, another for visitors like Wolf or, more famously, Herzl, who would also confer with him after the Kishinev pogrom. His widely recognized shrewdness came close to tacit acceptance of anti-Jewish excesses, so long as specific orders could not be traced to him.

---

[83] Urussov, *Kishinev*, 15.
[84] Cecil Roth, ed. *Essays in Jewish History by Lucien Wolf* (London, 1934), 68–9.

More to the point, Plehve did little to discourage the climate in which fanatics like Krushevan flourished. Urussov's memoirs note how Plehve, in ministerial meetings, openly spoke of his "war" against the Jews. Urussov was indeed much frustrated with Plehve's stubbornness on the issue. He reported that Plehve, highly capable and rational on most issues of state, would not listen to words defending the Jews.[85] Other observers, such as Witte, expressed similar opinions about Plehve.[86] Many of these observers suspected that Plehve, whatever his personal beliefs, knew the tsar would not condone a more favorable policy in regard to the Jews.

Many Jewish contemporaries recorded the Kishinev pogrom as a turning point for them, although in highly diverse ways. The issue of fighting back was now posed in a most direct and brutal form. Some Jewish activists lamented what they considered the cowardice of the Jews themselves at Kishinev. How could it happen that tens of thousands of adult Jewish males, of a total Jewish population of fifty thousand, were unable or unwilling to fend off several hundred rioters? As one reporter put it, "ninety percent of them [Jewish males] hid themselves, or fled to safer parts of the city for refuge."[87] There were isolated acts of Jewish bravery, as when Jewish butchers routed a gang of rioters in their neighborhood,[88] but such acts were apparently even less notable than the few incidents in which Christians risked life and limb to protect the Jews. In the searing words of the Jewish poet Bialyk, Jews in Kishinev reacted to their attackers "with trembling knees, concealed and cowering. . . . It was the flight of mice they fled, the scurrying of roaches was their flight; they died like dogs, and they were dead!"[89]

It was even more outrageous in the eyes of many activists that the poor suffered the most from the ravages of the pogromists. That was no doubt simply because there were so many poor in the city, but it was also because they were more vulnerable. A few rich Jews were attacked, but for the most part the richest of them "bribed the police with substantial sums of money to gain protection" or left town.[90]

In earlier times such passivity would have been elevated as martyrdom, not denounced as cowardice. But these were new times, with new lessons that young activists were anxious to learn or, really, to have others learn. Not long after the pogrom at Kishinev another broke out at the town of Gomel, which also had a large Jewish population (20,400 Jews in a pop-

---

[85] Urussov, *Kishinev*, 9, 172–5.
[86] Yarmolinsky, *Memoirs of Count Witte*, 190.
[87] Davitt, *Pale*, 170–1.
[88] *Die Judenpogrome in Russland: Herausgegeben im Auftrage des Zionistischen Hilfsfonds in London*, vol. 2 (Cologne, 1910), 12.
[89] Paul R. Mendes-Flohr and Yehuda Reinharz, *The Jew in the Modern World* (Oxford, 1980), 330–1.
[90] Dubnov, *History*, 719.

ulation of 36,800), but there the Jews of the town organized and fought back against the pogromists.[91] But the Gomel pogrom, which finally registered more victims than did Kishinev,[92] has not gone down in history, has not been the subject of searing poetry and indignant commentary like the Kishinev pogrom. Kishinev was the first, the one around which world attention centered, and thus it became a powerful symbol.

A lesson was learned at Kishinev that young Jewish activists already knew by heart and had been reciting for some time: Jews must fight back; Jews must learn to rely on their own resources; Jews must stop being physical cowards. A writer at the time observed that "the Kishinev pogrom ... met a new Jewish people, very sensitive to its human dignity, holding an enormous store of militant energy within itself. . . . In everybody, and before all else, there emerged the thirst for revenge."[93] A generation earlier, after the pogroms of 1881–2, that thirst had been notably weaker.

Approximately three hundred of the rioters at Kishinev were tracked down and arrested. However, the ensuing trial was a disappointment for a number of reasons. Although the governor and vice-governor were dismissed in disgrace and replaced by Prince Urussov, they were not charged with responsibility for the pogrom. Even more outrageous, Krushevan and those who worked with him escaped indictment. Only members of the mob who were accused of violent acts were arrested, not the ringleaders. Moreover, the testimony of many of the Jewish victims was often contradictory and filled with fantastic and implausible details for which no proof could be found. Thus, the lawyers appointed to defend the rioters often had an easy job discrediting Jewish witnesses; indeed, they exposed several of them to ridicule and laughter in the courtroom.

Jewish testimony, as noted, suffered from low regard on the part of the legal officials of the area; Jews themselves joked about how they lied before officialdom, and it was widely believed that Jews conspired in false testimony for their own clannish ends. Even Urussov, who by the time of the trial was being denounced by the anti-Semites for his "sentimental philo-Semitism," observed that Jewish testimony at this trial, as in others, was "often worthless. . . . The Jews, anxious to prove more than what really occurred, get extremely excited, fly into a passion, and exaggerate matters in their somewhat unwarranted testimony." Witnesses who first said they stayed in their cellar for the entire three days of the pogrom then provided graphic details of what they "saw" in other parts of the city; "witnesses identified different persons among the accused as the perpetrators of the murders they saw. . . . A bacchanalian orgy" of contradictory witnesses

[91] Baron, *Russian Jew*, 57; Frankel, *Prophecy and Politics*, 51–4.
[92] Frumkin, *Russian Jewry, 1860–1917*, 32.
[93] Frankel, *Prophecy and Politics*, 143.

arose, "confounding the unhappy judges" and throwing the lawyers for the Jewish plaintiffs into dismay.[94]

Urussov was also disappointed that the lawyers representing the Jewish victims seemed to be primarily interested in the trial as a political platform, a way of gaining political mileage by uncovering the responsibility of officials in St. Petersburg. Bringing the rioters to justice counted for relatively little. The lawyers did little to prepare the witnesses and did not check the reliability, consistency, or credibility of their stories.[95] But the testimony of many of the rioters was scarcely less bizarre and incredible. They freely admitted to "sinning a little;" they had stolen and committed vandalism, but they had not killed anyone, God forbid. Many testified that the Jews were "nice people," with whom they wanted to live in peace, except that now Jewish witnesses were "vexing them with false evidence."[96] Even more bizarre and perplexing testimony would mark the Beilis trial a decade later.

Some of this doubtful Jewish testimony had been published by the foreign press and further elaborated upon, so that the versions that reached foreign audiences were often even more sensational and unreliable.[97] It was, of course, a natural temptation for Jewish organizations, in their frantic efforts to elicit sympathy and funds for the victims and to discredit Russian authorities, to present the most damning, sensational accounts possible. The strict truth was at any rate difficult to obtain because of tsarist censorship; it was understandably easy to believe the worst – and to make maximum use of such worst-case fantasies. An indication of the lengths to which such fabrications about Kishinev ultimately could reach is seen in a letter from Chaim Weizmann (at the time of Kishinev a Zionist activist, later president of the state of Israel) to Dorothy de Rothschild:

> Eleven years ago, . . . I happened to be in the cursed town of Kishinev. . . . In a group of about 100 Jews we defended the Jewish quarter with revolvers in our hands, defended women and girls. . . . We 'slept' in the cemetary – the only 'safe' place, and we saw 80 corpses brought in, mutilated dead. . . . "

Thus Weizmann reports that he personally saw eighty mutilated corpses in a single place, when the death toll for the entire city was later generally recognized to be forty-five. But there is another problem with the account he provides. It is pure fantasy: Weizmann was in Warsaw at the time.[98]

---

[94] Urussov, *Kishinev*, 75–6.
[95] Ibid., 74–6.
[96] Ibid., 44.
[97] Cf. Singer, *Russia at the Bar*, passim. The tone of this volume, as well as the accounts of the atrocities in it, does suggest a lack of caution, if not exaggeration. There are internal contradictions and names are at times confused or badly misspelled.
[98] Reinharz, *Weizmann*, 151.

The pogrom at Kishinev was a terrible, revolting tragedy, but even such matters deserve to be described as dispassionately and accurately as possible. In their indiscriminate attacks on any and all, in their single-minded determination to get the maximum political mileage from the pogrom, some foreign Jewish publicists may have been unfair to individuals and to the general non-Jewish population of Kishinev. The presiding judge, Davydov, for example, was described not only as an anti-Semite (with the name "Davidovich") but as a man who himself had a part in planning the pogroms.[99] That account of him is difficult to reconcile with the account of Prince Urussov, who does not hesitate to condemn Krushevan, Ustrugov, and others but presents Davydov as an old and valued personal friend, a man of great personal honesty and judicial fairness and one who was not even in the area at the time of the pogroms.[100]

That such inaccurate and distorted accounts were published in the West, and that such ostensibly mendacious testimony was given by Jewish witnesses, further envenomed relations between Jews and tsarist officials, indeed between Jews and the rest of the population of Kishinev. Even Prince Urussov expressed frustration with accounts of the pogrom in the press, foreign and Russian. He became finally exasperated with those Jews who "exaggerated their cases to such an extent, and who ornamented them with such extravagant details, that it was absolutely impossible to give full credence to them."[101]

Urussov was also distressed by the tendency of Jewish spokesmen, who on other occasions expressed outrage that Jews were held collectively responsible for the acts of Jewish assassins, to hold the Christian residents of Kishinev collectively responsible for acts by non-Jewish criminals, with whom they by no means identified, even if they lacked the courage – or inclination – to risk their lives in defending Jews.[102] However, by all accounts he was able to soothe these various resentments and generally to reduce tensions in the city. It was impressive testimony to how the riots might have been avoided in the first place had competent and responsible authority been exercised.

Modern anti-Semitism in Russia

The Kishinev pogrom, and the reactions to it, may be seen as a portentous sign of political awakening on both the left and the right, among Jews and among anti-Semites. Mention has already been made of the socialist and liberal parties that were being established in the first years of the

[99] Singer, *Russia at the Bar*, 3–4.
[100] Urussov, *Kishinev*, 74.
[101] Ibid., 24–5.
[102] Ibid., 12.

century. On the right as well, organizational efforts were under way. However, as supporters of autocracy and as enemies of liberal democracy, right-wingers who sought to organize the masses inevitably involved themselves in contradictory activities. That is, mobilizing the people was considered by Russian conservatives to be a western, un-Russian activity.[103] Political parties and agitation by independent groups violated fundamental precepts of tsarist autocracy. In politics as in economic activity, independent initiative was distrusted by the authorities. Nevertheless, such groups began to proliferate, however confused and contradictory they were.

The most important of these right-wing organizations was the Union of the Russian People. It was the organization as well that went the farthest in terms of independent action, even of pressuring the authorities, albeit always under the guise of ardent support for the principle of tsarist autocracy. Those historians who have maintained that the tsar and his ministers consistently and actively conspired to provoke anti-Jewish pogroms have also accused those authorities of working hand-in-hand with the Union and similar organizations (all of which were often grouped under the imprecise designation of Black Hundreds). The Kishinev pogrom was, so these historians argue, only one example of a phenomenon that was endemic. Tsarist authorities used the Black Hundreds to provoke pogroms for reactionary purposes.

However, the coordination between government and organizations like the Union throughout Russia was both less extensive and less effective than such historians have supposed. The Union suffered not only from a confusion as to its goals but also from incompetent leadership and poor organization. It was torn by internal dissension and lacked staying power. For such reasons government officials were often chary of dealing with it.

The Russian right as a whole was scarcely more impressive than newer reactionary-populist organizations like the Union. The integration of traditional conservatism with newer forms of popular agitation was thus notably less developed in Russia than in countries like Austria or France. Partly because of its organizational and ideological weakness, the Russian right was tempted by terrorism and other forms of ruthless, disorganized violence.

Russian nationalist conservatives often come across as unsophisticated, frightened men with little vision. They were given to a kind of mystical pessimism, notably stronger than that of the cultural pessimists in Germany, in the face of powerful forces that they could not successfully resist

---

[103] Cf. Hans Rogger, *Jewish Policies and Right-Wing Politics in Imperial Russia* (Berkeley, Calif., 1986), 188 ff.

or even understand. Of course, the Russian right finally faced a much greater challenge than did the right in western and central Europe. The prospect of a socialist revolution in France, Austria, or Germany, however much it haunted the privileged and propertied, was in fact dim, whereas Russia exploded into revolution in 1905, one in which the institutions of tsarism barely survived. Thus it is not entirely appropriate to compare the relative moderation of anti-Semitic forces in western Europe with the often nihilistic violence of those forces in Russia. Of course, the "moderate" program of western anti-Semites was already in effect in Russia in that Jews there did not enjoy civil equality and were subjected to legislation designed to control them.

The pogroms instigated or exploited by the Union, or the Black Hundreds more generally, cannot be termed a success for the reactionaries. The random, senseless violence finally disgusted nearly everyone, including many anti-Semitic leaders. In Kiev, where the Beilis Affair would take place six years later, the principal participants and beneficiaries appear to have been the criminal elements of the city, much as had been the case in Kishinev. The general population was disgusted by the scenes of brutal pillage and rape.[104] The pogroms were intended to intimidate the left and to terrorize the Jews. Those goals may have been achieved to some degree but at the price of discrediting the regime and the reactionary cause more generally.

Many of those involved in the looting and violence in Kiev, as in Kishinev, were subsequently arrested and sentenced. Local officials in Kiev, or in the rest of Russia, were not uniformly corrupt, especially not those in the legal system. That system was one prominently surviving element of the reforms introduced by Alexander II in the 1860s, and it remained a source of hope and pride for Russian liberals and progressives.[105] It often worked well, or at least more effectively and independently than those accounts that strive to present an unrelieved picture of corruption and autocracy in Russia make clear to their readers.[106]

Nicholas II and the power of international Jewry

The nature of Russia's problems in the generation before World War I would have challenged the ablest of leaders. Nicholas II, who came to

---

[104] Samuel, *Blood Accusation*, 18.

[105] Cf. Kucherov, "Jews in the Russian Bar"; Samuel Kucherov, *Courts, Lawyers, and Trials Under the Last Three Tsars* (New York, 1953).

[106] Again, Dubnov, *History*, may be cited as a major and influential example of an emotional, one-dimensional account, serving polemical purposes rather than trying to provide a balanced picture.

the throne in 1894, turned out to be a weaker and less intelligent anti-Semitic reactionary than his father. Many had harbored hopes that Nicholas would be another reforming tsar, and in his first years he succeeded in giving the impression that he was a gentler, more humanitarian, and more peace-loving man than his father. He enjoyed a favorable treatment in the international press, in part because of his role in convening the International Peace Conference in The Hague, in 1899. Even in the Jewish communities of Russia, rumors spread that Nicholas was a friend of the Jews, that he would at last see to a general reform of the regulations that so oppressed them.

These hopes proved ill founded, for Nicholas soon surrounded himself with avowed Jew-haters. In conversations with his ministers, he habitually used the coarse and insulting Russian term *zhydi* (kikes) rather than the more polite *yevrei* (Hebrews). It gradually emerged that, rather than sympathizing with the Jews, he believed that they themselves were to be held responsible for provoking pogroms.[107]

The full measure of Nicholas II's inadequacies became clear in Russia's war with Japan in 1904–5. Revealingly, he habitually referred to the Japanese as "monkeys," even before Russia went to war with them. Many members of the ruling elite of Russia believed that a foreign war could resolve the country's internal problems by causing Russia's subjects to rally around the flag, and Nicholas, too, soon embraced those beliefs. However, the war with Japan proved a disaster for Russia, one that played a major role in provoking the revolution in 1905. Yet Nicholas showed little understanding of the wave of revolution that swept the country, and he was deeply shocked by the words and actions of the revolutionaries. He refused to believe that his "own people" could be ultimately responsible for such things. It had to be "foreign" people, above all the Jews.

Of perhaps even more pressing concern to Nicholas and his high officials was their belief that a number of powerful Jewish financiers outside of Russia were working ever more openly, diligently, and effectively to deny the country the financial aid it sought. These were not entirely fantasies: A most tenacious and effective enemy of tsarist Russia was Jacob H. Schiff, the American financier. Schiff played a crucial role not only in denying the Russians the bonds they sought in the international market to finance the war, but even more decisively in providing financial support for Japan, which then so humiliatingly defeated Russia.[108] In Great Britain Lucien Wolf, joined by the English Rothschilds, and in central Europe Paul

---

[107] Yarmolinsky, *Memoirs of Count Witte*, 190.

[108] Best, *To Free a People*, esp. 92 ff; Eric Herschler, ed., *Jews from Germany in the United States* (New York, 1955), 62–4; Edwin Black, *The Transfer Agreement* (New York, 1984), 30–3.

Nathan led the efforts to isolate Russia both economically and diplo-matically.[109]

By this time American Jews, especially Schiff, had begun to claim the leading role in international Jewish affairs that would become so important as the century progressed, paralleling the rise of the United States to the status of world power. Schiff delighted in the way that he and other Jews had been able to humble the great Russian Empire. He boasted that after its humiliation in the Russo-Japanese War Russia had come to understand that "international Jewry is a power after all."[110] When Count Witte came to the United States to negotiate the peace treaty with Japan, he was contacted by Simon Wolf, another American Jewish leader and long-time confidant of presidents, who told him that Russia needed two things, money and friends. "The Jews of the world, as citizens of their respective countries, control much of the first. . . . There is no use in disguising the fact that in the United States the Jews form an important factor in the formation of public opinion and in the control of finances. . . . By virtue of their mercantile and financial standing in this country they are exercising an all-potent and powerful [*sic*] influence."[111]

Much has already been said about the image of the powerful Jewish banker, up to this time personified by the Rothschilds. This boasting by Schiff and Wolf was transparently designed to impress the Russians, with the quite explicit goal of pressuring them to cease persecuting Jews inside Russia, but by 1905 such boasts were widely accepted as justified. Observers as different as Winston Churchill and Theodore Herzl firmly believed that international Jewry exercised enormous power in international relations. Even figures who passed as defenders of the Jews at this time made statements about Jewish power that appear today to be both extravagant and tinged with anti-Semitism. Arnold White, who praised Russia's Jews as the "most virtuous and prolific race" in the tsar's empire, wrote that the European press and international finance were in Jewish hands, that Jews "garnered most of the harvest that came from the blood shed by Boer and Briton," and that "the Prime Minister and the Cabinet of England alter their policy and abandon an important bill in parliament at the frown of the Rothschilds." He concluded that Jews were making "monotonous progress toward the mastery of the world."[112]

[109] Zosa Szajkowski, "Paul Nathan, Lucien Wolf, Jacob H. Schiff, and the Jewish Revolu-tionary Movements in Eastern Europe (1903–1917)," *Jewish Social Studies*, vol. 29, no. 1, Jan. 1967, 3–26.

[110] Best, *To Free a People*, 108.

[111] Ibid., 109.

[112] Singer, *Russia at the Bar*, 148–9.

Russia's minister of foreign affairs, Count Vladimir Nikolaevich Lams-dorf, was an ardent and anxious believer in the international power of the Jews. He informed the tsar that the Revolution of 1905 had been "actively supported and partly directed by the forces of universal Jewry," led by the Alliance Israélite Universelle, which had "gigantic pecuniary means" and an "enormous membership."[113] Lamsdorf had long opposed Russia's French alliance and hoped to break it up, to return to an alliance with Germany,[114] and his words partly reflected that agenda. Whether or not Lamsdorf's beliefs about the Alliance Universelle Israélite were justified, there is no question that Schiff was both supporting the Japanese and financing revolutionary socialist agitation among the Russian prisoners of war taken by Japan. His agent in that operation boasted that he had won over thousands of soldiers to revolutionary socialism.[115] In short, one of the more improbable fantasies of anti-Semites, that Jewish capitalists were supporting socialist revolutionaries, had at least this limited basis in fact.

Nicholas was a willing listener to those who spoke of a worldwide Jewish conspiracy against him. Especially after 1905 he was haunted by a fear that the Jews, their non-Jewish agents (which in his mind meant just about anyone on the left), and a network of Jewish financiers who had intimate contacts in the corridors of power in the West were out to undermine tsarist Russia, destroy his empire, and even to kill him personally. Although his mind worked in confused ways, although he entertained many absurd fantasies about the Jews (even that the ritual murder charge had sometimes been justified), he was correct that growing numbers of them, inside Russia and out, Marxist revolutionaries like Trotsky as well as sober financiers like Schiff, did want to destroy him and his empire. He was similarly justified in believing that large numbers of Jews everywhere rejoiced at his misfortunes. The delight felt by Chaim Weizmann (living in England but still a Russian subject) on hearing of Russia's defeats at the hands of Japan "was open and knew no bounds; he cheered the Japanese when they won battles" on land and sea, and remarked that, were he a believing Jew, he would see "the hand of God" aiding the commander of the Japanese forces, Heihachiro Togo.[116]

The Second Aliyah (Zionist immigration) to Palestine (1904–14), num-bering approximately forty thousand, was augmented by young Jews fleeing service in the tsar's armies, while at the same time thousands of

---

[113] Salo Wittmayer Baron, *Steeled by Adversity: Essays and Addresses on American Life* (Philadelphia, 1971), 331–2.
[114] Baron, *Russian Jew*, 62.
[115] Best, *To Free a People*, 107.
[116] Reinharz, *Weizmann*, 263.

Jewish recruits fought at the side of their non-Jewish compatriots against the Japanese. But it is no surprise that Jews of a wide variety of political persuasions and national origins were motivated by a firm determination to combat the policies of Nicholas, to put strong pressure on him to relent in his anti-Semitic stance, or even to bring down his rule. This was, of course, not a concerted, worldwide Jewish conspiracy of the sort supposed by those of Nicholas's mentality; it reflected, rather, a fairly wide international consensus among Jews and also among non-Jews of liberal to socialist persuasion. Still, it fed conspiratorial fantasies in Nicholas's mind and in the minds of many right-wing Russians. They were not wrong in asserting that Jews were a power in the world, and a rising one, particularly because of the influence they could exercise in the up-and-coming United States.

The revolutionary wave of early 1905 resulted in the tsar's granting of a Duma, or parliament, in which twelve Jewish deputies were elected, a remarkable figure in that Jews were a minority in all electoral districts. Moreover, it soon became clear that a majority of the deputies of the Duma was determined to grant the Jews civil equality and to abolish the descriminatory laws they faced.[117] These intentions were soon undermined by waves of counterrevolutionary violence at the end of the year and in 1906, waves that entailed anti-Jewish rioting on a scale that dwarfed the pogroms of Kishinev and Gomel in 1903. Jews were in many places attacked by soldiers who charged them with sympathies for the Japanese, if not with the revolutionaries. This new violence, however, was directed not only at Jews but also other minorities – and most of all at those who supported the revolution, overtly or covertly.

By this time the authority of the tsar and his ministers was much diminished as compared to 1903, as was their ability to control events. The anti-Semites, as fervent supporters of the tsar, naturally elicited both covert and more open support from tsarist officials, both at the local level and in St. Petersburg. Prince Urussov, whose memoirs cast doubt on the role of Plehve in the Kishinev pogrom, made a famous speech in early 1906 on the floor of the Duma denouncing the role of tsarist officials in the pogroms of that year and the year before. Witte, the prime minister, was himself appalled to discover that the secret police had been active in instigating a new pogrom in the town of Gomel.[118]

Even at this point the support of the government for anti-Semitic counterrevolutionaries was not part of a consistent policy, and certainly not one that Nicholas's ministers had all agreed upon. Rather than being committed to sinister and conspiratorial designs in regard to the Jews,

[117] Frumkin, *Russian Jewry*, 47.
[118] Urussov's speech and other related documents may found in E. Séménoff, *The Russian Government and Massacres* (Westport, Conn., 1972; first published, 1907), 149–60.

the government remained, again, divided and confused. With the events of 1905 (the strikes, mutinies, and uprisings), conservatives in Russia began to lose confidence in the ability of the government to maintain order, to protect itself or them. They were thus inclined, temporarily at least, to give support to organizations like the Union of the Russian People.

Unquestionably, the government gave financial support to the Union and to other right-wing, anti-Semitic organizations, and some officials lent other kinds of support to them. Tsar Nicholas openly praised the Union and met its delegations to him. But as one of the most careful historians of the subject has stated, "there were no concerted efforts on the part of the administration to create for itself a popular ally," to link autocracy to a modern mass movement of the right. Peter Stolypin, who would become the prime minister, had no use whatsoever for Dubrovin, a prominent leader of the Union; the government fined his newspaper, and Stolypin finally had him prosecuted for the murder of a liberal deputy.[119]

As noted, the anarchic violence in this period of the various anti-Semitic organizations, the Black Hundreds, finally repelled not only ordinary citizens but many leading conservatives. Many of them "began to recoil with distaste or even horror" from the methods of anti-Semitic mobs.[120] As the threat from the left receded, as public order was again restored, there emerged a wobbly consensus, at least in influential sectors of the conservative right, that such methods should not be used again, that the thugs and murderers of the anti-Semitic mass organizations were as much a threat to public order, and to conservative principles, as were the revolutionaries of the left.

Similarly, the government stepped up its measures against both left and right. Moving against the left, of course, also naturally entailed anti-Jewish measures, given the government's not unfounded belief that Jews constituted a large proportion of the revolutionaries. Stolypin thus not only arrested Dubrovnin but, as minister of interior, "devised one cruel anti-Jewish measure after another,"[121] in most cases merely enforcing with rigor and efficiency anti-Jewish legislation that had previously been ill enforced or subject to bribery and corruption.

In September 1911, when the revolution had been well contained and tsarist authority reestablished, Nicholas visited Kiev to dedicate a statue to his assassinated grandfather, Alexander II. Stolypin, now prime minister, standing a few feet from the tsar in the ceremonies, was shot down by a Jewish anarchist, police spy and double agent.

[119] Rogger, *Jewish Policies*, 215, 217.
[120] Ibid., 219.
[121] Reinharz, *Weizmann*, 341.

This would have been, it would seem, the ideal time for pogroms to break out in Kiev, if indeed such had been what the tsar and his ministers desired. No pogroms occurred. The calm in the city was all the more remarkable since, earlier in that year in Kiev, Mendel Beilis had been arrested and charged with the ritual murder of a young Russian boy.

1. Alfred Dreyfus stripped of his insignia. Reprinted courtesy of the Jewish Museum.

Coucou, le voilà!

La Vérité sort de son puits.

2. *Above:* Poster for *La Libre Parole*. Reprinted with the permission of J. Robert Maguire. Photograph by John Parnell, courtesy of The Jewish Museum, New York.

3. *Opposite:* Heading: "Peekaboo!" Caption: "Truth emerges from its well." Cartoons of the day, alluding to the emerging truth of Dreyfus's innocence, portrayed Truth as a woman emerging from a well. Zola's "well" is, in accordance with conservative thinking, a toilet (see p. 114). From *Psst . . . !,* June 10, 1899. Courtesy of The Jewish Museum, New York; Gift of Charles and Beth Gordon. Photograph by Emily Whittemore.

4. Drumont   5. Esterhazy

6. Henry   7. Picquart

4–7. By permission of the Houghton Library, Harvard University.

8. Zola. By permission of the Houghton Library, Harvard University.

9. Vandalized homes in Kishinev.

10. Mendel Beilis and his family after his acquittal.

11. Mendel Beilis.

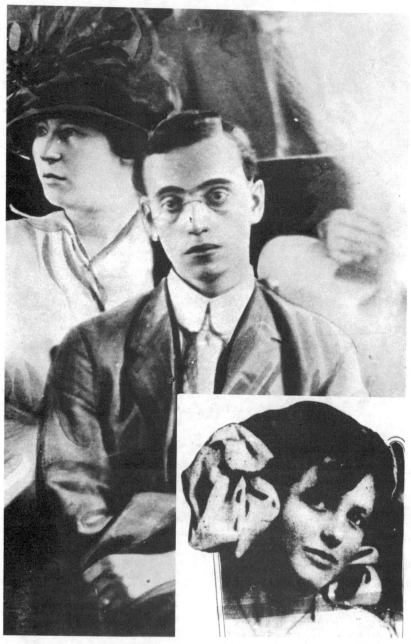

12. Leo and Lucille Frank at the Trial. From a 1915 issue of the *Atlanta Journal* or the *Atlanta Constitution*.

13. *Inset:* Mary Phagan. From the *Atlanta Journal*, April 28, 1913.

14. The lynching of Leo Frank. Courtesy, Georgia Department of Archives and History.

7

Blood libel; the Beilis Affair

The Jewish question is not only a Jewish question but a Russian question; the untruth and corruption uncovered at the Beilis trial is an all-Russian untruth and corruption. (V. G. Korolenko)

Now it becomes glaringly clear how this all-powerful international Jewry organizes its forces, and how incapable the Russian government is in a serious struggle with the Jews. (From a report of a government agent)

I had never imagined...that real Russians, non-Jews...would actually sacrifice their safety and positions, all in the interests of truth. Never will I...forget...these wonderful and enlightened men. [On a separate occasion:] What strange creatures these Russian people are! (Mendel Beilis)[1]

Beilis "case" or Beilis "Affair"?

The Beilis Affair and the Leo Frank Affair stand in the shadow of the Dreyfus Affair and cannot be understood in isolation from it. They occurred after the triumph of the Dreyfusards and Dreyfus's full exoneration, and they resemble the French affair in many ways, above and beyond the obvious ones that in each of them innocent Jews were accused of shocking crimes and that those accusations awakened a torrent of both emotional and opportunistic responses. Without the Dreyfus Affair and the perspectives it opened for anti-Semites, as for the enemies of anti-Semites, these two later affairs would not have developed as they did.

Yet there were many revealing differences in these three affairs. It might be concluded that an affair in Russia like the Dreyfus Affair was a near impossibility, since Russia was a backward country. Its embryonic political forms and the retarded state of its social institutions ostensibly precluded a modern, western-style mobilization of forces. One might simply refer to the Beilis "case," since inside Russia it provoked no mass action on a major, coordinated scale, no violence or marching in the streets, certainly no "Beilisist" or anti-Beilisist movement comparable to the Dreyfusard and anti-Dreyfusard movements. There had, of course, been a chaotic and finally abortive mass uprising in Russia less than a decade earlier, and both the left and right in Russia sought, if rather feebly, to exploit the Beilis case for their own purposes. More generally,

[1] Mendel Beilis, *The Story of My Sufferings* (New York, 1926), 169, 205–6.

174

Beilis's arrest and trial gained the rapt if relatively passive attention of millions of people inside Russia. But it was in the linkage of the case to the international arena, the way that Jews and non-Jews outside Russia reacted to it and attempted to exploit it, that the Beilis case involved "modern" organization and mobilization; it is the international dimensions of the Beilis case that are of particular and not immediately obvious significance. Even inside Russia, news of Beilis's arrest and sufferings in prison seemed to awaken emotions, if not actual deeds, throughout the country of an extraordinary, peculiarly Russian sort. In conjunction with the international dimensions, the distinctive emotional quality of the Beilis case may allow us, after all, to speak of an affair that developed out of the Beilis case.

In both the Dreyfus and Beilis affairs the tendency of many ostensibly factual accounts to present morality plays in black and white, heroes and villains, can be seriously misleading. To be sure, in the Beilis Affair there were more conspicuous examples of conspiratorial villains and blameless heroes than in the Dreyfus Affair, but the lines were by no means sharply drawn between Jew and non-Jew or even between philo-Semite and anti-Semite, for a number of non-Jews and even anti-Semites became active and influential defenders of Beilis. Some of Beilis's most important defenders included men whose anti-Semitism was more open and certainly more ideological than that of Picquart. In all of the affairs this curious assemblage of Gentile defenders suffered intimidation and death threats.

German Jews and Jewish organizations in both Germany and Austria played a decisive role in igniting the international agitation on Beilis's behalf, and that agitation outside Russia had a significant impact within the country. Yet even those German-Jewish leaders considered it of absolutely decisive importance to get non-Jews involved, especially eminent personalities, and they succeeded brilliantly in that goal.[2] Their success represented in a paradoxical way yet another kind of growing Jewish power, the power to mobilize influential Gentiles in defense of Jews – one that both impressed and dismayed anti-Semites. German Jews and Jewish organizations were able to set into action an international affair out of something that might otherwise have remained localized and of relatively minor significance. They, along with U.S. Jewish leaders, had already learned, in the international outrage expressed over the pogroms between 1903 and 1906, a great deal about how to apply pressure on

---

[2] Soza Szajkowski, "The Impact of the Beiliss Case on Central and Western Europe," *American Academy for Jewish Research, Proceedings*. vol. 31, 1963, 197–218, emphasizes the role of German Jews who saw in the Beilis case an opportunity to discredit Russia and possibly disrupt the Franco-Russian alliance. Szajkowski's perspective is somewhat different from mine; he emphasizes that "almost nothing was done without Jewish intercessions" (216).

Russia and to bring discredit upon her in the international community. Similarly, they had learned much inside their own countries since the late 1870s about how to organize against the anti-Semites.[3]

The role of German and U.S. Jews stands out in part because the Jewish community in Kiev remained extremely cautious in the course of the Beilis Affair. One young Jewish activist whose writings are a major source on the Beilis affair, having worked with Jewish leaders in the town, subsequently denounced them as "indecisive and timid." They "were AFRAID to wage open war" against the authorities.[4] However, his words must be evaluated with care. One detects in them echoes of young Léon Blum's disgust with the placid French Jewish bourgeoisie, or Bialyk's lament concerning the cowardice of Jews at Kishinev. There were signs of a generational conflict, as well as one of class and political persuasion, between those who wanted to work quietly behind the scenes and those who wanted an open fight, who preferred to take the issue to the streets. At any rate, other young Jews who had first-hand knowledge of the situation in Kiev were more charitable. One of them later rejected the charges of cowardice as "entirely without foundation"; it was necessary, he emphasized, in these "terribly dangerous years" to be cool-headed and "responsible."[5]

The situation for Jews in Kiev was not really comparable to that of Jews in Paris. It was even more delicate than elsewhere in Russia, for Kiev was considered a holy city, with special meaning for Orthodox Christianity. Therefore, although it was within the Pale of Settlement, it was in principle forbidden for Jews to settle in it. Those Jews allowed to reside in Kiev were both privileged and vulnerable, much as were those who were allowed to move outside the Pale. In the spring of 1910, as part of Stolypin's crackdown on Jewish dissidence, twelve hundred Jewish families were forced out of the city.[6] In such an atmosphere, the Jewish residents of Kiev were inclined to be more reticent than elsewhere in the Pale; they were undoubtedly more closely watched and knew that their privileges might easily be revoked. Jews in this holy city, especially the younger generation, were not immune to the new, more combative spirit that characterized Jews everywhere in the country. But in comparison to the Jews in cities like Odessa, Gomel, or other rapidly growing

---

[3] Cf. Richard S. Levy, *The Downfall of the Anti-Semitic Political Parties in Imperial Germany* (New Haven, Conn., 1975); Jehuda Reinharz, *Fatherland or Promised Land: The Dilemma of the German Jew* (Ann Arbor, Mich., 1975); Marjorie Lamberti, *Jewish Activism in Imperial Germany* (New Haven, Conn., 1978).

[4] Arnold D. Margolin, *The Jews of Eastern Europe* (New York, 1926), 242.

[5] J. M. Machover, "Reminiscences personelles," in L. Schneersohn, ed., *Du Pogrom de Kichinev à l'Affaire Beilis* (Paris, n.d.), 90–1.

[6] Jehuda Reinharz, *Chaim Weizmann: the Making of a Zionist Leader* (Oxford, 1985), 341.

cities with large Jewish populations, the Jews of Kiev were understandably inclined to caution.

It says something about the contradictions and puzzling intricacies of the scene in Russia by 1911 that in holy Kiev, "forbidden" to Jews, the Jewish population numbered roughly 5,000, around 1 percent of the total of 505,000. That was a much smaller proportion than in other large cities in the south, such as Odessa (200,000 out of 506,000 in 1911),[7] or middle-sized ones like Kishinev, but Jews in Kiev, even after Stolypin's measures against them, were still more numerous than in Moscow or St. Petersburg, especially after the mass expulsions that they had experienced in the 1890s. Moreover, Kiev's overall rate of growth had been comparable since the 1880s to that of new cities like Kishinev, with all the attendant problems of rapid growth. With this mere 1 percent of the population, Jews, supposedly not allowed to settle in Kiev, made up a larger proportion of the total than did the Jewish population of many cities in western Europe, where they could settle freely. Again, one notes how the absolute and relative number of Jews in Russia gave the Jewish Question a pervasively and qualitatively different character there.

Origins of the ritual murder charge in Kiev

The Beilis Affair began with the discovery, on March 19, 1911, of the body of thirteen-year-old Andrei Yushchinsky in a cave on the outskirts of Kiev. He had been killed eight days earlier. His face was beaten beyond recognition, and forty-seven stab wounds were counted on the body, thirteen of them purportedly inflicted to drain his blood. A pillowcase soaked with blood and containing traces of semen was found nearby. A large crowd of mourners attended the last rites of Andryusha ("Andy," as he was always affectionately called). But this was not to be an ordinary funeral: Along the funeral route and at the grave, leaflets were strewn among the mourners, announcing, "The kikes [*zhydi*] have tortured Andryusha to death!" The leaflets contained the old charge that Jews use the blood of Christian children to mix with their Passover matzot. The breathless text ended with the plea, "Avenge the unhappy martyr! It is time! It is time!"[8] These pamphlets resembled those distributed in Kishinev before the pogrom in 1903 and in the pogroms following the Revolution of 1905. However, by 1911 pogroms were no longer "tolerated" by the authorities. There is some evidence that Vladimir Golubev, a leader of the Union of the Russian People in Kiev, was organizing forces for a

---

[7] B. R. Mitchell, *European Historical Statistics, 1750–1975* (New York, 1981), 87–8.
[8] George Kennan, "The Ritual Murder Case in Kiev," *The Outlook*, Nov. 8, 1913; cf. Maurice Samuel, *Blood Accusation* (New York, 1966), 17.

pogrom at this time but was specifically warned against it by figures in the government with whom he had contact.[9]

Rumors concerning the crime spread far and wide in the spring and early summer of 1911, and anti-Semites throughout Russia angrily demanded that the purported ritual murderers of Andryusha be captured, but the general populace remained calm. It was not until a full four months after the murder that Mendel Beilis, the manager of a brick factory situated close to the cave where the mutilated body had been found, was arrested and charged with the crime. Initially the indictment was for murder alone, but subsequently the charge of ritual murder was added as the plans of the prosecution took shape – or, more accurately, as they shifted about uncertainly.

Differences from the Dreyfus Affair were from the beginning rather striking. Dreyfus was immediately believed by the overwhelming majority of people in France to be guilty, and French newspapers both spread and confirmed that mistaken belief. But in the Beilis case a large number of observers both inside the government and outside it had doubts about his guilt, whether the charge was simply murder or murder for ritual purposes. Those who genuinely believed him guilty seem to have been a mere fringe of fanatics. Even in their case one may doubt that sincere conviction, as opposed to political calculation, played a decisive role.

Whereas Dreyfus was convicted by a nearly unanimous popular press, incredulity concerning Beilis's guilt was expressed from the beginning by prominent newspaper editors and other influential public figures, keeping doubt alive rather than entrenching belief. Leaders on the left in Russia were particularly alert to how the government and its right-wing supporters might try to use a spectacular trial against a Jew for reactionary purposes. In that regard, the example of the Dreyfus Affair merely provided proof for left-wing Russians of the wider and more modern application in the West of a device that was all too familiar in their own country.

Some right-wing newspapers in Russia did attempt to exploit Beilis's arrest, to use the case to arouse the population against the Jews. In the immediately preceding years influential figures in the government had allocated large funds in support of a "literary" campaign against the Jews, as distinguished from the earlier recourse to violence. But the language in that campaign was at times one of extreme brutality, describing Jews as vermin worthy of extermination, and dredging up the old charges of ritual murder. The charges against Beilis may be seen as part of that campaign, as a different, less violent approach in the "war" waged by the tsarist government against its Jewish enemies. From the end of 1905 to 1916 the government "permitted the printing and distribution of over 14

---

[9] Alexander B. Tager, *The Decay of Czarism: The Beiliss Case* (Philadelphia, 1935), 45.

million copies of some 3,000 anti-Semitic books and pamphlets." The tsar himself allegedly contributed over 12 million rubles from his private fortune toward the dissemination of hate literature, including the *Protocols of the Elders of Zion*.[10]

To believe in Dreyfus's guilt and in the uprightness of the army became articles of urgent belief for millions in France; to believe in Beilis's guilt and the uprightness of the tsarist authorities was not so urgent for great numbers of Russians. If anything, an opposing tendency prevailed, given the deep discredit that anti-Semitic violence had earned in the past eight years. At any rate, the evidence against Beilis was from the beginning almost ludicrously weak, and the identity of the real murderers soon became reasonably clear.

Another difference in the two affairs was that Beilis was never found guilty, and thus no campaign developed to free an unjustly convicted man. Although he was imprisoned for twenty-six months awaiting trial and underwent tribulations in jail easily comparable to those suffered by Dreyfus on Devil's Island, Beilis was found innocent in the only trial that was held. The prosecuting attorneys forwarded the case with hesitations, frequent revisions, and long delays. Their uncertainties were all too apparent, as were the differences among them. Some prominent right-wingers, for example, the notorious Bessarabian anti-Semite Vladimir M. Purishkevich, openly fretted about the precedent of the Dreyfus Affair, since obviously that confrontation had not turned out well for the right in the long run. But others pressed on recklessly, pressuring the prosecution.

Whereas it took nearly four years for the Dreyfus case to become an affair, the arrest of Beilis provoked a relatively rapid rallying to his defense both inside Russia and abroad. The issues for Beilis's defenders were posed with relative clarity, as compared with the confused situation in France from 1894 to 1898. Protest manifestoes quickly appeared, an impressive outpouring of sympathy for Beilis and of indignation concerning what the legal authorities were attempting to put over on the Russian public. This activity, however, remained largely focused on obtaining legal remedy, on freeing Mendel Beilis, not on a larger political agenda.

On the international level, however, political motives soon mixed with legal and humanitarian-idealistic ones. Beilis's arrest offered enemies of tsarist Russia, and above all Jewish enemies, an irresistible opportunity to further discredit the already much discredited regime and in so doing to isolate Russia further from the world community and even, conceivably, to shake the Franco–Russian alliance. Jews had already played a

[10] Salo W. Baron, *The Russian Jew Under Tsars and Soviets* (New York, 1987), 61.

major role in the humiliation of the tsar and his ministers in 1904 and 1905, and many of them now perceived a further opportunity.

Jews in Germany and in Austria-Hungary, worried as they were about their countries' "encirclement" by France and Russia, took the lead in organizing international protest. Jews in France, in spite of the precedent of the Dreyfus Affair, were reticent to take part in the international agitation against France's valued Russian ally.[11] It will be recalled that even in the early 1890s, when the treaties between Russia and France were being worked out, French Jews had been charged with hostility to the alliance because of their outrage at the anti-Semitism of the Russian government. It is this international dimension of the Beilis case that helps to explain its enormous notoriety, a notoriety that the other ritual murder cases before 1911 failed to achieve. But that notoriety had to do as well with the larger, more blatant role played by the Russian authorities in this case.

The goals of the prosecution and the government

Again, the question must be asked, How much did this case represent a conscious conspiracy of the government? Was there a plan, reaching to the tsar, to convict Mendel Beilis of ritual murder? And once again, the evidence to support such charges is weak. As one of the more perceptive scholars of the matter has stated it, "There was no grand design; there had not even been a tactical plan."[12] On the other hand, there were conspirators of a sort, and some of them figured high in the Ministry of Justice, but issues were not so clear-cut, the conspirators did not work so smoothly as has often been assumed, and the tsar himself was not directly involved, whatever his indirect responsibility.

Exactly who was trying to frame Beilis, and why? The answer, insofar as it can be satisfactorily sorted out and simply stated, is that a few of Nicholas's officials, such as the archreactionary and unprincipled minister of justice, I. G. Shcheglovitov, concluded that the tsar would be pleased if a Jew in Kiev were convicted of ritual murder. In so pleasing the tsar, such men believed that they could advance their careers.

Shcheglovitov, it should be noted, was at this time playing havoc with Russia's esteemed legal system; "Shcheglovitov justice" became synonymous with injustice. However, the entire government was not involved, nor were even all officials in the Ministry of Justice. Indeed, the tsar

---

[11] Cf. Szajkowski, "Beiliss Case."

[12] Hans Rogger, "The Beilis Case: Anti-Semitism and Politics in the Reign of Nicholas II," *Slavic Review*, vol. 25, no. 4, Dec. 1966, 629. This article has been reprinted in Hans Rogger, *Jewish Policies and Right-Wing Politics in Imperial Russia* (Berkeley, Calif., 1986).

himself, while personally believing that Jews committed ritual murder, eventually concluded that Beilis was not guilty and openly expressed satisfaction when Beilis was found innocent.[13] Even the imperial couple's trusted "friend," the notorious monk Rasputin, did not think Beilis guilty, did not support the trial, and did not endorse the related persecution of religious and national minorities in Russia.[14]

Stolypin, the chief minister to the tsar at this time, was almost certainly not privy to plans to use the Beilis case for larger political motives, if such plans existed beyond the secretive and ill-coordinated initiatives of men like Shcheglovitov. Those who have believed in large-scale conspiracies in the Beilis case as in the various pogroms of 1903–5 have asserted that "officials" in St. Petersburg hoped that an emotional ritual murder trial at this time, one that could awaken and intensify suspicions of Jews in Russia, would lead to a defeat of the left in the forthcoming elections to the Duma, because the Jews and the left were so closely identified. Some right-wingers outside of the government may have reasoned in such ways,[15] but in 1911 Stolypin, even less than Plehve in 1903, was not likely to have tried something so outlandish,[16] even if he was willing to exploit bigotry and chauvinism in more subtle ways. A ritual murder trial was simply not his style. Stolypin was "no anti-Semitic firebrand."[17] On the other hand, he knew of the anti-Semitic feelings of those around him and did little to discourage their machinations in regard to the Jews. Even if he had been so inclined, he must have recognized the futility of open opposition to such men, given Nicholas's own well-known hostility to the Jews, his belief that they were bent on destroying the country and even on killing him.

Political calculations concerning what might discredit the Jews and their allies mixed in obscure ways with the machinations of the local branch of the Union of the Russian People in Kiev. It says something about the stature of the Union in Kiev that it was led by a nineteen-year-old student, Vladimir Golubev, who had a history of mental illness. It was he who was behind the leaflets distributed at Andryusha's funeral, and it was apparently he who lobbied most persistently among certain officials in favor of an accusation of ritual murder, as opposed to simple murder. That men of Golubev's stripe could ingratiate themselves with and then put pressure on local law-enforcement officers – and even on higher government officials – was the despair of Russia's more conscientious leaders. Sergei Witte, chairman of the Council of Ministers from October

[13] Rogger, "Beilis Case," 622.
[14] Maurice Samuel, *Blood Accusation* (New York, 1966), 277 (n. to p. 102)
[15] Ibid., 139 ff.
[16] Rogger, "The Beilis Case," 616.
[17] Ibid., 617.

1905 to January 1906, had this to say of the Union of the Russian People: "It is the embodiment of nihilistic patriotism, feeding upon lies, deceit, slander, savage and cowardly desperation. . . . Its leaders are unhanged villains. . . . And the poor, misguided Tsar dreams of restoring Russian grandeur with the aid of this party!"[18] Stolypin at times took measures against such "unhanged villains," but his efforts failed to intimidate the Union or other Black Hundreds organizations, in part because those organizations continued to get encouragement from other government officials.

Still, Golubev and other extreme right-wingers never held the government captive. His influence, and that of other reactionaries who pressed for a blood-ritual trial, remained of a more indirect and uncertain kind. Golubev did not have an easy time of it at first. He ran into resistance not only from the investigating magistrate, Vasili I. Fenenko, but also from other conscientious police officials in Kiev, most importantly from a Detective Mishchuk, who, in examining the evidence of the murder, concluded that Beilis could not be guilty. Like many police officials, Mishchuk detested the Union, which he knew was in league with criminal elements of the population. Like many respectable Russians, he wanted nothing to do with blood-ritual charges. The presence of men like Fenenko and Mishchuk on the local level, as the Beilis Affair began to unfold, was probably decisive to the eventual outcome of the case. They uncovered crucial information and put it into the public record. They also found clues that pointed to the real culprits, much as Picquart had done in France.

Golubev encountered greater receptivity, however, with the prosecutor of the Kiev Appellate Court, N. Chaplinsky, who seems to have concluded that he might forward his career by working with this young fanatic (or perhaps he feared the damage that Golubev might do to his career; both factors may have influenced his decisions). Chaplinsky tried to undermine Mishchuk's findings and to introduce false evidence, but his efforts were not particularly successful. Mishchuk stubbornly resisted, in spite of heavy pressure put on him. Like Picquart, he was subsequently arrested on trumped-up charges and sentenced to jail. Still, those who wanted to prove Beilis guilty did not succeed in destroying or discrediting all the evidence initially collected by Mishchuk, nor was the false evidence they patched together credible or consistent.

Mishchuk was led to the conclusion that the murder had been committed by a criminal gang associated with a colorful underworld character, Vera Cheberyak. Andryusha, who was a playmate of Vera's son, apparently threatened to reveal to the police information about robberies com-

[18] Samuel, *Blood Accusation*, 19.

mitted by Vera and her gang. They killed him and then mutilated his
body in order to make it appear a ritual murder. This same gang had
reaped a great harvest in the looting associated with the pogroms of 1905
and 1906. Mishchuk suspected that they hoped for a repeat performance.[19]

Reactions to Beilis's trial

After postponements by the prosecution lasting over two years, reflecting
its fumbling efforts to patch together a believable indictment, Beilis was
finally charged with ritual murder and brought to trial in the summer of
1913. At this point, too, vociferous dissents were registered by several
of the judges who were called to review the indictments. These judges,
not unlike those presiding at Kishinev a decade before, were themselves
"never noted for any great sympathy for the Jews." But they were uncomfortable that a case so lacking in evidence against the accused should
ever have come so far.[20] A comment made about French magistrates by
a historian of the Dreyfus Affair is applicable here: "Many of the judges
were anti-Semites but incapable of accepting any random infraction of
the law in the service of their prejudice."[21]

Reporters from most of the major nations of the world attended the
trial, and some of Russia's best legal minds volunteered their services to
defend Beilis. The courtroom was packed with over a thousand spectators,
including a large contingent of high-ranking officials and military men.[22]
The trial lasted six weeks and did not disappoint reporters in search of
colorful copy. During much of the summer of 1913, as the popular short-
story writer and liberal journalist Vladimir Korolenko wrote, "Never has
. . . a trial in Russia . . . attracted, to so great a degree, the attention of
the broad masses. . . . The Beilis Affair has pushed aside all other internal
and foreign affairs." Korolenko also expressed a belief that the Beilis trial
had led Russia's population to understand that "the Jewish question is
not only a Jewish question but a Russian question; that the untruth and
corruption uncovered at the Beilis trial is an all-Russian untruth and
corruption. . . . "[23] His opinion was seconded by many other luminaries
in Russia.

By this time, interest and concern outside of Russia had also spread
widely. By the spring of 1912 over two hundred prominent intellectuals

[19] Margolin, *Jews of Eastern Europe*, 192–3. Mishchuk was himself taken in by false evidence
given to him by criminals. His mistakes were used as a pretext to dismiss him and then
sentence him to jail.
[20] Samuel, *Blood Accusation*, 209–10.
[21] Jean-Denis Bredin, *The Affair: The Case of Alfred Dreyfus* (New York, 1986), 366–7.
[22] Beilis, *My Sufferings*, 133.
[23] Samuel, *Blood Accusation*, 243.

in Germany had signed a protest manifesto against the trial of Beilis. The signatories included Thomas Mann, Gerhardt Hauptmann, and Werner Sombart, the last of whom, interestingly, was considered an anti-Semite by many Jews at the time, and in fact would later become a Nazi sympathizer. An even more impressive list of protesters soon appeared in Great Britain, including the archbishops of Canterbury and York, the speaker of the House of Commons, the heads of colleges in Oxford and Cambridge, and scores of other intellectuals, religious leaders, and prominent citizens. A similar manifesto from France appeared at about the same time, although it elicited a narrower support since the French right, unlike the German right, hesitated to attack France's ally. From the United States, an appeal to Nicholas personally, signed by seventy-four leaders of various Christian denominations, appeared in the opening month of the trial. Mass meetings, demonstrations, and ardent protest speeches occurred in nearly every European country.[24]

In Kiev and in Russia as a whole, many ordinary people, by no means only or even mostly Jews, became engaged on Beilis's behalf. Although there was no full-fledged Beilisist movement, collections were taken up among common workers to help Beilis's family and to pay for his legal expenses. Even inside the jail Beilis encountered much sympathy from his fellow prisoners. However, one of them turned out to be a police agent, planted in the jail by the prosecution to win over Beilis's confidence. He later offered testimony that Beilis paid him to poison witnesses who might testify against him.[25] This was but one of a series of such efforts by the prosecution to build a case against Beilis.

The case for the prosecution

Mendel Beilis was apparently the only even remotely plausible Jew whom the prosecution could find who might have committed the crime, since he worked in the brick factory near where Andryusha's body was found. But the case the prosecutors finally made against him in the courtroom fell apart, often spectacularly. Their first and major mistake was in believing they could rely on a combination of prejudice and intimidation to frame this particular Jew. Mendel Beilis was a modest person, but he seems to have been one of the most respected, even beloved men in his neighborhood. That neighborhood, it should be noted, was composed entirely of Gentiles, since Beilis and his family, benefiting from special privileges, did not live in the Jewish districts of the city. The prosecution

[24] Ibid, 232–3.
[25] Ibid., 77–8.

was repeatedly frustrated in its efforts to get hostile testimony against Beilis. Time and again, those who knew him had only praise for "our Mendel," as they frequently put it. A number of the witnesses who had earlier offered incriminating testimony recanted on the witness stand, at times revealing official intimidation and bribery.

The prosecution had several goals, the first of which was to prove Mendel Beilis guilty of killing Andryusha. That entailed trying to discredit the ample evidence pointing to Vera Cheberyak and her band as guilty of the crime. The second goal, finally the more important one, was to prove that the murder was ritual in nature, even if it could not be proven that Beilis committed it, since proof of a ritual murder would supposedly blacken the name of the Jews collectively. That in turn would weaken the left, with its many Jewish leaders and its program of ending Jewish legal disabilities in Russia.

To prove that Beilis had murdered Andryusha in order to collect blood for matzot entailed, first of all, demonstrating that Beilis was an observant Jew, if possible a fanatically observant Jew, performing services (that is, getting Christian blood) for other observant Jews. The strategy of the prosecution may not have been quite so outlandish and improbable as it at first appears, since even among those who had no particular hatred of Jews, even among Jews themselves, there was uneasiness about the odd and unstable demeanor of some hasidim, to say nothing of the notorious reputation for corruption of some hasidic leaders. A few observers, again including Jews, expressed the opinion that even if the charges of ritual murder had no foundations in Jewish law, who could tell what some sort of wayward hasidic sect might conceivably have done.

Subjects of the Russian Empire were familiar with aberrant and bizarre activities among the country's Christian sects. Something comparable among the Jews, some criminally fanatical hasidic sect, did not seem wholly implausible, even if not a shred of credible evidence was ever produced for the existence of such a sect. Surrounding the figures of the hasidic "wonder rabbis" was an aura of magical powers, believed in not only by their own followers but even by the Russian peasants, who would, for example, bring their sick children to a *tsaddik* (a hasidic religious leader), hoping for a miraculous cure.[26] Such men, it was widely believed, used blood and other body fluids in various medicines and potions.

Efforts to prove that Beilis was a religious fanatic ran into large difficulties, however, for he was not even an observant Jew. A problem in this regard did arise for a short time, and perhaps here both Beilis and his defense counsel made a tactical error. Both believed that they had to

---

[26] Mark Zborowski and Elizabeth Herzog, *Life Is with People: The Culture of the Shtetl* (New York, 1969; first ed., 1952), 221.

demonstrate his utter ignorance of traditional Judaism. In striving to counter the charges of the prosecution that he was a fanatic, they made a few false and indeed unbelievable claims, arousing legitimate suspicions concerning their truthfulness. Jews did not have a good reputation in legal circles; as described above, they were believed by many magistrates to be inveterate liars and falsifiers of evidence. Even the investigating magistrate, Fenenko, who, along with Detective Mishchuk, ultimately played an important role in establishing the truth about the murder of Andryusha, initially suspected that Beilis was hiding something.

Fenenko may have had good reason, in his first interrogations of Beilis, to suspect that Beilis was not telling him the truth. For example, Beilis insisted that he, far from being a fanatical hasid, did not even know what a hasid was. Even more unbelievable, he said that he did not know what the *afikoman* was in the Passover Seder.[27] (It is a piece of matzo, taken from the middle of the three matzot on the table; it was customarily hidden from the children, and the child who found it was given a reward.) Beilis's father was a strictly orthodox Jew and had raised his children in the faith. A man raised as a Christian might have as plausibly claimed that he had never heard of the Christ child in the manger. In his autobiography Beilis wrote that he, too, had always been deeply concerned that his children get a Jewish upbringing and education. Such a man could not have remained so prodigiously ignorant about elementary matters of Judaism. These transparent falsehoods, such obvious stonewalling, at the beginning of his interrogations did not help Beilis's case.

But Beilis's initial missteps were finally small matters, not major problems, in the interrogation. The extent to which Beilis followed Jewish tradition cannot easily be determined from the evidence, but a key fact that emerged in the trial was that he had been working in the factory on the day that Andryusha was murdered, as his fellow workers amply confirmed. That day also happened to be the Jewish Sabbath, when work is strictly forbidden to observant Jews. Beilis's situation was in fact peculiar, and one not possible for a strictly observant Jew, for he was the only Jew at the brick factory. It was owned by the rich Jewish manufacturer Jonah Zaitsev, who was able to arrange, because of his special privileges as a Merchant of the First Guild, for Beilis to live on the grounds of the factory, in a district normally prohibited to Jews.

Their isolation from other Jews apparently did not mean that Mendel and his family lived in a tense relationship, surrounded by a hostile population. Their contacts with non-Jews seem to have been overwhelmingly harmonious. Even the Russian Orthodox priest in the area was on friendly terms with the family, since Beilis had arranged that funeral

[27] Beilis, *My Sufferings*, 46, 89–90.

processions be permitted to go through the brickyards on the way to the cemetery, a permission that had been denied by the Christian owner of an adjoining property.

In his autobiography, *The Story of My Sufferings*, Beilis offers ample testimony about a number of close friendships he maintained with conservative Russians, even with members of the Union of the Russian People, the very group whose leader, Golubev, was lobbying to have Beilis convicted of ritual murder. One of these friends, after Beilis's arrest, boarded the tram-car he was riding on the way from the court house to jail, embraced him, and said, "Brother, don't lose spirit! I am myself a member of the Double-headed Eagle [the Union], but I tell you that the stones of a bridge may crumble but the truth will out."[28] In the pogroms of 1905 and 1906 in Kiev, members of the Union had sent word to Beilis that he and his family would not be touched, and they were not.[29] Somehow nineteen-year-old Golubev had been subsequently able to counter such attitudes in the councils of the Union in Kiev.

The effort to prove that there had been a ritual murder, whether or not Beilis was the culprit, was also fraught with difficulties. The prosecution felt obliged to prove that ritual murders were a common occurrence in Russia, that Jews had frequently killed Christians for their blood throughout history, and that ritual murder was integral to Judaism. There was, however, some hedging and confusion on this last point. At times the prosecution seemed to assert that only a few Jewish sects used Gentile blood for ritual purposes, not all religious Jews. In a related way, the prosecution had to come up with evidence that proved Andryusha's wounds had been inflicted to collect his blood for ritual purposes, not simply to kill him.

The prosecution gathered much literature and "expert" testimony concerning ritual murder by Jews throughout history. Evidence about the suspicious nature of Andryusha's wounds was also introduced. One of the more colorful "experts" was Father Pranaitis, a defrocked Catholic priest and self-proclaimed authority on Jewish practices. It was characteristic of the frailty of the prosecution's case that no Orthodox priests could be found who were willing to testify in support of the charge of ritual murder, even though the Orthodox Church in Russia was anything but friendly to Jews. It apparently became necessary to resort to the likes of Pranaitis. He proceeded, through eleven hours of testimony – the judge tried in vain to get him to stick to the point – to paint a picture of Jews who, "hiding behind a human exterior, [were] ghouls, vampires, and fiends." He provided endless lists of uses to which Jews put Christian blood, quite

[28] Ibid., 49.
[29] Samuel, *Blood Accusation*, 59.

aside from Passover use.[30] It was a performance straight out of the Middle Ages, or perhaps a caricature of them.

Father Pranaitis claimed to know about such things because he had devoted deep study to the Talmud. The claim was transparently bogus, since his knowledge of the appropriate languages was thin. He was forced to answer "I don't know" to question after question about talmudic writings. The defense lawyers set a splendid trap for him by asking "When did Baba Bathra live and what was her activity?" Again, Pranaitis answered "I don't know." *Baba* in Russian is "grandmother," but in fact Baba Bathra is not a person at all; it is one of the best-known tractates of the Talmud, dealing with property laws, as even a beginning student of it knows. If an American defense lawyer had asked a similar "expert" on American history, "Who lived at the Gettysburg Address?" and received an answer of "I don't know," the effect would have been about the same. The Jewish members of the audience broke out into uncontrolled laughter.[31]

Conclusively discrediting the evidence that Andryusha's body had been drained of blood for ritual purposes proved more difficult, since the real murderers had ostensibly stabbed the body in order to leave just such an impression. Called to testify, medical experts differed. One professor of medicine came up with a hedged assertion that the body had been drained of blood in a ritual fashion, but it was later learned that he had been passed 4,000 rubles by the Ministry of Justice for that opinion. Most of the other experts consulted discounted the possibility of a ritual murder.[32]

The case for the defense

In the Beilis case it was not only the left, the defenders of Beilis, who heaped scorn on the case being made by the prosecution. If we are to find an equivalent in terms of sensational impact to Zola's *J'Accuse!*, it was not in the writings of sympathetic, left-wing journalists like Korolenko, but rather in an editorial by V. V. Shulgin, editor of the noted conservative and anti-Semitic newspaper in Kiev, the *Kievlyanin*. In words that caused an enormous uproar in Russia and intense embarrassment on the part of the prosecution, Shulgin denounced the trial as a sham, the evidence against Beilis "claptrap." He wrote, "One cannot help feeling ashamed for the Department of the Prosecution of the Kiev Court and for Russian justice as a whole, which has ventured to appear before

[30] Ibid., 212–3.
[31] Ibid., 216.
[32] Ibid., 211–21.

the world with such paltry equipment. . . . "[33] Both Shulgin and the recently deceased editor of the newspaper, N. Pikhno, had from the beginning shown an interest in the case and had actively aided Beilis's lawyers in building his defense.[34]

Shulgin and Pikhno were conservative nationalists who were deeply worried about the influence of Jews in Russia; they had no sympathy, however, for the likes of Krushevan and the violence provoked by him in Kishinev or with nineteen-year-old Golubev in Kiev. Shulgin prided himself on being what he termed an "honorable" anti-Semite; he believed only in "cold" pogroms (that is, nonviolent, legal action against Jews), not "hot," or violent, ones. Both he and Pikhno proclaimed that the ritual murder charges against Beilis reflected shame upon Mother Russia, not upon the Jews.[35]

Such men emerge with surprising frequency in this case, as in the Dreyfus Affair. They do not seem to have allowed their perceptions of Jews as political opponents, or outsiders in whatever sense, to overwhelm or corrupt the larger context of values in which they operated. Jews were for them human opponents, not fiends or demons. Even more, like Picquart, they were willing to face hostility, even personal danger, in standing up for those values – and it definitely was personally dangerous to cross the higher authorities associated with the minister of justice, Shcheglovitov, or, in a more directly physical sense, the thugs in the Black Hundreds. Interestingly, one of Beilis's defenders commented that when N. Pikhno died on July 29, 1913, just as Beilis's trial was about to begin, "Russian reaction lost one of its leading spirits. Beilis, however, lost in him the most powerful and influential of all his defenders. . . . " Beilis's wife and children reverentially laid wreaths on the grave of this nationalist, reactionary anti-Semite, whom they called "the kindly defender."[36]

These reactions may well be relegated to the realm of the exceptional rather than the typical. Yet a close examination of this trial, as of the Dreyfus and Frank trials, often reveals the decisive importance of the unexpected and exceptional. A no doubt less exceptional response of anti-Semites to the disappointing progress made by the prosecution in the trial may be seen in the confidential report of a government agent, who was present at the trial, to Minister of Justice Shcheglovitov:

> Now it becomes glaringly clear how this all-powerful international Jewry organizes its forces, and how incapable the Russian government is in a serious struggle with the Jews. . . . All of the

[33] Ibid., 165.
[34] Margolin, *Jews of Eastern Europe*, 190. Margolin was one of Beilis's lawyers and this book provides much first-hand information about the case.
[35] Ibid.
[36] Ibid., 212–3.

luminaries of the law, literature, medicine, and science are on the side of Jewry, which has succeeded in conditioning them. Against them stands the simple people, who have remained untouched by Jewish enlightenment. They will pronounce their incorruptible verdict, and this will be God's judgment on the Jews.[37]

The verdict and reactions to it

"The simple people" referred to in this report were the jurors. Those representing "Shcheglovitov justice" had done what they could to assure that only the most uneducated peasants, those believed most likely to be superstitious and easily intimidated, were called to serve on the jury. Beilis himself was dismayed when he learned of the composition of the jury: "The Russian peasant is known to be gullible, and the wilder the rumor, the more prone he is to believe it," he later wrote.[38] Seven of the twelve jurors turned out to be members of the Union of the Russian People. Shcheglovitov had also appointed a judge whom he felt confident would understand the requirements of his notion of justice; the lengthy instructions the judge gave to the jury were astonishingly prejudicial.[39] Beilis and his defenders faced as well an array of bribed or browbeaten witnesses, evidence that had been tampered with, and colorful testimony by rabid anti-Semites. There was thus cause for worry as the jury assembled to give its verdict in the last week of October 1913, after thirty-six days of trial.[40]

The indictment contained two parts, the first of which asked, "Has it been proved [that] . . . in one of the buildings of the Jewish surgical hospital [adjoining the Zaitsev brick factory] . . . Andrei Yushchinsky was gagged, and wounds inflicted upon him . . . and that after he had lost five glasses of blood, [other wounds] were inflicted upon him . . . leading to almost total loss of blood and to death?" To this question, the jury answered, "Yes, it has been proved."

Beilis and his supporters were stunned, inclined to despair. They listened with pounding hearts to the second part: "Is the accused guilty of having entered into collusion with others who have not been discovered . . . , in a premeditated plan prompted by religious fanaticism, to murder

[37] Samuel, *Blood Accusation*, 173.
[38] Beilis, *My Sufferings*, 135.
[39] Ibid., 134.
[40] Samuel, *Blood Accusation*, 170.

the boy Andrei Yushchinsky, and did he carry out his intentions . . . ?"
The answer was "No, not guilty."[41]

After a moment of uncomprehending silence, the courtroom broke into cheers, weeping, and the waving of handkerchiefs. Beilis's chest shook with nearly hysterical sobs. Celebration continued into the streets, not only of Kiev but of the rest of Russia, indeed of the world. Maurice Samuel described the universal jubilation: "Strangers embraced on the streets with shining faces and streaming eyes; Jews and gentiles congratulated each other, proud of their country and its 'simple citizens,' gloating over the happy ending and the humiliation of the administration."[42] (One of Beilis's lawyers, Oskar Grunzenberg, reported how close a call the matter had been: "Indeed, a miracle happened. The preliminary vote in favor of convicting Beilis was seven to five, but when the foreman began taking the final vote, one peasant rose to his feet, prayed to an icon, and said resolutely, 'I don't want to have this sin on my soul – he's not guilty.' "[43])

Beilis reported that in the courtroom "a gigantic Russian, weeping like a child," came over to him and, identifying himself as a merchant from Moscow, said, "Now, Lord be blessed, I can go home rejoicing. I am very happy to be able to shake hands with you. I wish you all the happiness in the world."[44]

Yet the prosecution maintained that it, too, had won an important victory, since it had been proved in court that a ritual murder had occurred, even if Beilis had not committed it. Anti-Semites were quick to pick up the line. Of course, the actual words "ritual murder" or even "Judaism" were not mentioned in the indictment, but the site of the crime, in one of the buildings of the surgical hospital in the Zaitsev grounds, and the "five glasses of blood" (rather than more neutral language, such as "five pints") implied both that it was a Jewish crime and that the blood was being collected in order to be drunk or consumed in some way. This was, to be sure, a cheap and paltry victory, especially since there was overwhelming evidence that the murder had been committed elsewhere, but it seems to have assuaged some of the humiliation felt by Beilis's accusers, for whom a "victory banquet" was arranged in St. Petersburg.

There was little doubt who had really won. The *Daily News* of London wrote that "the acquittal of Beilis was the most crushing blow to Russia since the Russo-Japanese War."[45] Officials in the tsar's government con-

[41] Ibid., 248–9.
[42] Ibid., 250.
[43] Oskar Osipovich Grunzenberg, *Yesterday: Memoirs of a Russian-Jewish Lawyer* (Berkeley, Calif., 1981; original Russian ed., Paris, 1938), 186.
[44] Beilis, *My Sufferings*, 250.
[45] Samuel, *Blood Accusation*, 252.

fidentially termed it among themselves "a second Tsushima" (after the naval battle in which the tsarist navy went down to defeat against Japan).[46]

It was as well, one might have said, the most notable victory for the Jews since that war and the ensuing revolution. But such a narrow interpretation reflected the attitudes of only a few. The more widespread belief was that the values of decency and truth, around which Jew and non-Jew could enthusiastically unite, had triumphed. Or even more optimistically, that the forces representing a new, modern Russia had emerged the winner. The *Times* of London concluded that the trial represented "possibly a final fight for existence on the part of the innermost powers of reaction against all modern forces in Russia."[47]

The jubilation inside Russia over the verdict continued for some weeks. Beilis became something of national hero, his home almost a shrine. By his own testimony he received seven to eight thousand visitors daily, over eleven thousand letters, seven thousand telegrams, twenty thousand visiting cards. Even his jailers, after the verdict and before his formal release, became suddenly respectful, in some cases downright obsequious and penitent. Several of them embraced him with tears in their eyes. One of the police captains, whom Beilis had earlier feared as "brutal," had a remarkable story for him. The captain's own daughter, a high school student, had followed the trial avidly, and "every time she read the papers and saw something had gone wrong with your case she wept like a child. She neglected her studies because of you." The captain begged Beilis to stay at the station for a moment so that his daughter could shake his hand. She arrived with a friend, and both told him that they had daily prayed for his release.[48] A Russian priest later arrived at Beilis's home, dropped to his knees, kissed Beilis's hand and asked for "forgiveness in the name of my people."[49]

But there was a more ominous side as well. Messages arrived from the Black Hundreds threatening him with death, and those threats against him and his family finally persuaded him to leave Russia. He could only comment, "What strange creatures these Russian people are!"[50] His words made clear that he, like most Jews in Russia, did not consider himself a part of "these" Russian people, even if he could not suppress warm feelings for many of them. He first left for Palestine in 1914 and then, unable to make a living there, emigrated to the United States in 1922.

Beilis's defenders, the liberal forces representing a new and modern Russia in the eyes of some foreign observers, were unable to translate

[46] Grunzenberg, *Memoirs*, 123.
[47] Ibid., 181.
[48] Beilis, *My Sufferings*, 199–201.
[49] Ibid., 205.
[50] Ibid., 205–6.

their judicial victory into the kind of political victory that the Dreyfusards had won in France, partly because war broke out within a year. There were, however, some intriguing, if minor, parallels in Russia to developments in France in what has been called the "judicial murder" of War Minister Sukhomlinov's protégé, Colonel S. N. Miasoedov. "The liberals, who had shown great courage for the cause of human rights in the notorious Beilis case, this time lent a hand in the miscarriage of justice."[51] In short, these champions of justice against raison d'état in 1911–13 proved themselves, much like many Dreyfusards, capable of supporting an unfair trial a few years later when it served their own political agenda.

Looking back across the years upon the sense of victory and jubilation by the pro-Beilis forces, the modern observer is naturally inclined to feelings of irony, given the coming horrors that Jews and liberal Gentiles were to face in Russia. Nevertheless, to many contemporaries it seemed beyond question that another great victory, like that in France, against the forces of reactionary anti-Semitism had been won, that the forces of decency and toleration, if only they would stick together and fight, could prevail even in a country like tsarist Russia. There, too, the "gathering storm" of anti-Semitism seemed less ominous than it would appear in retrospect to later generations.

At this very moment yet another battle was taking shape on a distant continent where most Jews believed they were safer and more secure than anywhere else in the world – a continent to which millions of Russian Jews had fled in order to escape tsarist autocracy. And this battle would have a far less happy outcome.

[51] Tsuyoshi Hasegawa, *The February Revolution: Petrograd, 1917* (Seattle and London, 1981), 29.

8

America, the "exception"

Here individuals of all nations are melted into a new race of men (J. Hector St.-Jean de Crèvecoeur)[1]

America is our Palestine: here is our Jerusalem. (Rabbi Max Lillienthal, 1867)

Liberty is born in them [the Jews]. They threaten tyranny and superstition everywhere. (Editorial in W. R. Hearst's *Chicago American*, May 22, 1903)[2]

Twenty-five years of education resulted in making the colored women more immoral and the men more trifling. . . . Negroes are intellectually, morally, and physically an inferior race – a fact none can deny. (Editorial in the newspaper *The Jewish South*, 1896)

American exceptionalism

Scholars have long debated the extent to which American history is some-how qualitatively different from the history of Europe. A widely accepted generalization about the situation of Jews in the United States is that it has always been "exceptional," distinctly less oppressive than anywhere else in the world in modern times. Only qualified dissent has been registered against that consensus, and it has been based primarily on a complaint that historians of the United States have not sufficiently recognized the importance of anti-Semitism in American history.[3] Rarely has the claim been made that things have been worse for Jews in the United States than elsewhere. Leading Jewish spokesmen have repeatedly described the United States as fundamentally different from the countries of Europe, a place where Jews could at last feel genuinely at home.

[1] Quoted in John Higham, *Send These to Me: Immigrants in Urban America*, rev. ed. (Baltimore, 1984), 178.
[2] Cyrus Adler, ed., *The Voice of America on Kishineff* (Philadelphia, 1904), 293.
[3] Cf. Leonard Dinnerstein, *Uneasy at Home* (New York, 1987); Michael N. Dobkowski, *The Tarnished Dream: The Basis of American Anti-Semitism* (Westport Conn., 1979). Unfortunately, passages in Dobkowski's book were taken verbatim, without proper acknowledgment, from the writings of John Higham – one of the scholars, ironically, that he criticizes for inadequate attention to American anti-Semitism. Dobkowski's overall arguments can be found also in his "American Anti-Semitism: A Reinterpretation," *American Quarterly*, vol. 29, 1977, 167–90. His argument, although one-sided and polemical, is not without merit. Similarly, however unfortunate the lapse in using Higham's words, Dobkowski has done valuable research.

In historical perspective, the hyperbole in such statements is obvious. We have seen how Jews in Hungary and France by mid-nineteenth century made similar claims, and indeed the Jews of many European countries, Italy perhaps most prominently, have claimed "exceptional" histories, largely free of the anti-Semitism of other countries.[4] In a broader context, many scholars have questioned how appropriate it is to term the American experience exceptional.[5] The issue of national exceptionism became a staple of debate among historians in the 1970s and 1980s, especially in terms of Germany's opposite kind of exceptionalism, or its "special path" (*Sonderweg*). In reviewing this debate, one historian has appropriately concluded that "upon scrutiny every nation had its own exceptionalism."[6]

Historical perspective also suggests that most Jews come to the United States for immediate, pressing reasons, poverty most of all, not primarily because they perceived the country as a haven of cultural pluralism where there was little anti-Semitism. Similarly, long-resident Americans accepted Jews not because they were impressed by Jewish "immigrant gifts," the cultural contributions that Jews would make to American civilization, but because the labor of Jews and other immigrants was needed to build and populate the country. These hard realities have at times been glossed over by what one scholar has termed "ethnic myths," by a romantic portrayal of the degree of freedom and tolerance in the United States.[7]

Recognizing the hyperbole and myth-making, the case to be made for American exceptionalism in regard to Jewish–Gentile relations remains compelling. Even many Italian or Hungarian Jews recognized that relations between Jews and non-Jews in the New World were freer of friction than in the Old. This recognition was linked to the tendency of at least some Europeans to idealize the New World, to praise it as a place where the prejudices of the Old World had been left behind. In the early nineteenth century the words of the great German poet Goethe were often quoted: "*Amerika, du hast es besser!*" (America, you have it better). It was a common but by no means unanimous opinion, as we will see.

Historians of anti-Semitism in the United States have been concerned

[4] Cf. Dan Antonio Segre, *Memoirs of a Fortunate Jew: An Italian Story* (Bethesda, Md., 1987).
[5] Cf. Daniel Bell, "The End of American Exceptionalism," *The Public Interest*, no. 41, 205, where he emphasizes that Americans "have not been immune to the corruptions of power. We have not been the exception." Also, Alexander Deconde, "Historians, the War of American Independence, and the Persistence of the Exceptionalist Ideal," *The International History Review*, vol. 5, no. 3, 399–430.
[6] Charles S. Maier, *The Unmasterable Past: History, Holocaust, and German National Identity* (Cambridge, Mass., 1988), 108.
[7] Cf. Stephen Steinberg, *The Ethnic Myth: Race, Ethnicity, and Class in America* (Boston, 1981).

primarily with issues of lingering stereotypes, social exclusion, and obstacles to equality of opportunity, all of which loomed large enough in the lives of individual American Jews. During the nineteenth and early twentieth centuries Jews found many prestigious and lucrative occupations effectively closed to them. However, hostility to Jews in America has been mostly latent and ambiguous, not overt, militant, or violent. One historian has written that in the United States "no decisive event, no deep crisis, no powerful social movement, no great individual is associated primarily... with anti-Semitism."[8] The worst that Americans have been accused of is not opening their doors wide enough, not aiding Jews as much as they might have.[9] Another historian has concluded that if the United States "has not been utter heaven for Jews, it has been as far from hell as Jews in the Diaspora have ever known."[10]

Prior to World War I there were no significant American ideologists or popularizers of anti-Semitism comparable to Dühring or Marr, Barrès or Drumont, Pobedonostsev or Khrushevan. Even the underlying expectation that Jews should "disappear" once they had been given civil equality – that delicate issue, so central to the European scene by the late nineteenth century – was less explicitly and forcefully formulated in the United States. To be sure, prior to the mid-twentieth century, few if any non-Jewish Americans had much sympathy for Jewish separatism, and the insistence of American ruling elites that immigrants conform to Anglo-Saxon linguistic and cultural norms was typically unyielding. But that insistence gradually weakened as American identity grew more diffuse, less narrowly associated with notions of a single "truly American" race, religious tradition, and integral culture.

What is perhaps most exceptional in American history has been the process of redefinition of what it means to be an American, in the painfully slow but gathering consensus that American identity is properly pluralistic and open to all people. In that process American Jews played an important role, both theoretical and practical.[11] That the Statue of Liberty, the symbol of the United States for much of the world by the early twentieth century, had placed at its base, in 1903, a bronze plaque with a poem composed by a Jewish American, Emma Lazarus ("Give me your tired,

---

[8]There are few overall introductions to the subject; perhaps the best is Charles Hebert Stember, ed., *Jews in the Mind of America* (New York, 1966), especially the essay in it by John Higham, "American Anti-Semitism Historically Reconsidered," from which the preceding quotation is taken. The essay may be found also in Leonard Dinnerstein, ed., *Anti-Semitism in the United States* (New York, 1971), 63–77. See also, David Gerber, ed., *Anti-Semitism in American History* (Chicago and Urbana, Ill., 1986).

[9]Cf. David S. Wyman, *The Abandonment of the Jews: America and the Holocaust, 1941–1945* (New York, 1984).

[10]Jonathan D. Sarna, "Anti-Semitism and American History," *Commentary*, vol. 71, no. 3, March 1981, 47.

[11]Steinberg, *Ethnic Myth*, 45 ff, 253.

your poor, your huddled masses, yearning to breathe free . . . "), suggests the importance of that role. (The poem, with its reference to the immigrants as "wretched refuse," is also not without awkward ambiguities; Lazarus, as will be discussed below, was not an admirer of the Jewish element of those huddled masses, and she unquestioningly embraced Anglo-Saxon cultural preeminence.)

The rise of the Jews has been nowhere more obvious, significant, and lasting than in the United States, as is attested by many Jewish observers. "It is as if centuries of Jewish energies and ambitions . . . found here a sudden and stunning release. . . . "[12] "More than any other immigrant group, Jews have found their way into almost every interstice of American life, have taken just about every opportunity this nation has to offer, and have given back to America in enriching ways that are wondrous."[13]

But that rise has not entailed a significant non-Jewish backlash. The nightmare of European nationalists, "jewification" of their national identity, has not been a major or lasting concern of non-Jewish Americans. From at least the mid-nineteenth century, a Jewish contribution to American civilization has been tacitly and increasingly recognized, just as have contributions of, say, the Irish or Germans. Even those who were most adamant in their insistence upon the identity of the United States as an Anglo-Saxon, Protestant nation, were, unlike such European integral nationalists as Treitschke and Barrès, often also warm defenders of the contributions of Jews to American civilization and saw no dangers in those contributions, no important contradictions between Jewish and American values.

The blending of Jewish cultural traditions (notably humor), language (the numerous Yiddishisms that became part of American speech), and tastes (food especially) into a modern American amalgam has been held up, particularly by the mid-twentieth century but still with origins going well into the nineteenth, as a good example of how in the United States cultures can blend and find strength in the blend, of how American identity is relatively optimistic and lacking in the kind of paranoia and fear of the future so characteristic of countries like Russia or Romania. Similarly, American nationalism in the nineteenth and twentieth centuries remained extraordinarily robust and self-confident. Citizens of the richest and most powerful country in the world were relatively unaffected by fears of invasion or subversion. The "people of plenty," in historian David Potter's phrase,[14] lived in a different world from the great mass of Euro-

---

[12] Leonard Fein, *Where Are We? The Inner Life of America's Jews* (New York, 1988), xvii.

[13] Howard Simons, *Jewish Times: Voices of the American Jewish Experience* (Boston, 1988), 7.

[14] David M. Potter, *People of Plenty: Economic Abundance and American Character* (Chicago, 1954).

peans, who were still insecure in their national identities, fearful of national survival, and haunted by visions of poverty and want.

The issue of fantasy versus reality in Jewish–Gentile relations takes on revealing forms in American history, for fantasy about Jews has played a relatively small role; normal social and economic frictions have been less exaggerated by ideological inflation than elsewhere. The more grotesque of the fantasies, such as the blood libel, have been almost entirely absent. Even the perception of Jews as culturally destructive has not turned against them to the degree that it has elsewhere. Their large role in the American left, as a dissenting minority among other dissenting minorities, has been as much a source of admiration as of resentment by non-Jewish Americans. Mommsen's description of Jewish critical destructiveness as useful in the building of a new national character could hardly find a better example than in the role of left-wing Jews in the emerging, ever-changing American national character. Right-wing Jews and those close to the political establishment have also played an important role, so the notion of Jews as invariably left-wing has had less plausibility.

No doubt an important reason that the rhetoric in favor of American exceptionalism was at one time so unqualified and prone to myth-making was that the Jews who came to the United States found comfort in an image of themselves as opponents of European tyranny and bigotry, as a courageous people pursuing freedom, rather than as "wretched refuse" driven by poverty. They pictured themselves as resisting not only the tyranny of European Gentile leaders but also that of rabbinical authorities and the Jewish upper classes, both of whom typically cooperated with Gentile authorities. Many Jewish immigrants to the United States long retained simmering resentments against the European Jewish establishment.[15]

Even when the American reality was bitterly disappointing, as it often was, public statements by Jewish leaders were heavily influenced by a sense of how much worse things were in Europe, above all in Russia, and it was, of course, from that despotic land that the great majority of American Jews by the first decades of the twentieth century had recently come. As some Jewish observers would later recognize, Jews were inevitably tempted to exaggerate not only European sins but also American virtues.[16]

Earlier generations of Jewish scholars felt with particular force the need to stress how Jews had blended into American society, how they had become good Americans. The most recent generation of Jewish-American historians, coming of age in the 1960s, with a different, often

---

[15]These resentments form a key theme in Arthur Hertzberg, *The Jews in America: Four Centuries of an Uneasy Encounter* (New York, 1989).
[16]Cf. Steinberg, *Ethnic Myth*, 49–51.

explicitly contrasting consciousness from that of earlier historians and taking their Americanness more for granted, have often felt freer to point out conflict and dissonance in the United States' past.[17]

At any rate, without some strong sense of the European reality, and its own important variations from country to country, descriptions of the dark side of American history in regard to its Jewish citizens may become mired in provincialism, in unbalanced and morally absolutist condemnations, or in sweeping statements that anti-Semitism was stronger than "previously thought." Yet "strong" and "weak," without the concrete reference points that comparative history provides, remain uncomfortably vague, too prone to purely subjective evaluations.

Jews and non-Jews: the structures of the relationship

In the seventeenth and eighteenth centuries the Jewish population in the American colonies was extremely small and mainly Sephardic. Even more than the Sephardim in France, Jews in America by the mid-1700s were accepted by the surrounding society and desired acceptance by it, although many colonial legislatures passed measures limiting their rights in the earlier part of the century. The American states and France both wrote constitutions in the late eighteenth century; revealingly, in America the issue of civil equality for Jews played almost no role, whereas there were rancorous exchanges in France in the early 1790s and prologued debates in Germany throughout the nineteenth century. Individual states of the union introduced restrictions on Jewish office holding, against which Jews fought persistent and often frustrating legal battles,[18] but Jewish civil rights were on the whole more secure and more extensive than in any country of Europe, particularly before the latter half of the nineteenth century.

Many of the Founding Fathers seem to have had friendly feelings toward the Jews, insofar as they expressed themselves on the matter, and only occasionally did they express disdain for them.[19] George Washington, the symbolic father of the nation, whose words and advice carried unusual weight for average Americans, was well known for his welcoming "the children of the stock of Abraham." He expressed hope that they would

---

[17] These issues are provocatively explored in John Patrick Diggins, "Comrades and Citizens: New Mythologies in American Historiography," *The American Historical Review*, vol. 90, no. 3, June 1985, 614–49.

[18] One of the most recent and useful studies is Morton Borden's, *Jews, Turks, and Infidels* (Chapel Hill, N.C., 1984).

[19] Ibid., 26 ff.

"continue to merit and enjoy the good will of other inhabitants," under a government that "gives to bigotry no sanction."[20] Interestingly, the words "gives to bigotry no sanction" were suggested to Washington by Jewish leaders who had congratulated him on becoming president. Almost all histories of the Jews in the United States quote them.

At the Constitutional Convention, the framers of the Constitution did not even debate whether Jews should have civil equality. Article VI specifically prohibits a religious test for office in the United States, in this regard in advance of the British constitution; the issue of Jews' holding high office in Britain would be contested well into the nineteenth century. The First Amendment specifically prohibits any federal law that would establish a national church or limit the free practice of any religion. There was no comparable restriction on the states, however, and in a number of them religion and politics became deeply enmeshed. In a few an established church lasted for many years. Naturalization also became the subject of a prolonged and often rancorous debate. It was by no means widely accepted at this time that large numbers of immigrants should be welcomed to the country, nor was it accepted that immigrants could easily or quickly become good citizens.[21]

America's own men of the Enlightenment, influential figures like Thomas Jefferson, Benjamin Franklin, and John Adams, did not harbor the enmity to Jews so typical of European intellectuals like Voltaire and Diderot or even the more subtle and abstract denigration of Jewish religion and ritual to be found in the writings of Kant. Adams did find it "hard work," in practice, to extend to Jews, with their "asperities" and "peculiarities" of character, the love he believed proper in principle,[22] and that sense of difficulty would find frequent echo in the years to come. But the example of the American Enlightenment puts into question the assertion, found in many studies, that the pagan or pre-Christian heritage operated as a powerful, self-perpetuating ideology, sometimes combining with Christian elements, that fostered anti-Semitism or was a fundamental cause of it.[23] In this regard, too, pagan "fantasies" required "realities" to cause them to come to life, and those realities were lacking in America at this time as compared to Europe.

Interestingly, in the 1760s Franklin did openly fret, not about "jewification," but rather about the dangers of "germanization" in Pennsylvania, where there was a large and growing German population. His concerns to preserve the Anglo-Saxon culture of the country were widely shared

---

[20] Quoted in Jehuda Bauer and Paul Mendes-Flohr, eds., *The Jew in the Modern World* (Oxford, 1980), 363.
[21] Steinberg, *Ethnic Myth*, 11–12.
[22] Hertzberg, *Jews in America*, 86–7.
[23] Cf. Arthur Hertzberg, *The French Enlightenment and the Jews* (New York, 1968).

by the Founding Fathers and were reiterated by prominent Americans well into the nineteenth and twentieth centuries. Similarly, nearly all of the Founding Fathers were hostile to the idea of large-scale immigration because they feared its divisive, disruptive potential. It is highly improbable that they would willingly have accepted the millions of non-English-speaking immigrants who entered the country a century later.

The argument was made in Chapter 4 that France's Jews were overwhelmed and powerfully drawn away from their own traditions by the combination of a prestigious civilization and their relatively small numbers. A contrary process was described in Chapter 6: Russia's Jews, because of their great numbers, retained a kind of critical mass, one that was not much tempted to integrate into Slavic culture, moreover, since it held that culture in low regard. The first of these arguments holds at least as strongly for America, where the Jewish population was, until the latter part of nineteenth century, proportionately even smaller than that of France and much less concentrated in single areas with historic traditions of their own.

Similarly, there were not many Jews in the first hundred years of the American republic who hewed "stubbornly" to orthodox practice and social separatism or who seemed to non-Jewish Americans to exhibit the kind of religious separatism that would prevent their becoming good, productive citizens. Jews simply played a less visible role in the early stages of American life, both in a negative and a positive sense, than their counterparts in Europe. Although Jefferson, in a typically Enlightened way, seems to have accepted as valid the frequent deprecation of the Talmud and Jewish morality of his time,[24] he did not attack Jews with the ferocity and monomania of Voltaire. On the other hand, Americans did not have a Lessing, a Mendelssohn, a Heine, a Marx, or a Disraeli. The extremes are missing in the first centuries of American history, as is no doubt some of the richness that characterized the European scene.

American culture did not have the drawing power that the great cultures of Europe at the time had for Jewish secular intellectuals. Rather than being attracted, most Jewish intellectuals in Europe were repelled, especially by the late nineteenth and early twentieth centuries. Figures as diverse as Scholem Aleichem, Leon Trotsky, and Sigmund Freud held things American in low regard. Religious Jews were even more profoundly repelled by American life, but whether religious or secular, European Jewish intellectual elites were almost unanimous in rejecting American culture as inferior – raw, vulgar, and crassly material.

Nevertheless, for ordinary Jews – and it was they, rather than the European Jewish bourgeoisie and intellectual elites, who came to the

---

[24] Lester J. Cappon, *The Adams–Jefferson Letters*, vol. 2 (Chapel Hill, N.C., 1959), 383.

United States in great numbers – American culture, as a variety of English culture, remained decidedly in the ranks of the higher civilizations of the time. Jews who were little attracted to the predominantly peasant and premodern cultures of eastern Europe, the Romanians, Ukrainians, Slovaks, or, even the Russians and Poles, could still feel pride in entering into the ranks of one of the world's highest civilizations by becoming Anglo-Americans. An activist among the Yiddish-speaking workers of Russia reported that, in the evening classes he taught, the "life of the peoples" began with primitive tribes and ended with the pinnacle of contemporary civilization: "the English, their parliament and trade unions."[25] Jews who came to the United States were, if possible, even more concerned to assimilate culturally than were Jews in France, Germany, or Hungary. If they offered resistance to the adamant demands that they conform to Anglo-Saxon ideals, it was feeble, especially by the second generation; most of them, rather than resisting, energetically learned English and sought in other ways to become culturally like their hosts. Much the same may be said about religious adaptation, insofar as it can be distinguished from cultural assimilation: American Reform Judaism, even more than its German or Magyar counterparts, took giant steps in the direction of becoming like Protestant Christianity.

The Christian churches in the United States, whether Protestant or Catholic, were less hostile to Jews than were their counterparts in Europe. The United States' predominant Christian traditions, related as they were to those of England, contained important tendencies toward philo-Semitism. The American Puritans fancied themselves modern versions of the ancient Hebrews; their religious beliefs owed relatively much to the Old Testament and relatively little to the New. The crucifixion and the Jews' responsibility for it were less central to their beliefs. Similar remarks hold for American fundamentalist and anabaptist sects; they did not typically demonize or seek to oppress those that they often admiringly referred to as "the People of the Book." Jewish refusal to believe in Christ, and more generally the "stubbornness" of Jews, although often mentioned by American Christians, does not seem to have evoked the same quality of resentment in the United States that it did in much of Europe.

Still, the large ambiguities of Christian belief and tradition concerning Judaism played a role in the United States. Christians there as elsewhere could hardly ignore the potently anti-Judaic and anti-Jewish passages of the New Testament. Negative images of Jews were amply propagated in Sunday schools and pulpits in nineteenth-century America. Remarks about Jewish stinginess, the vengefulness and unforgiving character of

---

[25] Ezra Mendelsohn, *Class Struggles in the Pale: The Formative Years of the Jewish Workers' Movement in Tsarist Russia* (Cambridge, 1970), 35.

Jews, and the backward, "medieval" quality of orthodox Judaism are to be widely found in nineteenth-century sermons, speeches, novels, and editorials.[26] But, again, such remarks do not seem to have evoked the same quality of disdain as elsewhere, no doubt in part because they were not backed up legally or institutionally to a major degree, nor did they mesh with historical traditions. Jews in America had never been part of a medieval-style corporate body, and they had not been legally isolated in ghettos. They never formed a distinct commercial caste, nor were they ever required to wear distinctive clothing.

Even Catholics in America, who in the eighteenth century were also small in numbers and without the kind of political power they exercised in many countries of continental Europe, eventually came to esteem toleration between religious communities, Jews included, no doubt because Catholics themselves suffered from intolerance. The most serious religious hostility that existed throughout most of the history of the United States – and it was often severe, sometimes murderous – was between various Protestant denominations or between Catholics and Protestants or even between Reform and Orthodox Jews, not typically between Jews and Christians. The controversies within Jewish denominations, broadly reproducing those in German- and Magyar-speaking central Europe, were more prominent and certainly more passionate than Christian–Jewish controversies. Over the long run, the United States' identity as a haven from religious persecution by the state became ever more central, and Jews inevitably benefited from that identity. Indeed, they helped powerfully to shape it.

Anglo-American political and cultural traditions, which blended inextricably with religious preferences, also emphasized toleration and compromise. From the late seventeenth century on, the notion of toleration for both political and religious dissent and the related conviction that the state "had no legitimate interest in the religious beliefs of obedient citizens" gradually became widely accepted among the English-speaking peoples.[27] Jeffersonian distrust of centralized political power, above all when that power was used to enforce religious conformity, linked to a strong insistence on personal freedoms, posed a powerful obstacle to national legislation hostile to Jews. The American frontier supported the Yankee's preference for putting distance between himself and the central government and in a broader way permitted escape from the confinements of tradition and custom. Jews, like other Americans who headed westward, had unparalleled opportunities to do and be what they wanted, without

[26] Dobkowski, *The Tarnished Dream*, 14, 28–9.
[27] Todd Endelman, *The Jews of Georgian England, 1714–1830: Tradition and Change in a Liberal Society* (Philadelphia, 1979), 44.

fear of central government, repressive rabbinical authority, or more subtle community pressures.

The perceived kinship of Americans and Jews

The concept of American exceptionalism merges into another: that American ideals and Jewish ideals have similar roots, a deep kinship, exceeding that of Jews with any other modern nation. It was a notion often put forth by Jewish leaders in the nineteenth and early twentieth century, especially by assimilated German Jews. Supreme Court Justice Louis Brandeis argued that the "fundamentals of American law, namely life, liberty, and the pursuit of happiness are all essentially Judaistic and have been taught by [Jews] for thousands of years."[28]

Rhetorical exaggerations concerning this kinship there undoubtedly were, both by Jewish and non-Jewish spokesmen, and the openly expressed attitudes of Jews and non-Jews to one another naturally varied according to the audience and the occasion. A revealing example of how a particular historical occasion could influence what was publicly expressed about Jews can be seen in American reactions to the Kishinev massacres in Russia in 1903. The preceding two decades had seen a rising alarm in the United States about the mass migration of Jews out of Russia, but with the news of the pogrom, there was a remarkable outpouring of moral indignation against Russia's leaders, accompanied by fulsome praise for Jews as desirable citizens. Sermon after sermon, editorial after editorial, political speech after political speech praised the Jews as sober, productive, and "inoffensive" (a telling and frequently used adjective). Jews were champions of the oppressed, enemies of fanaticism, upholders of equality.

One editorial concluded that "the Jews of Russia are persecuted now because they talk in Russia as our forefathers talked here in 1776."[29] Other editorials expressed utter puzzlement as to why any country would want to persecute and drive out those people who "have the money, who are the money lenders and the money savers." One noted that Spain's decline began with its expulsion of the Jews.[30] The Jews of Russia, one might have concluded from these hundreds of editorials and sermons, were brothers-under-the-skin to Americans. These authors seemed oblivious to the denigration of the Jews from eastern Europe, so common in Europe

---

[28] Quoted in Irving Howe, *World of Our Fathers* (New York, 1976), 208.
[29] From an editorial of Hearst's *Chicago American*, May 22, 1903, in Adler, *Voice of America*, 296.
[30] From an editorial of the Janesville, Wis., *Gazette*, May 29, 1903, in Adler, *Voice of America*, 312.

by this time, and hardly unknown in the United States, as we will see.
Critical or hostile remarks about the bizarre behavior of the hasidim or
the socially destructive Jewish criminals, white slavers, assassins, anarchists, and revolutionaries – hardly inoffensive in the eyes of other
observers on other occasions – seemed to find, at this juncture at least,
almost no echo in the United States.

There was important symbolism in President Theodore Roosevelt's
meeting, following upon the Kishinev pogrom, with a Jewish delegation.
He expressed deep sympathy for the Jewish victims in Russia and delivered a speech full of praise for Jews in the United States and for Jews in
general. The secretary of state at the time, John Hay, also commonly
made pro-Jewish public statements. Both of them, like many prominent
American politicians, had established intimate contacts with leading
American Jews.[31] On the other hand, many of the ruling elite of the
country at this time, Hay included, were known to make disparaging
private remarks about Jews. Similarly, Roosevelt was strongly represented
among those who believed in an Anglo-Saxon America and who attacked
the idea of "hyphenated" Americans, as distinguished from those who
were "one hundred percent" American.

One only need consider how unthinkable it would have been for Nicholas II and Plehve to have met with a Jewish delegation in 1903, offering
remarks similarly full of praise, to gain some sense of the utterly different
situation of Jews in the two countries in relation to the political authorities.
Roosevelt emphasized with obvious pride that no major power had been
so diligent as the United States in protecting the rights of Jews. He made
a special point of how one of his most valiant officers in the Spanish-
American War was Jewish. He similarly described how, when he was
chief of police in New York, many of his most valued officers were Jewish.[32]
Plehve, too, was capable of a grudging recognition of the usefulness of
certain Jews, but even when putting on a good face for foreign visitors,
he would never have spoken as had President Roosevelt.

These statements of mutual admiration reached a crescendo in the
celebrations held on Thanksgiving Day, 1905, to commemorate the two
hundred fiftieth anniversary of the settlement of Jews in North America.
Many non-Jewish dignitaries, including the governor of New York, addressed the various assemblages, and President Roosevelt sent a letter,
noting with admiration that even in the colonial period Jews had been
essential to the "upbuilding of this country." Jacob Schiff, who chaired
the meeting in New York, hammered home the point that Jews "are

---

[31] Cf. Gary Dean Best, *To Free a People: American Jewish Leaders and the Jewish Problem
in Eastern Europe, 1890–1914* (Westport, Conn., 1982), 68 ff, and passim.

[32] The full text of the speech may be found in Henri Dagan, *L'Oppression des juifs dans
l'Europe orientale* (Paris, 1903).

justified in the claim that this is our country." Jews throughout the world, he intoned, look "longingly and hopefully toward these shores." Other speakers recalled the recent pogroms in Russia and appealed to the tradition of the Pilgrims who, it was claimed, had come to America to assure that there would always be a shelter for the poor and persecuted.[33]

Just as England became known as a land of commercial enterprise, a "nation of shopkeepers," and thus Jewish in the eyes of many continental anti-Semites, so America's Yankee traits were ones easily identified with Jewish ones (love of material gain, esteem gained through money accumulated, saving money, deferred gratification, and so forth). The noted German scholar, Werner Sombart, one of the "anti-Semitic" signers of the petition against Beilis's arrest, in a widely discussed study published in the first years of the century, had made much of the similarity of the Jews and the Anglo-Americans. He noted, for example, that both believed the acquisition of material wealth was a sign of divine favor.[34] German conservatives typically made a distinction between *Helden* and *Händler*, heroes and tradesmen, and while such conservatives often harbored ambiguous feelings about the English, they typically saw the Yankees as the most ignoble of money-grubbers. Nicholas II and those around him professed to see the English and the Jews as having the same kind of commercial souls; the English, the tsar often commented, also were *zhydi*.[35]

The power of commercialism in the United States was hardly to be denied. The English themselves were often taken aback by the commercial scramble in the United States in the nineteenth century, by the "Jewish" souls of the Yankees. Frances Trollope, the mother of the famous novelist, recorded her impressions and those of other English visitors to the country in the 1820s. She wrote that one "never heard Americans conversing without the word DOLLAR being pronounced between them."[36] Nearly a century later, Sigmund Freud saw only one reason to have anything to do with Americans: to get their money, for they were "useful for nothing else." They were, one and all, "savages" and "swindlers."[37] His sneering attitude to the American *Dollaronkel* (dollar uncle) and the sneering tone of his private remarks about Americans was strikingly like that of German aristocrats in regard to the *Geldjuden* (money Jews). Richard Hofstadter's *American Political Tradition* suggestively speaks of the United States as a "democracy of cupidity rather than a

[33] Hertzberg, *Jews in America*, 185–6.
[34] Werner Sombart, *The Jews and Modern Capitalism* (Berlin, 1911); cf. the discussion in Gerald Krefetz, *Jews and Money* (New Haven, 1982), 42; Marcus Arkin, *Aspects of Jewish History* (Philadelphia, 1975), 143–8.
[35] Cf Maurice Samuel, *Blood Accusation* (New York, 1966), 97–118.
[36] Nancy McPhee, *The Book of Insults* (New York, 1978), 96.
[37] Peter Gay, *Freud, a Life for Our Times* (New York, 1988), 563–4.

democracy of fraternity."[38] A democracy of fraternity, whatever its merits, is also likely to be more difficult and precarious for outsiders to enter, especially if it is linked to notions of integral nationalism, as in France, or racist, *völkisch* identities, as in Germany.

In the United States Jews who showed a taste for commercial gain and individual success were less likely to encounter hostility, particularly not aristocratic, anticommercial snobbery, than in Europe. They were more likely to be admired, if grudgingly. Prevailing attitudes towards commercialism in Europe were notably different. The followers of Richard Wagner in Germany maintained that the only interest Jews had in art was to sell it. Artistic production in Germany, so the Wagnerians argued, necessarily came from those who had long been part of the *Volk*, and that Volk had been Christian for over a thousand years. True art emerged mystically from the memory of shared experiences as a people. Barrès's ideas were similar.

The linkage of art and commercial gain became more important in the United States than in any other country in history. Indeed, individual gain became a holy of holies. Barrès complained that for Jews, rootless, eternal wanderers, France was merely a place "where their self-interest is best pursued." The patriotism of French Jews was necessarily opportunistic, shallow, and fleeting, whereas for the true Frenchman the *patrie*, the fatherland, was the resting place of his ancestors beyond memory and thus the source of a deep, unshakable, and selfless attachment.[39] Americans, an emigrant people, could not make such exalted claims and were less likely to denigrate Jews as recent arrivals. Compared to Europeans, Americans were nearly all rootless wanderers, at home in a democracy of cupidity, commercialism, and narrow self-interest.

The lack of a landed aristocracy and titled nobility similarly meant that Jews faced fewer obstacles to gaining social acceptance in the United States. A. J. Langbehn, an influential spokesman for German antimodernist, aesthetic anti-Semitism, remarked at the end of the nineteenth century that "the crude cult of money is a North American, and at the same time Jewish, trait. . . ."[40] European anti-Semites were nearly unanimous in seeing the United States as a "jewified" land, without a sense of honor, of history, of aristocratic virtue.

Revealingly, influential Jews in the United States made many of the same points but found merit where Europeans found fault. Brandeis spoke

[38] Richard Hofstadter, *The American Political Tradition and the Men Who Made It* (New York, 1957), v–xi; cf. Diggins, "Comrades and Citizens," 615.
[39] Paula Hyman, *From Dreyfus to Vichy: The Remaking of French Jewry, 1906–1939* (New York, 1979), 13.
[40] P. G. J. Pulzer, *The Rise of Political Anti-Semitism in Germany and Austria* (New York, 1964), 240.

glowingly of the United States as a land of "cultural pluralism," where Jews could remain Jews and be perfectly at home. He asserted that "the Jewish spirit . . . is essentially modern and essentially American." In the same period, Drumont equated "Americanism" and "Semitism," but he viewed them both as soullessly modern and destructive of cherished French traditions and values.[41]

Brandeis eventually became a Zionist, but of a peculiarly American sort, one who differed in fundamental ways from most European Zionists. For them anti-Semitism was not only an important cause for their becoming Zionists; it was also a bitter personal experience. For him it was neither. Like many other leading American Jews, Brandeis expressed faith in the goodwill of the non-Jewish majority, and he had few if any experiences of anti-Semitism that left him with bitter memories.[42] He did come to believe in a Jewish homeland – but for others, not for American Jews.

Since the Jews who arrived in the United States, especially in the latter half of the nineteenth century, were to an important extent those who cared relatively little for Jewish religious tradition or eastern European Jewish custom *(minhag)*, the United States was all the more attractive to them. Few immigrants could claim illustrious Jewish lineage *(yikhus)*. Many yearned to escape from their Jewish identity, or at least from certain elements of it that prevailed in eastern Europe at that time. Jewish "self-made men" were legion in the United States. If many of them lacked polish, it was not particularly important in this new land. The commonly criticized "tactlessness" of Jews, their lack of civility, their loud and pushy ways – all were less of an issue in a country where manners were generally coarse and civility, genteel style, and patrician culture in the European sense were likely to be suspect or even to be viewed as "un-American." Even American speech, considered by educated Europeans to be nasal, sloppy, and vulgar in form, corresponded to the views of assimilated European Jews concerning Yiddish; both were dismissed as whining, debased dialects, with the tonal and formal qualities appropriate to hawkers and peddlers, to a materialistic people who were indifferent to high culture and correct, aesthetically pleasing speech. In these regards, too, Jews and Yankees blended with relative ease.

Many observers of the American Jewish scene have not only noted the overlap of Jewish and Yankee manners but have argued that Jewish culture, with its emphasis on literacy and learning, was an essential ingredient of Jewish success relative to other immigrants from eastern and

[41] Drumont, *La France Juive*, vol. 2, 258–60; from Frederick Busi, *The Pope of Anti-Semitism: The Career and Legacy of Edouard-Adolphe Drumont* (Lanham, Md., 1986), 72.
[42] Peter Grose, *Israel in the Mind of America* (New York, 1984) 55–6.

southern Europe. That argument has merit, but it has also suffered from exaggeration and myth-making. Evidence suggests that it was not so much Jewish learning and literacy per se, but the higher degree of urbanization and a related familiarity with modern economic activity that best explain the upward mobility of Jewish immigrants. Revealingly, Italian immigrants to the United States who came from an urban background in northern Italy did even better than Jewish immigrants. Some observers have insisted that Jewish learning in its traditional form was no advantage at all, but rather a burden, involved as it was in rote learning and sterile hair-splitting. At any rate, urban experience appears to have been crucial; Tevye the milkman had great emotional appeal for later generations of Jews, but his life in the shtetl was in truth the direct experience of only a minority. As noted in Chapter 6, only 25 percent of Jewish immigrants to the United States from eastern Europe came from villages and shtetlekh.[43]

Racism and social conflict

The preoccupation with race in Europe in the late nineteenth century definitely had its counterparts in the United States, yet in ways that may have decreased rather than increased anti-Semitism. Belief in superior and inferior races was probably even more important in the United States than in Europe; the country's large Black population was believed by the majority of nineteenth-century White Americans to be racially inferior, and the findings of nineteenth-century "science" that confirmed Black inferiority were welcomed as a modern justification of slavery, or at least of social separation and political disenfranchisement of Blacks.

Jews were accepted as Whites; potential hostility to them as "different" was minimized since Blacks were incomparably more different – and threatening, decidedly not "inoffensive." Just as religious hostility in the United States was significantly deflected from Jews, finding expression between Christian sects, so American racial hostilities, which were almost certainly more intense than religious hostilities by the middle of the nineteenth century, tended to be between Blacks and Whites, while Jews were accepted as Whites by non-Jews.

Insofar as the notion of racial inequality among Whites was espoused in the middle years of the century, it was in regard to the newly arriving Irish, who came as an impoverished mass to the United States in large numbers from the midcentury on and who encountered often virulently racist antipathies. In these years, Jews themselves typically shared the

[43] Steinberg, *Ethnic Myth*, 94 ff.

Anglo-American negative evaluations of both Blacks and Irish. Rabbi Isaac Mayer Wise, a prominent Jewish spokesman at midcentury, of generally liberal sentiments and active in Reform Judaism, energetically defended Black slavery. He believed it just to buy and sell "savages," and to "place them under the protection of the law, [securing for them] the benefit of civilized society."[44] He further commented that "either one must say that the Negro was created to be a beast of burden . . . or you must say he is just as good as you are." Wise was bitterly opposed to Abraham Lincoln, whom he described as an "imbecile."[45]

Wise did not speak for all Jews in the United States. Most Northern Jews were supporters of Lincoln, and he became undoubtedly the most popular president among Jews – indeed, some of the unsophisticated among them thought he was Jewish – until Franklin Delano Roosevelt. It is nevertheless possible to recognize in Wise's words the same kind of language used by nationalistic, and racist, German and Hungarian Jews in denigrating the Slavic or Romanian peasant peoples around them in the late nineteenth century. To repeat, on the issue of race, the evidence suggests that Jewish attitudes, until the turn of the century, did not differ markedly from non-Jewish.

The Ashkenazic German-speaking Jews from central Europe who began to come in increasing numbers after the failures of the revolutions in Europe in the late 1840s were perceived by native-born Americans primarily as Germans rather than as Jews. That was, again, usually the way such Jews identified themselves. Germans were, after the English, the largest ethnic group in the country and were widely considered an up-and-coming people. Hostile images of the Irish derived not only from their origin as an impoverished, illiterate peasant people from a backward land but also from their attachment to an especially detested "popery." German-speaking Jews were on the whole more educated and less inclined to alcoholic abuse and violence than were the Catholic Irish. (The Protestant Irish, who came earlier, were also numerous but were not generally the subject of the hostile imagery that the Catholic Irish were.) A majority of German Jews quickly rose in wealth and in social position by the latter part of the nineteenth century, much as they did in Germany and Austria.

However, from their own standpoint, their acceptance by non-Jewish elites was often incomplete and unsatisfactory. Even highly successful German Jews in the United States occasionally faced insulting stereotypes and social ostracism. A few episodes have loomed large in accounts of the history of American Jews, especially those that have sought to emphasize how anti-Semitism in the United States has been inadequately recognized.

[44] Hertzberg, *Jews in America*, 125.
[45] Grose, *Israel*, 28.

During the Civil War, Jews in some areas encountered a sudden up-surge of hostility. They were accused of being unpatriotic and driven by greed, profiteering from the misfortunes of others.[46] General Grant's infamous Order No. 11 charged Jews, "as a class," with "violating every regulation of trade" established by the authorities; they were given twenty-four hours to get out of the war zone in question. But Order No. 11 was reversed within a few weeks, as soon as President Lincoln heard of it – and, significantly, before Jewish representatives reached him with their protests. Wars are notorious for bringing out the worst, as well as the best, in people, or the worst and best potential in any given society. In balance, Grant's order appears to be more a contretemps than an appropriate symbol of a deeper problem. With some important but not long-lasting exceptions, Jews were not made into scapegoats or blamed for the tragedies of the war, even in the South.

It is significant that the charges against Jews in the Civil War, whether at the level of cabinet officer or front-line peddler, appear to have been exaggerated or simply false.[47] Although there were unscrupulous Jews who sought to make profit from the war, such individuals were to be found of all religious backgrounds; the evidence does not indicate that Jews were war profiteers more often than others. It is possible that Jews were noticed more because they were different and also because their profiteering was small-scale and without powerful protectors, whereas some of the Gentile profiteers operated on a larger scale and had friends in influential places. But however important these negative impressions of Jews may have been, individual Jews on both sides of the American war served with bravery on the battlefield, and both sides honored them with abundant recognition. Many non-Jews stepped forward, in the South as in the North, to defend Jews against their accusers and to note that non-Jews were also war profiteers.

Even Grant, the apparent anti-Semitic villain, had friends who were prominent Jews, a number of whom he later appointed to high office.[48] Such friendships are by no means positive proof of the absence of anti-Semitic belief, for a surprising number of European anti-Semites (Lueger, Wagner, Barrès, Marr) had intimate friendships with Jews. But in Grant's case his war-time orders do not seem to have reflected any special hatred for Jews. Indeed, he regretted those orders for the rest of his life. As

[46] Cf. Bertram W. Korn, *American Jews and the Civil War* (Philadelphia, 1951); this study includes a chapter on violent expressions of anti-Semitism both in the South and in the North, part of which has been reprinted as "American Judaeophobia: Confederate Version," in Leonard Dinnerstein and Mary Dale Palsson, eds., *Jews in the South* (Baton Rouge, 1973) 135–55.

[47] Cf. Korn, "American Judaeophobia."

[48] Alan Edelstein, *An Unacknowledged Harmony: Philosemitism and the Survival of European Jewry* (Westport, Conn., 1982), 24, n. 32.

president, in response to appeals from Jews in the United States, he lent his support to protests against the persecutions of Jews in Romania, and he told Jewish representatives that "the sufferings of the Hebrews of Roumania profoundly touch every sensibility of our nature."[49]

The shift at the turn of the century

The financial scandals that marked the end of the liberal era and the beginning of the economically troubled 1870s and 1880s in Europe had plentiful counterparts in the United States. Corruption in high places became even more of an issue in the United States than in Europe at that time. Yet, unlike the situation in Europe, Jews were not conspicuous in or blamed for difficulties in those years, difficulties that were often striking in their general similarity to those in Europe: the stock market crash of September 1873; the scandal over the Credit Mobilier (beginning in the year before and having to do with the financing of railroads); the so-called Salary Grab of 1873 (involving questionable increases in congressional and presidential salaries); the Whisky Ring scandal (having to do with corruption in the Treasury and War departments).

In Europe, the anti-Semitic agitators of the 1870s and 1880s could plausibly identify Jews as having a major role in financial crashes, bribery, corruption in high places, and spoliation of the landscape. These matters were of concern in the United States as well, but Jews were rarely blamed for them, certainly not to the degree that they were in the Gründerzeit scandals in Germany or the Panama scandals in France. In those cases there were many Jewish culprits, whereas in America there were few if any.

By the turn of the century problems of a more profound and lasting sort for Jews began to emerge in the United States. The mostly latent hostility to Jews in America, the potentials of existing negative stereotypes and religious imagery, now began to connect more solidly and abundantly with objective problems, with real conflict between Jews and non-Jews. Hundreds of thousands of Jews from eastern Europe were moving into the country. Simultaneously, the earlier Jewish immigrants, the upwardly mobile and often sensationally successful German Jews, started to impinge as never before upon the terrain – economic, social, and cultural – of older Anglo-American elites. Perhaps even more important, newly rich Jews began to compete with newly rich Gentiles for positions in high society, and the Gentile nouveaux riches were even less inclined than the older American elites to mix socially with Jews.

[49] Best, *To Free a People*, 6–7.

In this regard, there seem to have been faint echoes in the United States of the kind of anti-Semitism that began to develop in central and eastern Europe in the late nineteenth and early twentieth centuries. In those areas, a native, highly nationalistic bourgeoisie began to form among primarily peasant peoples; this new bourgeoisie encountered a most unwelcome competition – incomparably greater than in the United States – from the Jews who had previously monopolized trade and commerce.

In short, a palpable, irritating Jewish presence began to be a more important reality in the United States, particularly on the Eastern Seaboard, in areas of considerable Jewish density, such as in New York. Jews and Gentiles began to compete and clash as never before for positions in boardrooms and resort hotels, factories and neighborhoods. The exclusion of Joseph Seligman, a wealthy Jewish businessman and confidant of presidents Rutherford B. Hayes and Ulysses S. Grant, from the Grand Union Hotel in Saratoga as early as 1876, provoked widespread indignation. Complaints about prejudice and similar exclusions had already filled the pages of Jewish newspapers, but this incident made the national press, and the indignation expressed, significantly, was now by non-Jews at least as much as by Jews. The episode came to dramatize and symbolize problems of social exclusivity against Jews.[50]

At the other end of the social scale, trade union leaders feared that the new eastern European hordes would take the jobs of American workers and lower wages. Liberals and progressives, concerned with issues of public morality, feared political corruption, bossism, and a swelling of the ranks of the Democratic Party (three closely related phenomena in their eyes). Urban gangs and organized crime were cause for further, related alarm. Social conservatives pointed to the large numbers of Marxists and anarchists among the immigrants, especially among the Jews and the Italians.

Conflicts of this sort characterized the end of the century everywhere in Europe. In the United States as in Europe, those challenged by the Jews were tempted by anti-Semitic fantasies, but in America there was so far relatively little about the response to Jewish–Gentile conflict that was fundamentally different from "ordinary" conflict, whether ethnic, economic, social, or religious, involving other groups. It is difficult, in other words, to see how inherited hostile imagery about Jews significantly intensified anti-Semitism in the United States at this time.

There was, however, one area of revealing parallels between Europe and the United States. Just as certain European intellectuals bemoaned

---

[50] Further examples and particulars are to be found in Salo Wittmayer Baron *Steeled by Adversity: Essays and Addresses on American Jewish Life* (Philadelphia, 1971), 323–4; cf. also, Charlers E. Silberman, *A Certain People: American Jews and Their Lives Today* (New York, 1985), 47–8.

the advent of a materialistic, atomistic, industrial society, so now certain American intellectuals, themselves usually of the older Anglo-American elites, began to express a basically aesthetic revulsion from what was happening to their country by the late nineteenth century. Whereas Jefferson had known only a few Jews and had extended a friendly hand to them, Henry Adams, a man of roughly comparable intellectual eminence, saw growing numbers of them in the late nineteenth century and increasingly disliked what he saw (among those he could scarcely ignore, it should be noted, was the husband of his sister; a Jew, in short, had became a member of the Adams clan).

Adams was a member of a venerable American family, the closest equivalent one can find in the North of the United States to a native aristocracy, and he felt shunted aside by an emerging industrial America and mass society. Moreover, that society deeply offended his aesthetic sensibilities. He seemed at times consumed with hatred for "infernal Jewry," and that hatred was inextricably mixed into his aesthetic concerns about the modernization of his native land. He believed that "we are in the hands of the Jews. They can do what they please with our values. . . . " He wrote to a friend, "The Jew makes me creep."[51]

Nevertheless, Adams was widely considered to be an irascible crank on this particular issue, especially in his old age; his complaints never assumed the dimensions, and never attracted the same attention, that parallel complaints of anti-Semitic antimodernists in Europe did. His remarks on Jews were mostly private and often ambiguous. ("The atmosphere [in 1914] really has become a Jew atmosphere. It is curious and evidently good for some people, but it isolates me. . . . We seem to be more Jewish every day."[52]) He did not try to bring his anti-Semitic ideas into the political arena; his was not the crusading, populist, and scurrilous anti-Semitism of a Drumont or a Krushevan, nor did it have the range and subtlety to be seen in the writings of Barrès, Treitschke, or even Pobedonostsev. Similar remarks hold for other American anti-Semitic brahmans, such as James Russell Lowell, who saw Jewish machinations everywhere and exclaimed that the rise of the Jews to world power was driving him mad. But when he began to rant about the Jews, he was more often mocked than respectfully listened to.[53]

Other prominent Americans of Adams's and Lowell's class, such as the previously mentioned John Hay, William James, or William Dean Howells, were forthright critics of anti-Semitism and generally friendly to

[51] W. C. Ford, ed., *Letters of Henry Adams, 1892–1918*, vol. 2 (New York, 1938), 338, 620; from Paul R. Mendes-Flohr and Jehuda Reinharz, *The Jew in the Modern World, A Documentary History* (Oxford, 1980), 370.
[52] Ibid., 110 ff.
[53] Grose, *Israel*, 42.

Jews.[54] Howells warmly and effectively supported the work of aspiring Jewish authors, earning deep-felt gratitude from many of them. Even Henry James, inclined to a distant, condescending snobbery in relation to Jews – probably the most common attitude of America's upper classes – did not stoop to viciousness. On returning to the United States from England in 1907, he was bewildered by the changes he saw. American cities looked "alien" to him, especially New York, which he termed "New Jerusalem." Yet he was willing to grant that the emerging culture might become "the most beautiful on the globe and the very music of humanity," even if it was different from the English culture that he and others of his class considered most genuinely, or at least originally, American.[55]

At the end of the nineteenth century the structures of the United States' economy, like those of most of the economies of Europe, were shifting in ways that threatened as never before the welfare of those involved in small-scale production. The ever-increasing concentration of industrial capital, the powerful and impersonal sway of market forces, economic modernization in its many guises, threatened many small producers, above all small family farms in the South and West. Imagery that laid blame on the Jews for these developments, with potential connections to long-standing anti-Semitic fantasies, started to appear and to take on a more rancorous, resentful, and ugly tone, especially following the depression that hit with unprecedented fury in 1893–4, a period that Allan Nevins has called "the *année terrible* of American history between Reconstruction and the World War." Unemployment rose to record levels in the cities, as did bankruptcies and ruined farms in the countryside.[56]

The destitute eastern European Jews who were arriving in such unprecedented numbers were no less shocking in hygiene, manners, and religious practices to many Americans than they were to western Europeans in the same years. Secretary of State Walter Quintin Gresham declared them "degraded and undesirable persons, unfitted in many respects for absorption into our body politic."[57] Undeniably, many of the recent arrivals were less prepared for what they would encounter in the United States, more reticent than had been earlier Jewish immigrants about becoming part of American society.

A much larger percentage than before of Jewish immigrants wanted as little as possible to do with the American Goyim – feelings that they quickly learned were mutual. The very idea of assimilation was less familiar to these immigrants, and the new American world shocked

---

[54] Ibid., 42.
[55] Baron, *Steeled by Adversity*, 321.
[56] Allan Nevins, *Grover Cleveland: A Study in Courage* (New York, 1932), 649; C. Vann Woodward, *Tom Watson: Agrarian Rebel* (Savannah, Ga., 1972), 223.
[57] Grose, *Israel*, 41.

their sensibilities. These sensibilities had evolved within the confines of a millions-strong, separatist, Yiddish culture. Of course, many eastern European Jews also merged into American society with unbounded enthusiasm. In the end, the overwhelming majority of them assimilated in one way or another, but not before a long and painful process of adjustment, on their side more extensive and painful than on the side of non-Jewish Americans. They were, in short, "americanized" incomparably more than non-Jewish Americans were "jewified."

In the United States, as in Europe, dismay at the manners and beliefs of eastern European Jews was often more pronounced among the established Jewish population than among the Gentiles because of the largely justified concern by such Jews that these new arrivals, these backward, unwashed, and strange-looking Jews, would provoke Gentile hostility, would undermine the steady progress that Jews had made in the country up to that time.

There was as well an economic, social, and cultural chasm between these two Jewish communities; they would remain distant from one another until the mid-twentieth century. Jews from eastern Europe often brought with them a distaste for rich bourgeois Jews, in part because of the way many such Jews in Russia had cooperated with the authorities. To that was added a distaste for the stiff manners and aura of superiority of German Jews (*yekkes* was the derogatory Yiddish term for them). German Jews in the United States shared the racist views of the surrounding society, including a belief in the racial inferiority of eastern and southern Europeans. Eastern European Jews were – to put it mildly – not welcome in German-Jewish country clubs, even when they could afford them, which was not often. Ironically, Jews from eastern Europe were shunned socially by German Jews in much the same way that German Jews were shunned by Gentile nouveaux riches and older, more established Anglo-American elites. Such invidious stratifications occur, of course, in nearly all societies, but nevertheless the way that German Jews treated eastern European Jews undermined the moral basis for their own expression of indignation when they experienced exclusion at the hands of Gentile elites.

On the other hand, charities of great importance and variety were organized by German Jews to benefit the newly arriving Jews from eastern Europe and to speed their integration into American society – so long as this charitable activity did not entail sitting down at the same dinner table with them. As one Jewish observer put it, the German-Jewish elite did what it could to americanize the east European Jews, yet "despised them cordially."[58] Even when racism was not predominant or explicit, many

[58] Ibid., 43.

Americans of northern and western European background, Jews among them, feared an array of evils arriving with the new immigrants: disease, crime, prostitution, revolutionary activity, unemployment, indigence. American Jewish leaders took an active part in the campaign against white slavery (international prostitution), in which, as they recognized with intense shame, Jews from eastern Europe played a prominent role.[59]

Thus, even the highly favorable remarks made about Jews on the occasion of Kishinev must be appreciated in context. Writers of sermons and editorials at that time were mostly concerned to contrast the moral stature and cultural level of Americans and Russians. It was not the appropriate time to express concern about any perceived defects of the Jewish victims. Certainly by 1903 not all Americans, whether non-Jew or Jew, were enthralled with Russian Jews; very few really considered them brothers-under-the-skin.

Still, among the eastern and southern European peoples, to say nothing of those from Asia, that were newly entering the United States at this time, Jews undoubtedly had the most favorable press. At the time of Kishinev, the Jews were described in a Wisconsin newspaper as a "thrifty, energetic, far-seeing race," whereas "their Slavic neighbors [were] too sodden with drink and too bestial by nature to take any thought for the morrow."[60] Twelve years earlier, in 1891, when President Benjamin Harrison had expressed his "serious concern" about the estimated one million Russian "Hebrews" that would be coming to the United States in the next few years, he nevertheless remarked that "the Hebrew is never a beggar; he has always kept the law . . . even under severe and oppressive civil restrictions."[61]

Ironically, many American editors, in defending the Jews, implicitly and unwittingly seemed to accept the point made by many Russian nationalists and government officials – that the peasants were no match for the Jews and would inevitably come under their power. The *Commercial Gazette* of Pittsburgh, Pennsylvania, for example, in an editorial that strongly condemned the civil inequalities of the Jews in Russia, noted, in praise and sympathy for the Jews, that "in competition with the weak and thriftless Russian peasant, the Jew acquires all the trade and prosperity."[62] A few years earlier, Mark Twain, in a light-spirited article that obviously intended to praise the Jews and counter anti-Semitic charges, had written that it would be wise for Gentiles to prevent the establishment

---

[59] Edward J. Bristow, *Prostitution and Prejudice: The Jewish Fight Against White Slavery, 1870–1939* (Oxford, 1983), 146 ff.

[60] Adler, *Voice of America*, 314.

[61] James A. Richardson, *A Compilation of the Messages and Papers of the Presidents, 1789–1908*, vol. 9 (Washington, D.C., 1908), 188; quoted in Salo W. Baron, *The Russian Jew Under Tsars and Soviets* (New York, 1987), 49.

[62] Adler, *Voice of America*, 445.

of a Jewish state: "It will not be well to let that race find out its strength. If horses knew theirs, we should not be able to ride any more." He similarly commented that in the Mississippi valley, the Jews were just like the Yankees; both were able to outsmart and exploit the poor Whites and Blacks. Twain wrote at some length concerning the intellectual superiority of the Jewish race to the non-Jewish, using the term "Jewish race" unapologetically, as did nearly all of his contemporaries. That Jews should be disliked was no surprise to him, for the Jew "is substantially a foreigner wherever he may be, and even the angels dislike a foreigner."[63]

Even more remarkable was how much prominent Jews in America seemed to corroborate precisely what Russian officials maintained about Russia's Jewish population: It was clannish, religiously fanatical, and bent on domination. Isaac Mayer Wise said that it was "impossible . . . to identify ourselves with that half-civilized orthodoxy," and Emma Lazarus, whose poem was placed at the base of the Statue of Liberty, was not so sure about the huddled masses of Jews from Russia. She suggested that another place, not the United States, should be found for that unappealing "mass of semi-Orientals, Kabbalists, and Hassidim."[64] Walter Lippmann wrote that Jews had "many distressing personal and social habits . . . selected by a bitter history and intensified by a pharisaical theology." He believed that if American universities were to take in more than 15 percent Jews, the result would be a "disaster."[65] Quotas in Russia were defended by the ministers of the tsar in much the same language.

Ethnic riots occurred in the United States in the troubled years around the turn of the century, but they were directed against Italians and Chinese, not Jews. The characteristic form of American "pogrom," lynchings of Blacks, occurred with great regularity and stomach-turning brutality. Nineteen Italians were lynched in Louisiana in the 1890s, apparently because they appeared to fraternize with Blacks.[66] Many of the editorial writers in 1903, on the occasion of the Kishinev pogrom, were obviously troubled by the similarities between Russia and the United States in regard to such violence. They were quick to dismiss as inaccurate and unfair any suggestions that the two countries suffered from similar problems, since the authorities in the United States did not encourage these actions (an assertion that certainly might be contested, at least in terms of local authorities).

[63] Mark Twain, *Concerning the Jews* (Philadelphia, 1985), 18–27. [From the March 1898 issue of *Harper's New Monthly Magazine*.]
[64] Grose, *Israel*, 32.
[65] Ronald Steel, *Walter Lippmann and the American Century* (London, 1980), 194; Johnson, *History of the Jews*, 469. Lippmann, it should be noted, was referring to the Jewish population in general; but his fear of a Jewish takeover in education, which was incomparably less likely in the United States than in Russia, is the point here.
[66] Leonard Dinnerstein, *The Leo Frank Affair* (New York, 1968), 65.

What particularly irked many American editorial writers was that the Russian ambassador to the United States, in responding to the criticism of his country surrounding the Kishinev pogrom, had freely recognized that the lower orders in the Russian Empire, when driven to frenzy by race and religious hatred, and when under the influence of alcohol, were capable of violence – "just like Americans." He observed that Americans had recently lynched Blacks or attacked unpopular minorities in many parts of the country and in numbers that exceeded the number of Jews who were killed or injured at Kishinev.

The closest that Jews in the United States at this time experienced to riots against them was in New York City in July 1902. In this case, the Jews themselves had violently attacked a factory whose mostly Irish workers had insulted a Jewish funeral in progress, throwing refuse on the mourners. Called in to restore order, the police officers, also mostly Irish, themselves went out of control. One Jewish observer remarked shortly afterward that "it was a thing that even a Russian, with all his dislike of our people, would have been ashamed of."[67] The Jews in this instance were provoked beyond measure, and their vigorous response might well have occurred at any period in history, but on the other hand, there was no little symbolism in the episode: The old stereotype of the cowed and defenseless Jew was increasingly being challenged. It was being replaced by an image of an active and self-respecting Jewish citizen who was un-afraid to stand up and fight with fists and physical violence for his dignity, a transformation, as we have seen, that was well under way in Russia. The episode also reflected real conflict between two ethnic groups, the Irish, established in the city, and the Jews, who were rapidly increasing in numbers and threatening to change the character of the Lower East Side in ways that were unacceptable to the Irish. In broad outlines it paralleled the conflict in cities like Vienna, Berlin, Kiev, or Kishinev. A key difference was the relatively unimportant linkage of ideological fantasy in the United States. That linkage, however, was not entirely lacking.

Potential areas of conflict; American anti-Semitic ideology

Although the mesh, or fit, of inherited Jewish manners and traditions with native American manners and traditions was extensive, it was by no means perfect. In a few regards there were rather deep-rooted differences, ones that began to become more visible by the late ineteenth century. Re-

---

[67] Leonard Dinnerstein, "The Funeral of Rabbi Jacob Josepth," in Gerber, *Anti-Semitism in American History*, 287; Howe, *World of Our Fathers*, 124.

spect for manual labor, in particular for working the land with one's own hands, was a central American virtue. Such respect was not a part of a European Jewish tradition, both for what might be termed cultural-religious reasons[68] and for reasons having to do with history, that is, the Jews' own preference since ancient times for trade and mobile occupations, linked to the restrictions imposed on Jews in many areas concerning ownership of land. Americans who worked the land, like the peasantry of Europe, were inclined to think of their labor as both "real" and "honest." The work of men who sold the goods produced by others was naturally suspect, and even more suspect were the moneylenders, bankers, and financiers. Their wealth was unearned, and they manipulated the economy in devious ways to gain unnatural wealth by exploiting those who worked honestly, by the sweat of their brow.

Such perceptions and reasoning were central to European democratic radicalism and to socialism, especially its Proudhonian varieties. They have points of contact even with Marxism. Their anti-Semitic potential, the possibility of making them part of an ideology of anti-Semitism, is obvious. In the United States distrust of those who manipulated money rather than doing "honest" work was one of the points of departure for the Populist movement, which gained an ardent following in the depression years of the 1890s around the themes of protecting the small farmer against the incursions of "money power" and the "international Gold Ring." American Populists were in many regards similar to the Christian-social movements in Europe at the turn of the century; important parallels with the republicanism of the Paris shopkeepers can also be seen.[69]

A debate raged for some time among American historians about how much the Populists, like the parallel movements in Europe, were anti-Semitic. More generally, the role of bigotry, racism, and xenophobia in the movement has been debated. Without delving into the considerable intricacies of the matter,[70] it is clear that a few leading Populists attacked Jews and that the mass of increasingly impoverished small farmers in the South and West during the 1890s were aroused by Populist denunciations of financiers, such as the Rothschilds, as well as of other powers in the international and American economy, such as the (non-Jewish) Rockefel-

---

[68] "For a man 'who comes from yikhus' [who is of distinguished lineage] to engage in manual labor, even under the stress of economic necessity, is a calamity, for manual labor has come to symbolize the antithesis of the social ideal – a life devoted entirely to study." Mark Zborowski and Elizabeth Herzog, *Life Is with People: The Culture of the Shtetl* (New York, 1969), 78.

[69] Cf. Philip G. Nord, *Paris Shopkeepers and the Politics of Resentment* (Princeton, N.J., 1986), 488, who particularly emphasizes the important left-wing and progressive elements in both ideologies.

[70] See James Turner, "Understanding the Populists," *Journal of American History*, vol. 67, no. 2, Sept. 1978, 354–73, for balanced discussion of the problem, with ample bibliographical references.

lers and Morgans. In this area, potential for anti-Jewish feeling, and for a linkage of real conflict and ideological fantasy about Jews, had always existed; that potential now began to be realized, especially among the dirt farmers, who were desperately clinging to their land but who found the market price for their produce steadily declining. For them, modern times, in the form of new market forces, were undoubtedly threatening. As in Europe, the visibility of Jews as symbols of market forces was increasing, and for uneducated and despairing farmers the Jewish financier was an obvious, tempting target. Such farmers could easily share Henry Adams's perception: Their country was being taken over by un-American, parasitic Jews.

There is little question that the Jews were a people on the rise, whereas the small farmer was in decline. It is by no means clear, however, that significant numbers of small farmers actually saw things in such terms or that many of them turned to anti-Semitic ideologists who were capable of supplying focus and coherence to their resentments. Anti-Semitic ideology in the United States remained undeveloped; even intellectuals like Adams and Lowell did not attempt to integrate their disappointments and aversions into a modern ideology of anti-Semitism designed to attract a mass following. About as close as any major American writer or thinker in the late nineteenth century came to formulating a modern anti-Semitic ideology, of being an American equivalent to the likes of Marr, Drumont, or Krushevan, was Ignatius Donnelly (1831–1901), a prominent figure in the Populist movement and author of the ringing preamble of the party platform in 1892.

In the middle years of the century Donnelly had served in Minnesota as lieutenant governor, as congressman, and as member of the state legislature. He edited the weekly *Anti-Monopolist* in the late 1870s and the Populist *Representative* in the 1880s. His political and literary interests ranged widely, including works on Bacon and Shakespeare, but his best-known work was the novel *Caesar's Column* (1891), where he set forth his views, among other things, on the destructive role of the Jews in the modern world.

Donnelly is sometimes dismissed as an unbalanced eccentric; he has been called "the prince of cranks." Yet there was genuine content to his thought, and some observers have praised his sagacity, even his intellectual generosity. His attitude to Jews was more complex and even ambiguously sympathetic than brief résumés of his work might suggest. Like Marr, Donnelly portrayed the Jews in social-Darwinistic terms: They were tough, having survived centuries of persecution; they had now become "as merciless to the Christian as the Christian had been to them."[71]

---

[71] Quoted in Baron, *Steeled*, 322.

Unlike Marr, however, Donnelly was not a racist, since he saw Jewish character as formed by the experience of Jews in history. He did not develop that perspective with the acuity of a Barrès, but it was nevertheless different from the racist determinism of many European anti-Semites. Still, like Barrès, Donnelly was a man of some learning, and, also like Barrès, his sympathy for the downtrodden was genuine. He worked long and hard to help the common people.[72]

Donnelly's work helped to spread negative images about Jews when many in the American nation were primed to receive them. In most regards those images resembled images already frequently described: contempt for non-Jews, uncontrollable greed, lust for power, secretiveness, and indifference to national allegiance. But one of the images, or a set of interconnected ones, is of particular relevance in examining the background to the Frank Affair: the Jew as unclean, lecherous, and lusting after Gentile women. One of Donnelly's principal Jewish villains, Prince Cabano, hungers for the Anglo-Saxon woman Estella Washington.

It is difficult to know how widespread or widely believed such images were around the turn of the century in the United States, but they popped up in sometimes surprising quarters, not simply in the fictionalized imaginings of a man like Donnelly. E. A. Ross, a prominent Progressive and highly respected sociologist, wrote in 1914 that "pleasure-loving Jewish businessmen . . . pursue Gentile girls," which "excites bitter comment."[73]

This negative stereotype, associated as it was with sexuality in an epoch of sexual repression, was almost by definition one that could not be openly discussed. Even today determining its appeal as a fantasy is difficult. Some observers have argued that fear of Jewish sexuality explains the special vehemence and irrationality of Hitler's anti-Semitism,[74] and related fears unquestionably played an important role in Nazi propaganda against Jews.[75] Even among Jewish observers the sexuality of Jewish males and their alleged special attraction to non-Jewish females has been a perennial topic, especially in fiction. The longed-for *goldene shikse* (golden Gentile girl) is a central theme in much recent, best-selling fiction by American Jews[76] and appears even in such unexpected places as the life of Chaim Weizmann, the Zionist leader and first president of Israel.[77]

---

[72] Cf. the perceptive and balanced discussion in Frederic Cople Jaher, *Doubters and Dissenters* (New York, 1964), 130–40; reproduced in Dinnerstein, *Anti-Semitism*, 78–86.

[73] E. A. Ross, "The Hebrew of Eastern Europe in America," *The Century Magazine*, vol. 88, Sept. 1914, 787; from Dinnerstein, *Frank*, 198.

[74] Johnson, *History*, 475.

[75] Cf. Dennis E. Showalter, *Little Man, What Now? Der Stürmer in the Weimar Republic* (Hamden, Conn., 1982).

[76] Cf. Philip Roth, *Portnoy's Complaint* (New York, 1969); Mordecai Richler, *Joshua, Then and Now* (New York, 1980).

[77] Jehuda Reinharz, *Chaim Weizmann: The Making of a Zionist Leader* (Oxford, 1985), 367–72.

At any rate, in the Frank Affair the issue of Jewish sexuality would assume a central importance, as would the related one of the Jew as publically upright but privately perverse and dishonest.

The South and the Jews

The largely harmonious relations of Jews and Gentiles in the country as a whole may seem irrelevant, in that Frank's arrest, conviction, and lynching was the result of specifically Southern mentalities and conditions. Most Americans certainly thought of the Frank case as a Southern matter, a tragedy that could not have happened in the North. There is much to be said in favor of that perception. However, important qualifications must also be applied to it.

The American South in the eighteenth and nineteenth centuries was different from the rest of the country and might be described as resembling European nations, especially those in eastern Europe. The South might then be expected to suffer from European afflictions, such as anti-Semitism, more than the rest of the country. Well into the nineteenth century the South remained premodern, or preindustrial, in social structures and values; southerners revered tradition, feared change, and distrusted the outsider. A planter aristocracy ruled over large estates worked by servile Black labor, interspersed with an impoverished and benighted White peasantry (in the language of the South, "rednecks" or "crackers"), known for cruel outbursts of violence. Large cities and towns in the South were rare and unimportant as compared to the North; the middle class, or bourgeoisie, was small in numbers and without political significance. Charm and grace, brutality and ignorance mixed in ineffable ways.

These intriguing comparisons of the Old World and the American South can be deceptive, especially in regard to anti-Semitism, for it was less important there than readers unfamiliar with that region might suppose, certainly less important than it was in most countries of Europe. There has been a minor debate among historians about what might be termed Southern exceptionalism in regard to the Jews. Some have argued that, in spite of the well-known religious bigotry, xenophobia, and racism in the South, Jews found a friendlier, more welcoming environment there than they did in the rest of the country.[78] Nativism, which appears repeatedly in American history, in nearly all parts of the country, especially in times of trouble, was unquestionably strong in the South, stronger than in most of the rest of the nation, but nativism in regard to Jews was

---

[78] One of the most recent discussions of this issue, with ample bibliographical citations, can be found in Abraham Peck, "That Other 'Peculiar Institution': Jews and Judaism in the Nineteenth Century South," *Modern Judaism*, vol. 7, no. 1, Feb. 1987, 99–114.

less strong than it was against other outsiders, whether Yankees, Italians, Greeks, or Slavic Europeans.

Jews in the South were less numerous and more thinly distributed than in almost any country of Europe in the nineteenth century, let alone the United States. By 1907 only 5 percent of the Jewish population of the United States lived below the Mason–Dixon Line.[79] Eastern European Jews did not migrate there in significant numbers, and those Jews who settled in the South embraced southern mores even more unreservedly and unanimously than German Jews elsewhere accepted the mores of the rest of the country.

Southern leaders from the 1880s on invited settlers but expressed reservations about receiving eastern and southern European immigrants. If it was not possible to have a continued immigration of the English and Scots-Irish stock from which most Southerners sprang, they preferred Germans and Scandinavians. The first Jewish immigrants in the South in the nineteenth century were largely German in background and undoubtedly benefited from the prestige of the German culture with which they openly identified.

Jews did not function as a dissenting minority in the South in the nineteenth century. Before the Civil War, Jewish entrepreneurs bought and sold slaves; individual Jews owned them. Slave-owning Jews included rabbis and other prominent members of the Jewish community. One of the most careful historians of southern Jewry has concluded that the attitudes of southern Jews to slavery did not differ significantly from those of southern Christians.[80] He adds that "no Jewish figure of the Old South ever expressed any reservations about the justice of slavery or the rightness of the Southern position." He also notes that "people of color" were not allowed in Jewish congregations, even if they were the product of sexual unions between Jewish slaveholders and their female slaves. Unlike Christians, Jewish owners did not educate their slaves into their faith,[81] and conversions of Blacks in the South to Judaism were extremely rare. Southern rabbis commonly justified slavery from Old Testament texts, much as Christian Whites did. Southern Jews were inclined, like southern White Christians, to construct romantic mythologies about their racially superior and aristocratic origins (Anglo-Norman in the case of the Christian Whites; Sephardic – thus aristocratic, because of the high social

[79] Steven Hertzberg, *Strangers Within the Gate City: The Jews of Atlanta, 1845–1915* (Philadelphia, 1978), 3.

[80] Bertram Korn, "Jews and Negro Slavery in the Old South," *Publications of the American Jewish Historical Society*, vol. 50, March, 1961; reprinted in Dinnerstein and Palsson, *Jews in the South*, 89–134.

[81] Korn, "Jews and Negro Slavery," 115, 123.

standing of the Jews of Spain and Portugal in the Middle Ages – in the case of Jews).[82]

Well into the twentieth century Jews in the North were less successful in gaining major political office than were Jews in the South. Judah P. Benjamin held cabinet-level positions in the Confederacy during the Civil War and had been U.S. senator from Louisiana before that. He owned a plantation with hundreds of slaves. A number of other southern Jews gained similar prominence and identified wholly with southern racist, slaveholding society. After the war southern Jews commonly expressed regret at the passing of the institution of slavery. Solomon Cohen wrote that slavery was "refining and civilizing to whites" and "the only institution that could elevate the Negro from barbarism and develop the small amount of intellect with which he is endowed."[83] There are even examples of Jewish participation in the Ku Klux Klan.[84] In 1896, an editorial of *The Jewish South*, published in Richmond, Virginia, observed that "Twenty-five years of education resulted in making the colored women more immoral and the men more trifling. . . . Negroes are intellectually, morally, and physically an inferior race – a fact none can deny."[85] A decade later a Jewish member of the Carnegie Library Board in Atlanta, Georgia, voted with the majority to reject a petition to admit Blacks to the library.[86] These were not isolated incidents.

Some southern Jews offered a religious basis for their racism. A Jewish editor, Jacob N. Cardozo, explained that "the reason the Almighty had made the colored black" was to mark them as inferior, to provide an obvious, God-given approval of their natural status as slaves.[87] Other basic texts of the Old Testament could, of course, be used to oppose slavery; Christian abolitionists cited them for their purposes, but until the late nineteenth century Judaism in the United States did not begin to realize its potential for social justice and reform. American Jews had not, for the most part, accepted a sense of responsibility, as Jews, for the larger society around them, and when they later did so, southern Jews were much behind those of the North.

The talmudic injunction that "the law of the land is the law," which traditional Jews in Russia regarded as a command to remain faithful to the institutions of tsarist autocracy, also allowed American Jews in the

---

[82] Peck, "Jews and Judaism in the South," 101.
[83] Korn, "Jews and Negro Slavery," 127.
[84] Dinnerstein, *Frank*, 68.
[85] *The Jewish South*, July 10, 1896, 2; quoted in Peck, "Jews and Judaism in the South," 109.
[86] Hertzberg, *Strangers*, 193.
[87] *Reminiscences of Charleston* (Charleston, 1866), 10; quoted in Korn, "Jews and Negro Slavery," 125.

South to defend slavery as the law of the land. However, many Jewish defenders of slavery used racist arguments that went well beyond what was necessary in following that talmudic injunction. It was only later that northern Jews, especially the politically left-wing masses of the northern cities in the twentieth century, began massively to express sympathy for the plight of Blacks in America. German Jews in Europe cited Torah and Talmud to support a divine sanction for the new German Reich; French Jews did the same for the Third Republic. Quite aside from the above-cited talmudic injunction, the use of sacred texts to support opportune causes is hardly an unfamiliar phenomenon, whether for Jews or for Christians.

In the South any different attitudes towards Blacks by Jews in the nineteenth and early twentieth century would almost certainly have provoked ferocious hostility by southern Christian Whites. For this reason, it is not surprising that "there was not a single abolitionist among the Jews of the South."[88] Those rare Jews who chose to seek their fortune in the South were certainly aware of the danger of challenging southern mores – or very soon became aware of it.[89] They almost necessarily were the sort who, even more than Jews in the rest of America, were not deeply attached to the outward forms of traditional Judaism. "Judaism was not their whole life," as one historian has remarked.[90] They were reticent to let religious tradition interfere in a major way in their ambitions and careers. There were other places in the country, mostly in northern urban centers, where observant Jews could settle, where the concentrated numbers of Jews and the supporting institutions (religious schools, rabbis, ritual slaughterers, ritual baths, cemeteries, and so forth) made a more strictly observant life possible.

In a purely practical sense, the isolated, itinerant Jewish peddler or even the established merchant in the South was obliged to put aside traditional practices and beliefs if he was to be able to do business with southerners. When a Jewish peddler by the name of Schwartz was invited into an Alabama farmhouse, it became immediately clear to him that the people there did not have much to eat except pork. When he was served and began to eat heartily, the farm lady expressed surprise. She had been told, she said, that "Moses ordered the Jews not to eat any hog meat."

---

[88] Korn, "Jews and Negro Slavery," 130.

[89] But cf. Korn, who argues that there is no evidence that "would lead us to believe that these Jews gave conscious support to the slave system out of fear of rousing anti-Jewish prejudice. Any such motivation for their behavior and attitudes, if it existed at all, was well hidden in the unconscious psyche." "Jews and Negro Slavery," 132.

[90] Bertram W. Korn, "Factors Bearing upon the Survival of Judaism in the Ante-Bellum Period," *American Jewish History Quarterly*, vol. 13, 1964, 344; quoted in Peck, "Jews and Judaism in the South," 106.

Schwartz amiably replied, "Ah, madam, if Moses had traveled through Perry County, Alabama, he never would have issued such an order."[91]

These adjustments to southern realities by Jews who settled in the South go a long way toward explaining why southern attitudes tended toward philo-Semitism more than northern. Similarly, southern forms of Christianity, even more than northern, tended to overlook or play down the anti-Semitic potential of the New Testament. One Jewish observer has insisted that "the Protestant fundamentalism of the South greeted the Jew with unusual generosity."[92] Another has remarked that many small-town southerners took care of "their" Jews "with a zeal and devotion otherwise bestowed only on the Confederate monument in the square."[93]

Even those southerners who, by the late nineteenth century, began to express outrage at what they perceived as the secretive machinations of the Jewish Money Men, or who resorted to anti-Semitic imagery from the New Testament, often expressed admiration for individual Jews. "Our Mr. Levy" existed in a separate category from the Money Men, and so did the local Jewish families, well known and personally esteemed as decent, law-abiding, hard-working citizens, people who did not – this was essential – offend southern mores. In an episode that strikingly recalls the experiences of Mendel Beilis with the Black Hundreds in Kiev, a Southern Jew, Irving Engel, was preparing to flee from Birmingham, Alabama, and was intercepted by an emissary of the Ku Klux Klan who told him, "Don't go away. You're not the kind of Jew we are after."[94] The Straus family, stung by denunciations of Jewish merchants during the Civil War, prepared to leave the small southern town in which they were living at the time; to their surprise and confusion nearly the whole town turned out to beseech them to remain, to insist that the attacks on Jewish merchants had by no means been directed at them personally.[95] In the philo-Semitic pronouncements that accompanied the condemnations of the Kishinev pogrom, southern ministers and southern editors were prominent.[96]

Aside from the perceived religious compatibilities of Southern Protestantism and Judaism, the economic and social position of southern Jews helped to ensure a warm welcome and continued hospitality for them.

---

[91] Quoted in Peck, "Jews and Judaism in the South," 106.
[92] Hasia R. Diner, *In the Almost Promised Land: American Jews and Blacks, 1915–1935* (Westport, Conn., 1977), 20.
[93] Harry Golden, "Jew and Gentile in the New South: Segregation at Sundown," *Commentary*, vol. 20, Nov. 1955, 403–4.
[94] Quoted in Peck, "Jews and Judaism in the South," 107.
[95] Korn, "American Judaeophobia," 147. For a more general treatment of this phenomenon, see Jonathon D. Sarna, "The 'Mythical Jew' and 'the Jew Next Door' in Nineteenth-Century America," in Gerber, *Anti-Semitism*, 57–74.
[96] Cf. Adler, *Voice of America*.

Put in simple terms, southern Jews satisfied many practical needs in the South, for rich and poor, Black and White, while offering little cause for offense. The situation recalls that of Hungary, in that southern Jews were perceived by the ruling elite as useful; they made up for the weakness of a native merchant and business class. In both Hungary and the South Jewish immigrants did not for the most part push out or threaten a preexisting, native commercial middle class, since there was only a very small one. Similarly, and probably even more importantly, southern Jews, like Hungarian Jews, enthusiastically identified with and bolstered a "threatened" culture, even to the degree of becoming prominent and articulate defenders of southern mores, thus naturally earning the gratitude of many southerners. Judah P. Benjamin, for example, was known as one of the most "eloquent defenders of the Southern way of life" in the history of the South.[97]

There were, to be sure, occasional complaints about the economic role of the Jews in the South. In 1856 Frederick Law Olmstead, a northerner on a southern tour, wrote that "a swarm of Jews, within the last ten years, has settled in nearly every southern town, many of them men of no character, opening cheap clothing and trinket shops, ruining, or driving out of business many of the old retailers. . . ."[98] But as in Hungary, such complaints were of relatively minor importance. Even in the bitter years during and immediately following the Civil War, when the Jews of the South were natural targets for frustrations of the time, hatred directed at them remained mixed and equivocal. Jews, as owners and operators of general stores, became a vital element of the southern rural economy, providing a system of capitalization and distribution in a ravaged and bankrupt region.[99] This Jewish class of general-store owners developed a network of face-to-face, personalized relationships with their rural customers, which goes a long way to explain how they, even if of foreign origin, even if they were "capitalists" of a sort, retained the affections of at least a part of the rural poor.

By the last decades of the nineteenth century, "there was a [Jewish] furnishing or general store at almost every crossroad in the South,"[100] but the ruling southern elites, the large plantation owners, were not threatened by this Jewish bourgeoisie since it remained narrowly concerned with making a living, politically unambitious as a class, and deferential to the powers-that-be. What one historian has called the "antimerchant

[97] Korn, "Jews and Negro Slavery," 123.
[98] Quoted in Burton Rascoe, *An American Reader* (New York, 1939), 226; from Korn, "American Judaeophobia," 139.
[99] Thomas D. Clark, "The Post–Civil War Economy in the South," in Dinnerstein and Palsson, *Jews in the South*, 166, 161.
[100] Ibid., 162.

refrain," which was a central feature of the anti-Yankee, agrarian southern ideology before the Civil War, had never, up to that point, been turned against the Jews of the South.[101] After the war, it again receded.

Revealing comparisons with Russia, as well as with Hungary, suggest themselves, for in Russia, too, many observers emphasized that for much of the nineteenth century Jews were welcomed by peasants in isolated areas, since Jews brought new goods and a measure of economic prosperity, while threatening no existing class in the villages. Anti-Semitic violence by the common people, uncommon in Russia in the nineteenth century until the 1880s and the unprecedented social changes of those years, had its origin, according to this persuasive line of argument, in the rapidly growing cities and towns of the late nineteenth century, to which great masses of Jews were flocking and where they came into competition with non-Jews in a way that was different from that of the villages and small towns in years past.

Jewish–Gentile Relations in Atlanta, Georgia

Comparisons with Russia suggest one further point of importance, in that Atlanta, Georgia, was one of the fastest growing urban centers in the South, a city that grew up from almost nothing, an American equivalent of Kishinev. In the experiences of the two cities may be seen a number of interesting parallels. Both were new, open cities that attracted Jewish as well as many other immigrants and that experienced helter-skelter growth, with major problems arising from poor planning, inadequate and incompetent police forces, and corrupt officials. In 1906, the year of a major race riot in the city, a reporter described Atlanta as "the very worst of American cities," filled with the "riff-raff that the mining towns of the West used to relieve us of."[102]

Yet Atlanta, a city that would later bill itself as "too busy to hate," offered powerful attractions to Jews. Just as America's openness and newness offered unparalleled opportunities to Jews willing to cast off their Old World habits, so it was with Atlanta. The city was not caste ridden as were older southern cities such as Richmond or New Orleans; there were no old-money families that resented newcomers. Businessmen were respected, and Jewish enterprise was generally welcome. Thus, the comparison to Kishinev also breaks down. Atlanta more resembled Budapest or Berlin in that Jewish settlement was widely accepted as useful to the city's growth, not denounced as a "plague" by government officials.

[101] Jonathan M. Wiener, "Planter–Merchant Conflict in Reconstruction Alabama," *Past and Present*, vol. 68, Aug. 1975, 88.
[102] Quoted in Dinnerstein, *Uneasy at Home*, 108.

The number of Jews involved was also radically different. On the eve of the Civil War, the Jewish population of the city had been minuscule, about fifty souls. It grew to around four thousand by 1910, an increase from 0.5 to 2.5 percent of a rapidly expanding total (Atlanta's total population was about 155,000 in 1910). Kishinev was only slightly smaller in total population by the first decade of the twentieth century, but its Jewish population was about fifty thousand, approximately fifteen times the Jewish population of Atlanta. Moreover, a large proportion of Kishinev's Jewish population remained extremely poor, lacking in skills, and not "useful," and a visible minority of Jewish youth in the town was involved in revolutionary activity, neither of which was true in Atlanta.

Atlanta became the capital of Georgia, the state's largest city, and the city with the largest number of Jews of any in the South. Georgia, similarly, had about twice the Jewish population of any other southern state. However, these growing numbers of Jews, both absolutely and relatively, resulted in very little hostility or jealousy on the part of the Gentile business class of Atlanta; there was much "space" for economic and social ambition, for Jews as for non-Jews. Jewish upward mobility was more striking in Atlanta than in most northern cities,[103] yet Gentiles in Atlanta seemed little concerned about a Jewish takeover. After 1890 there began a rapid increase in the number of Jews from eastern Europe in Atlanta; by the eve of World War I, they had become a majority of the Jewish population of the city. Still, the percentage of Jews of Atlanta remained between 2 and 3 percent, scarcely more, in other words, than in Kiev, where they were allowed to settle only under special dispensation.

The Reform rabbi of the city, David Marx, was very popular with the city's Gentiles. He established closer, more harmonious relations with the Unitarian, Universalist, Presbyterian, Baptist, and Methodist clergy in Atlanta than he ever did with the Orthodox rabbis who represented the new immigrants. His interpretation of Reform Judaism in many ways imitated Protestant Christianity. That kind of Reform Judaism found strong approval from the German-Jewish elite of the city, no doubt in part because it facilitated Gentile good will and added to the social respectability of upwardly mobile Jews.

Rabbi Marx and other German Jews in the city were not reticent to describe the newly arriving Russian Jews as barbaric and ignorant. German Jews went as far as to charge that the new arrivals were unaware of such fundamental concepts as the Ten Commandments.[104] Atlanta's German Jews, as German Jews elsewhere, feared that these backward Jews would awaken anti-Semitism where it had been notably absent. Once the

[103] Cf. Hertzberg, *Jews of Atlanta*, Ch. 6.
[104] Ibid., 128–9.

Frank Affair exploded in Atlanta, Rabbi Marx bitterly blamed the eastern European Jews for creating a climate that made Frank's arrest and conviction possible – events, he insisted, that would have been inconceivable a few decades earlier.[105]

By the first years of the twentieth century, the Jewish elite of Atlanta had entered into the social and political establishment of the city to an extent that had few parallels in the North. A number of Jewish–Gentile law partnerships were formed in Atlanta, as elsewhere in the South. In the 1880s four Jews were elected to the Atlanta city council. In the generation before the war a large number of Jews served on the grand jury. Jews were regularly chosen as officers of the Chamber of Commerce, and a Jew from Atlanta was elected to the Georgia House of Representatives. Jews were extremely active in the city's fraternal orders, the Elks, Shriners, and especially the Masons. In the Masonic lodges in Atlanta the Jews constituted from 25 to over 35 percent of the membership by the eve of the war. From the 1860s on Jews were repeatedly elected to the highest offices in those lodges.[106]

As in the North, there were a few clubs that remained closed to Jews, but that limited exclusion did not prevent the German-Jewish elite from mixing widely and easily in Atlanta society. Jews in Atlanta in the 1880s and 1890s openly and proudly declared that their social situation was far better than that of Jews in the North. Atlanta's Jews did not face significant discrimination in housing, education, employment, or public accommodation.

The change in climate at the end of the century, however, did affect the Jews in Atlanta, if in more subtle ways than in the North. Long-resident Jews in Atlanta began to worry that the widespread esteem that they had enjoyed was beginning to fade, that the fulsome praise heaped upon Jews by prominent Gentiles in the city, the quite explicit philo-Semitism, was somehow less in evidence than it had been in the immediately preceding decades. And Rabbi Marx was not the only one to blame the new Jewish arrivals for this disturbing change, although all were aware of the role of economic hardship and rapid change. After the turn of the century a number of Jewish candidates for city council failed to be elected. Their loss was certainly not because of open anti-Semitism in the campaigns, but still the Jews in the city were apprehensive. As in the rest of the nation at this time, there were new sources of friction between Jews and Gentiles, and in truth the worries of the German-Jewish elite about the negative impact of the newly arriving eastern European Jews in the city were not without foundation.

---

[105] Ibid., 212.
[106] Ibid., 168–9.

Temperance had long been a divisive issue in the South, and non-Jews generally recognized that Jews overwhelmingly opposed prohibition. No doubt part of the reason that the issue did not much disturb Jewish–Gentile relations for much of the century was that Jewish community was also known as an unusually sober one; its reservations about outlawing the sale of alcohol could be explained as related to the role of wine in Jewish religious ceremonies. Open and rancorous differences between Jews and Gentiles over the issue of the sale and consumption of alcohol did not assume much importance until the early twentieth century, and then public ire was not so much directed against the German-Jewish producers of alcohol, by this time mostly wealthy, established citizens, as against the Russian-Jewish saloon keepers. It was charged that they sold alcohol to the Blacks of the city, contributing to the rising levels of public drunkenness, street violence, indigence, and crime. The charge resembled that made in central and eastern Europe, in regard to the role of Jewish innkeepers and the peasantry. Allegations were also widely made that Russian-Jewish pawnbrokers were receiving stolen goods, and even selling weapons to Blacks.[107]

The issue of Jews' selling alcohol and weapons to Blacks was much envenomed in 1906 by what has been termed "the worst race riot America has ever suffered."[108] Provoked by reports that two White women had been savagely murdered by Blacks, mobs of Whites went on a rampage, attacking Blacks – men, women, and children – at random. For over a week armed men roamed the streets of Atlanta, at times breaking into stores to get more guns and ammunition.

As in Kishinev, the riot was marked by police bungling and apparent complicity (in regard to Blacks, not Jews, who were not attacked by the rioters); order was finally restored by the National Guard. Ten Blacks were reported killed, as were two Whites, and approximately seventy people were injured. A number of saloon licenses held by Jews were revoked immediately after the riots.[109] In the following years, Christian temperance leaders openly attacked the Jews for their role in the liquor trade, for what they described as Jewish greed and pursuit of profit at the expense of public health and morality.

Yet in these same years powerful counterimages were also presented. In 1907 Governor J. M. Terrell reported that only one Jew was to be found among the thirty-five hundred inmates in Georgia prisons. Time and again the Atlanta press marveled at how law-abiding Jews were.[110] Similarly, prominent Jews were quick, in this period of racial tension, to

[107] Ibid., 186.
[108] Harry Golden, *A Little Girl Is Dead* (Cleveland, 1965), 40.
[109] Hertzberg, *Jews of Atlanta*, 162, 186–7.
[110] Ibid., 178.

make clear their identification with White supremacist attitudes. The Jewish journalist, Frank Cohen, went as far as to condone lynching Blacks who violated "the sanctity of the white man's home" or who committed "the unmentionable crime against women." A recent immigrant from Poland remarked with dismay that he "heard the term 'nigger' used by Jewish sons of immigrants with the same venom and contempt that the term 'zhid' was used in the old country."[111] Black spokesmen at times expressed their sense of disappointment in these southern Jewish attitudes. Upon the death of the White supremacist Jewish senator from Maryland, Isador Rayner, a Black journalist lamented that, although Rayner was of a race that had known suffering and oppression, "he invoked upon his colored neighbor the terrors of Kishinev."[112]

Another source of friction and potential anti-Jewish feeling in Atlanta at the end of the century was the Populist movement. However, that potential found little expression in the city in the 1890s. Tom Watson, a leading Populist in the South and editor of the extremely influential *People's Party Paper*, published in Atlanta, at this time explicitly rejected anti-Semitism. He and other Populist leaders could hardly ignore the open, often adamant opposition of Jewish business interests to the Populist movement, in particular to the idea of free silver. Even so, Jewish merchants bought advertising space in Watson's paper, and Watson often praised the city's Jews and notably avoided calling attention to anti-Populist sentiment among them.[113]

Watson's lack of animus against Jews extended surprisingly far. He defended the Jewish anarchist, Emma Goldman, at this time a notorious figure in the eyes of the respectable public, while eloquently denouncing the "true destroyers" of Jeffersonian democracy, the Goulds, Rockefellers, and Vanderbilts.[114] This disinclination of Watson and American Populists more generally to denounce left-wing Jews stands in particularly stark contrast to the Christian socials and most other European anti-Semites of the period.

The opposition of southern Jewish businessmen to the Populist movement suggests another area of potential anti-Jewish sentiment, related to the perception of Jews as people who avoided manual labor, who did not do real or honest work. There was no Jewish proletariat in the South, like the one in the North at the turn of the century, and Jews in the South, even when establishing friendly relations with the common people, were not part of them in the sense of sharing their sufferings, of working together in labor unions and political campaigns, as working-class Jews

[111] Ibid., 193.
[112] Ibid., 200.
[113] Ibid., 163 ff.
[114] Woodward, *Tom Watson*, 224.

increasingly did in the North. Nor did southern Jews openly or prominently sympathize with the plight of the lower orders, whether Black or White. A historian of Hungarian Jewry has noted that "by identifying itself unconditionally and uncritically with a basically reactionary regime whose favors it enjoyed and to which it was indebted, Hungarian Jewry alienated itself from the oppressed classes. . . . "[115] A similar situation held in the South; in the uncritical identification by Jews with the culture and values of the establishment lurked a potential vulnerability. Even if the leaders of the Populist movement, men like Tom Watson or William Jennings Bryan, did not exploit the Jewish issue, a few did, and a potential for lower-class resentment was certainly there, resentments that were easily linked to nativist perceptions of Jews as outsiders and Populist perceptions of Jews as exploiters.

[115] Randolph L. Braham, *The Politics of Genocide: The Holocaust in Hungary* (New York, 1981), 2.

9

The Leo Frank Affair

The Frank case is enough to depress the most hopeful student of the times. It has shown us how the capitalists of Big Money regard the poor man's daughter. It has shown us what our daily papers will do in the interests of wealthy criminals. It has shown us how differently the law deals with rich man and the poor. (Tom Watson)[1]

> Leo Frank he met her
> With a brutish heart and grin;
> He says to little Mary,
> "You'll never see home again."
>
> . . .
>
> The Christian doers of heaven
> Sent Leo Frank to hell. . . . ("The Ballad of Mary Phagan")

Images and interpretations of the Frank Affair

Both France and the United States were widely considered to be progressive and tolerant countries where Jews could find just treatment and unusual opportunities. Yet whereas Dreyfus and Beilis eventually became free men, Leo Frank was found guilty. His guilt and the fairness of his trial were repeatedly reaffirmed by higher judicial authorities. He was nearly murdered while in prison, and he was then dragged from prison and lynched. No legal decision has ever fully or explicitly exonerated Frank of killing Mary Phagan,[2] nor have those who lynched him ever been identified and punished. The emotions his trial unleashed appear as ugly and primitive as any to be found in France or in the most backward areas of eastern Europe.

Here would seem to be an excellent example, better than the Dreyfus Affair, of how anti-Semitic fantasies, surviving in a realm of their own,

---

[1] Leonard Dinnerstein, *The Frank Case* (New York, 1968), 202.

[2] In March 1986 Frank was pardoned, after lengthy proceedings and a refusal by the Georgia Board of Pardons to grant a pardon in December 1983. The pardon studiously avoided declaring Frank innocent. Rather, it recognized the failure of the state to protect "the person of Frank and thereby preserve his opportunity for legal appeal of his conviction." The statement also expressed a desire to "heal old wounds." Still, it stated that "it is impossible to decide conclusively the guilt or innocence of Leo M. Frank." (Quoted in Mary Phagan [Kean], *The Murder of Little Mary Phagan* (Far Hills, N.J., 1987), 306.

can suddenly explode in unpredictable and incomprehensible ways. The Frank Affair might also be cited as proof, for those more inclined to insist on the importance of real historical forces, that tensions between Jew and non-Jew in the United States were finally more important than historians have been willing to recognize. However, the available evidence does not offer very solid support for either of those conclusions. Furthermore, that evidence even puts into question the assertion that anti-Semitism, whether as a product of a self-perpetuating fantasy divorced from reality or as a reflection of tensions in the real world, was of decisive importance in the Frank case.

Had Frank not been Jewish, but only a northerner or an Italian or a rich man or simply a man with his personal appearance and idiosyncrasies, he still might have been arrested and convicted of the crime. Frank's Jewishness weighed at least as much in his favor as against him. Italians or Greeks enjoyed a distinctly less friendly press in Atlanta and in the South generally. They encountered a lower regard in public opinion and were more generally perceived as outsiders who were insensitive to southern traditions. They were people of racial and religious types that were not welcome in the South, which was not the conclusion generally reached about Jews.

To be sure, if Frank had not been Jewish, there might not have been an affair emerging out of the case, since innocent men of other races and religions might not have enjoyed the respect and connections that he and other influential Jews of Atlanta did, nor might they have attracted the attention of selfless and powerful individuals, Jewish and non-Jewish, who both rallied defenders and provoked a widespread hostility in Georgia (that is, helped to make an affair of the Frank case). Similarly, and even more important, national and world attention might not have focused so sharply on the plight of an innocent Italian or Greek, since there had been nothing recently comparable to the Dreyfus or Beilis affairs for Italians or Greeks. The plight of an innocent Jew was both newsworthy and likely to attract the attention of powerful people.

These are, of course, speculations. They are placed here as a way of trying to gain perspective in order to approach the case as open-mindedly as possible. This effort is necessary because, as in the two other affairs, charges of anti-Semitism, both at the time of the trial and in later historical accounts, have been burdened with preconceptions that project onto the available facts of the case an interpretation that those facts fail to substantiate. People then and later have in some sense wanted to find anti-Semitism. They have not been entirely disappointed in their search, but they have also been inclined to dramatize inappropriately or exaggerate what they found of it.

There is no doubt a danger of carrying this argument too far. Certain negative stereotypes about Jews in late nineteenth-century America did come into play as the Frank case became an affair. But they were not decisive; if they had not been present, the case might plausibly still have developed toward a guilty verdict and a lynching. A point of central importance is that Frank's lawyers and his other defenders, in order to strengthen their case, overstated the role of anti-Semitic prejudice in his arrest – understandably, perhaps, but also mistakenly and in ways that may have damaged Frank's chances of acquittal as well as setting in motion and encouraging subsequent exaggerations of the role of anti-Semitism.

Leo Frank: respected businessman or vulnerable Jew?

Leo Frank was born in Texas of German-Jewish parents, although soon after his birth his family moved to the East Coast. He graduated from Cornell University and moved from New York to Atlanta, Georgia, in 1908, when he was twenty-four years old, to assume the position of superintendent in a pencil factory of which his wealthy uncle was the majority stockholder and in which he also held stock. In 1911 he married the daughter of a wealthy manufacturer in Atlanta. As a college graduate, an American-born German Jew, he was considered, according to one Jewish observer, a "catch" for any Jewish woman in Atlanta.[3] His background and education also helped him earn almost immediate acceptance into the elite of the Jewish community. He was soon elected president of the Jewish fraternal organization B'nai B'rith in Atlanta. He was not yet thirty years old.

That organization was of considerable importance to Jews in Atlanta. For many Jews in the city, especially those who found Jewish ritual or even synagogue membership and attendance an unsatisfactory expression of their sense of Jewishness, the B'nai B'rith served as a secular substitute.[4] Ironically, as president of the organization one of Frank's first concerns, probably because of what he was told by German Jews who had lived in the city for a longer time, was to do something about the recent subtle change for the worse in the attitudes toward Jews in Atlanta. He appointed a committee, in early 1913, just before his arrest, "to investigate the complaints against Jewish caricatures that are becoming so frequent on the local stage."[5]

[3] Harry Golden, *A Little Girl Is Dead* (Cleveland, 1965), 18.
[4] Deborah Dash Moore, *B'nai Brith and the Challenge of Ethnic Leadership* (Albany, N.Y., 1981), 28.
[5] Steven Hertzberg, *Strangers Within the Gate City: The Jews of Atlanta, 1845–1915* (Philadelphia, 1978), 180.

Frank was obviously not the kind of man that one would expect to be arrested for a brutal murder. All indications are that he enjoyed an excellent reputation. He seems to have encountered no significant difficulties related to his Jewishness in his five years as supervisor. Difficulties of that sort would at any rate have been unlikely for a man of his position in Atlanta. His northern origins, a more likely source of difficulty, never seem to have been a problem either. In short, he appears to have been a typical member of the German-Jewish bourgeois elite of the city, widely recognized as law abiding, hard working, and inoffensive.

Yet, if this is an accurate picture of Frank's standing in Atlanta, it is undoubtedly surprising that popular opinion could turn so rapidly against him, that so many of Atlanta's citizens, and not merely the uneducated common people, were willing to jump to conclusions about him. Many observers, whether or not they continued to believe Frank guilty, later marveled at how suddenly he was assumed to be guilty, how he was rapidly transformed in the public eye from respected businessman and community leader to loathsome murderer and sexual pervert. In attempting to explain this change in opinion, it has been frequently assumed that his Jewishness was decisive, that, moreover, initial suspicion was directed at Frank simply or largely because he was Jewish. By this assumption, his investigating officers were driven by anti-Semitic prejudice and arrested him on insufficient grounds; he was thereafter convicted on the basis of inadequate evidence, again because of prejudicial feelings about him as a Jew.

That interpretation was aggressively forwarded by Frank's lawyers: During the trial, they told the jurors that the case was "the greatest frame-up" since the Dreyfus Affair; "if Frank had not been a Jew, there never would have been any prosecution against him."[6] The jury was not convinced by this argument, nor was the general public in the city. Even many Jews in Atlanta long remained doubtful about the importance of Frank's Jewishness in his arrest and conviction. They could hardly ignore the much-heightened tensions between Jew and non-Jew in the city as a result of the trial, as a result particularly of the widespread belief, after Frank's conviction, that the Jews were trying, through devious means, to arrange that a convicted murderer be freed. But that was an issue separate from the reasons that he was initially arrested and then convicted.

Students of the Frank Affair have been harsh in their judgment of Frank's lawyers. It does seem that they erred seriously in making anti-Semitism such a prominent part of his defense. Even more than in the arrest of Dreyfus, a persuasive argument can be made that the reasons for suspecting Frank and for arresting him in the first place had less to

[6] Quoted from the trial transcript in Phagan (Kean), *Murder*, 142.

do with his Jewishness than with his peculiar personality, with pressure to find a suspect quickly, and with a mounting body of evidence against him, evidence of far greater substance and persuasiveness than that presented against Dreyfus.

On the other hand, Frank appears to have been in a position of much latent tension and symbolism – matters inherently more difficult to evaluate. He supervised the work of nearly a hundred women in the pencil factory, many in their early teens. Their pay was not particularly low, and the work of manufacturing pencils was less arduous than that in the great cotton mills of the city, but Frank's own pay, at 180 dollars a week (to which was added his share of the profits), vastly exceeded Mary Phagan's, at 12 cents an hour, or her father's at the mills (20 cents an hour, perhaps $10 for a normal work week).[7] Frank was a hard-driving, efficient, no-nonsense supervisor. The potential symbolism of his position, and the fantasy that might be derived from it, is all too obvious, although the relative power of the specifically anti-Semitic element of it cannot be determined. Leo Frank was a representative of Yankee capitalism in a southern city, with row upon row of southern women, often the daughters and wives of ruined farmers, "at his mercy" – a rich, punctilious, northern Jew lording it over vulnerable and impoverished working women.

There was, of course, the stereotype, apparently spreading at this time, of wanton young Jewish males who hungered for fair-haired Gentile women. Jewish sensuality and Jewish violation of sexual norms were common themes in Europe, as was the related identification of Jews with saloons, prostitution, white slavery, and pornography. These European concerns seem to have taken on life in Atlanta with the arrival of eastern European Jews, from the 1890s on, particularly because of the saloons they owned and all that was associated with those saloons – drunkenness, prostitution, and crime.

Fear of Jewish sexuality may have had a special explosiveness in Atlanta at this time because of the way it could easily connect to a central myth, or cultural theme, in the South – that of the pure, virtuous, yet vulnerable White woman. The peculiar sense of honor and chivalry of southern males was expressed in a deep concern for "protecting their women." Perceived threats to southern women touched a raw nerve and often provoked a fierce reaction. Blacks were routinely lynched in the South at the merest suggestion of sexual advances on their part toward White women – an alleged glance was sometimes enough. The race riot of 1906 in Atlanta had been sparked by rumors of the murder of two White women by Blacks.

[7] Golden, *A Little Girl*, 5–6.

There is little question that poor Whites, ruined farmers moving from the countryside, were offended by much of what they saw in the new industrial cities like Atlanta. White males were humiliated by the necessity of sending their wives and daughters from the protection of the home into the factories, which were widely viewed, often for good reason, as places of immorality and sexual license, where working women were vulnerable to the advances of their bosses.

But there was more involved than symbolism in Frank's arrest, and whatever the role of that symbolism, the detectives who came to suspect Frank had concrete reasons to do so. Moreover, the peculiar sequence of events of late April 1913 were of crucial importance, for Frank's arrest constituted the first stage of what now appears to be a strange and tragic chain reaction, gathering in force and irrationality, much as in the Dreyfus Affair.

The murder of Mary Phagan and the arrest of Leo Frank

On April 27, 1913, fourteen-year-old Mary Phagan, an employee of Frank's pencil factory, was found murdered in the basement of the factory. Her body was covered with dirt, around her neck was a noose, and she had deep gashes on her head. Here it was: the ultimate nightmare for southerners. "Little Mary Phagan," or "the little factory girl," as she was often referred to thereafter, had met a grisly death.

A murder of this sort would shock any community, but the popular response in Atlanta and in the surrounding counties was remarkable, difficult for outsiders to comprehend. It far exceeded the reaction in Kiev to the even more horrible death of "Andy." Around ten thousand mourners arrived to view the body at the morgue, "the largest crowd that ever viewed a body in Atlanta," and over a thousand attended the funeral. During the ceremonies, described in full detail by the local press, Mary's mother fainted, and at the burial, in the town of Marietta, Mary's birthplace, relatives loudly wept, Mary's aunt let out a "piercing scream," and her mother fainted again.[8]

The emotions provoked by this murder went beyond mere public grief; they suggest qualities of a religious dimension. One observer has written that "Mary's People," the wretched and exploited common people of Georgia, were nursing a "fanatical grievance" and were "haunted by the purposelessness of their lives." They now turned with fury in a blind

[8] Dinnerstein, *Frank*, 11.

search for the murderer,[9] lending a fevered, wholly irrational atmosphere to the events that followed. The appropriateness of this loaded and condescending language may be questioned; the emotionalism of the Jewish masses in northern cities had many similarities, particularly in evidence at funerals, yet has not normally been described as fanatic, blind, or an aspect of the purposelessness of their lives. The most recent and popular of such descriptions has urged that a sympathetic understanding be extended for the exaggerated emotionalism of these poor and oppressed people.[10] A similarly sympathetic understanding might be extended to Mary's People, no less poor and oppressed.

The resemblances in the emotional tone of the crowds in Atlanta at this time and those that rallied to Populist banners in the 1890s are striking. In describing the Populists, too, observers have spoken of an exalted, religious quality, different from other political phenomena of the time.[11] Mary Phagan in tragic death gained a status close to that of a popular saint in Catholic cultures, with the attendant rituals. For years after her burial, thousands of people made a solemn pilgrimage to her grave. The epitaph there spoke of her "heroism . . . , an heirloom of which there is nothing more precious among the old red hills of Georgia," and ended with the words "many an aching heart in Georgia beats for you, and many a tear from eyes unused to weep, has paid tribute too sacred for words."[12]

The initial expressions of shock and grief were rapidly followed by vociferous demands that the murderer be found. It was at first assumed that the Black nightwatchman, Newt Lee, who had found the body, was the culprit. The newspapers in town claimed to have conclusive evidence that it was he who "mistreated and murdered pretty Mary Phagan"; a bold headline announced: "Lee's guilt proved!"[13] He was browbeaten and roughed up by the police to extract a confession, common practices at the time, especially when dealing with Blacks, but he continued to insist that he was innocent, and the evidence against him turned out to be very weak. Still, the police continued to believe that he knew something that he was not telling. Handwriting experts called in on the case declared that the crude, barely literate notes left by the body were in Lee's handwriting, but little else about the case against him made any sense, and it later turned out that the opinions of these "experts" were little more reliable or consistent than those consulted in the Dreyfus case.

[9] Leonard Dinnerstein, "Atlanta in the Progressive Era: A Dreyfus Affair in Georgia," in Leonard Dinnerstein and Mary Dale Palsson, eds., *Jews in the South* (Baton Rouge, 1973), 195–6.

[10] Irving Howe, *World of Our Fathers* (New York, 1976), 169ff.

[11] C. Vann Woodward, *Tom Watson, Agrarian Rebel* (Savannah, Ga., 1976; first published, 1938), 210 ff.

[12] Phagan (Kean), *Murder*, xi.

[13] Dinnerstein, *Frank*, 14.

As in the Dreyfus Affair, tremendous pressure developed to find the culprit quickly. The pressure may have been even more intense in Atlanta, since the police, unlike the French military, suffered from a particularly low regard in the public eye. The city's police officers were portrayed by their critics as hayseeds, overwhelmed by the challenge of maintaining public order in a bustling metropolis like Atlanta. Eighteen Black women had been murdered in the past several years, but none of their assailants had been found. The case of Little Mary Phagan, however, was incomparably more important, for it involved a respectable and pretty White girl. The mayor openly threatened the police: "Find this murderer fast or be fired!" The newspapers spoke of the police force as being "on trial."[14]

Attention began to turn to Leo Frank for a number of perfectly legitimate reasons having nothing to do with his Jewishness. First, he was one of the few in the factory on the day, a Saturday and holiday, of the murder. Since it was never seriously questioned that the murder took place in the factory, he automatically became one of a few natural suspects. A fateful linkage was then made to his alleged sexual proclivities, for at the inquest of the coroner's jury several female employees of the pencil factory complained that Frank regularly made improper advances to them. Moreover, a young male acquaintance of Mary's testified that she had complained to him of Frank's unwelcome familiarity with her in the factory. Two days after the inquest a police officer reported that he had earlier apprehended Frank in the woods with a young woman, intent on immoral purposes.

This kind of information began to pile up, and each new bit of news upped the emotional intensity and increased the tendency to jump to conclusions. Among those bits were the following, all amply trumpeted in the press: Frank had rented a room in a boardinghouse of doubtful reputation on the day of the murder; he had often visited a local bordello to indulge in perverse sexual practices; he and another man had often used the offices of the pencil factory on Saturdays for sexual encounters with various women; it was even reported that he had formed a "delicate relationship with an office boy."[15]

Any young man in Frank's position might have been suspected of taking advantage of his position as factory superintendent, and certainly no one believed that only Jews visited houses of prostitution or were philanderers. Frank's Jewishness was not much stressed in these reports; his northern origins were more an issue, as was his wealth.

There was still more that drew suspicion in his direction, including hair and bloodstains, believed to be Mary's, in the room next to his office.

[14] Ibid., 16.
[15] Ibid., 19.

However, on later examination much of this information proved demonstrably false (mistaken identity in the case of the police officer and the couple in the woods; a confused rumor in regard to the boardinghouse) or of uncertain validity (Mary's male friend was an unreliable witness, as were at least some of those women employees who reported Frank's lewd advances in the factory; the "bloodstain" may not have been blood at all, and the hair may not have been Mary's). Unfortunately, the doubtful reliability of these "revelations" did not become clear until later; qualifying information was often relegated to the inner pages of the newspapers, whereas the unreliable initial news releases were placed on the front page, usually in bold headlines.

Frank's initial contacts with the police, before he was charged with the crime, proved seriously detrimental to his case. Like Dreyfus, Frank was not a gregarious or affable man, or at least he had few likable traits in the eyes of ordinary southerners, the kind of men who were his arresting officers. He was uncommunicative, humorless, inflexible, and habitually ill at ease, chain-smoking cigars, "the nervous, bilious temperament which at first repels rather than attracts,"[16] as one of his business associates put it. A high social position, an aura of respectability, might well have been enough to shield such a person in normal circumstances (and Frank tried his best to use that shield), but these were not normal circumstances.

Frank had another problem, again difficult to evaluate but impossible to ignore: He was physically unattractive or at least unimpressive and odd looking in terms of southern models of manhood. It may simply have been that Frank was unphotogenic, that the photos of the day were crude and cruel, especially when reproduced in a newspaper, but his odd physical qualities would be the source of much comment, even among those who watched him daily during the trial, whose observation of him in other words was not limited to crudely reproduced photos in the newspapers. Frank's physical appearance unquestionably helped many to view him as alien and capable of heinous acts – the kind of man concerning whom negative fantasies easily grew up.

Frank's photos seem to have been his worst enemies. There was something "wrong," repellent about his looks; such was a frequent observation. He "looked like a pervert," as one observer who appeared otherwise lacking in hostility to Frank put it. Those looks made it all the easier to believe him guilty of attacking Little Mary Phagan.[17] Another observer, Tom Watson, who was by this time anything but objective and whose articles on the trial were very widely read, called Frank a "lascivious pervert" and regarded as clear evidence of his perversion his "bulging,

[16] Ibid., 6.
[17] Ibid., 172–7.

satyr eyes . . . the protruding fearfully sensual lips; and also the animal jaw."[18]

Few in the South of the United States spoke of Aryans and Semites at this time, but Frank could easily have satisfied those who used such language. He was five feet six inches tall, thin, with thick lips, thick glasses, and bulging eyes. Whether or not his physical and mental traits meant that he "looked Jewish" or "acted like a Jew" may certainly be questioned, for other prominent Jews in town did not look or act that way, but a man with a different physical appearance and more appealing mannerisms would have had a better chance to escape initial prejudice and suspicions.

From the autopsy performed on Mary Phagan it was concluded that, although her hymen was no longer in place, she had not been raped. However, even among those who accepted the coroner's conclusion, and not everyone did, the suspicion remained that something sexual was involved in her murder. Such lingering suspicions were powerfully fed when a local madam, operator of the above-mentioned bordello, reported that Frank visited her house regularly but was interested only in "perverted" sex. As it later emerged, this apparently meant that Frank was either not interested in or capable of normal genital intercourse; he preferred to use his hands or mouth. The language of the day was delicately indirect in such matters, and thus it is not always clear what was being intimated. However, the "perversity" of oral sex was punishable by death in the state of Georgia at that time.

The issue of Frank's personality and physical attributes, at least as it began to emerge in the popular press, strikingly resembles that in the Dreyfus case. That is, if Frank had seemed less a distant and superior outsider, if he had been a more familiar type – if not a "good ol' boy," at least a more typical southern Jew, easy and affable in manner, with more significant personal friendships among the Gentile establishment of the city – then matters might have developed differently. Those who began to suspect him would have been less comfortable with that suspicion; they might have been slower to charge him, and, as evidence accumulated, a whole chain of different events might have developed. In short, if a different Jew had been in either Frank's or Dreyfus's position, a different course of events might have occurred. That being the case, it is not reasonable to maintain that blind prejudice, an anti-Semitism asserting that all Jews are the same, played a larger role than did the accident of personality.

Frank almost certainly benefited from a competing nexus of positive images surrounding Jews, especially in the case of a brutal murder, since

[18] Woodward, *Watson*, 379–80.

Jews enjoyed such a widely accepted reputation of being nonviolent, family oriented, and law abiding. If one is to speak of "prejudice," in the sense of prevailing, preconceived notions about Jews at that time and place, the prejudice of the non-violent, law-abiding, familial Jew was almost certainly more prevalent than the prejudice of Jews as sexually aggressive or deviant. As a Black writer complained, "it is so rare for a Jew to commit a crime, . . . [and even more] to be brought to the courts for heinous ones, that when he does commit one, every reasonable doubt is in his favor."[19]

Frank resorted to racial stereotypes in his own defense. He insisted that Mary must have been killed by some sort of violent, primitive brute – in short, a Black, not a Jew. Frank's lawyers were energetic in insisting that murder of this sort was not a Jewish crime, and they did not hesitate to exploit anti-Black bigotry. They referred to Jim Conley (as we will see, the prime suspect, if Frank could be shown to be innocent) as a "dirty, filthy, black, drunken, lying nigger," and they denounced the prosecution for trying to make this "dirty nigger" look so "slick."[20] Even making concessions for the kinds of things commonly said by Whites about Blacks at this time, there was something a little incongruous and hypocritical about such men, denouncing the bigotry against Jews that they asserted was responsible for the charges against Frank, yet resorting to a far more explicit and vicious bigotry against Blacks in his defense. Significantly, the prosecution avoided racial stereotyping, at least of this blatant sort.

Still further evidence, much more palpable and persuasive, pointed in Frank's direction. When the police had first contacted him and asked if he knew Mary, he replied that he did not. Yet, shortly before her murder, as he later recognized, she had come to his office and received her pay envelope from him. Employees testified that he often called her by name in the factory. Similarly, he gave seriously conflicting accounts concerning what he had said to Mary when she came to pick up her pay, as if he suddenly realized the need to change his alibi.[21]

The officers who first questioned Frank considered him unusually shifty in manner, extraordinarily nervous and thus perhaps trying to hide something. That he immediately called in both a private detective and a lawyer, when he himself was only being questioned and before he had been charged with anything, also led them to suspect that he had a guilty conscience.

But the most incriminating inconsistency in the information that Frank initially provided the police concerned his activities around noon on the day of the murder. Frank told the police that he had remained in his

[19] Hertzberg, *Jews of Atlanta*, 198.
[20] Phagan (Kean), *Murder*, 141.
[21] Golden, *A Little Girl*, 35.

office, after giving Mary her paycheck, until he went home about an hour later. However, another employee, Maureen Stover, also in search of her paycheck, came into his office shortly after Mary had been there and found the room empty. After waiting in the hall for five minutes or so, she left. Stover, unlike those who accused Frank of making improper advances to them, was not suspected of harboring grudges against him; she testified that he was a kind man and in fact well liked by the women employees.[22] Frank could not satisfactorily explain this episode, except to speculate that he may have gone to the bathroom when Maureen came to his office.

Frank, furthermore, was never able to provide a widely persuasive account of what he was doing during the hour (12 to 1 o'clock) when it was believed, according to autopsy evidence, that Mary was murdered. In the evening following the murder he repeatedly called the factory, finally reaching the nightwatchman, Newt Lee, and asked if everything was all right (this was before Lee had found the body). Frank's explanations for making these calls, that the nightwatchman was fairly new and that he was worried about a recently fired employee, were judged inadequate by many, especially since Frank had never made such calls before this.

The "set" of opinion against Frank: the popular press

The newspapers in the city exploited the case for all it was worth in sales. It undoubtedly was great copy, and the city's newspapers at this time were in wild competition with one another. William Randolph Hearst's *Atlanta Georgian* had just appeared in the city the year before, determined to dominate the journalistic scene as the Hearst papers were doing in other cities. In many of their initial articles, the city's papers simply assumed Frank's guilt – "the strangler," or "the monster," as they termed him, had been "caught." No headlines announced, significantly, that "the Jew" had been caught.[23] In astonishingly irresponsible competition with one another for sensational details, they simply fabricated stories or resorted to the most lurid, absurd speculations. If the argument that opinion in certain segments of Atlanta's population rapidly hardened into something like a religious faith has merit, then there is little question that these early sensationalistic releases by Atlanta's newspapers were essential to the process.

But there is little evidence that anti-Semitic instincts lay behind the

[22] Ibid., 60–1.
[23] Ibid., 44.

irresponsible behavior of Atlanta's newspapers. The *Constitution*, which seemed the most firmly persuaded of Frank's guilt and which apparently enjoyed insider contacts with the police, had a Jewish editor and had been, in preceding years, a central vehicle for favorable reporting about Atlanta's Jewish community. A recent editorial in it had, for example, emphasized that "no single betrayal of trust and honor has ever been chargeable to them."[24] Similarly, the Hearst press was widely recognized by the Jews themselves as friendly. William Randolph Hearst had many close Jewish friends; he had been among the first to contribute to the Kishinev charities a decade before, and at this very time his northern papers were amply decorated with Happy Passover greetings. The Hearst papers, like most of the American press, whether yellow or respectable, had almost unanimously supported Dreyfus[25] and denounced the charges against Beilis.[26] Although undoubtedly capable of whipping up xenophobic hysteria, the yellow press in the United States had not notably turned against the Jews. In this way the American journalistic scene was distinctly different from the European.

Quite the opposite of exploiting anti-Semitism, Hearst was widely suspected in Atlanta of pro-Jewish sympathies and illicit connections with powerful Jews. As rumors began to spread that Jews were resorting to bribery to rig Frank's trial and to get him free, Hearst's paper became suspect, especially after an article in it suggested that Jim Conley was the more likely culprit. Some Atlantans angrily dismissed the article as planted by Jewish intriguers. Hearst's paper, they believed, was putting up a "patsy" in order to get Frank off the hook, much as the Dreyfus family was believed to have done in the case of Esterhazy.

The truth was a little less lurid, if also, as in the case of Mathieu Dreyfus's activities, palpably connected to the rumor: Hearst's Jewish advertisers in the North did let him know that they were shocked at the initial articles in the *Atlanta Georgian*. Jewish merchants in Atlanta as well criticized the paper for inflaming popular passions. Whether because of such pressure or simply because of the new evidence that appeared, the paper began to change its posture, eventually calling for a new trial. So did most other newspapers that had at first assumed Frank's guilt. But in other quarters Hearst was denounced as a "half-Jew" who was "taking orders" from Nathan Straus and R. H. Macy.[27] It was a fatal turn of events for the *Atlanta Georgian*. Its circulation, which had risen to forty thousand

[24] Hertzberg, *Jews of Atlanta*, 157.
[25] Egal Feldmann, *The Dreyfus Affair and the American Conscience* (Detroit, 1981), 78–89.
[26] E. Lifschutz, "The Repercussions of the Beilis Trial in the United States, *Zion*, vol. 28, 1963, 206–22; Dinnerstein, *Frank*, 73–4.
[27] Golden, *A Little Girl*, 44–5.

copies a day in the opening stages of the trial, giving it the largest circulation in the South, began to decline, and it folded in a few years.

Frank's family and friends were, of course, active in his defense, but
on the whole the Jewish community in Atlanta remained cautious in the
opening stages of the trial and maintained a low profile throughout. Much
like the Jewish bourgeoisie in France at the beginning of the Dreyfus
Affair, the characteristic response of Atlanta's Jewish establishment was
to urge respect for the authorities and to express their belief that Frank
would get a fair trial. Even later, as Atlanta's Jewish community became
more involved in the struggle on Frank's behalf, its leaders remained
painfully aware of how much a militant, public defense of Frank endangered their standing in the city, above all if that defense resorted to
charges of anti-Semitism as, of course, he and his lawyers were doing.

Jews in France at first assumed Dreyfus to be guilty, and few of them
knew him personally. But Atlanta's German-Jewish elite constituted a
smaller, closer community, and those who knew Frank well could not
believe him guilty of such a crime. Even the Jewish law partner of the
solicitor general (that is, public prosecutor, the man who brought charges
against Frank), openly expressed utter disbelief in the murder charges.[28]
At the same time, a few Atlantan Jews wrote to influential Jews and Jewish
organizations in the North before the trial began, urging them to avoid
public comment on the case since it would only antagonize Georgians all
the more and not help Frank's chances for acquittal.[29] And in that judgment they were certainly correct.

The fear that Frank would escape justice because of his wealth and
assumed powerful connections contributed significantly to the way that
popular opinion set against him. Quite aside from the ill-advised scramble
to find the murderer, the anxiety that, once found, he would somehow
escape the grasp of justice became the central issue for the anti-Frank
faction. And just as suspicions that Hearst was responding to Jewish
pressure had some basis in fact, so popular fears about what influential
Jews might do on Frank's behalf once he had been convicted were also
not without foundation.

It was not only the newspapers that acted irresponsibly in the opening
stages of the Frank case; many others in authority, or who otherwise
enjoyed popular confidence, spoke at first as if there was no doubt that
the guilty man had been found. General Mercier's confident declaration
that Dreyfus was guilty beyond a doubt caused many obedient soldiers
to believe in that guilt; Solicitor General Hugh Dorsey similarly spoke
with great assurance that Frank was guilty and would be easily convicted.

---

[28] Hertzberg, *Jews of Atlanta*, 211.
[29] Golden, *A Little Girl*, 227.

He repeatedly dropped hints about further decisive evidence that he was saving for the trial. Others who became involved in the case, not only the Atlanta police but even those whom Frank himself had called in – Pinkerton detectives and agents from the famous Burns detective agency – all publicly expressed their confidence that Frank was guilty beyond any question.

Ordinary people are not always capable of appropriately sifting through legal evidence, even when they have access to reliable information, which was hardly the case in the weeks immediately following the murder. They have even more difficulty in maintaining an attitude of suspended judgment over a long period – a difficult act for even the most sophisticated. Moreover, ordinary people are inclined to look to respected figures for guidance – an inclination also not unknown among the sophisticated. In Atlanta ordinary people could observe what seemed near unanimity on the part of respected and presumably disinterested figures, men known for their friendliness to the Jewish community, not only that Frank was guilty, but also that the evidence of his guilt was overwhelming. Those who spoke up against that presumption of guilt, like the editors of Hearst's paper, were less respected and trusted. "Mary's people" did not need to engage in the intellectually taxing effort of sifting the accumulating mass of increasingly confused and contradictory evidence; they did not have to endure the psychologically difficult process of suspending judgment any longer. The "monster" had been caught, and what a satisfying conclusion! Later, as disturbing new evidence began to appear, it would be psychologically very difficult, humiliating even, for many ordinary people to abandon their loudly espoused and nourishing convictions, to move away from beliefs that had taken on a near religious form, especially when most authority figures in Atlanta continued to insist on Frank's guilt, dismissing the new evidence as insubstantial, unreliable, or the result of Jewish money at work.

The role of anti-Semitism in the trial

However the evidence of anti-Semitism in Frank's arrest is evaluated, however prejudicial the handling of his case by the newspapers, a finer, more difficult question must be posed: How much did anti-Semitism affect the calculations of the prosecution and eventually those of the judge and jury? The legal system and trial by jury are, after all, supposed to be a bulwark against both popular excitement and unwarranted actions by police authorities. Here, too, the evidence is slim that anti-Semitism played a decisive role. This is a conclusion, however, that requires some important qualifications.

A key figure – and a key puzzle among several others in the case – was the solicitor general. The popular writer Harry Golden, in his book *A Little Girl Is Dead*, has put together a potent indictment of Hugh Dorsey, itself based on an earlier study.[30] According to this view, which also finds qualified support in the most scholarly of the studies of the Frank Affair,[31] Dorsey was a ruthlessly ambitious man, one who harbored anti-Semitic beliefs and who knew perfectly well that Frank was not guilty. Dorsey persisted in his prosecution of an innocent man because he "realized" that the case represented the "chance of a lifetime." If Dorsey could convict Frank, so Golden argues, "there was probably no office in the state to which he could not succeed," since he would become a popular hero in bringing the rich, northern Jew to justice.[32] (Dorsey did run for governor of the state in 1916 and won by an overwhelming majority.)

By this interpretation, Dorsey played a role similar to that attributed by the Dreyfusards to the "clerico-military" conspirators in France. Those charges of conspiracy lack both consistency and evidence in the Dreyfus Affair, whether when put forth by Dreyfusards at the time or when expounded by historians like Halasz in subsequent years. There are some interesting resemblances in the quality of Golden's book and that of Halasz; both have something in common with what has been termed "morality tales," and both have had a large influence on the way the cases have been understood by the general public, in no small part because they offer colorful, dramatic, and emotionally satisfying accounts, "finding" what they already "knew."

Dorsey is supposed to have actually suppressed evidence that put Frank's guilt in question. At the same time Dorsey purportedly elicited false testimony against Frank, intimidating and bribing various witnesses. Dorsey allegedly did something even more unscrupulous and finally horrifying than eliciting false testimony: He elaborately, day after day, drilled Jim Conley in false testimony, so that he would be able to withstand cross-examination by defense lawyers. All the while Dorsey knew, without any doubt, so Golden and others maintain, that Conley was the actual murderer.

Without further information, above all some sort of in-depth study of Dorsey himself and access to his personal papers, if relevant ones still exist, it is difficult to know how to deal with these extraordinary charges. They assume a conspiracy, to say nothing of a moral turpitude, on Dorsey's part, of a staggering dimension. Was Hugh Dorsey so driven by ambition or by hatred of Jews, so utterly unprincipled, and so reckless that he could hatch an elaborate scheme to see an innocent man put to death

[30] Charles Samuels and Louise Samuels, *Night Fell on Georgia* (New York, 1956).
[31] Dinnerstein, *Frank*.
[32] Golden, *A Little Girl*, 50; Samuels and Samuels, *Night Fell on Georgia*.

and a guilty one – a lawless and dangerous one, as Conley undoubtedly was – escape the hangman?

These charges against Dorsey give pause in part because of what is known about him prior to the Frank Affair. They also merit careful scrutiny because of the further light they shed on the role of anti-Semitism in the Frank Affair. Hugh Dorsey was almost certainly not driven by hatred of Jews, nor is there much evidence, whether in his earlier or later career, that would suggest a man of such awesome immorality, even granting the kinds of rationalizations that lawyers have perfected in terms of what they permit themselves to do in the performance of their legal duties.

The same lack of previous anti-Semitism may be noted in the case of those who assisted Dorsey and who must have thus been, if one believes in a conspiracy of the prosecution, co-conspirators in framing Leo Frank: Frank Hooper, a successful corporation lawyer who had himself earlier served as solicitor general, and the assistant solicitor general, Edward Stephens.[33] In more general ways, Dorsey was not notably bigoted. He was known in town as a moderate liberal in dealing with the Black population; he had consistently refused to pander to anti-Black prejudice. One of his law partners was Jewish, and he had had a Jewish roommate in college. He was invited to lecture at the Jewish Educational Alliance in early 1912, and when he ran for the solicitorship that same year, he received the endorsement of twelve Jewish lawyers.[34] This record, to which similar details could be added, hardly suggests that he was known as a man of ruthless, unprincipled ambition or anti-Semitic sentiments, even covert ones.

The case that Dorsey built against Frank was not based in any overt way upon anti-Semitism. Five Jews sat on the grand jury that indicted Frank. It seems safe to conclude that they were persuaded by the concrete evidence that Dorsey presented, not by his pandering to anti-Jewish feeling (the grand jury met before Conley's testimony against Frank was known, it should be noted). And at the trial Dorsey vigorously countered the charges of the defense that Frank was the victim of an anti-Semitic frame-up. In his summation to the jury, Dorsey explicitly denounced racial anti-Semitism, indeed, indulged in some of the common philo-Semitic rhetoric of the day, with references to Disraeli ("the greatest prime minister that England has ever produced"), Judah P. Benjamin ("as great a lawyer as ever lived in America"), prominent Jewish-American businessmen, and Atlanta's Rabbi Marx (whom he knew and "honored"). But he also mentioned recently notorious Jewish criminals and a Jewish

[33] Stephens was termed "the real genius of the prosecution" in a study of the trial, written under the sponsorship of the Anti-Defamation League of B'nai B'rith in 1948. See DeWitt Roberts, *The Story of Mass Hysteria* (Atlanta, 1948).

[34] Hertzberg, *Jews of Atlanta*, 309, n. 7.

political boss known for his insatiable sexual appetites. He concluded that "these great people [the Jews] are amenable to the same laws as you and I and the black race. They rise to heights sublime, but they sink to depths of degradation."[35]

These remarks may be dismissed as hypocritical, but they are consistent with Dorsey's record before Frank was arrested. He was well known as one of those public officials who stood for due process, who firmly opposed lynch law (against the opinion, as we have seen, of some Jewish editors in the South), and who had formed extensive bonds of friendship, profession, economic interest, and respect with Atlanta's German-Jewish elite.

In short, Atlanta was not Kishinev or Kiev; government officials, the police, the political establishment in general had never acted prejudicially against Jews, individually or collectively, openly or covertly. Dorsey was not an anti-Semite, nor was he operating in a previously existing anti-Semitic climate. Attacks on Jews had not been used in the past to gain popularity or public office.

One possible explanation of Dorsey's actions is that, rather than satanically plotting from the beginning to derive political advantage by convicting an innocent man of murder, he may at first have become genuinely convinced of Frank's guilt, as did other reasonably astute observers. Dorsey may not have embraced the idea of Frank's guilt with a religious tenacity, but he did invest a large degree of personal prestige in asserting that guilt. Having committed himself so unequivocally, he may have lacked the moral strength to back down.

Further, it may not have been simply a matter of moral courage since he may never have been persuaded of Frank's innocence. Many others were not, including some who had friendly contacts with Atlanta's Jewish community and who lacked Dorsey's alleged motivations to frame Frank. In particular Dorsey seems to have been firmly persuaded of Frank's bad moral character, of his perverse sexual escapades, about which he claimed to have an overwhelming mass of evidence, most of which he did not introduce at the trial.[36]

If Dorsey had reversed his initial confident remarks about Frank's guilt, it is certain that some Atlantans would have accused him of having sold out to the Jews, especially since he had a Jewish law partner. Such an accusation could have ruined his career, even endangered his life. Furthermore, since Dorsey had recently failed to convict two murderers, he might have felt that another failure, in a case of such great importance, would have disastrous implications for his personal future.[37] These moral dilemmas were similar to those faced by Picquart. It seems clear enough

[35] From trial transcript, as quoted in Phagan (Kean), *Murder*, 143–4.
[36] Dinnerstein, *Frank*, 172.
[37] Ibid, 19.

that Dorsey was not a man of Picquart's ultimate moral courage and integrity. Still, we have seen that Picquart was not oblivious to his own interests, that he was not simply a shining hero; he was a prig and an anti-Semitic one at that. It is at least possible that there is another side to Dorsey's case, that he was not simply a calculating, loathsome villain but a more human mix of virtues and vices.

The matter may finally come down to an initial – portentous – miscalculation by Dorsey, when he spoke up so confidently about Frank's guilt, when he jumped to a most injudicious if also opportune conclusion. But surely, Dorsey must have had the option for some time to charge Conley with the crime, even if this drunken, criminal Black was not so "big" and satisfying a catch as a northern capitalist. If Dorsey knew from the very beginning and without any doubt in his own mind that Conley was the murderer and Frank innocent, and if he was willing to see Frank hanged and Conley jailed on a lesser charge (all of which are certainly plausible hypotheses), then he must have been indeed a morally corrupt man. On the other hand, if he had at first firmly believed in Frank's guilt, and if his main, or initial, moral failing had been to announce too early and too confidently that he had caught the guilty man, then we can see a more complicated situation morally, above all if Dorsey remained unimpressed by the mounting evidence of Conley's guilt and Frank's innocence.

Dorsey may have thus become entangled in a web of circumstances not entirely of his choosing. He may have been able to convince himself that even falsifying evidence and putting pressure on witnesses was necessary in order to assure the conviction of a guilty man, since that man had so many fancy lawyers, rich connections, and tricks up his sleeve. Dorsey's moral weakness was not thus anti-Semitism but opportunism and a lack of judicial caution. However his actions are explained, the irony is heavy: Picquart and Shulgin, the anti-Semites, come to the rescue of Dreyfus and Beilis; Dorsey, the friend of Jews, fights to see Frank convicted and then hanged.

Just how Dorsey coached Conley to testify against Frank is a key point, yet remains unclear. The solicitor general apparently reasoned that Conley, like most Blacks of his class, was an inveterate liar, a conclusion that was perfectly natural for a southern White, even one who was liberal in his views of Blacks, in confronting such a man as Conley. Indeed, in Conley's case that conclusion was also wholly justified: He *was* an inveterate liar, a perfect example of the "lying nigger" of southern mythology; he lied constantly, blithely admitting as much. Faced with transparent lie after lie from Conley, Dorsey could continue to question him until the truth emerged, until Conley "finally" told the truth, as southern lore maintained would ultimately happen with a "lying nigger."

That "truth" offered graphic, overwhelming evidence of Frank's guilt.

We may never know how much of Conley's testimony had any basis in fact, although there is persuasive evidence that he was still lying when he "finally told the truth" to Dorsey.

The real murderer: Conley or Frank?

The best evidence now available indicates that the real murderer of Mary Phagan was Jim Conley, perhaps because she, encountering him after she left Frank's office, refused to give him her pay envelope, and he, in a drunken stupor, killed her to get it. However, many unresolved questions concerning his guilt remain, and no court of law has ever made a judgment concerning it. Simply stated, the evidence against Conley, although never subjected to the elaborate scrutiny of due process, appears stronger than that against Frank, who, of course, did have a regular trial. More to the point, we can now see that Frank, in spite of some strong evidence against him, was not guilty beyond a reasonable doubt, especially in light of the evidence that later emerged.[38]

But that reasonable doubt did not emerge clearly enough at the trial. The trial was when much of the prejudicial evidence that had been released to the newspapers in the days following Mary's murder could be discredited by Frank's lawyers and when unreliable testimony could be revealed as such by cross-examination. It was the time, in other words, when what seemed like an overpowering accumulation of damning evidence could be exposed as doubtful.

Conley's testimony was new, concrete, and direct. It may have been decisive in Frank's conviction, just as Henry's may have been in Dreyfus's. In its final version, Conley's story was that Frank regularly used his office at the pencil factory for his perverse sexual encounters and that he employed Conley as a lookout. Conley was providing that service, he testified, on the day that Mary Phagan went to Frank's office. Shortly after she entered the office, Conley heard a scream, and then, an hour or so later, Frank called him to his office. Frank was, in Conley's words, "shivering and trembling and rubbing his hands" – in which he held a rope similar to that found around Mary Phagan's throat.[39]

According to Conley, Frank reported that when Mary refused to give

[38] Much has recently made of the testimony of Alonzo Mann, an office boy at the time of the murder, who came forward in the mid-1980s to say that he had seen Conley in the factory, carrying Mary Phagan's body. As we will see, this was not the only testimony implicating Conley, but since Mann's recollections, after so many years, have not been subjected to in-court cross-examination, it is difficult to know how to evaluate them. It should be noted that Mann did not testify that he actually saw Conley commit the murder. The issue is discussed in Phagan (Kean), *Murder*.

[39] Golden, *A Little Girl*, 121.

in to his desires, he hit her and she fell, striking her head. Conley found Mary's lifeless and bloodied body in an adjoining room, with a rope around her neck. Together, he and Frank carried the body to the basement, by way of the elevator. Frank then gave Conley $200 and told him to burn Mary's body in the furnace. Conley refused, and Frank took the money back, telling him to keep his mouth shut and promising, "If you get caught, I will get you out on bond and send you away." Frank then urged Conley to come back that night and burn the body.

Conley left but did not come back. He did not see Frank again until the following Tuesday, three days later, when Frank approached him with the warning "Keep your mouth shut." Frank complained to him, "If you'd come back on Saturday and done what I told you to do . . . there wouldn't have been any trouble."[40]

Why would anyone believe this story, provided as it was by a Black known to be drunken, thieving, and mendacious, in a region where the testimony of a respectable Black against a White traditionally carried little weight? This testimony was against not just any White man, but rather one who was a member of the reputable and wealthy bourgeoisie of the city, who was the member of a race known to be unusually law abiding and not inclined to violence. Again, it has often been argued that anti-Semitism – and more particularly the potent image of the alien, lascivious Jew – explains why Conley was believed. Yet, still again, the evidence for this explanation is weak.

Conley's testimony was extraordinarily rich in details, sometimes of the most minute and graphic sort. Many observers simply could not believe that a southern Black, a man with Conley's supposedly limited mental powers, could make up such an intricate story or even repeat a story in which he had been coached by Dorsey, without tangling himself in contradictions. His testimony had to be based, so was a widespread conclusion at the time, on something he had actually seen himself. (It will be remembered how, in the Tiszaeszlár Affair, the defense lawyer had demolished the testimony of Móric Scharf by showing that he could not have possibly seen what he said he saw through the keyhole of the synagogue.)

Frank's lawyers, recognized as among the most experienced and sharpest legal minds in the South, grilled Conley for sixteen hours without breaking his story, without being able to point to inconsistencies of enough importance to discredit it. Many doubted that a highly intelligent White, experienced in the courtroom and trained in the law, could have successfully defended a false, wholly concocted story against such lengthy, expert cross-examination. Even today, one must wonder how Dorsey himself could have embarked on such a risky enterprise as coaching Con-

[40] Ibid., 125–6.

ley in a fabricated testimony, knowing him to be guilty and surely knowing what experts in cross-examination could do to a witness who had concocted an elaborate false testimony. It seems, moreover, unbelievable that Dorsey and the other lawyers for the prosecution, Hooper and Stephens, could have been so reckless as to thus risk a humiliating collapse of their case against Frank. And what might have happened to their reputations and future careers if Conley, having broken down in full courtroom, had testified that Dorsey coached him in false testimony?

Frank himself puzzlingly refused a pretrial offer of a confrontation with Conley. It was another example, among many, of what appears to be bad judgment on his part, of a foolish inflexibility. For many observers it was yet further evidence of his guilt, as was his long period of absolute silence after being arrested and before the trial. Much else about Frank's attitude toward Conley raised serious questions. He at first tried to direct suspicion toward two other Black employees; he did not even mention Conley to the police until it was unavoidable, as if he feared to have Conley interrogated. Moreover, Frank knew perfectly well that Conley could write (a key point because of the notes left at the scene of the murder) but remained silent when Conley initially denied that he could.

Even those who were not convinced that Frank had murdered Mary Phagan suspected that he was trying to hide something, most likely something in which he and Conley were involved. Such people were inclined to think that Frank's puzzling reticences and inconsistencies derived from his ill-conceived efforts to cover up certain sexual peccadillos that, if revealed, would have shattered the image that he cultivated of indignant, high-minded innocence. He had good reason to fear that once accusations of sexual misconduct had been levied at him any admission of guilt in that regard would have resulted in a jail term, or at least the ruin of his career. Even the death penalty could not be ruled out, given the severity of Georgian law in regard to "perversities" such as oral sex.

Frank may have preferred to hew to a pretense of spotless virtue, a "win all or lose all" approach, and in the process himself became tangled in a web from which he could not break free. These are, of course, speculations, based on slim evidence, only slightly bolstered by Dorsey's claim to have at his disposal a "fearful mass of testimony" concerning Frank's sexual exploits, which he would use only if the defense forced him to. Frank and his lawyers, significantly, did not call Dorsey's bluff – if it was that – reinforcing a belief that they feared what Dorsey might reveal.[41] Similarly, on several occasions during the trial, even Frank's attorneys seemed to accept implicitly that their client may not have always been a model of propriety in sexual matters – "We are not trying this

[41] Dinnerstein, *Frank*, 172.

case on whether you or I or Frank have been perfect in the past . . . Let him who is without sin cast the first stone".[42] Further suggesting that there may have been some substance to the allegations concerning Frank's sexual activities, Dorsey later vowed that if Frank were freed by higher courts, he would have him indicted on other charges, including criminal assault and sexual perversion.[43]

The guilty verdict

To question or to qualify the role of anti-Semitism at various stages of the Frank Affair is not to deny the role that bigotry and prejudice in a broader sense finally played in Frank's conviction and even more in his death. Frank's trial was in some regards even more a mockery of justice than were those of Dreyfus and Beilis. Still, careful distinctions must be made, especially if we are to understand how so many intelligent and otherwise unprejudiced people concluded that Frank was guilty, both in fact and in law, and, moreover, how countless appeals to higher courts failed to gain a new trial for him.

Judge Roan, who presided over the case, was widely respected. His conduct of the trial was, on the whole, a model of judiciousness, and he personally was free of the taint of anti-Semitic feeling. The jury selection was laborious and careful: The defense used eighteen out of twenty of its peremptory challenges, and thus ostensibly had ample opportunity to eliminate those who seemed prejudiced against Frank because he was a Jew. (An ironic aspect of the process – and yet so typical of all three anti-Semitic affairs – was that one member of the jury, apparently impaneled without his revealing his anti-Semitic convictions, was the only one who at first expressed doubts, in jury deliberations, about Frank's guilt.) Further, Frank's lawyers could have called for a change of venue if they had been persuaded that an impartial jury could not be found in Atlanta. Yet they did not do so, nor did Judge Roan, who also had the authority, indeed the responsibility, to make such a change if he felt a fair trial was not possible in Atlanta.

Those who have criticized the trial have not emphasized the inadequacies of the judge or of the procedural niceties in selecting a jury. They have insisted, rather, that these were unimportant when compared to other factors, above all the pressure of public opinion, most palpably the mob outside the courtroom. These critics have also blamed Frank's lawyers, in spite of their recognized brilliance (or perhaps because of it), for

[42] Phagan (Kean), *Murder*, 141.
[43] Robert Seitz Frey and Nancy Thompson-Frey, *The Silent and the Damned: The Murder of Mary Phagan and the Lynching of Leo Frank* (Lanham, Md., 1988), 71.

overconfidence and for a series of crucial mistakes, both tactical and strategic, among which was failing to move for a change of venue. According to these critics, the chants, jeers, and threats of the crowd – such as "Hang the Jew or we'll hang you!" – made it impossible for the jury to deliberate in a proper atmosphere. Yet others have denied that such was the case: "Not one newspaper ever reported any of the spectators shouting 'hang the Jew'.... "[44] Members of the jury, when asked, denied that they felt intimidated, and in later appeals the Georgia Supreme Court ruled that pressure from the mob did not have a decisive impact on the jurors.[45]

But these denials are puzzling and finally difficult to believe. It is also questionable whether a change of venue would have avoided the problem of jury intimidation. Historians of the Sacco and Vanzetti trial have argued that the two Italian anarchists could not have found a fair trial by jury anywhere in the state of Massachusetts or even in the country as a whole, given the pervasiveness of prejudice against men of their background and persuasion. Such may have been the case with Frank as well, at least to the extent that public opinion in Georgia had so firmly set against him, and it had become so dangerous to defend him, that no jury in the state at the time could have been expected to find him innocent. Such may have finally been the conclusion of Judge Roan; he apparently calculated that a lynching could be averted and that Frank had a better chance of surviving if he were first found guilty, passions allowed to cool, new evidence given wide publicity, and then a new trial arranged.[46]

When the jury brought in its verdict of "guilty," the jubilation in the streets of Atlanta was extraordinary, of such wild abandon that the hypothesis concerning the psychological need of "Mary's People" for a guilty man of Frank's dimensions, "big" in a way that a simple Black would not have been, takes on added plausibility. There was a striking and also suggestive similarity to this jubilation and the popular joy expressed in Russia when the jury found Mendel Beilis innocent. In both cases the powerless experienced a moment of exhilaration in seeing the defeat and humiliation of a normally powerful and inaccessible oppressor (tsarist ministers in one case, the rich and well connected in the other). The poor people of Georgia had cornered a representative, or a symbol, of those distant power brokers and Money Men who had been "raping" them for the past fifty years. And in spite of payoffs and fancy lawyers, he had not gotten away.

[44] Phagan (Kean), *Murder*, 25.
[45] Golden, *A Little Girl*, 240.
[46] Dinnerstein, *Frank*, 80.

The Frank case becomes an affair:
the opposing forces

The trial of Leo Frank did not at first attract great attention outside Georgia. It was only after Frank's conviction and in the long process of trying to find legal redress that the Frank case began to take on a larger, national, indeed international shape, to become the Frank Affair. Opposing forces began to align and arguments to take on more of an ideological form, although the concrete issue centered on whether Frank should be hanged as expeditiously as the law allowed or his death sentence should be postponed because of doubts about the justice of the trial.

There were comparable developments, the gathering of forces on each side, in the Dreyfus and Beilis cases, and similarly, when the often misleading and hypocritical rhetoric of the day is put aside, an unexpected, bewildering mixture of motives in the opposing camps is to be seen. In the Frank Affair, too, the issues were defined in abstract, moralistic ways by Frank's defenders, as truth and justice against bigotry and mendacity, and by his enemies, as equal justice against special treatment for the rich and well connected. But motives on both sides were less than one hundred percent pure.

A political motive of a most immediate and palpable sort soon became obvious in the anti-Frank camp. In March 1914 an editorial of the *Atlanta Journal*, widely recognized as the organ of U.S. Senator Hoke Smith, demanded that Frank be given a new trial and concluded that to execute him would constitute "judicial murder."[47] Hoke Smith and Tom Watson, the Populist leader, were at this time bitter political opponents, so much so that Watson's "desire to bring disgrace upon Hoke Smith" had become "a blinding obsession."[48] In 1910, in spite of frantic efforts by Watson to defeat Smith in the elections of that year, Smith had been elected by an overwhelming majority. Watson was convinced that the article in the *Atlanta Journal* was evidence that Smith was receiving money and political support from Frank's family and defenders ("Jewish money"), and he quickly perceived an issue by which he might gain advantage over his old political enemy, who was up for reelection.

Up to this point, that is, about a year after Frank's arrest, Watson and other politicians had steered clear of the case, expressing confidence in the judicial system, in due process, to assure justice for Frank. To be sure, Hearst's paper in Atlanta had begun to express reservations about Frank's guilt, and so had other papers, but major political figures had not

[47] Woodward, *Watson*, 378.
[48] Ibid., 358.

tried to gain mileage from the issue. Senator Smith's initiative in openly defending Frank changed that. Watson explained his entry into the case as being provoked by the deplorable efforts of rich Jews and northerners to free a murderer who had, in Watson's opinion, received as fair a trial as any man was likely to get.

A year earlier, upon Frank's arrest, his family had contacted Watson and offered him a substantial fee if he would defend Frank. Watson enjoyed a formidable reputation for successfully defending those charged with murder, and he had previously expressed principled opposition to the death penalty. Indeed, what had turned him so single-mindedly against Senator Smith was Smith's refusal, six years earlier, when he was governor of Georgia and when he and Watson were political allies, to commute the sentence of Arthur Glover, a convicted murderer. Glover's guilt was not in question, but he had been a Populist supporter of Watson in the 1890s, acting as personal bodyguard. In that capacity he had once saved Watson's life from a hostile mob.[49] Watson asked Smith that Glover's death sentence be commuted to life imprisonment as a personal favor, but Smith refused, and Glover was executed.

Watson never forgave Smith. In any event, when approached by Frank's family, Watson refused to take Frank's defense. Similarly, he refused, when approached shortly afterward, to assist the prosecution. (His subsequent assertion that the trial had been a fair one stood in stark contrast to his observation, when first contacted by Frank's family, that trying Frank in Atlanta "would be like trying a rat before the old cat and her kittens." He advised the family to seek a change of venue.[50])

By 1913 Watson had attained a nearly legendary stature in the South, remarkably similar to the position of the now more famous Huey Long of Louisiana. It was Watson, more than any other single man or organization, who made an affair out of the Frank case. Frank's defenders, particularly certain influential Jews in the North, had, to be sure, begun a process of publicizing the case as a judicial error, but that was not enough to make an affair of it. Opposing forces had to be mobilized, and in that regard Watson's efforts were decisive. It was he who gave the case a particular kind of publicity, one with ideological connections derived from Populism. He articulated and played upon the growing fears of Mary's People that Leo Frank would somehow escape justice. If we are looking for a Drumont or a Krushevan in the Frank Affair, Tom Watson is the best candidate.

Yet a careful comparison of Watson with European anti-Semites again reveals important differences between the United States and the Old

[49] Ibid., 334–7.
[50] Ibid., 378.

World. Watson was, up to this point, not known as an anti-Semite. On the contrary, as earlier described, he had repeatedly expressed friendly words for Jews in his various publications, and Jewish merchants, even if hostile to Populism, had regularly bought advertising space in those publications. Obviously, Frank's friends and family would not have approached Watson to defend Frank if Watson had been known to be anti-Semitic.

Tom Watson was as colorful, enigmatic, and tragic a figure as ever appeared in American history. Theodore Roosevelt, another politician who had often expressed friendship and admiration for Jews, was a long-time Republican opponent of Watson's but still admired him personally, claiming to recognize in him a "spiritual kin." Before the Frank Affair Roosevelt had eulogized Watson as "fearless, disinterested, and incorruptible."[51] And that was not simply political hyperbole. Watson had early in his career fought tirelessly for the small farmer, both Black and White. He was exceptional at that time in his willingness to appear as a speaker alongside Black leaders of the day. With colorful imagery and homespun wit, he denounced eastern financiers, oppressive industrialists, and corrupt government.

In Europe in these same years, the 1880s and 1890s, men like von Schönerer, Lueger, and Drumont were similarly denouncing rapacious business interests and a corrupt government in the name of peasants, craftsmen, and shopkeepers. The parallels are instructive, but there was an important difference: Watson did not exploit racial hatred. On the contrary, he was a voice for reconciliation of the races, and he bemoaned that racism was exploited by the rich to keep the poor, Whites and Blacks, divided and unable to recognize their true enemies and exploiters. Still, Watson's ardent following among the common people resembled that of von Schönerer and other European radical-democratic or populist politicians; they were, all of them, embraced as secular saviors by desperate, frightened, and resentful people.

Watson's efforts in the early 1890s on behalf of the Populist movement provoked unrelenting retribution from the Democratic Party in Georgia, which resorted to violent intimidation of voters, ballot-box stuffing, and an array of other ruthlessly corrupt practices.[52] Watson met defeat after defeat in the elections of those years. Yet he was undeniably popular in the state; his defeats were clearly the result of Democratic tampering with the electoral process. In 1896 he became Populist candidate for vice-president, alongside presidential candidate William Jennings Bryan. After the resounding defeat of the Populist ticket in that year, a defeat that was

[51] Ibid., 315.
[52] Ibid., 232 ff.

deeply humiliating to him personally, Watson retired to private law practice and to writing.

The lengthy process by which Watson's early idealism began to fade cannot be described here, but he was, it seems, irreparably wounded by his defeats in the 1890s. He wrote: "How near I came to loss of mind only God who made me knows. . . . If ever a poor devil had been outlawed and vilified and persecuted and misrepresented and howled down and mobbed and threatened until he was well nigh mad, I was he."[53] Perhaps the most notable change in Watson was his abandonment of the idea of political cooperation between Whites and Blacks. With growing fervor he took up the cause of White supremacy, in part because he concluded that social justice for Whites and political equality for Blacks were, realistically, incompatible ideals. Whites would never accept Blacks as equals. In other areas as well, disillusionment and bigotry replaced his earlier idealism and tolerant humanity. The Catholic Church and the pope became special objects of vicious, mean-spirited attacks by Watson.

Yet a humane and libertarian side also remained; he never abandoned certain essential elements of his Populist faith. He continued to fight for the material welfare of the common people, above all the rural population. He remained as well a stubborn defender of popular liberties, even if his sense of what those liberties entailed did not always correspond to classical definitions of liberalism. Because of his deep-rooted attachment to freedom for the common people, his attacks on the Church had a kind of consistency; they reflected his belief, a very common one at the time in America as in Europe, that the Church supported the forces of repression and hatred for popular rule. Still, after the turn of the century Watson's speeches and articles gradually began to lose their earlier cogency and focus. His earlier penetrating analysis of plutocracy and corruption in high places gave way to an ill-focused sensationalism, the purported sexual activities of priests, nuns, and popes gaining a prominent position.

Until March of 1914, when the article favoring a new trial for Frank appeared in the *Atlanta Journal*, Watson's growing taste for sensationalism and bigotry rarely and only in inconsequential ways touched upon Jews. If Frank had been a Catholic, it is nearly inconceivable that Watson would have so scrupulously refrained from comment about the case for over a year. Thus, the question that has been asked repeatedly – how significant was anti-Semitism? – must again be answered with "not very" or at least "less than might be assumed." Watson was not attracted to the case because of his personal hatred for Jews or even because he believed that anti-Semitism represented a potentially powerful political device. Once engaged, however, he began, in his characteristic way, to pull out the

[53] Ibid., 285–6.

stops, to conjure up graphically vicious remarks about Jews. But, unlike anti-Catholic sensationalism, anti-Semitic sensationalism was a new venture for him in 1915.

The most immediate and certainly most palpable stimulus for his decision was his feud with Hoke Smith. A second cause, related to the first, was Watson's mania, dating back to his earliest public activities, about the power of the rich, a mania all the more consuming if their wealth was connected to modernizing big business and yet more consuming if that industry had northern connections. That rich men escaped scot-free for doing things that brought down harsh punishment upon the poor – his friend Glover is the obvious example – was something that Tom Watson found unbearable, and always had.

Watson was also much concerned about protecting southern womanhood, and once he began to involve himself in the Frank case, the sexual angle played a role in his pronouncements that was nearly as important as the image of a rich man using his influence to escape justice. Such interlocking factors came down to a potent combination for Watson: Leo Frank was allied with and supplying money to Watson's detested political enemy, Hoke Smith, who had recently bested him in a humiliating way; Leo Frank was a rich man with even richer friends and relatives; Leo Frank was a capitalist from the North, a college graduate trained in efficiently exploiting the labor of the wives and daughters of ruined farmers; Leo Frank had attempted to impose himself in a perverse way upon a southern girl and then had murdered her when she resisted; Leo Frank was now trying to escape by exploiting the legal system, which he could do because of his money and connections.

Leo Frank's Jewishness blended into all these factors and may have intensified them in Watson's mind, as in the minds of others. Yet if that Jewishness had been absent and all the others had remained, it seems almost certain that Watson would have reacted in much the same way. That being the case, it is difficult to consider anti-Semitism to have been a factor of decisive importance.

Moreover, Watson's attacks on Frank as a Jew and on the Jews who were trying to help Frank lacked the dimensions, texture, and consistency of most European anti-Semitic attacks. Put in other terms, it bonded only weakly with full-bodied anti-Semitic fantasy or with modern anti-Semitic ideology. It has been mentioned before that Watson came to the defense of the Jewish anarchist Emma Goldman. He subsequently established friendly connections with Jewish activists in New York during his muckraking period in the first years of the twentieth century. At that time, he came to fear that the socialists were making inroads into the ranks of the younger Populists, and he did attack socialist theory, making derogatory, if extremely brief, remarks about Marx's Jewish background. But Watson knew pitifully little about Marxism and ostensibly even less about European theories of anti-Semitism. It apparently did not even occur to him to describe socialism as a characteristic product of the Jewish mind and Jewish race, as was commonly done at this time by European anti-Semites. Revealingly, in 1919, when Watson was fighting a rear-guard battle against the postwar Red Scare, he eulogized Rosa Luxemburg, the epitome of the destructive Jewish revolutionary for European anti-Semites, because she had tried to defend ordinary recruits against the brutalities of their officers.[54]

It is tempting to conclude that Watson was concerned only about rich Jews, not about Jews generally or Jews as a race or even a distinct ethnic group. His attacks repeatedly focused on the wealth and powerful connections of Frank's supporters. Among his first comments on the case were warnings that a "gigantic conspiracy of Big Money" was at work to corrupt the state's courts, its governor, and its newspapers to free a rich "Sodomite." "Frank belongs to the Jewish aristocracy, and it was determined by the rich Jews that no aristocrat of their race should die for the death of a working-class Gentile."

But Watson's charges were so ill focused that they implicitly touched all Jews, rich and poor. Moreover, they incorporated images with unmistakable, if weakly developed, connections to modern anti-Semitic ideology. Frank was described as a "typical young libertine Jew," the kind "dreaded and detested by the city authorities of the North" because such Jews "have an utter contempt for law, and a ravenous appetite for . . . the girls of the uncircumcised."[55] Similarly, in his various threats and warnings Watson was unmistakably talking not only to rich Jews. He accused Frank's lawyers of having "blown the breath of life into the monster of Race Hatred: AND THIS FRANKENSTEIN, *whom you created at such enormous expense*, WILL HUNT YOU DOWN!"[56]

In looking at those who began to line up in support of Leo Frank, it is difficult to find much in the way of narrow or immediate political interest, of men who hoped to gain political advantage from the Frank Affair. It will be recalled that French Marxists charged that the agitation on behalf of Dreyfus was being manipulated by Jews who hoped, by proving Dreyfus innocent and exposing the bigotry behind the Anti-Dreyfusard cause, to exonerate "all the Jews and Jew-lovers among the Panama men," washing away the "filth of Israel." But American Jews by the time of the Frank case, although they had been embarrassed by a few notorious cases of Jewish criminality and were concerned to counter charges about lawless and libertine young Jewish males, faced a different

[54] Ibid., 350 ff, 408.
[55] Ibid., 379.
[56] Ibid., 382.

public opinion and public press in the United States. The "filth of Israel" was not being regularly denounced on the eve of the Frank Affair – neither by the press of the right nor by that of the left, as in France.

At most one might speculate that some Jewish leaders welcomed the chance to expose and demolish the charges against Frank with the hope that in some ill-defined way a successful campaign on behalf of Frank, resulting in a clear demonstration of his innocence and a reversal of his first conviction, would exonerate Jews in the public eye, thus quashing ugly rumors and stereotypes. But saving Frank's life was foremost in all of their minds, in a way that concern for Dreyfus's personal welfare was not always so clear on the part of the Dreyfusards. Similarly, whether or not Hoke Smith accepted money from Frank's supporters, the article in the *Atlanta Journal* must be seen as an act of political courage rather political opportunism on his part. The article did nothing to forward his political career, already crowned with many successes, and it is difficult to believe that Jewish financial support, if it indeed played a role, was worth the cost to Smith in terms of the loss of popularity he risked in supporting a new trial for Frank.

There were important differences in the way that defenders of Frank responded to the case, differences that in general outline are by now familiar but that are scarcely vulnerable to charges of political opportunism. On the one hand were the German-Jewish leaders in Atlanta, who wanted as little publicity and public excitement as possible, a strictly legalistic approach, and were reticent to make an issue of anti-Semitism. On the other hand were those, mostly in northern cities and mostly of eastern European origin, who looked to mass demonstrations and popular campaigns on Frank's behalf and were lightning-quick to bring up charges of anti-Semitism in this as in other matters.

For the lower-class activists, as with Mary's People, the Frank Affair merged into something like a public ritual, one that offered emotional sustenance, that allowed an accumulation of frustrations and resentments to surge forth and find focus – in an immigrant people inclined at any rate to emotionalism – in the campaign to free Leo Frank. But the Jewish masses of the northern cities were not threatening to lynch anyone. There was no immediate object on which they might direct violence – no disrespectful factory workers to provoke Jewish mourners, for example; no high-placed anti-Semitic officials, as in Russia, to be targets for Jewish assassins; no pimps and prostitutes to assault, as in Warsaw in 1905.

Members of the German-Jewish elite in Atlanta began to work on the Frank case not long after his conviction. Just as European Jewish leaders like Lucien Wolf and Paul Nathan believed it essential to engage non-Jews in the battle on behalf of Mendel Beilis, and succeeded impressively in that goal, so influential northern Jews like Louis Marshall, once alerted to the case by Jews in Atlanta, concentrated on winning over Gentile public opinion. He and other Jewish leaders in the North were sharply aware of the danger of polarization, of making this seem a narrowly Jewish issue, as distinguished from an issue of justice, pure and simple. They tried to operate as unobtrusively as possible. However, such behind-the-scenes activity by American-Jewish "notables," their quiet contacts with non-Jewish men of power and influence, nourished anti-Semitic visions of Jewish conspiracies, in the United States as in Europe.

Marshall, like Mathieu Dreyfus, avoided public statements or efforts to mobilize mass demonstrations. One of his preferred strategies was to contact the editors of southern newspapers, privately, and try to persuade them to defend Frank. The Hearst papers were, of course, already on his side, and Marshall was able to get the Jewish publisher of the *New York Times*, Adolph Ochs, to launch an extensive campaign on behalf of Frank. Similarly, Albert D. Lasker, a Jewish millionaire from Chicago, devoted much of his time to the case, both in raising money for Frank's legal expenses (he himself donated $160,000) and in contacting newspaper editors and urging them to defend Frank.[57]

Watson and others who demanded that Frank be hanged as any other man found guilty would be hanged were aware of these many efforts. Watson repeatedly observed that a non-Jewish convicted murderer, no matter how flagrantly unjust his trial, would never have benefited from such a massive infusion of money, nor would a non-Jew have benefited from such a network of men who had privileged access to those who formed public opinion in the United States. He may have had a point, but of course not one that justified hanging Frank. Moreover, within the not too distant future non-Jewish victims of what was perceived as prejudice and judicial error (Sacco and Vanzetti [1921], the Scottsboro Boys [1931]) would win a perhaps even wider public support than Frank's.

The activities of Jews like Marshall and Lasker seem to have been fruitful, although it is difficult to distinguish where they had a decisive effect by careful, nonpublic contacts with powerful Gentiles, and where it was simply an issue of editors and other important men examining the case on their own and concluding that an injustice had been done. At any rate, most of the editors of newspapers in Atlanta, after having acted so irresponsibly in the opening stages of the case, now began to draw back, to ask whether the case should be reconsidered.

These new words of caution seem to have had little effect on public opinion in Atlanta, or in Georgia as a whole. Mary's People had made up their mind. It made little difference to them that the very newspapers that, only a short time before, had published headlines about Frank, the

[57] Dinnerstein, *Frank*, 91–8.

"monster," being "caught," were now calling for a more careful examination of evidence, were criticizing Dorsey's methods, and were publishing information that put much of the initially published information into doubt. Indeed, Hearst's newspaper even ran a headline, "Plot to hang Frank!"[58] but at this point such sensationalism was widely dismissed as the result of Jewish money, pressure, or deception.

Although the confrontation of Frank's supporters and those who wanted to see him hanged did not take on the institutional and explicitly ideological forms that the confrontation of Dreyfusards and Anti-Dreyfusards did, one might still suggestively speak of "two worlds," or two separate cultures, confronting one another in the Frank Affair. These two worlds had much to do with the by now familiar contrast between liberal-notable politics and the new politics of populist democracy. On the one hand, there was the cultural and intellectual world of those who believed in the law, in the efficacy of due process and the jury system, who believed in a larger but related way that truth would out in an open discussion between honest and rational men. If a mistake had been made in convicting Frank, that mistake could be undone. On the other hand, there were Mary's People, bitter, resentful, and having little attachment to, or understanding of, such liberal virtues as suspended judgment and due process.

Those who believed in due process did not fail to speak up in Atlanta. A majority of the Christian ministers in the city signed a petition urging the commutation of Leo Frank's sentence.[59] But Mary's People far outnumbered those who came to question the justice of Frank's sentence. Many Atlantans also came to feel that this case was one that engaged the pride of Atlanta, of Georgia, and of the South generally. For them, there was a powerful symbolism in the opening days of the trial: On Frank's side of the courtroom was a bevy of high-priced lawyers and expensively dressed relatives from the North. On the other side was Mary's grief-stricken and impoverished mother. How could she hope for justice? There was an answer, of course. Mrs. Phagan had only Hugh Dorsey to see that her daughter's murder was avenged, that this rich, Jewish pervert would not escape justice through lawyers' tricks.

Frank's lawyers petitioned the higher courts of Georgia and of the United States, all the way to the Supreme Court, some thirteen different times. But no higher court was willing to agree that Frank was legally entitled to a new trial. The issues in the petitions were mostly technical, not easily summarized, and the judgments by no means constituted thirteen different legal reaffirmations of Frank's guilt. Still, there were many

[58] Ibid., 85.
[59] Seventeen of them are listed in the John Marshall Slaton Collection (AC 00–070); cited in Frey, *Silent and Damned*, 88.

who saw them as that, or at least as an overwhelming affirmation that
Frank had been given a fair trial. Such was especially the case in Georgia,
where a rising indignation could be sensed that these legal shenanigans
might go on forever. Many in Atlanta took pride that the lynch mob had
been restrained, the legal system respected. But now it was time for this
loathsome murderer of Little Mary Phagan to hang.

Outside Georgia opinion was radically different. Throughout the United
States, large numbers of Americans, by no means only or even primarily
Jews, responded as if this was another Dreyfus or Beilis affair, a horrible
miscarriage of justice, unthinkable in the United States – or perhaps
possible only in the bigoted South. There was an enormous outpouring
of letters, over one hundred thousand at final count, to the governor of
Georgia and to the Prison Commission, urging that Frank's sentence be
commuted to life imprisonment.

As in the earlier affairs these letters were more than a reflection of a
campaign led by Jews and their organizations, even if those often played
a catalytic role or a role behind the scenes. The letters were signed by
every imaginable kind of figure, including senators and governors of other
southern states, presidents of major corporations and universities, writers,
clergymen, and labor leaders. Thousands of petitions flowed in as well,
containing over a million signatures. In a single day in May of 1915 Frank
received over fifteen hundred letters. In Georgia itself, some ten thousand
residents were courageous enough – and this did take courage in Georgia
at this time – to sign a petition on behalf of Frank.[60]

The role of Governor Slaton

If one is to find a heroic figure in this drama, one who might be compared
to Picquart in terms of the personal risks taken to see that justice was
done, it was the governor of Georgia, John M. Slaton, even if in his case,
as in the case of Picquart, there are considerations that put his heroic
stature into question. In the long line of appeals, both for a retrial and
for a commutation of the death sentence, he was the final person to
consider the case before Frank's sentence was to be carried out. Slaton
had before him much information not available, or usable, by other reviewing agencies. He had, for example, a letter from Judge Roan, describing the death sentence as a mistake and requesting that the mistake
be rectified. He had as well a communication revealing that Conley had
confessed the murder to his lawyer, which in fact that lawyer had also
made public. Finally, he had a letter from another informant, now an

[60] Dinnerstein, *Frank*, 118–19.

inmate in the state prison, who said that he had seen Conley struggling with Mary Phagan on the day of the murder.

Slaton also went over the trial transcripts with great care and insight. He noticed a number of details whose significance had somehow escaped the attention of Frank's lawyers. In particular, he detected a major flaw in Conley's testimony, one that might have fatally discredited that testimony during the trial if Frank's defense lawyers had pointed it out. According to the detectives who first went to the factory, a pile of excrement was crushed by the elevator in the factory, producing a strong odor, when they used it to go to the basement on the day following Mary's murder. Conley later testified that he had deposited the excrement there earlier on the day of the murder. He also testified that he and Frank used the elevator to bring Mary's body into the basement. Yet detectives had earlier seen the excrement, as yet not crushed, when searching the area after they had found Mary's body. The excrement was not crushed, in other words, until the next day. Thus, Conley's elaborate testimony, which included using the elevator with Frank to take the body to the basement, was put into question.

There were a number of other, if somewhat less striking, problems with the case that Dorsey had made against Frank that were now cogently exposed in Slaton's analysis. Indeed, Frank's lawyers had not wholly failed in their own efforts to discredit Conley's testimony. They had, no less than Slaton, pointed to problems with timing in that testimony, how Frank and Conley could have done the many things he described in the brief period that Frank was in the office. Similarly, Frank's lawyers had called a mechanic to the stand who had been in the factory until around 3 P.M.; he remarked that if the elevator had been used, the noise would have been considerable, and he would certainly have heard it, but had not. None of these problems was decisive enough to crack Conley's testimony during the trial, or at least to persuade the jury that he had made up the entire story. Only in connection with the new points brought up by Slaton did these other points take on added weight.

At this stage for Slaton to commute Frank's sentence to life imprisonment (a right he had as governor, when there was doubt concerning the guilt of a convicted man) made him vulnerable to charges of being bought by the Jews or being of their tool. There was another awkward problem with his decision to review the case: He was a law partner of Frank's attorney, Luther Rosser. Yet further raising eyebrows, Slaton and Rosser had been partners with Benjamin Z. Philips, a Jewish attorney, in the 1880s. Slaton's partnership with Rosser, many believed, constituted a conflict of interest, one that should have caused Slaton to refuse to review the case personally. Slaton's earlier partnership with a Jew could also lead to the suspicion that he retained special connections with Jews, even if such partnerships were common (Dorsey himself had one). At any rate, Slaton insisted that he felt no conflict of interest and refused to disqualify himself. The decision was made in his very last days of office; his successor had publicly stated that he would refuse to commute Frank.

That decision must have been difficult. He received over a thousand letters threatening to kill him and his wife if he let Frank live. He nonetheless persisted, commenting, "I can endure misconstruction, abuse, and condemnation, but I cannot stand the constant companionship of an accusing conscience."[61]

As predicted, his commutation order set off a storm of indignation in Georgia. Even more than the entry of northerners into this case, Slaton's actions inflamed the common people of Georgia. News of the commutation was similar in its effect to Zola's *J'Accuse!* Angry men from the surrounding area arrived in Atlanta by the thousands. Tom Watson urged them on, repeatedly approving the idea of popular violence, even lynching, as the only remaining way for the common people to find justice, since Slaton had refused to do his job, had sold out to the Jews and their agents.

However, unlike France or Russia, in Atlanta there was never any suggestion of collusion between the forces of order and the mob. The local police and the state troopers effectively protected property; the sheriff, upon hearing of the commutation, warned Jewish leaders in Atlanta of a possible riot and even authorized some of them to carry firearms. Earlier accounts of this period, particularly Golden's *A Little Girl Is Dead*, presented a picture of Jewish panic, of exodus from the city, but a more recent and careful scholar has concluded that "there was no dramatic exodus or panic. The Jews were frightened, but most went about their business as usual and no serious incidents occurred."[62]

A mob formed in town, but rather than attack Jews or their property, it marched to the governor's mansion, armed with an array of weapons, including dynamite, and chanting, "Slaton, king of Jews!" State troopers at the mansion were finally able to disperse the mob, after much violence. Again, there is no question that in this mob there were anti-Semites, but it is also significant that their indignation appeared to be focused on Frank and Slaton, rather than on Jews in general. Even efforts at an economic boycott of Jews at this time had little success (cards were sent to thousands of Atlantans urging them to buy from "Americans," not those who used their profits to help a murderer escape from justice[63]).

Aside from such actions, Jews in Atlanta felt new hostility in the air, sensed new suspicions of them, but overt or concrete manifestations of anti-Semitism were few. In what has been called a "referendum" on the

[61] Frey, *Silent and Damned*, 88–9.
[62] Hertzberg, *Jews of Atlanta*, 213.
[63] Ibid., 213.

Frank Affair in Atlanta, a by-election to the city council pitted Joseph Loewus, a rich Jewish manufacturer, against Oscar W. Williamson, a railway conductor. Loewus said that a vote for him would constitute a repudiation of "the fanaticism . . . which has libeled the good name of our city." Williamson won by a landslide.[64] However, anti-Semitism was only indirectly an issue here; it is a fair bet that a non-Jewish rich manufacturer would have fared little better against Williamson. In the same period a Jew, Victor Kriegshaber, was elected president of the Chamber of Commerce, and the existing Jewish officers in the various Masonic lodges retained their posts. But no Jew ran for public office again in Atlanta for another twenty years, and it would not be until 1969–73 that the city elected a Jewish mayor.

The lynching

The attack on the governor's mansion occurred in mid-June 1915. On July 17, at the Milledgeville Prison Farm, where Frank was incarcerated, William Creen, a twice-convicted murderer, crept up on Frank while he was asleep and cut his throat from ear to ear. Only the speedy attention of a surgeon, himself serving a sentence for murder, saved Frank's life, although it hung in the balance for several weeks. The governor's office was deluged with demands for Creen's pardon, even his immediate release.[65]

Other efforts were also underfoot to assure that Frank did not "escape justice." A group calling itself "the Knights of Mary Phagan" had sworn over her grave to avenge her murder. The Knights were not a lynch mob in the sense normally understood. They were headed by what must be termed, for lack of a better word, "respectable" citizens. Among their members were a former superior judge, a former sheriff, and a clergyman. They had taken care to exclude from their ranks the more unruly sorts, the redneck riff- raff that typically made up the southern lynch mob. Their argument, moreover, was legalistic, one that Watson had also made: They had long waited for the legal system to work, but it had not. The people of Georgia were thus merely carrying out what that system had failed to do.

The Knights planned an attack on the Milledgeville Prison Farm on the night of August 16–17 with the thoroughness and efficiency of an elite commando detachment. It took them about ten minutes, once they had arrived at the prison, to break into the grounds, overcome the guards,

[64] Ibid., 213–14.
[65] Golden, *A Little Girl*, 286–7.

seize Frank, and return to their cars. They then headed for Marietta, Mary Phagan's home town and the place where she was buried.

Frank's wounds from the knife attack had scarcely healed. When he was hanged from a tree on the outskirts of Marietta, his neck wounds opened, spilling blood over his shoulder. An excited crowd gathered to view Frank hanging from the tree. The body was kicked and stamped upon when cut down. Plans to dismember and then burn it were narrowly prevented. Snapshots taken of the dangling body were reproduced in great number. They became a popular item in Georgia, sold in rural markets throughout the state for many years.

Horror, indignation, and dismay over the lynching were expressed throughout the United States, even by most of the authorities in Georgia. However, the grand jury that investigated the lynching reported that it could find no evidence and obtain no testimony against the Knights, in spite of widespread knowledge of who they were. Mary's People closed ranks. Tom Watson seemed to express popular opinion when he wrote, "In putting the Sodomite murderer to death the Vigilance Committee has done what the Sheriff should have done, if Slaton had not been in the mold of Benedict Arnold. LET JEW LIBERTINES TAKE NOTICE! Georgia is not for sale to rich criminals."[66]

[66] Ibid., 299.

Epilogue and conclusion

The Jewish Question exists wherever Jews live in appreciable numbers.
. . . Naturally, we move where we are not persecuted; our appearance then
leads to persecution. This is a fact and is bound to remain a fact everywhere.
. . . (Theodore Herzl)

However horrifying the lynching of Leo Frank, however much it and the
events surrounding it stood in flagrant violation of the ideals of American
democracy, one may still legitimately question whether the Frank Affair
represented a victory, in a deeper sense, for the forces of anti-Semitism
in the United States or even in the South. It may be argued that the
Frank Affair contributed to the articulation and dissemination of an American variety of anti-Semitic ideology, particularly as expressed by Tom
Watson, but to speak of a gathering storm of anti-Semitism in the United
States makes little sense, or at least less than similar arguments – themselves problematic – made for France and the rest of Europe.

To be sure, there is evidence of rising tension between Jews and Gentiles in the United States, with some sharp ups and downs, from the 1890s
until the early 1950s. Watson would be followed by men like Henry Ford
and Father Charles Coughlin, who attracted a following throughout the
United States and who made more solid connections with main-line anti-
Semitic traditions. Yet even their anti-Semitism pales in comparison with
that found in Europe. It is indicative of American reality that Ford, a
man whom Hitler and the Nazis lionized, finally backed away from his
anti-Semitism, even openly apologized for it.[1] There is little evidence
that he gained in popularity because of his anti-Semitism, and there is
much evidence that he abandoned public espousal of it in part because
of the popular disfavor it incurred.

In the United States, as in Europe, one may speak of a "rising tide"
against anti-Semitism, one that paralleled, opposed, and stifled efforts of
the anti-Semites to organize and to spread their ideas. Mobilization and
institutionalization of forces opposed to anti-Semitism in the prewar
world, especially by Jews themselves, was in certain regards even more

[1] Cf. Albert Lee, *Henry Ford and the Jews* (New York, 1980); Michael N. Dobkowski, *The
Tarnished Dream: The Basis of American Anti-Semitism* (Westport, Conn., 1979).

impressive in the United States than in Europe.[2] The Frank Affair did not in fact play a major role in initially galvanizing these forces, since they had begun to organize a number of years before his arrest. Moreover, in the Frank Affair there was no clear-cut victory, as there was in France and Russia. The forces that came together to oppose Frank's conviction did not go on to win power in Congress, as the Dreyfusards did in the French Chamber of Deputies, nor was there violent revolution against those who supported anti-Semitism, as in Russia.

Still, the Frank Affair touched on basic issues of American identity in a most painful way and almost demanded expressions of regret as expiation. This was, after all, the country whose president, just a decade before, had boasted that no other country in the world had done so much to protect the rights of Jews. It was, to say the least, awkward that in the same year that Mendel Beilis was freed by a jury of peasants – and was cheered as national hero by millions of ordinary Russians – Leo Frank was found guilty, in an atmosphere of mob violence, by a jury of middle-class Americans, and subsequently was lynched by an organization of "respectable" citizens.

Americans had abundantly expressed their indignation at the pogrom at Kishinev. They had expressed outrage over Beilis's arrest, and there had been an enormous outpouring of sympathy for Dreyfus in the United States, from all corners of the nation and all political persuasions. The sympathy expressed for Frank was unquestionably more broad-based in the United States than was the hatred for him personally; those who spoke out against anti-Semitism at this time outnumbered by far those who sought to exploit it. Among those Americans, in the nation at large, who took an interest in the matter, those who called for a new trial were more prominent and incomparably more numerous than those agitating for his execution, even if among the latter were those whose convictions were potent enough to lead them to violence. If we can accept the paradoxical conclusion that the Kishinev pogrom marked a rising Jewish combativeness, it is no less paradoxically accurate to conclude that the reaction to the Frank Affair underlined the existence of a more friendly environment for Jews, in the sense that their enemies were weaker than in other countries, their friends more willing to identify openly with the struggle for toleration and decency in regard to their fellow Jewish citizens.

By the time of the Frank Affair American Jews who were long-time residents had come to appreciate more than ever before the dilemmas and ambiguities of life among the Gentiles, but they did not give up on the idea of living in their midst; they did not conclude that the future

---

[2] Cf. Naomi W. Cohen, *Not Free to Desist: The American Jewish Committee, 1906–1966* (Philadelphia, 1972).

was impossibly bleak. As influential Jews saw it, anti-Semitism had raised its ugly head in the Frank Affair, but it had been defeated or at least widely discredited. Jews were obliged to recognize once again what had always been obvious, that they had numerous and powerful enemies. But they also had numerous and powerful friends. Or if that overstates the matter, Jews could take some comfort that their enemies faced even more powerful enemies – who, to be sure, were not necessarily friends of the Jews. Such twisted formulations, even more appropriate for the situation in France and Russia, are often necessary to suggest the ambiguous texture of Gentile–Jewish relationships, but those relationships were nevertheless not widely considered to be without hope prior to 1914.

The "Zionist lessons" of the Frank Affair were even less persuasive to the overwhelming majority of American Jews than were the Zionist lessons of the Dreyfus Affair to French Jews. In Russia, of course, the spread of Zionism much predated the Beilis Affair, but even there, where by the eve of World War I it had won over many more followers than in the West, it attracted only a minority of the total Jewish population. French Jews felt so confident after the victory of the Dreyfusards that a major French-Jewish journal commented, "in giving birth to the Dreyfus Affair, anti-Semitism had died."[3] Much the same can be said for the attitudes of Jews in the rest of western and most of central Europe, where, as a leading scholar has stated, "relative security and well-being characterized the middle classes, and [where] the differences which had rent apart nations like France seemed to have ended in compromise."[4] Some Jewish observers, in utter contrast to Herzl, went as far as to argue that the Dreyfus Affair had ultimately had a positive effect, in that anti-Semitism had been fatally exposed: It was not directed really or exclusively at Jews but rather at tolerance, at humane, modern values more generally,[5] and thus all people of good will had an interest in combating it.

Even in Atlanta, where the Jewish community was deeply shaken by the Frank Affair and where Jewish leaders long opposed efforts to reha-bilitate Frank because of the hostility such efforts might revive, Jews continued to move into the city in numbers no less impressive than before the Frank Affair. The Jewish population of Atlanta more than doubled by the end of World War II, quadrupled by 1968.[6] In the long run, the

---

[3] "La nouvelle revision," *Univers Israelite*, June 22, 1906. Quoted in Paula E. Hyman, "The French Jewish Community from Emancipation to the Dreyfus Affair," in Norman L. Kleeblatt, ed., *The Dreyfus Affair: Art, Truth, Justice* (Berkeley, Calif., 1987), 22.

[4] George L. Mosse, *Toward the Final Solution: A History of European Racism* (New York, 1980), 168.

[5] Michael Marrus, *The Politics of Assimilation: The French Community at the Time of the Dreyfus Affair* (Oxford, 1970), 280.

[6] Steven Hertzberg, *Strangers Within the Gate City: The Jews of Atlanta, 1845–1915* (Philadelphia, 1978), 217.

economic opportunities in the city outweighed any reputation it had for being anti-Semitic. Similarly, a leading historian of French Jewry has remarked on how little the Dreyfus Affair seemed to affect native French Jews in the long run. Rather than abandoning their belief in assimilation, they "remained practically unchanged, and the most important anti-Semitic crisis of nineteenth-century France appeared as only a ripple in the smooth course of Jewish life in that country."[7] Similar remarks appear appropriate for Atlanta, to say nothing of the rest of the country.

The world before 1914 was still a basically hopeful and optimistic one, whatever the brooding of intellectual and artistic elites. But that world was soon to change fundamentally. Even as Leo Frank was being lynched, hundreds of thousands of young men were falling in senseless slaughter across the Atlantic. The cataclysmic and brutal decade between 1914 and 1924 would transform, as nothing so far had, the relations of Jews and Gentiles, in both Europe and the United States. Those events would also transform the way that subsequent generations viewed the decades immediately preceding the Great War. That is another story.

* * * * * *

A central argument of this work has been that in the generation before World War I, anti-Semitism, especially violent or overt expressions of it, is best understood in terms of real factors, most notably the rise of the Jews, but also the growing rivalry of nation-states, and the fears that modern times meant the end of established, familiar, and cherished patterns of life. Inherited prejudice, reformulated in a modern anti-Semitic ideology, mushroomed in the soil of such conditions; where and when they were less important, it withered. It remained perennially in the background as a potential, but it did not have an independent or self-generating power of its own to stimulate large numbers of people into action.

Another key argument has been that negative impressions of Jews were countered and for the most part overwhelmed by positive ones, that while anti-Semitic ideology found confirmation to some degree in the actions of real Jews, it was also undermined by the actions of real Jews who proved themselves "useful" rather than destructive or threatening, who did not correspond to the fantasies of inherited prejudice. Similarly, evidence is weak that anti-Semitic ideology, prejudice against Jews, was the decisive factor in the arrest and conviction of Dreyfus and Frank, however important the role of anti-Semitism in the affairs that developed thereafter. And anti-Semitic ideology, even when ambiguously sustained by the power of the state, was not sufficient to persuade a jury of simple

[7] Marrus, *Assimilation*, 282.

peasants that Mendel Beilis – by all accounts a good and decent man – was guilty of ritual murder. Jew-hatred was at best a rough and unwieldy political device, even in tsarist Russia.

Another reflection of the unwieldiness of anti-Semitic belief was the war of conflicting imagery and moral obligation that raged within the breasts of strategically placed anti-Semites in the Three Affairs. Jew-haters like Drumont or Khrushevan may have been utterly consumed and corrupted by anti-Semitic fantasy, but others, such as Picquart and Shulgin, suppressed their anti-Semitic prejudice in the name of the higher ideals of truth and justice. Even figures like Lueger or Watson, while capable of exploiting anti-Semitic hatred, were not immune to the power of those higher ideals.

The rise of the Jews has appeared in these pages as a matter of key importance, one that has not always been given its due in historical accounts, and one whose complex and often paradoxical nature is more clearly revealed by a comparative approach – showing, for example, that a rapid rise, as in Hungary or the United States, did not necessarily result in a correspondingly rapid rise in anti-Semitism. Many non-Jews welcomed rising Jews as partners in a new world of progress, prosperity, and hope for the future. Yet some of those in the generation before World War I who pondered the implications of the prominent, often brilliant participation of Jews in modern civilization came to troubled and troubling conclusions. In this sense, the Three Affairs evoked with particular drama certain fundamental questions about Jewish–Gentile relations – or about "rising" Jews – with echoes back through the centuries. These questions vexed the more penetrating Zionist thinkers, first of all Herzl himself, and they have not been put to rest by the last decades of the twentieth century.

Zionists did not, of course, attract many followers before World War I, especially not in western Europe or in the United States. Yet the musings of some of them now appear disturbingly prescient. They asked, in ways that often seemed to parallel questions posed by the anti-Semites, if the continuing rise of the Jews would not inevitably provoke resentment from non-Jews. Chaim Weizmann, in writing his memoirs, argued that "whenever the quantity of Jews in any country [he was discussing Great Britain in 1905] reaches the saturation point, that country reacts against them. . . . [This] reaction . . . cannot be looked upon as anti-Semitism in the ordinary or vulgar sense of that word; it is a universal social and economic concomitant of Jewish immigration and we cannot shake it off."[8]

Weizmann's reflections, which, of course, echo those of Herzl, suggest

---

[8] Chaim Weizmann, *Trial and Error* (New York, 1949), 90; cf. Jehuda Reinharz, *Chaim Weizmann: The Making of a Zionist Leader* (Oxford, 1985), 486.

larger ones: Would the steadily rising wealth of Jews, their dazzling in-
tellectuality and verbal acuity, their remarkable concentration in certain
prestigious and influential professions, their political finesse at some point
inevitably provoke those less successful than they? Did the many virtues
and impressive talents of modern Jews add up to some sort of modern
fulfillment of Jewish chosenness, of an eventual "right to rule" in the
societies where they lived? If Jews resisted blending fully into those
societies, if they refused to "disappear" by abandoning their particularist
identity with its intimations of moral superiority, would not anti-Semitism
emerge, sooner or later, and in free societies perhaps more explosively
than in those where Jews are subject to controls designed to prevent their
rise? And when adversities occurred, as they inevitably would (economic
depressions, wars, revolutions, even accidents of nature or pandemic
disease), would the Jews not always remain tempting scapegoats, to be
"accused" again and again?

Such questions took on profoundly renewed meaning in the three decades after the Three Affairs, when a quantum leap in the virulence of
anti-Semitism occurred, when far greater numbers were drawn to the
banners of anti-Semitic movements, when fantasies about Jews in the
form of racist ideologies ripened as never before, and when – perhaps
most important of all – the opponents of anti-Semitism weakened in their
resolve and in their popular support. A central concern of this volume
has been to describe how, before the Great War, anti-Semitism appeared
different in quality both to Jews and to non-Jews than in the interwar
period, and how the opponents of anti-Semitism appeared triumphant.
This emphasis is not meant to suggest that Jews before World War I did
not feel threatened by anti-Semitism or did not suffer from it. Rather,
the point is that large numbers of them believed time was on their side;
they continued to harbor hopes for the future, to believe in rationality,
progress, and the prospects of ethnic and religious harmony. World War
I and the Russian Revolution opened up vistas of human irrationality and
bestiality that nineteenth-century Europeans and Americans had considered securely a thing of the past. But the Three Affairs, or even the rash
of pogroms from 1903 to 1906 in Russia, did not fundamentally shake the
optimism of most Jews about the future.

We know things now that have irreparably altered our reactions to the
issue of Jewish–Gentile relationships in the nineteenth century. What we
know not only colors our perception of events before 1914 but inclines
us to a skewed vision, to "see" a rising hatred of Jews but pay little
attention to opposing trends, to the powerful opposition to anti-Semitism
that is so well illustrated in the Three Affairs. We can now see that anti-
Semitic fanatics like Drumont and de Morès, dismissed as incompetent
and incapable of a successful challenge to the political powers-that-be,

would be succeeded by men like Julius Streicher and Adolf Hitler, who moved to center stage and, indeed, whose eventual success was paradoxically related to the lingering conviction, bolstered by prewar experiences, that men like them could never succeed in politics.

The rise of the Jews was inextricably part of certain broad historical trends, such as the rise of the middle class, population growth, industrialization, and urbanization, most of which can themselves be subsumed under the awkward and now much criticized rubric of "modernization." These pages have presented the Three Affairs solidly in the context of such impersonal forces, as distinguished from presenting them in psychologically appealing accounts of heroism or in the framework of one-dimensional, moralizing narrative, as stories of personal villainy or national sickness and corruption. On the other hand, Jews have been presented, individually and collectively, as active agents, as modern, responsible, and flawed human beings, not merely as passive martyrs or as uncomprehending objects of impersonal forces. A key point has been that personal character and moral choices, Jewish and non-Jewish, in the anti-Semitic affairs were crucial. Those moral choices in some elusive sense ultimately stood outside historical determinants.

Even if the rise of modern anti-Semitism in these years can be understood in the same way that other trends are understandable, unpredictable or accidental factors were at times crucial. Much about anti-Semitism can be comprehended with the generalizing tools of the social scientist, yet much else remains irreducibly unique, and more properly in the realm of historical-humanistic understanding. However, calling for such understanding is not the same as accepting the assertion that we can only describe anti-Semitism – recognize, isolate, and condemn it, contenting ourselves with a flat narrative.

Description and understanding are not so easily distinguished from one another. At any rate the argument here has been that anti-Semitism is not inapproachably mysterious; there is nothing about it that makes it essentially beyond human ken. Whether we are speaking of "objective" anti-Semitism, arising out of normal competition in the real world, or "fantastic" anti-Semitism, derived from ancient myths, hatred of Jews can be studied just as hatred of other peoples – and understood, if we do not impose an impossibly strict definition on that term.

To make this assertion is not to accept that Jew-hatred is essentially like other hatreds. Its uniqueness derives from the peculiar way that normal or "objective" tensions link up to peculiar fantasies, the way that ordinary human friction between Jews and non-Jews fuses with ancient and enduring myths of great power and complexity. As has been repeatedly emphasized, the most challenging task for the historian is to understand the changing nature of that fusion, to place it concretely in history, and to be sensitive not only to the remarkable differences of time but also to those of place. It may be that at times those myths generate hatred with little connection to real, living Jews. It also may be that at times friction between Jews and non-Jews remains largely normal, similar to friction between other groups, without a significant bonding to anti-Semitic fantasy. But for the most part, certainly in the generation before World War I, there has been an extensive interplay of myth and normality, fantasy and reality. Such, of course, is true of many hatreds; Whites and Blacks may also tap potent myths or fantasies about one another, thus exhancing or exaggerating ordinary or objective kinds of tension.

Human personality is also unique, hard to capture with the generalizations of social science. The role of personality in the Three Affairs was decisive, and to the degree that human character remains elusive we may also term that role mysterious. Who could maintain that these affairs would have occurred as they did without the accidental or unpredictable uniqueness of the personalities of Dreyfus, Beilis, and Frank? Even more, who could deny the crucial yet unforeseeable and often astonishing roles played by figures like Móric Scharf, Picquart, Zola, Mishchuk, Shulgin, Dorsey, Conley, or Watson? The issue is more than their attachment, or lack of it, to moral values; it relates to such random idiosyncracies as conviviality – Beilis was saved in part because he was likable; Dreyfus and Frank might have been spared their sufferings had they not been so stiff and distant.

The evidence assembled in these pages about the background and evolution of the Three Affairs makes it difficult to agree with those observers who describe anti-Semitism as an ideology of great inherent or independent power, or at least it suggests the need for a careful definition of the nature of that power and how it comes to express itself. Modern anti-Semitism is rent by internal contradictions and weakened by demonstrable absurdities. It opportunistically attaches itself to, or is pulled into, more potent forces, but it has little coherent carrying force of its own and thus withers when those forces weaken. At the same time, to be sure, it has demonstrated a remarkable ability to persist, to revive time and again through the ages, an ability that is obviously related to the way that Jewish themes are inextricably intertwined in the fundamental identity of western civilization. Whether hated or admired, Jews have perennially fascinated members of that civilization.

Modern anti-Semites like Marr, Drumont, or Krushevan insisted that they were denouncing real Jews, their power and malevolence, not fantasies about them. It might at first seem that to recognize the role of real factors is to lend support to the arguments of such men. However, to pick up a point made in the Introduction, to ignore real factors or dogmatically to deny their importance finally plays into the hands of anti-

Semitic propagandists. A prominent right-wing Russian dissident (and distinguished mathematician), Igor Shafarevich, has argued that a powerful alliance of international Jews effectively shouts down any effort to examine Jewish influence in the world. He has bitterly complained about a "deeply rooted, internalized inhibition," where "any thought that somewhere in some period actions of some Jews harmed other peoples – even any objective study which does not from the start rule out such possibility – is considered reactionary, not intellectual enough, impure." As the many references in this work should make clear, including those of numerous Jewish scholars, Shafarevich's complaints are ill founded, in spite of what might seem a ring of plausibility. He continues by lamenting that Jews use charges of anti-Semitism "as a device to stir emotions, consciously ignoring logic."[9] Again, it is the partial truth of this assertion that gives it a dangerous plausibility.

This study has tried to show that claims about the decisive role of anti-Semitism in key stages of the Three Affairs have at times been based on intuition and a readiness to believe rather than on evidence. To be sure, there were also those, like Alfred Dreyfus and his wife, whose faith ran in the opposite direction, who tenaciously and repeatedly refused to believe that anti-Semitism could so cruelly corrupt the personalities of people they had respected and trusted. Yet even in the case of Dreyfus's superiors one must wonder how much the decisive issue for most of them was anti-Semitism rather than less complicated moral failings – incompetence and the related inability to accept responsibility for disastrously bad decisions, mixed with opportunism. The evidence for such a play of factors, rather than for anti-Semitism, is even more persuasive in the case of Hugh Dorsey. Obviously, such an explanation cannot deny that anti-Semitic prejudice played any role in the actions of such men; most likely in the Dreyfus Affair, as in the Beilis and Frank affairs, anti-Semitic feelings, spineless irresponsibility, and opportunism mixed in ways that can never be untangled. But even Watson, for all his vicious ranting about Jews, was drawn into the Frank Affair by his rivalry with Hoke Smith and his hatred of rich northerners, not by long-standing and deep-seated hostility to Jews based on, or driven by, the influence of anti-Semitic ideology. He in truth knew little about modern anti-Semitic ideology and unconsciously contradicted a number of its central tenets.

It is intriguing and thought-provoking that Picquart, a traditional anti-Semite who made no secret of his aversion for Alfred Dreyfus and his disgust – to the very end – for the Dreyfus family, courageously came to Dreyfus's aid, whereas Dorsey, a traditional southern philo-Semite with

---

[9] Quoted in Liah Greenfeld's review of Igor Shafarevich's *Russophobia*: "The Closing of the Russian Mind," *The New Republic*, Feb. 5, 1990, 30–4.

many friendly connections to the Jewish community of Atlanta, stubbornly worked for Frank's conviction and execution. These paradoxical cases may be offered as symbolic of how little anti-Semitic – or philo-Semitic – convictions may determine action at a given historical moment, whatever one may conclude about anti-Semitism as a more fundamental determinant in history. That Frank was lynched whereas Beilis went free may also serve as a symbol of how in specific situations the relative strength of anti-Semitism in the surrounding society or in the state itself by no means determines the outcome of crucial events.

How unexpected and puzzling it is that men like Pikhno and Shulgin, prominent ideological anti-Semites in Russia, proclaiming the need for "cold" pogroms, should come to Beilis's aid. And how ironic that a man like Zola, who before the Dreyfus Affair had written vicious things about Jews, has become for Jews a hundred years later a familiar symbol of the courageous Gentile, steadfastly struggling for justice and humanity. The example of Zola may also serve to show how history, especially that transparently serving political agendas, can become hopelessly tangled in a web of misperception. Clio, the Muse of History, is deceitful. The lessons we sometimes think we have learned from her are no lessons at all.

Bibliography

The following list of works cited in the footnotes is provided for the convenience of the reader. No effort has been made to provide a bibliography of all relevant works or even of all works that have influenced the author.

Books

Adler, Cyrus, ed. *The Voice of America on Kishineff*. Philadelphia, 1904.

Arendt, Hannah. *The Origins of Totalitarianism*. New York, 1963.

Arkin, Marcus. *Aspects of Jewish History*. Philadelphia, 1975.

Aschheim, Steven. *Brothers and Strangers: The Eastern European Jew in Germany and German Jewish Consciousness, 1800–1923*. Madison, Wis., 1982.

Ausubel, Nathan. *A Pictoral History of the Jewish People*. New York, 1953.

Avishai, Bernard. *The Tragedy of Zionism*. New York, 1985.

Baron, Salo Wittmayer. *Steeled by Adversity: Essays and Addresses on American Life*. Philadelphia, 1971.

Baron, Salo W. *The Russian Jew Under Tsars and Soviets*. New York, 1987.

Barrows, Susanna. *Distorting Mirrors: Visions of the Crowd in Late Nineteenth-Century France*. New Haven, Conn., 1981.

Bauer, Yehuda, and Mendes-Flohr, Paul, eds. *The Jew in the Modern World*. Oxford, 1980.

Beilis, Mendel. *The Story of My Sufferings*. New York, 1926.

Bensimon-Dorath, Doris. *Sociodemographie des Juifs de France et d'Algérie*. Paris, 1976.

Berger, David, ed. *The Legacy of Jewish Migration: 1881 and Its Impact*. New York, 1983.

Best, Gary Dean. *To Free a People: American Jewish Leaders and the Jewish Problem in Eastern Europe, 1890–1914*. Westport, Conn., 1982.

Biale, David. *Power and Powerlessness in Jewish History*. New York, 1986.

Black, Edwin. *The Transfer Agreement*. New York, 1984.

Blitzer, Wolf. *The Territory of Lies*. New York, 1989.

Blum, Léon. *Souvenirs sur l'Affaire*. Paris, 1929, 1982.

Boehlich, Walter, ed. *Der Berliner Antisemitismusstreit*. Frankfurt am Main, 1965.

Borden, Morton. *Jews, Turks, and Infidels*. Chapel Hill, N. C., 1984.

Braham, Randolph L., ed. *Hungarian-Jewish Studies*. New York, 1966.

Braham, Randolph L. *The Politics of Genocide: The Holocaust in Hungary*. New York, 1981.

Bredin, Jean-Denis. *L'Affaire*. Paris, 1983. English translation, *The Affair: The Case of Alfred Dreyfus*. New York, 1986.

Bristow, Edward J. *Prostitution and Prejudice: The Jewish Fight Against White Slavery, 1870–1939.* Oxford, 1983.

Brogan, Denis W. *The Development of Modern France, 1870–1939.* New York, 1966.

Burns, Michael. *Rural Society and French Politics: Boulangism and the Dreyfus Affair, 1886–1900.* Princeton, N.J., 1984.

Busi, Frederick. *The Pope of Antisemitism: The Career and Legacy of Edouard-Adolphe Drumont.* Lanham, Md., 1986.

Byrnes, Robert. *Anti-Semitism in Modern France.* New Brunswick, N.J., 1950.

Cappon, Lester. *The Adams–Jefferson Letters.* Vol. 2. Chapel Hill, N.C., 1959.

Caron, François. *An Economic History of Modern France.* New York, 1979.

Chapman, Guy. *The Dreyfus Case: A Reassessment.* London, 1955.

Cherikover, Elyohu, ed. *Geshikhte fun der yidisher arbeter bavegung in der fareyniker shtatn.* New York, 1943–5.

Cohen, David. *La Promotion des Juifs en France à l'époque du Second Empire.* Vol. 2. Aix, 1980.

Cohen, Naomi W. *Not Free to Desist: The American Jewish Committee, 1906–1966.* Philadelphia, 1972.

Coleman, Hugh, ed. *The Jews of Czechoslovakia.* Philadelphia, 1968.

Dagan, Henri. *L'Oppression des juifs dans l'Europe orientale.* Paris, 1903.

Davitt, Michael. *Within the Pale: The True Story of Anti-Semitic Persecution in Russia.* New York, 1903.

Diner, Hasia R. *In the Almost Promised Land: American Jews and Blacks, 1915–1935.* Westport, Conn., 1977.

Dinnerstein, Leonard, ed. *Anti-Semitism in the United States.* New York, 1971.

Dinnerstein, Leonard. *The Leo Frank Affair.* New York, 1968.

Dinnerstein, Leonard. *Uneasy at Home.* New York, 1987.

Dinnerstein, Leonard, and Palsson, Mary Dale, eds. *Jews in the South.* Baton Rouge, 1973.

Dobkowski, Michael N. *The Tarnished Dream: The Basis of American Anti-Semitism.* Westport Conn., 1979.

Dubnov, Simon. *History of the Jews: From the Congress of Vienna to the Emergence of Hitler.* Vol. 5. New York, 1973. First English edition, 1920.

Edelstein, Alan. *An Unacknowledged Harmony: Philosemitism and the Survival of European Jewry.* Westport, Conn., 1982.

Eidelberg, Philip Gabriel. *The Great Rumanian Peasant Revolt of 1907: Origins of a Modern Jacquerie.* Leiden, The Netherlands, 1974.

Endelman, Todd. *The Jews of Georgian England, 1714–1830: Tradition and Change in a Liberal Society.* Philadelphia, 1979.

Eötvös, Károly. *A Nagy Per.* 3 vols. Budapest, 1904.

Fast, Howard. *The Jews, Story of a People.* New York, 1982.

Fein, Leonard. *Where Are We? The Inner Life of America's Jews.* New York, 1988.

Feldmann, Egal. *The Dreyfus Affair and the American Conscience, 1895–1906.* Detroit, 1981.

Field, Geoffry. *Evangelist of Race: The Germanic Vision of Houston Stewart Chamberlain.* New York, 1980.

Fischer, H. H. *Out of My Past: Memoirs of Count Kokovtsev.* Stanford, Calif., 1935.

Fitzpatrick, Sheila. *The Russian Revolution.* Oxford, 1982.

Ford, W. C., ed. *Letters of Henry Adams, 1892–1918.* Vol. 2. New York, 1938.

Frankel, Jonathan. *Prophecy and Politics: Socialism, Nationalism, and the Russian Jews, 1862–1917.* Cambridge, 1981.

Frederick, Harold. *The New Exodus: Israel in Russia.* London, 1892.

Frey, Robert Seitz, and Thompson-Frey, Nancy. *The Silent and the Damned: The Murder of Mary Phagan and the Lynching of Leo Frank.* Lanham, Md., 1988.

Frumkin, Jacob, et al., eds. *Russian Jewry.* New York, 1966.

Furet, François, ed. *Unanswered Questions: Nazi Germany and the Genocide of the Jews.* New York, 1989.

Gay, Peter. *Freud, a Life for Our Times.* New York, 1988.

Geehr, Richard S. *Karl Lueger, Mayor of Fin de Siècle Vienna.* Detroit, 1990.

Gérard, Patrick. *Les Juifs de France de 1789 à 1860.* Paris, 1976.

Gerber, David, ed. *Anti-Semitism in American History.* Chicago and Urbana, Ill., 1986.

Gitelman, Zvi. *A Century of Ambivalence: The Jews of Russia and the Soviet Union.* New York, 1988.

Goguel, François. *La Politique des partis sous la IIIe République.* Paris, 1958.

Goldberg, Harvey. *The Life of Jean Jaurès.* Madison, Wis., 1962.

Golden, Harry. *A Little Girl Is Dead.* Cleveland, 1965.

Green, Nancy L. *The Pletzl of Paris: Jewish Immigrant Workers in the "Belle Epoque."* New York, 1986.

Greenberg, Louis. *The Jews in Russia: The Struggle for Emancipation.* Two vols. New Haven, Conn., 1965.

Grose, Peter. *Israel in the Mind of America.* New York, 1984.

Gruenzenberg, Oskar Osipovich. *Yesterday: Memoirs of a Russian-Jewish Lawyer.* Berkeley, Calif., 1981. Original Russian edition, Paris, 1938.

Halasz, Nicholas. *Captain Dreyfus, the Story of a Mass Hysteria.* New York, 1955.

Hamerow, Theodore S. *Reflections on History and Historians.* Madison, Wis., 1987.

Handler, Andrew. *Blood Libel at Tiszaeszlár.* New York, 1980.

Handler, Andrew. *Dori: The Life and Times of Theodor Herzl in Budapest, 1860–1878.* Tuscaloosa, Ala., 1984.

Handler, Andrew. *An Early Blueprint for Zionism: Győző Istóczy's Political Anti-Semitism.* New York, 1989.

Hasegawa, Tsuyoshi. *The February Revolution: Petrograd, 1917.* Seattle and London, 1981.

Hepp, Alexandre. *Paris tout nu.* Paris, 1885.

Herschler, Eric, ed. *Jews from Germany in the United States.* New York, 1955.

Hertzberg, Arthur. *The French Enlightenment and the Jews.* New York, 1968.

Hertzberg, Arthur. *The Jews in America: Four Centuries of an Uneasy Encounter.* New York, 1989.

Hertzberg, Steven. *Strangers Within the Gate City: The Jews of Atlanta, 1845–1915*. Philadelphia, 1978.

Higham, John. *Send These to Me: Immigrants in Urban America*. Revised ed. Baltimore, Md., 1984.

Hoffmann, Robert Louis. *More Than a Trial: The Struggle over Captain Dreyfus*. New York, 1980.

Hofstadter, Richard. *The American Political Tradition and the Men Who Made It*. New York, 1957.

Holmes, Colin. *Anti-Semitism in British Society: 1876–1939*. New York, 1979.

Howe, Irving. *World of Our Fathers*. New York, 1976.

Hyman, Paula. *From Dreyfus to Vichy: The Remaking of French Jewry, 1906–1939*. New York, 1979.

Irvine, William D. *The Boulanger Affair Reconsidered: Royalism, Boulangism, and the Origins of the Radical Right in France*. Oxford, 1989.

Jaher, Frederic Cople. *Doubters and Dissenters*. New York, 1964.

Johnson, Douglas. *France and the Dreyfus Affair*. New York, 1966.

Johnson, Paul. *A History of the Jews*. New York, 1987.

Die Judenpogrome in Russland: Herausgegeben im Auftrage des Zionistischen Hilfsfonds in London. Vol. 2. London, 1910.

Katz, Jacob. *From Prejudice to Destruction: Anti-Semitism, 1700–1933*. Cambridge, Mass., 1980.

Katzburg, Nathaniel. *'Antishemiut Be-Hungaria, 1867–1964*. Tel Aviv, 1969. In Hebrew.

Kedward, H. R. *The Dreyfus Affair, Catalyst for Tensions in French Society*. London, 1965.

Kelley, Robert. *The Cultural Pattern in American Politics*. New York, 1979.

Kershaw, Ian. *The 'Hitler Myth': Image and Reality in the Third Reich*. Oxford, 1989.

Kleeblatt, Norman L., ed. *The Dreyfus Affair: Art, Truth, and Justice*. Berkeley, Calif., 1987.

Klier, John Doyle. *Russia Gathers Her Jews: The Origins of the "Jewish Question" in Russia, 1772–1825*. Dekalb, Ill., 1986.

Kochan, Lionel, and Abraham, Richard. *The Making of Modern Russia*. New York, 1963.

Korn, Bertram W. *American Jews and the Civil War*. Philadelphia, 1951.

Krefetz, Gerald. *Jews and Money*. New Haven, Conn., 1982.

Kucherov, Samuel. *Courts, Lawyers, and Trials Under the Last Three Tsars*. New York, 1953.

Lamberti, Marjorie. *Jewish Activism in Imperial Germany*. New Haven, Conn., 1978.

Langer, William L. *Political and Social Upheaval: 1832–1852*. New York, 1969.

Lee, Albert. *Henry Ford and the Jews*. New York, 1980.

Levy, Richard S. *The Downfall of the Anti-Semitic Political Parties in Imperial Germany*. New Haven, Conn., 1975.

Lewis, Bernard. *The Jews of Islam*. Princeton, N.J.

Lifton, Robert J. *The Nazi Doctors: Medical Killing and the Psychology of Genocide*. New York, 1986.

Maier, Charles S. *The Unmasterable Past: History, Holocaust, and German National Identity*. Cambridge, Mass., 1988.

Malino, Frances, and Wasserstein, Bernard, eds. *The Jews in Modern France*. Hanover, N.H., and London, 1985.

Margolin, Arnold D. *The Jews of Eastern Europe*. New York, 1926.

Marrus, Michael. *The Politics of Assimilation: the French Community at the Time of the Dreyfus Affair*. Oxford, 1971.

Massing, Paul. *Rehearsal for Destruction*. New York, 1967; first published, 1949.

Maurer, Trude. *Ostjuden in Deutschland, 1918–1933*. Hamburg, 1986.

Mayer, Alfred G. *Leninism*. New York, 1963.

Mayer, Arno J. *The Persistence of the Old Regime: Europe to the Great War*. New York, 1981.

McCagg, William O., Jr. *Jewish Nobles and Geniuses in Modern Hungary*. New York, 1972.

McPhee, Nancy. *The Book of Insults*. New York, 1978.

Mendelsohn, Ezra. *Class Struggles in the Pale: The Formative Years of the Jewish Workers' Movement in Tsarist Russia*. Cambridge, 1970.

Mendes-Flohr, Paul R., and Reinharz, Yehuda. *The Jew in the Modern World*. Oxford, 1980.

Mitchell, B. R. *European Historical Statistics, 1750–1975*. New York, 1981.

Moore, Deborah Dash. *B'nai B'rith and the Challenge of Ethnic Leadership*. Albany, N.Y., 1981.

Mosse, George. *Toward the Final Solution: A History of European Racism*. New York, 1978.

Nathan, Paul. *Der Process von Tisza-Eszlar: Ein Antisemitisches Culturbild*. Berlin, 1892.

Nettl, J. P. *Rosa Luxemburg*. Oxford, 1969.

Nevins, Allan. *Grover Cleveland: A Study in Courage*. New York, 1932.

Nord, Philip G. *Paris Shopkeepers and the Politics of Resentment*. Princeton, N.J., 1986.

Novick, Peter. *That Noble Dream: The "Objectivity Question" and the American Historical Profession*. Cambridge, 1988.

O'Brien, Conor Cruise. *The Siege: The Saga of Israel and Zionism*. New York, 1986.

Pawel, Ernst. *The Labyrnth of Exile: A Life of Theodor Herzl*. New York, 1989.

Phagan (Kean), Mary. *The Murder of Little Mary Phagan*. Far Hills, N.J., 1987.

Poliakov, Léon. *The History of Anti-Semitism*. Vol. 3. New York, 1975.

Potter, David M. *People of Plenty: Economic Abundance and American Character*. Chicago, 1954.

Prajs, Lazare. *Péguy et Israël*. Paris, 1970.

Pulzer, P. G. J. *The Rise of Political Anti-Semitism in Germany and Austria*. New York, 1964.

Rabi. *Anatomie du Judaisme français*. Paris, 1962.

Rascoe, Burton. *An American Reader*. New York, 1939.

Rebérioux, Madeleine. *La République radicale*. Paris, 1975.

Reinach, Joseph. *Histoire de l'Affaire Dreyfus*. 7 vols. Paris, 1901–11.

Reinharz, Jehuda. *Fatherland or Promised Land: The Dilemma of the German Jew.* Ann Arbor, Mich., 1975.

Reinharz, Jehuda. *Chaim Weizmann: The Making of a Zionist Leader.* Oxford, 1985.

Richardson, James A. *A Compilation of the Messages and Papers of the Presidents, 1789–1908.* Washington, D.C., 1908.

Richler, Mordecai. *Joshua, Then and Now.* New York, 1980.

Ritterband, Paul, ed. *Modern Jewish Fertility.* Leiden, 1981.

Roberts, DeWitt. *The Story of Mass Hysteria.* Atlanta, 1948.

Rogger, Hans. *Jewish Policies and Right-Wing Politics in Imperial Russia.* Berkeley, Calif., 1986.

Roth, Cecil. *A History of the Jews In England.* Oxford, 1964.

Roth, Cecil, ed. *Essays in Jewish History by Lucien Wolf.* London, 1934.

Roth, Philip. *Portnoy's Complaint.* New York, 1969.

Rozenblit, Marsha L. *The Jews of Vienna, 1867–1914: Assimilation and Identity.* Albany, N.Y., 1983.

Samuel, Maurice. *Blood Accusation.* New York, 1966.

Samuels, Charles, and Samuels, Louise. *Night Fell on Georgia.* New York, 1956.

Sartre, Jean-Paul. *Anti-Semite and Jew.* New York, 1967. First French edition, Paris, 1946.

Schmitt, Hans A. *Charles Péguy, the Decline of an Idealist.* Baton Rouge, 1967.

Schorske, Carl. *Fin-de-Siècle Vienna, Politics and Culture.* New York, 1980.

Segre, Dan Vittorio. *Memoirs of a Fortunate Jew: An Italian Story.* Bethesda, Md., 1987.

Séménoff, E. *The Russian Government and Massacres.* Westport, Conn., 1972; first published in 1907.

Seton-Watson, R. W. *Racial Problems in Hungary.* New York, 1972. First published, 1908.

Showalter, Dennis E. *Little Man, What Now? Der Stürmer in the Weimar Republic.* Hamden, Conn., 1982.

Silberman, Charles E. *A Certain People: American Jews and Their Lives Today.* New York, 1985.

Silberner, Edmund. *Sozialisten zur Judenfrage.* Berlin, 1962.

Simons, Howard. *Jewish Times: Voices of the American Jewish Experience.* Boston, 1988.

Singer, Isadore. *Russia at the Bar of the American People: A Memorial of Kishinef.* New York, 1904.

Sombart, Werner. *The Jews and Modern Capitalism.* Berlin, 1911.

Sorel, Georges. *La Révolution dreyfusienne.* Paris, 1911.

Sorlin, Pierre. *"La Croix" et les Juifs (1880–1899): contribution à l'histoire de l'antisémitisme contemporaine.* Paris, 1967.

Stanislawski, Michael. *Tsar Nicholas I and the Jews: The Transformation of Jewish Society in Russia, 1824–1855.* Philadelphia, 1983.

Steel, Ronald. *Walter Lippmann and the American Century.* London, 1980.

Steinberg, Stephen. *The Ethnic Myth: Race, Ethnicity, and Class in America.* Boston, 1981.

Stember, Charles Hebert, ed. *Jews in the Mind of America.* New York, 1966.

Sternhell, Zeev. *La Droite révolutionnaire: 1885–1914: Les origines françaises du fascisme*. Paris, 1978.

Stillman, Norman A. *The Jews of Arab Lands*. Philadelphia, 1979.

Stone, Norman. *Europe Transformed, 1878–1919*. Cambridge, Mass., 1984.

Tager, Alexander B. *The Decay of Czarism: The Beiliss Trial*. Philadelphia, 1935.

Thomas, Marcel. *L'Affaire sans Dreyfus*. Paris, 1961.

Tuchman, Barbara. *The Proud Tower: A Portrait of the World Before the War, 1890–1914*. New York, 1966.

Twain, Mark. *Concerning the Jews*. Philadelphia, 1985. [From the March 1898 issue of *Harper's New Monthly Magazine*.]

Urussov, Prince Serge Dmitriyevich. *Memoirs of a Russian Governor: The Kishinev Pogrom*. New York, 1908. Reprinted, 1970.

Verdès-Leroux, Jeannine. *Scandale financier et antisémitisme catholique: le krach de l'Union générale*. Paris, 1969.

Villier, Marjorie. *Charles Péguy, a Study in Integrity*. London, 1965.

Weber, Eugen. *France: Fin de Siècle*. Cambridge, Mass., 1986.

Weizmann, Chaim. *Trial and Error*. New York, 1949.

Whiteside, Alexander. *The Socialism of Fools: Georg Ritter von Schönerer and Austrian Pan Germanism*. Berkeley, Calif., 1975.

Wilson, Stephen. *Ideology and Experience: Anti-Semitism at the Time of the Dreyfus Affair*. East Brunswick, N.J., 1982.

Winnocker, Rudolf. *Papers of the Michigan Academy of Science, Arts, and Letters*. Vol. 30. 1936.

Wistrich, Robert S. *Revolutionary Jews from Marx to Trotsky*. New York, 1976.

Wistrich, Robert S. *Socialism and the Jews: The Dilemmas of Assimilation in Germany and Austria-Hungary*. East Brunswick, N.J., 1983.

Wistrich, Robert S. *Hitler's Apocalypse: Jews and the Nazi Legacy*. New York, 1985.

Woodward, C. Vann. *Tom Watson: Agrarian Rebel*. Savannah, Ga., 1972.

Wyman, David S. *Paper Walls: America and the Refugee Crisis*. New York, 1968.

Wyman, David S. *The Abandonment of the Jews: America and the Holocaust, 1941–1945*. New York, 1984.

Yarmolinsky, Abraham, ed. and transl. *The Memoirs of Count Witte*. Garden City, N. Y., 1921.

Zborowski, Mark, and Herzog, Elizabeth. *Life Is with People: The Culture of the Shtetl*. New York, 1969. First ed., 1952.

Zeldin, Theodore. *France, 1848–1945*. Oxford, 1973.

Zimmermann, Moshe. Wilhelm Marr: *The Patriarch of Anti-Semitism*. New York, 1986.

Zipperstein, Steven J. *The Jews of Odessa: A Cultural History, 1794–1881*. Stanford, Calif., 1985.

Articles

Articles cited from collections in books are here cited for the convenience of the reader. The books from which they are taken are also cited under "Books."

Aronson, Michael. "Geographical and Socioeconomic Factors in the 1881 Anti-Jewish Pogroms in Russia." *The Russian Review*, vol. 39, no. 1, Jan. 1980, 18–31.

Barany, George. "Magyar-Jew or Jewish-Magyar." *Canadian-American Slavic Studies*, vol. 8, 1974, 1–23.

Bell, Daniel. "The End of American Exceptionalism." *The Public Interest*, no. 41.

Birnbaum, Pierre. "Anti-Semitism and Anticapitalism in Modern France." In Frances Malino and Bernard Wasserman, eds., *The Jews in Modern France*. Hanover N.J., 1985, 214–23.

Bole, William. "The Pollard Affair: Did the Punishment Fit the Crime?" *Present Tense*, vol. 16, no. 2, Jan.–Feb. 1989, 12–15.

Burns, Michael. "The Dreyfus Family." In Norman L Kleeblatt, ed., *The Dreyfus Affair: Art, Truth, and Justice*. Berkeley, Calif., 1987, 140–52.

Clark, Thomas D. "The Post–Civil War Economy in the South." In Leonard Dinnerstein and Mary Dale Palsson, eds., *Jews in the South*. Baton Rouge, 1973.

Deconde, Alexander. "Historians, the War of American Independence, and the Persistence of the Exceptionalist Ideal." *The International History Review*, vol. 5, no. 3.

Diggins, John Patrick. "Comrades and Citizens: New Mythologies in American Historiography." *The American Historical Review*, vol. 90, no. 3, June 1985, 614–49.

Dinnerstein, Leonard. "Atlanta in the Progressive Era: A Dreyfus Affair in Georgia." In Leonard Dinnerstein and Mary Dale Palsson, eds., *Jews in the South*. Baton Rouge, 1973.

Dinnerstein, Leonard. "The Funeral of Rabbi Jacob Joseph." In David Gerber, ed., *Anti-Semitism in American History*. Chicago and Urbana, Ill., 1986.

Dobrowski, Michael. "American Anti-Semitism: A Reinterpretation." *American Quarterly*, vol. 29, 1977, 167–90.

Funkenstein, Amos. "Theological Interpretations of the Holocaust." In François Furet, ed., *Unanswered Questions: Nazi Germany and the Genocide of the Jews*. New York, 1989, 275–303.

Goldberg, Andy. "The Proud Parents." *Jerusalem Post, International Ed.*, week ending Apr. 1, 1989, 6.

Golden, Harry. "Jew and Gentile in the New South: Segregation at Sundown." *Commentary*, vol. 20, Nov. 1955, 403–4.

Greenfeld, Leah. "The Closing of the American Mind." *The New Republic*, Feb. 5, 1990, 30–4. (Review of Igor Shafarevich's *Russophobia*.)

Hamerow, Theodore S. "The Transformation of History into an Academic Discipline Has Diminished Its Role." *The Chronicle of Higher Education*, vol. 34, no. 43, A40.

Higham, John. "American Anti-Semitism Historically Reconsidered." In Charles Herbert Stember, ed., *Jews in the Mind of America*. New York, 1966.

Hutton, Patrick. H. "Popular Boulangism and the Advent of Mass Politics in France." *The Journal of Contemporary History*, vol. 11, 1976.

Hyman, Paula. "The French Community from Emancipation to the Dreyfus Affair." In Norman L. Kleeblatt, ed., *The Dreyfus Affair: Art, Truth, and Justice*. Berkeley, Calif., 1987, 25–36.

Kennan, George. "The Ritual Murder Case in Kiev." *The Outlook*, Nov. 8, 1913.

Korn, Bertram W. "American Judaeophobia: Confederate Version." In Leonard Dinnerstein and Mary Dale Palsson, eds., *Jews in the South*. Baton Rouge, 1973, 135–55.

Korn, Bertram W. "Factors Bearing upon the Survival of Judaism in the Ante-Bellum Period." *American Jewish History Quarterly*, vol. 13, 1964.

Korn, Bertram W. "Jews and Negro Slavery in the Old South." *Publications of the American Jewish Historical Society*, vol. 50, March 1961. Reprinted in Leonard Dinnerstein and Mary Dale Palsson, eds., *Jews in the South*. Baton Rouge, 1973, 89–134.

Kucherov, Samuel. "Jews in the Russian Bar." In Jacob Frumkin et al., eds., *Russian Jewry*. New York, 1966, 220–28.

Kusnets, Simon. "The Immigration of Russian Jews to the United States: Background and Structure." *Perspectives in American History*, vol. 10, 1975, 35–124.

Lambroza, Shlomo. "The Tsarist Government and the Pogroms of 1903–06." *Modern Judaism*, vol. 7, no. 3, Oct. 1987, 287–96.

Lavaillant, R. "La Génèse de l'antisémitisme sous la troisième République. *Revue des études juives*. Cited in Hannah Arendt, *The Origins of Totalitarianism*. New York, 1963.

Levine, Burton. "Justice for the Pollards?" *Present Tense*, vol. 16, no. 2, Jan.–Feb. 1989, 15–19.

Lifschutz, E. "The Repercussions of the Beilis Trial in the United States." *Zion*, vol. 28, 1963, 206–22.

Lindemann, Albert S. "Anti-Semitism: Banality or the Darker Side of Genius?" *Religion*, vol. 18, 1988, 183–95.

Machover, J. M. "Reminiscences personelles." In L. Schneersohn, ed. *Du Pogrom de Kichinev à l'Affaire Beilis*. Paris, n.d.

Martin, Benjamin. F. "The Dreyfus Affair and the Corruption of the French Legal System." In Normal L. Kleeblatt, ed., *The Dreyfus Affair: Art, Truth, and Justice*. Berkeley, Calif., 1987, 37–49.

Mitchell, Allan. "The Xenophobic Style: French Counter-espionage and the Emergence of the Dreyfus Affair." *Journal of Modern History*, vol. 52, no. 3, Sept. 1980, 414–25

Nadler, Allen. "Piety and Politics: The Case of the Satmar Rebbe." *Judaism*, vol. 31, 1982, 132–51.

Nochlin, Linda. "Dégas and the Dreyfus Affair: Portrait of the Artist as an Anti-Semite." In Norman L. Kleeblatt, ed., *The Dreyfus Affair: Art, Truth, and Justice*. Berkeley, Calif., 1987, 96–116.

Peck, Abraham. "That Other 'Peculiar Institution': Jews and Judaism in the Nineteenth Century South." *Modern Judaism*, vol. 7, no. 1, Feb. 1987, 99–114.

Podhoretz, Norman. "J'accuse." *Commentary*, vol. 74, no. 3, Sept. 1982, 21–31.

Rogger, Hans. "The Beilis Case: Anti-Semitism and Politics in the Reign of Nicholas II." *Slavic Review*, vol. 25, no. 4, Dec. 1986, 615–29.

Rubinow, Israel. "The Economic Condition of Jews in Russia." *Bulletin of the Bureau of Labor*, no. 72. Washington, D.C., 1907, 487–583. Cited in Stephen Steinberg, *The Ethnic Myth: Race, Ethnicity, and Class in America*. Boston, 1981.

Sarna, Jonathan D. "Anti-Semitism and American History." *Commentary*, March 1981, 42–7.

Sarna, Jonathan D. "The 'Mythical Jew' and 'the Jew Next Door' in Nineteenth-Century America." In David Gerber, ed., *Anti-Semitism in American History*. Chicago and Urbana, Ill., 1986.

Schuker, Stephen. "The Origins of the 'Jewish Problem' in the Later Third Republic." In Frances Malino and Bernard Wasserstein, eds., *The Jews in Modern France*. Hanover N.H. and London, 1985, 135–80.

Stanislawski, Michael. "The Transformation of Traditional Jewish Authority in Russian Jewry: The First Stage." In David Berger, ed., *The Legacy of Jewish Migration: 1881 and Its Impact*. New York, 1983, 23–30.

Sternhell, Zeev. "The Roots of Popular Anti-Semitism in the Third Republic." In Frances Malino and Bernard Wasserstein, eds., *The Jews in Modern France*. Hanover, N.H. and London, 1985, 103–34.

Szajkowski, Zosa. "The Impact of the Beiliss Case on Central and Western Europe." *American Academy for Jewish Research, Proceedings*, vol. 31, 1963, 197–218.

Szajkowski, Zosa. "Paul Nathan, Lucien Wolf, Jacob H. Schiff, and the Jewish Revolutionary Movements in Eastern Europe (1903–1917)." *Jewish Social Studies*, vol. 29, no. 1, Jan. 1967, 3–26.

Tugan-Baranowsky. "Anti-Semitism in Contemporary Russia." *Monthly Review*, Jan. 1904. Cited in Isador Singer, *Russia at the Bar of the American People: A Memorial of Kishineff*. New York, 1904.

Turner, James. "Understanding the Populists." *Journal of American History*, vol. 67, no. 2, Sept. 1978, 354–73.

Wasserman, Neil. "Regular Police in Tsarist Russia, 1900–1914." *The Russian Review*, vol. 44, 1985, 45–68.

Wiener, Jonathan M. "Planter–Merchant Conflict in Reconstruction Alabama." *Past and Present*, vol. 68, Aug. 1975.

Index